Contents

PROBLEM SOLVING WITH DATA STRUCTURES USING JAVA™

A MULTIMEDIA APPROACH

Mark Guzdial and Barbara Ericson

College of Computing
Georgia Institute of Technology

Prentice Hall

Upper Saddle River   Boston   Columbus   San Francisco   New York
Indianapolis   London   Toronto   Sydney   Singapore   Tokyo   Montreal
Dubai   Madrid   Hong Kong   Mexico City   Munich   Paris   Amsterdam   Cape Town

Vice President and Editorial Director, ECS: *Marcia J. Horton*
Editor-in-Chief: *Michael Hirsch*
Executive Editor: *Tracy Dunkelberger*
Assistant Editor: *Melinda Haggerty*
Editorial Assistant: *Allison Michael*
Vice President, Production: *Vince O'Brien*
Senior Managing Editor: *Scott Disanno*
Production Liaison: *Jane Bonnell*
Production Editor: *Pavithra Jayapaul, TexTech International*
Senior Operations Supervisor: *Alan Fischer*
Marketing Manager: *Erin Davis*
Marketing Assistant: *Mack Patterson*
Art Director, Cover: *Jayne Conte*
Cover Designer: *Axell Designs*
Cover Image: *Photobank.kiev.us/Shutterstock*
Art Editor: *Greg Dulles*
Media Editor: *Daniel Sandin*
Media Project Manager: *Danielle Leone*
Composition/Full-Service Project Management: *TexTech International*

Java is a trademark of Sun Microsystems, Inc. Company and product names mentioned herein are the trademarks or registered trademarks of their respective owners.

Library of Congress Cataloging-in-Publication Data

Guzdial, Mark.
    Problem solving with data structures using Java : a multimedia approach / Mark Guzdial and Barbara Ericson.
        p. cm.
    Includes bibliographical references and index.
    ISBN 0-13-606061-7 (alk. paper)
    1. Data structures (Computer science) 2. Java (Computer program language) 3. Multimedia systems.
    I. Ericson, Barbara. II. Title.
    QA76.9.D35G894 2010
    005.7′3–dc22   2009038567

Prentice Hall
is an PRENTICE Hall

PEARSON

www.pearsonhighered.com

10 9 8 7 6 5 4 3 2 1
ISBN-13: 978-0-13-606061-1
ISBN-10:   0-13-606061-7

Dedicated to our families.
We are grateful for their support.

PROBLEM SOLVING
WITH DATA STRUCTURES
USING JAVA™

4   SIMULATIONS: PROBLEM SOLVING WITH DATA STRUCTURES   339

14   Using an Existing Simulation Package   341

15   Introducing UML and Continuous Simulations   365

16   Abstracting Simulations: Creating a Simulation Package   391

Preface

In 1961, the MIT Sloan School hosted a symposium on "Computers and the World of the Future." The speakers were a who's who of computer science pioneers, including Grace Hopper, John McCarthy, J.C.R. Licklider, and Alan Perlis, the first ACM Turing Awardee. Perlis's lecture [3] argued that everyone should take computer science as part of a modern liberal education. He listed the topics of a computer science class for everyone, which included:

> *Representation.* The data organization in each problem may have a "natural" representation for one phase of a computation and a different one for another. Transformations between representations must always balance in the student's mind the ease of processing versus the work involved in transformation ...

> *Simulation.* It is important for the student to realize that a process possibly not even associated with, and operating external to, a computer may to varying degrees of approximation be imitated on a computer ...

This book addresses these two points. Most texts on data structures deal with *representation*, but few also deal with *simulation*. The combination provides the opportunity to think about the reason for the representations. This book addresses data structures as tools that you can use to solve problems that arise in modeling a world and executing (simulating) the resultant model. We cover the standard data structure topics (e.g., arrays, linked lists, stacks, queues, trees, maps, and graphs) but in the context of modeling. The execution of the model results in a simulation, which often generates an animation. The last section of the book challenges the reader to think about structure and behavior more abstractly, and how they interrelate. The following are some of the strengths of this book:

- The same problem is addressed in multiple ways, increasing in sophistication and power with each iteration. For example, Chapter 6 considers the problem of supporting music composition on a computer. First, we consider arrays of notes, then linked lists of MIDI (music) note segments. We develop several different kinds of linked lists, with increasing flexibility for music composition and expression. In Chapter 7, we consider the problem of laying out images to define a scene, and work through several iterations of linked lists and finally develop scene graphs, a common data structure in computer animation. That's the first kind of tree that students see in this book. Simulations are introduced through the use of an existing simulation package in Chapter 14, then a simple predator–prey simulation is created based on our `Turtle` class in Chapter 15, and a complete general continuous simulation package is developed in Chapter 16, and finally, discrete event simulations are covered in Chapter 17.

- The same data structure is seen in multiple contexts. Chapter 6 introduces linked lists for MIDI notes, Chapter 7 introduces linked lists for images, Chapter 9 uses linked list (with recursive traversals) for sampled sounds, and then a generalized form of linked lists (for any kind of data) is developed in Chapter 10. A similar progression is used with trees, using images in Chapter 8, sounds in Chapter 9, and creating the generalized structure in Chapter 10. In this way, we believe that students develop an abstract notion of data structures.

- Since we are using a movie context, our data can be images and sounds instead of just numbers. For example, we create linked lists of musical phrases and trees of images and sounds. The advantage to this approach is that students find the exercises much more motivating than the traditional abstract ones. This approach also allows for open-ended assignments that encourage the students to be creative. In our use of this book at Georgia Tech, 70% of the students reported that working with media made the class more interesting, and 66% of the students reported spending extra time on a project to make the outcome look "cool" [6].

HOW TO USE THIS BOOK

Many teachers will want to tailor how they use this book.

- If students already know Java, then skip sections 2.1–2.3 and section 3.1. You may think that you can also skip some of Chapter 4, but the concepts introduced here are used in later animations and simulations.

- Chapter 5 can be skipped if your students are already familiar with traversing and modifying one-dimensional arrays.

- Chapters 6, 7, 8, and 9 introduce linked lists and trees using different media. These might be used stand-alone (e.g., using these chapters within the context of an existing data structures class) or used selectively (e.g., just Chapter 6 for music, or just Chapters 7 and 8 for pictures). Chapter 10 generalizes on the previous linked lists and trees, so it does presume that some of the previous chapters have been visited.

- Chapter 13 is about user interfaces. It can be skipped, but you might want to at least cover section 13.2, which explains how user interfaces relate to trees. And section 13.3 uses a stack to allow users to undo previous operations.

- Part 4 of the book (Chapters 14–17) is about simulations. This is where the data structures get put together to create new kinds of solutions. This part could be used as a final project in a more traditional data structures class.

EXPECTATIONS OF THE READER

The presumption is that the reader has had some previous programming experience. We expect that the reader can build programs that use variables, iteration, and conditionals and that the reader can assemble programs using subprograms (functions/methods) that pass input via arguments. The reader should also be familiar with arrays. We don't care what language the reader's previous experience is in.

We use DrJava in the examples in this text. *It is not necessary to use DrJava to use this book!* The advantages of DrJava are that it has a simple interface and a powerful Interactions Pane. The Interactions Pane allows us to manipulate objects without writing new classes or methods for each exploration. Rapid iteration allows students to explore and learn more quickly than they might if each exploration required a new Java class and/or method.

INSTRUCTOR AND STUDENT RESOURCE MATERIAL

- PowerPoint Lecture Slides
- Companion Website containing links to all software and media

To access these materials, please visit the Companion Website or the publisher's website:

Companion Website: www.mediacomputation.org
Publisher's Website: www.pearsonhighered.com/guzdial

For username and password information please contact your Pearson Representative.

TYPOGRAPHICAL NOTATIONS

Examples of Java code look like this: x = x + 1. Longer examples look like this:

```java
public static void main(String[] args) {
    System.out.println("Hello, World!");
}
```

When showing something that the user types in with DrJava's response, it will have a similar font and style, but the user's typing will appear after a prompt (>):

```
> int a = 5;
> a + 7
12
```

User interface components of DrJava will be specified using a small-caps font, like the EDIT menu item and the LOAD button.

There are several special kinds of sidebars that you'll find in the book.

Example Java Code 1: An example program

A program creates a model of interest to us.

```java
import jm.music.data.*;
import jm.JMC;
import jm.util.*;
import jm.music.tools.*;
```

```
6    public class Dot03  {
         public static void main(String[] args) {
8            Note n = new Note(JMC.C4,  JMC.QUARTER_NOTE);
             Phrase phr = new Phrase(0.0);
10
             phr.addNote(n);
12           Mod.repeat(phr, 15);

14           Phrase phr2 = new Phrase(0.0);
             Note r = new Note(JMC.REST,  JMC.EIGHTH_NOTE);
16           phr2.addNote(r);
             Note n2 = new Note(JMC.E4,  JMC.EIGHTH_NOTE);
18           phr2.addNote(n2);
             Note r2 = new Note(JMC.REST,  JMC.QUARTER_NOTE);
20           phr2.addNote(r2);
             Mod.repeat(phr2, 7);
22
             Part p = new Part();
24           p.addPhrase(phr);
             p.addPhrase(phr2);
26
             View.show(p);
28       }
     }
```

Computer Science Idea: An example idea

Powerful computer science concepts appear like this.

A Problem and Its Solution: The problem that we're solving

We use data structures to solve problems that arise when we model a world. In these sidebars, we explicitly identify the problem and its solution.

Common Bug: An example

Common things that can cause your program to fail appear like this.

Debugging Tip: An example

If there's a good way to keep those bugs from creeping into your programs in the first place, they're highlighted here.

Making It Work Tip: An example

Best practices or techniques that really help are highlighted like this.

ACKNOWLEDGMENTS

Our sincere thanks go out to the following organizations and people:

- The National Science Foundation, which gave us the initial grants that started the Media Computation project.
- Robert "Corky" Cartwright and the whole DrJava development team at Rice University.
- Andrew Sorensen and Andrew Brown, the developers of JMusic.
- Monica Sweat, Colin Potts, David Smith, and especially Jay Summet, who used this text at Georgia Tech and gave us feedback on it.
- Most importantly, Matthew, Katherine, and Jennifer Guzdial, who allowed themselves to be photographed and recorded for Mommy and Daddy's media project.
- We also thank our (then anonymous) reviewers for all their useful comments on the draft of this manuscript: Jim Bohy, Mount Mercy College; Charles Fowler, Gainesville State College; Helen H. Hu, Westminster College; Tim Huang, Middlebury College; Kam Fui Lau, Armstrong Atlantic State University; Kathy Liszka, University of Akron; John Neitzke, Truman State University; Dale J. Skrien, Colby College; Robert Sloan, University of Illinois; and Tom Wulf, University of Cincinnati.

About the Authors

Mark Guzdial is a professor in the School of Interactive Computing in the College of Computing at Georgia Institute of Technology. He is one of the founders of the ACM's International Computing Education Research workshop series. Mark's research focuses on learning sciences and technology, specifically, computing education research. His first books were on the programming language Squeak and its use in education. He was the original developer of "Swiki" (Squeak Wiki), the first wiki developed explicitly for use in schools. Mark has published several books on the use of media as a context for learning computing, which have influenced undergraduate computing curricula around the world. He serves on the ACM Education Board as vice-chair and is on the editorial boards of the *Journal of the Learning Sciences* and *Communications of the ACM*.

Barbara Ericson is a research scientist and the Director of Computing Outreach for the College of Computing at Georgia Tech. She has been working on improving introductory computing education since 2004. She enjoys the diversity of the types of problems she has worked on over the years in computing including computer graphics, artificial intelligence, medicine, and object-oriented programming.

PROBLEM SOLVING WITH DATA STRUCTURES USING JAVA™

PART 1

INTRODUCTION TO JAVA: OBJECT-ORIENTED PROGRAMMING FOR MODELING A WORLD

1

Objects for Modeling a World

1.1 MAKING REPRESENTATIONS OF A WORLD

1.2 WHY JAVA?

In the 1994 Disney animated movie *The Lion King*, there is a scene when wildebeests charge over the ridge and stampede the lion king, Mufasa (Figure 1.1). Later, in the 1996 Disney animated movie *The Hunchback of Notre Dame*, Parisian villagers mill about, with a decidedly different look than the rest of the characters (see the bottom of

FIGURE 1.1
Wildebeests in *The Lion King*. Images © Disney Enterprises, Inc.

FIGURE 1.2
Parisian villagers in *The Hunchback of Notre Dame*. Image © Disney Enterprises, Inc.

Figure 1.2). These are actually related scenes. The wildebeests' stampede was one of the rare times that Disney broke away from their traditional hand-drawn cel animation. The wildebeests were not drawn by hand at all—rather, they were *modeled* and then brought to life in a *simulation*.

A model is a detailed description of structure and behavior. The model of the wildebeests for *The Lion King* described what wildebeests looked like, how they moved, and what they did during a stampede. The villagers' model described what they did when milling about and how they reacted as a group to something noteworthy, like the entrance of Quasimodo. A simulation is an execution of the model—simply let the wildebeests start responding to one another and to the obstacles on the ridge, according to the behavior defined in their model. Then, in a sense, simply "film" the screen.

This is a different process than what Pixar used when it created *Toy Story*. There was a model for Woody, which described how Woody looked and what parts of him moved together when he smiled or walked. But *Toy Story* wasn't a simulation. The movements and character responses of *Toy Story* were carefully scripted. In the wildebeest or villagers simulations, each character is simply following a set of rules, usually with some random element (e.g., should the wildebeest move left or right when coming up against the rock? when should the villagers shuffle or look right?). If you run a simulation a second time, depending on the model and the random variables you used, you may get a different result than you did the first time.

This book is about understanding these situations. The driving questions of this book are, ***"How did the wildebeests stampede over the ridge?"*** and ***"How did the villagers move and wave?"*** The process of answering those questions will require us to cover a lot of important computer science concepts, like how to choose different kinds of *data structures* to model different kinds of structures, and how to define behavior and even combine structure and behavior in a single model. We will also develop a powerful set of tools and concepts that will help us understand how to use modeling and simulation to answer important questions in history, science, or business.

1.1   MAKING REPRESENTATIONS OF A WORLD

When we create models we construct a representation of the world. Think about our job as being the job of an artist. Specifically, let's consider a painter. A painter creates a model of the world using paints, brushes, and a canvas. We will use the programming language *Java* to create model worlds.

Is there more than one way to model the world? Can you imagine two different paintings, perhaps *radically* different paintings, of the same thing? Part of what we have to do is to pick the software structures that best represent the structure and behavior that we want to model. Making those choices is solving a *representation problem*.

You already know about mathematics as a way to model the world, though you may not have thought about it that way. An equation like $F = ma$ is saying something about how the world works. It says that the amount of force (F) in a collision (for example) is equal to the amount of mass (m) of the moving object times its acceleration (a). You might be able to imagine a world where that's not true—perhaps a cartoon world where a slow-moving punch packs a huge wallop. In that world, you'd want to use a different equation for force F, and that would be a different model.

The powerful thing about software representations is that they are executable—they have *behavior*. They can move, speak, and take action within the simulation that we can interpret as complex behavior, such as traversing a scene and accessing resources. A computer model, then, has a *structure* to it (the pieces of the model and how they relate) and a *behavior* to it (the actions of these pieces and how they interact).

Are there better and worse *physical structures*? Sure, but it depends on what you're going to use them for. A skyscraper and a duplex home each organize space differently. You probably don't want a skyscraper for a nuclear family with 2.5 children, and you're not going to fit the headquarters of a large multinational corporation into a duplex. Consider how different the physical space of a tree is from a snail shell—each structure has its own benefits for its purpose, and would not work at all for the other. A snail shell is not going to support a bird's nest, and a tree is completely wrong for hosting a shell-less snail.

Are there better and worse information structures, or *data structures*? Imagine that you have a representation that lists all the people in your department, some 50–100 of them sorted by last names. Now imagine that you have a list of all the people in your work or academic department, but grouped by role, e.g., teachers vs. writers vs. administrative staff vs. artists vs. management, or whatever the roles are in your department. Which representation is *better*? It depends on what you're going to do with it.

- If you need to look up the phone number of someone whose name you know, the first representation is probably better.

- If the artistic staff gets a new person, the second representation makes it easier to write the new person's name in at the right place.

Computer Science Idea: Quality of data structures depend on use

A structure (data or physical) is better or worse than another structure depending on how it's going to be used—both for access (looking things up) and for change. How will the structure be changed in the future? The best structures allow you to find things quickly and also allow you to add or remove items quickly and easily. Often, you have to make trade-offs between options to get the best structure (highest quality) for your purpose. ∎

Structuring our data is *not* something new that appeared when we started using computers. There are lots of examples of structuring data and using representations in your daily life.

- Consider the stock listing tables that appear in your paper. For each stock (arranged vertically into rows), there is information such as the closing price and the difference from the day before (in columns). A *table* appears in the computer as a *matrix* which is also called a *two-dimensional array*.
- Our daughter, Katie, used to create treasure hunts for the family, where she hid notes in various rooms (Figure 1.3). Each note referenced the next note in the list. This is an example of a *linked list*. Each note is a link in a chain, where the note tells you (links to) the next link in the chain. Think about some of the

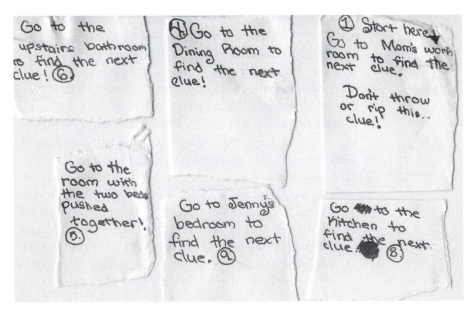

FIGURE 1.3
Katie's list of treasure hunt clues.

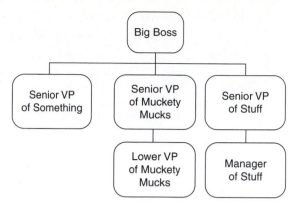

FIGURE 1.4
An organization chart.

advantages of this structure: the pieces define a single structure, even though each piece is physically separate from the others; and changing the order of the notes or inserting a new note only requires changing the neighbors (the ones before or after the notes affected).

- An organization chart (Figure 1.4) describes the relationships between roles in an organization. It's just a representation—there aren't really lines extending from the feet of the CEO into the heads of the presidents of a company. This particular representation is quite common—it's called a *tree*. It's a common structure for representing *hierarchy*.

- A map (Figure 1.5) is another common representation that we use. The real town actually doesn't look like that map. The real streets have other buildings and things on them. The real streets are wonderfully rich and complex. When you're trying to get around in the town, you don't want a satellite picture of the town. That's too much detail. What you really want is an *abstraction* of the real town, one that just shows you what you need to know to get from one place to another. We think about Interstate I-75 passing through Atlanta, Chattanooga, Knoxville, Cincinnati, Toledo, and Detroit, and Interstate I-94 going from Detroit through Chicago. We can think about a map as *edges* or *connections* (streets) between points (or *nodes*) that might be cities, intersections, buildings, or places of interest. This kind of a structure is called a *graph*.

These data structures have particular *properties* that make them good for some purposes and bad for others. A table or matrix is really easy for looking things up (especially if it's ordered in some way). But if you have to insert something into the middle of the table, everything else in a table has to move to make room. When we're talking about space in the computer (*memory*), we're literally talking about copying each element in memory separately to a new place. On the other hand, inserting a new element into a linked list or into a graph is easy—just add edges (links) in the right places.

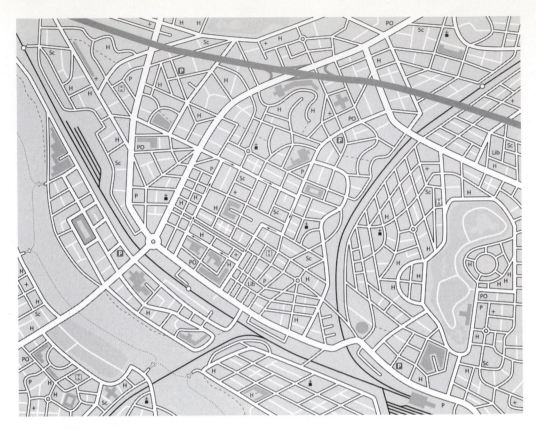

FIGURE 1.5
A map of a town. Courtesy of Robert Adrian Hillman/Shutterstock.

Why does the structure matter? It matters because of the way that computer memory works. You can think of memory as being a whole bunch of mailboxes in a row, each with its own address. Each mailbox stores exactly one thing. In reality, that one thing is a binary pattern, but we can interpret it any way we want, depending on the encoding. Maybe it's a number, or maybe it's a character, or maybe it is the address of another mailbox.

A table (a matrix or an array) is stored in consecutive mailboxes. So, if you have to put something into the middle of a table, you have to move the things already in there somewhere else. If you put something new where something old used to be, you end up overwriting the something old.

To make it clear, let's imagine that we have a table that looks something like this:

Name	Age	Weight
Arnold	12	220
Kermit	47	3
Ms. Piggy	42	54

Let's say that we want to add "Fozzie" to the list, who's 38 and weighs 125 pounds. If we add him alphabetically, he would go below Arnold and above Kermit, but if we just put him after Arnold, we would overwrite Kermit. So, the first thing we have to do is to make room for Fozzie at the *bottom* of the table. (We can simply add more mailboxes after the table.)

Name	Age	Weight
Arnold	12	220
Kermit	47	3
Ms. Piggy	42	54

Now we have to copy everything down into the new space, opening up a spot for Fozzie. We move Ms. Piggy and her values into the bottom space, then Kermit into the space where Ms. Piggy was. That's two *sets* of data that we have to change, with three values in each set.

Notice that that leaves us with Kermit's data duplicated.

Name	Age	Weight
Arnold	12	220
Kermit	47	3
Kermit	47	3
Ms. Piggy	42	54

Once we add the information for Fozzie in the space where Kermit was originally, the table will look like this:

Name	Age	Weight
Arnold	12	220
Fozzie	38	125
Kermit	47	3
Ms. Piggy	42	54

Now let's compare that to a different structure, one that's like the treasure trail of notes that Katie created. We call that a linked list representation. Consider a note (found in a bedroom) like the following:

"The next note is in the room where we prepare food."

Let's think about that as a note *in* the bedroom that *references* (says to *go to*) the kitchen (Figure 1.6).

In terms of memory mailboxes, think about each note as having two parts: a current location, and where the *next* one is. Each note would be represented as two memory mailboxes (Figure 1.7).

bedroom ————————→ kitchen

FIGURE 1.6
Bedroom note refers to the kitchen.

Current Location: bedroom	Next Location: kitchen

FIGURE 1.7
Memory mailboxes for bedroom note.

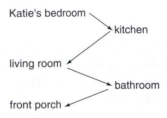

FIGURE 1.8
Treasure hunt trail.

So let's imagine that Katie has set up a trail that looks like the one in Figure 1.8.

Now, she changes her mind. Katie's bedroom shouldn't refer to the kitchen; her bedroom should point to Matthew's bedroom as the next location. How do we change that? We simply put a new note in Katie's bedroom that refers to Matthew's bedroom as the next location. We move the note that was in Katie's bedroom to Matthew's bedroom. It will still refer to the kitchen as it's next location. None of the other notes need to move or change as shown in Figure 1.9.

In terms of memory mailboxes we added a new memory mailbox with a current location of Matthew's bedroom and a next location equal to the original next location of the first memory mailbox in the trail, the kitchen. Then we changed the next location of the first memory mailbox in the trail to refer to Matthew's bedroom.

Adding to a linked list representation is much easier than adding to a table, especially when you're adding to the middle of the table. But there are advantages to tables, too. They can be faster for looking up particular pieces of information.

Much of this book is about the trade-offs between different data structures. Each data structure has strengths that solve some sets of problems, but the same data structure probably has weaknesses in other areas. Each choice of data structure is a trade-off between these strengths and weaknesses, and the choices can only be made in the context of a particular problem.

These data structures have a *lot* to do with our wildebeests and villagers.

- The visual structure of villagers and wildebeests (e.g., how legs and arms attach to bodies) is typically described as a tree or graph.
- Tracking which villager is next to do something (e.g., move around) is a queue.

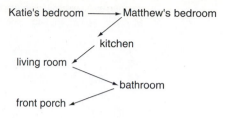

FIGURE 1.9
Modified treasure hunt trail.

- Tracking all of the wildebeests in the stampede is often done in a *list* (like a linked list).

- The images to be used in making the villagers wave or the wildebeests run are usually stored in a list.

1.2   WHY JAVA?

Why is this class taught in Java, instead of another language, like Python?

- Overall, Java is faster than Python (and definitely faster than Jython). We can do more complex things faster in Java than in Python.

- Java is a good language for exploring and learning about data structures. It makes explicit how you're connecting data through *references*.

- More computer science classes are taught in Java than Python. So if you go on beyond this class in data structures, knowing Java is important.

- Java has "resume-value." It's a well-known language, so it's worth it to be able to say, even to people who don't really know computer science, that you know Java. This is important—you'll learn the content better if you have a good reason for learning it.

- Java has a huge library of pre-built classes that make creating programs easier. For example, it has components for creating professional-looking graphical user interfaces, for reading information from files or from networks, and for working with relational databases.

Getting Java Set Up

You can start out with Java by simply downloading a Standard Edition (SE) *JDK* (*Java Development Kit*) from `http://www.java.sun.com` for your computer. With that, you have enough to get started programming in Java. However, that's not the easiest way to *learn* Java. In this book, we use *DrJava* which is a useful *IDE* (*Integrated Development Environment*)—a program that combines facilities for editing, compiling, debugging, and running programs. DrJava is excellent for learning Java because it provides an Interactions Pane where you can simply type in Java code and try it out.

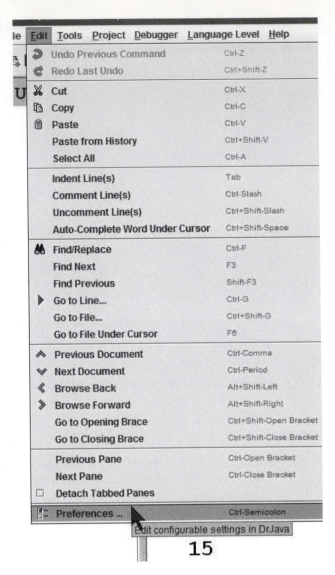

FIGURE 1.10
Open the DrJava Preferences by clicking on Edit and then Preferences.

If you'd like to use DrJava, follow these steps:

- Download DrJava from `http://www.drjava.org` and install it.
- Download *JMusic* from `http://jmusic.ci.qut.edu.au/` and install it.
- Make sure that you grab the `media-source` and `java-source` from the book Web site: `http://www.mediacomputation.org`.
- You'll need to tell DrJava where to find the classes that we created for this book and the libraries for JMusic. You use the Preferences in DrJava (see Figure 1.10) to

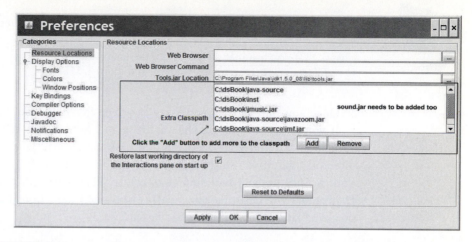

FIGURE 1.11
Adding `java-source`, the JMusic libraries, and the jars in `java-source` to the classpath in DrJava.

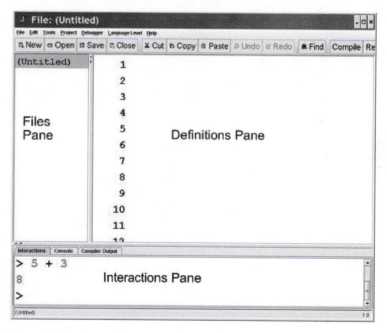

FIGURE 1.12
Parts of the DrJava window.

add the `java-source` directory, the JMusic *jar file* (`jmusic.jar`), the instruments directory (`inst`), and all the jar files (`jmf.jar`, `javazoom.jar`, and `sound.jar`) in the `java-source` directory (Figure 1.11) to the list of locations to look for unknown classes. This list of places to look for unknown classes is known as the *classpath*. Once you have added all items to the classpath, click on APPLY and OK.

Making It Work Tip: Keep all your Java files in your `java-source` directory
Once you add `java-source` to your classpath, this is the location DrJava will look for classes that you use that aren't part of the Java language. If you move your source code to a different directory, it won't be found (Figure 1.11).   ∎

Once you start DrJava, you'll have a screen that looks like Figure 1.12.

If you choose *not* to use DrJava, that's fine. Set up your IDE and be sure to install JMusic and set up your classpath to access the JMusic jar (`jmusic.jar`), the `inst` directory, the `java-source` directory, and the jars (`jmf.jar`, `javazoom.jar`, and `sound.jar`) in the `java-source` directory. This book will assume that you're using DrJava and will describe using classes from the Interactions Pane, but you can easily create a class with a `main` method instead.

2

Introduction to Java

Chapter Learning Objectives

We will be using Java for modeling the worlds which we will simulate, like the ridge where the wildebeests charged down. In this chapter, we start introducing Java while using it for manipulating media.

The computer science goals for this chapter are:

- Explain why Java is relevant to modeling and simulation.
- Give the basic syntax details for variables, arrays, iteration, and conditionals.
- Explain how to create a class and a subclass.

The media learning goal for this chapter is:

- Give the user a brief introduction to the manipulation of pictures, sounds, and music.

2.1 WHAT'S JAVA ABOUT?

Java programs contain interacting *objects*. In *object-oriented programming*, the programmer cares about more than just *specifying* a process. In other languages, like Python or Visual Basic, you mostly tell the computer, "First do this, then do that." In object-oriented programming, you care about who (or what) does each task in the process, and how the overall process *emerges* from the interaction of different objects. The software engineering term for this is *responsibility-driven design*—we don't just care about how the process happens; we care about who (which object) does which part of the process.

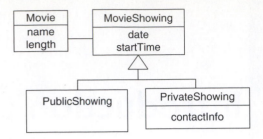

FIGURE 2.1
UML class diagram of movie types and movie showings.

An example might help. When you go to the movies there are people that sell tickets, people that take the tickets, people that sell drinks, popcorn, and candy, and people that clean the theaters. Each job has a set of responsibilities. Each job has skills that people doing the job must have and information that people doing the job need to know. People that sell tickets need to be able to process payment and need to know which movies are sold-out. People that take the tickets need to know where the theaters are in order to direct people to the theater. A job *classification* identifies the required skills for the job.

In Java we create *classes* that identify the things that objects of the class can do (called *methods*) and the information (called *fields*) that objects of the class need to keep track of. When creating a Java program to model a movie theater, we would create a class for each job classification. We would also create classes for other objects at a movie theater like movie, food, ticket, theater, etc. Each movie has a name and a length. A movie can be shown several times a day so we will need an object for each showing. Each showing will have a date and start time. There could be private showings as well as public ones. A private showing will have contact information as well as the usual showing information. In object-oriented programming we call the relationship between movie and a showing of a movie an *association* or a *has-a* link which is shown as a solid line in Figure 2.1. The relationship between showing and private showing is an *inheritance* or an *is-a-type-of* relationship which is shown as an open triangle pointing toward the *parent class* in Figure 2.1. In inheritance the *child class* (private showing) inherits data and behavior from the *parent class* (movie showing). Figure 2.1 is a *UML class diagram* which is used to show classes and the relationships between them. UML is short for *Unified Modeling Language*, which defines standard notations for object-oriented programming. In a UML class diagram, each class is shown in a box with the name of the class at the top of the box. Under the class name, you can show the fields (the data each object will have).

Object-oriented programming dates back to a programming language called *Simula*, which was a programming language for creating simulations. The idea was to describe the world that you cared about in the Simula language; e.g., how customers work their way through a store, how material flows through a factory, how deer and wolves balance each other ecologically in an ecosystem. That description is called a *model*. When Alan Kay used Simula in the late 1960s, he realized that all programs can be thought of as modeling some world (real or imaginary) and that all programming is about simulation. It was this insight that led to his programming language *Smalltalk* and our current understanding of object-oriented programming. Java is an object-oriented programming language based on ideas from Smalltalk.

Thinking about programming as modeling, and simulation means that you *should* do responsibility-driven design—you need to spread control over what happens in the overall process across many objects. That's the way that the real world works. Setting aside theological arguments, there is no great big for loop telling everything in the real world to take another time step. You don't write one big master program in Java—your program arises out of the interaction of lots of objects, just like the real world. Most importantly, in the real world, no *one* object **knows** everything and can **do** everything. Instead, in the real world and in Java, each object has things that it *knows* and things that it can *do*.

2.2   BASIC (SYNTAX) RULES OF JAVA

This section contains the basic rules for doing things in Java. We'll not say much about classes, fields, and methods here—we'll introduce the syntax (rules) for those as we need them. These are the things that you've probably already seen in other languages.

Declarations and Types

If your past programming experience was in a language like Python, Visual Basic, or Scheme, the trickiest part of learning Java will probably be its *types*. All variables and values in Java have a type. You must declare a variable before you can use it. To declare a variable, specify the type and the name of the variable.

```
TYPE NAME;
```

You can also initialize the value of the variable to the result of an expression when you declare it.

```
TYPE NAME = EXPRESSION;
```

The type of a variable can be either the name of a class or one of the primitive types. Java stores integer numbers, floating point numbers, single characters, and Boolean values as primitives (not objects). It does this in order to make calculations quicker.

When primitive variables are declared, memory is set aside to hold a value of that type and the variable name is associated with that memory. When you use the name again in your program, the name will be used to find the memory that stores the value and the value will be substituted for the name in expressions.

In the following Java code we are declaring a variable named a that can hold integer values. We then set the value of a to 5 and then add 7 to the value in a. The value stored in a was 5, so the result is 12. If you enter a statement in the Interactions Pane of DrJava and do not add a semicolon at the end of the statement, DrJava will print out the result of the statement.

```
> int a = 5;
> a + 7
12
```

You can also print the output of the result of an expression using the Java code `System.out.println(EXPRESSION)`, which will output the result of the expression followed by the end of a line.

```
> System.out.println(a + 7);
12
```

If you declare another variable with the same name in the Interactions Pane you lose any way to refer to the original variable's value. You can't reserve two different sections of memory with the same name. The computer would not know which one you would mean when you used the name. You can *change* the value of the variable (the value in memory) as often as you want.

```
> int a = 6;
> System.out.println(a);
6
> a = -8;
> System.out.println(a);
-8
```

How much memory is used for a variable? Some types take up more memory than others. The type `int` is used to store positive and negative integers such as 352 and -20. The amount of space used to store `int` variables is 32 bits long and the values are stored using *two's complement notation* (a standard way of representing integer values in binary patterns). "Bit" is short for binary digit, and each bit can store the value 0 or 1. The type `char` is used to store single characters such as 'a' or 'T'. A `char` variable is 16 bits long and the value is stored using the Unicode format. The length of the type `boolean` is not specified, but it could be stored in just one bit with 0 for `false` and 1 for `true`. The values `true` and `false` are literals in Java.

```
char firstLetter = 'a';
System.out.println(firstLetter);
'a'
> boolean flag = true;
> System.out.prinln(flag)
true
```

In Java there are two types that can be used to represent floating point (decimal) numbers such as 25.321 or -3.04. The types are `float` and `double`. The type `double` can be used to store more significant digits than the type `float` since a `double` is stored in 64 bits and a `float` is stored in 32 bits. A floating point variable is stored in *IEEE 754 floating point format* (a standard format for representing numbers with decimal points in binary patterns). As you can see below, you must use the letter 'f' after a number with a decimal in it if you want it to be of the type `float` because otherwise the compiler will assume that the number is a `double`.

```
> float f = 13.2f
> f
13.2
```

Notice that you don't get what you might expect from the below addition (26.431). Floating point numbers are not exactly represented in computers. Calculations involving floating point numbers do not always give exact results.

```
> double d;
> d = 13.231;
> d
13.231
> d + f
26.43099980926514
```

You can't put a floating point number into an integer because an integer doesn't store a fractional part.

```
> a = f
Error: Bad types in assignment
```

You can tell the computer to make a double value fit into an integer variable by throwing away the fractional part. Use a *cast* to do this. A cast is indicated by specifying the type to cast to inside of a pair of parentheses in front of the value or expression to be cast. This is like casting clay to form a new shape.

```
> a = (int) f
13
```

Strings

You can represent a series of characters using the class String. Note that the String object is not just an array of characters, like it is in some languages. You can assign a value to a String object by enclosing a series of characters in a pair of double quotes. The class String is defined as part of the Java language.

```
> String s = "This is a test";
> System.out.println(s);
"This is a test"
```

There are many things you can do to String objects in Java. You can create a new String that has the same characters as the original String, but in which, all the characters are lowercase. In Java String objects are *immutable*. Immutable means that they can't change. If you try changing a String in Java you get back a new String object.

```
> String start = "UPPERCASE LETTERS ARE LIKE SHOUTING";
> String lower = start.toLowerCase();
> System.out.println(lower):
uppercase letters are like shouting
> System.out.println(start)
UPPERCASE LETTERS ARE LIKE SHOUTING
```

You can look for something in the String. If the thing isn't found in the String, it returns the value −1. If the thing is found in the String, it returns the position that it was found at. The first character in a string is at position 0.

```
> int position = start.indexOf("IS")
> System.out.println(position);
-1
> int posU = start.indexOf("U");
> posU
0
```

There are many more things that you can do with String objects. We recommend that you take a look at the documentation for the String class if you want to learn more. The String class is in the java.lang package. Java contains hundreds of classes. Classes are organized into *packages*. A package is a collection of related classes. The classes in the java.lang package are the core classes in Java. The classes in package java.io handle input and output. The classes in the java.net package work with networks. Go to java.sun.com and find the *API* (application programmer interface) for the version of Java you are using. Then click on the package name java.lang to see all the classes in that package. Click on the String class (Figure 2.2) and scroll down to the methods section of the documentation; this is an alphabetical list of the things you can do with strings.

Object Variables and Primitive Variables

When you declare a variable using a class name in Java, a variable is created in memory that has as its value a way to find the actual object of that class in memory. This is called a *reference* to an object. This is different from how variables of primitive types work.

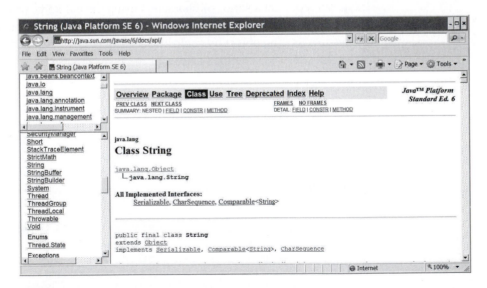

FIGURE 2.2
Showing the API for the String class.

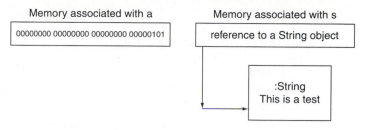

FIGURE 2.3
Showing memory for an `int` variable and a `String` variable.

When you declare a primitive type, the memory associated with the variable name holds the value. So if we declare an `int` variable a to have a value of 13 and a `String` variable s to have a value of "This is a test", we would get the memory map shown in Figure 2.3.

Why don't we just store the object in the memory associated with the variable like we do for primitive types? The problem is that when you declare a variable with a type that is a class name, then that variable can be used to refer to an object of that class name or an object of any subclass (child) of that class. An object of a subclass can be larger than an object of the class. For example, the `String` class in Java is a child of the `Object` class. You can declare a variable o that is of the type `Object` and set the value to a new `String` object.

```
> Object o = new String("hi");
> System.out.println(o);
"hi"
```

Since an object of the `String` class is bigger than an object of the `Object` class, it wouldn't fit in the variable if we had allocated only enough memory for an `Object`. So instead when we declare a variable with a type that is a class name, memory is allocated that stores a reference to an object. The reference is used to find the actual object in memory.

You can think of a reference to an object as being like a tracking number on a package. A package tracking number is the same size regardless of the size of the package and is used to find the actual package. The reference is used to find the actual object in memory. The class allocates memory for an object when you create it since the class knows the information (fields) defined for each object of the class.

There is a special value in Java called `null` that indicates that a reference doesn't refer to any object. So, if we declare a new `String` variable but do not assign it to a valid `String` object, we get the value `null` when we print the variable.

```
> String s1;
> System.out.println(s1);
null
```

Assignment

```
VARIABLE = EXPRESSION
```

The equals sign (=) is used for assignment. The VARIABLE should be replaced with a declared variable, or (if this is the first time you're using the variable), you can declare it in the same assignment, e.g., `int a = 12;`. If you want to create an object (not a *literal* like the numbers and strings in the last section), you use the term `new` with the name of the class (and perhaps include input for use in initializing the object fields). For example, we have created a `Picture` class that you can use to display (show) and modify digital pictures.

```
> Picture p = new Picture(FileChooser.pickAFile());
> p.show();
```

Semicolons

Java statements are ended by a semicolon. Statements can take up several lines. You can think of a Java statement like an English sentence, except that it ends in a semicolon, not a period. So you do need a semicolon at the end of an assignment statement since you are saying, "set the value of the variable to the result of the expression," which is a complete sentence.

Common Bug: Forgetting a semicolon at the end of a statement
If you forgot to add a semicolon at the end of a statement, the compiler will report: "Error: ';' expected". This is a very easy error to fix. Just click on the highlighted line in the compiler output and it will take you to the statement that is missing the semicolon. Add the semicolon and recompile. Occasionally the actual error lies above where it shows it in the code, so check if the statement above the current one looks okay.   ∎

Conditionals

You can conditionally execute a statement when an expression is true.

```
if (EXPRESSION)
    STATEMENT
```

```
> int x = 3;
> if (x == 3)
      System.out.println("x is 3");
x is 3
```

Notice that while = is used to assign a value to a variable, == is used to test for equality.

You can also execute a block of statements when an expression is true. A block of statements is enclosed in a pair of curly braces.

```
if (EXPRESSION) {
    STATEMENT
    STATEMENT
    ...
}
```

In the example above you may notice that the open curly brace is at the end of the line after the `if`. This is the Java style standard, but some some people prefer the open curly brace at the beginning of the next line. It doesn't matter to Java if you put the open curly brace at the end of a statement or on the next line. Some people find it easier to match curly braces when the open curly brace is at the beginning of an empty line. But, this does make the code longer. We will use the Java style standard in this book.

```
int y = 2;
if (y  <  2)
    System.out.println("y is  >= 2");
    System.out.println("done");
System.out.println("after if");
```

Do try the example above. Type it exactly as-is. Do you get the output you expect?

If you have more than one statement following an `if` that you want executed when the condition is true, be sure to put the statements in a block defined by a pair of open and close curly braces. The *indention* (extra spaces at the beginning of a statement) is ignored by Java. We just indent code to make it easier for us to see the blocks.

Debugging Tip: Always use a block of statements with conditionals

Even though you don't need to put a single statement following an `if` inside a pair of curly braces, it will make your code safer if you do. A common bug is to add more than one statement after an `if`, but forget to add the curly braces to form a block of statements. When the code executes, only the first statement following the `if` is executed as part of the conditional.

An expression in Java is pretty similar to a logical expression in any other language. One difference is that a logical *and* is written as **&&**, and an *or* is written as **||**.

You can execute one statement or block of statements when the expression is true, and a different statement or block of statements when the expression is false using an `if` and `else`.

```
if (EXPRESSION)
    THEN-STATEMENT OR BLOCK OF STATEMENTS
else
    ELSE-STATEMENT OR BLOCK OF STATEMENTS

int z = 3;
if (z < 3) {
    System.out.println("z < 3");
}
```

```
else {
  System.out.println("z >= 3");
}
```

Common Bug: Watch out for extra semicolons

Remember that a semicolon is one way to end a Java sentence. A block is another way. So we don't need to add a semicolon at the end of a block, but Java won't care if you do. But, if you add a semicolon in the middle of a conditional statement (after the Boolean expression), you end the statement, which can lead to some very unexpected results. ∎

Arrays

To declare an array, you specify the *type* of the elements in the array followed by open and close *square brackets*. (In Java all elements of an array have the same type.) `Picture[]` declares an array of type `Picture`. So `Picture[] myArray;` declares `myArray` to be a variable that refers to an array of Pictures.

To actually create the array, we might say something like `new Picture[5]`. This declares an array of references to five pictures. This does *not* create the pictures, though! Each of those have to be created separately. Java indices start with zero, so if an array has five elements, the minimum index is zero and the maximum index is four. The fifth array reference (as seen below) will result in an error—`ArrayIndexOutOfBoundException`.

```
> Picture[] myArray = new Picture[5];
> Picture background = new Picture(800,800);
> FileChooser.pickMediaPath();
> myArray[0]=new Picture(FileChooser.getMediaPath("katie.jpg"));
> myArray[1]=new Picture(FileChooser.getMediaPath("jungle.jpg"));
> myArray[2]=new Picture(FileChooser.getMediaPath("barbara.jpg"));
> myArray[3]=new Picture(FileChooser.getMediaPath("flower1.jpg"));
> myArray[4]=new Picture(FileChooser.getMediaPath("flower2.jpg"));
> myArray[5]=new Picture(FileChooser.getMediaPath("butterfly.jpg"));
ArrayIndexOutOfBoundsException:
  at java.lang.reflect.Array.get(Native Method)
```

You can also initialize the contents of an array when you declare it. The size of the array will be the number of items inside the open and close curly braces. Separate the array items with commas. Arrays are objects and they know their length. You can get the number of items in an array using `NAME.length`. Note that there are not any parentheses after `length`, since it is a *public field* and not a method. Public means that anyone (any class) can see the field and directly access the value using `objectRef.fieldName`.

```
> numArray.length
4
```

Iteration

As of Java 1.5 (also called Java 5) you can use a `for-each` loop to loop through the elements of an array or collection and repeat a statement or block of statements.

```
for (TYPE NAME : ARRAY)
    STATEMENT OR BLOCK OF STATEMENTS
```

A concrete example will help to explain this. I can create an array of integers and then total them.

```
> int[] gradeArray = {90, 80, 85, 70, 99};
> total = 0;
> for (int grade : gradeArray)
    total = total + grade;
> System.out.println(total);
424
```

This will loop through each element of the array. Each time through the loop, the grade variable will be set to the next array element. The current value of the grade variable will be added to the total. So, the first time the grade variable will have the value 90, and the second time it will have the value 80, and so on until the last time through the loop it will have the value of 99.

You can also use a `while` loop to repeat a statement or block of statements as long as an expression is true.

```
while (EXPRESSION)
    STATEMENT OR BLOCK OF STATEMENTS
```

There is a `break` statement for exiting the current block. There is also a `continue` statement that will jump to the next execution of the loop.

Probably the most confusing iteration structure in Java is the `for` loop. It really combines a specialized form of a `while` loop into a single statement.

```
for (INITIAL-EXPRESSION;
     CONTINUING-CONDITION;
     ITERATION-EXPRESSION)
    STATEMENT OR BLOCK OF STATEMENTS
```

A concrete example will help to make this structure make sense.

```
> for (int num = 1 ; num <= 10 ; num = num + 1)
    System.out.print(num + " ");
1 2 3 4 5 6 7 8 9 10
```

The first thing that gets executed *before anything inside the loop* is the INITIAL-EXPRESSION. In our example, we're creating an integer variable num and setting it equal to 1. We'll then execute the loop, testing the CONTINUING-CONDITION before each time through the loop. In our example, we keep going as long as the variable num is less than or equal to 10. Finally, there's something that happens *after* each time through the loop—the ITERATION-EXPRESSION. In this example, we add one to num. The result is that we print out (using `System.out.print`, which is the same as `print` in many languages) the numbers 1 through 10. The expressions in the `for` loop can actually be several statements, separated by commas. Notice that `System.out.println` printed the result of the expression and then moved to a new line, while `System.out.print` prints the value of the expression and stays on the same line.

The phrase `VARIABLE = VARIABLE + 1` is so common that a short form has been created (`VARIABLE++`).

```
> for (int num = 1 ; num <= 10 ; num++)
        System.out.print(num + " ");
```

Strings versus Arrays and Substrings

A Java *string* is not an array of characters like it is in some languages. But, you can create a string from an array of characters. Characters are defined with single quotes (e.g., `'a'`) as opposed to double quotes (e.g., `"a"`) which define strings.

```
> char characters[]={'B','a','r','b'}
> characters
[C@1ca209e
> String wife = new String(characters)
> wife
"Barb"
```

You cannot index a string with square brackets like an array. You can use the `substring` method on a string to retrieve part of the string (*substrings*) within the string. The `substring` method takes a starting and ending position in the string, starting with zero. It does not include the character at the ending position.

```
> String name = "Mark Guzdial";
> name
"Mark Guzdial"
> name[0]
Error: 'java.lang.String' is not an array
> name.substring(0,0)
""
> name.substring(0,1)
"M"
> name.substring(1,1)
""
> name.substring(1,2)
"a"
```

2.3 USING JAVA TO MODEL THE WORLD

We have talked about the value of objects in modeling the world, and about the value of Java. In this section, we use Java to model some objects from our world. Let's consider the world of a student.

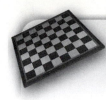

A Problem and Its Solution: What should I model?

When you model something in the world (real or virtual) as an object, you are asking yourself, "What's important about the thing that I am trying to model?" Typically, that question is answered by considering what you want from the model. Why are you creating this model? What's important about it? What questions are you trying to answer?

If you are creating a model of students, then the question that you want to answer determines what you model and how you model it. If you want to create a model in order to create a course registration system, then you care about the students as people with class sections. If you wanted to model students to answer questions about their health (e.g., how dormitory food impacts their liver, or how lack of sleep impacts their brains), then you want to model students as biological organisms with organs like livers.

For our purposes in this chapter, let's imagine that we are modeling students in order to explore registration behavior. Given the previous, that means that we care about students as people. At the very least then, we want to define a class Student and a class Person.

A Problem and Its Solution: How much should I model?

Always try for the minimal model. Model as little as possible to answer your question. Models grow in complexity rapidly. The more attributes that you model, the more that you have to worry about later. When you model, you are always asking yourself, "Did I deal with all the relationships between all the variables in this model?" The more variables you model, the more relationships there are to consider. Model as little as you need to answer your question.

We are going to define the class Student as a *subclass* of Person. There are several implications of that statement.

- Class Person is a *superclass* of Student. We also say that Person is the *parent class* of Student, and Student is the *child class* of Person. We should be able to think about the subclass, Student, as being "a kind of" (sometimes shortened to *kind-of*) the superclass. A student is a kind of person—that's true, so it's a reasonable superclass-subclass relationship to set up.

- All *fields* or *instance variables* of the class Person are automatically in instances of the class Student. That does not mean that all those variables are directly accessible—some of them may be *private*, which means that they are defined in the parent class, they are directly accessible in the parent class, but they are not directly accessible in the methods of the subclass.

- All *methods*, except private methods, in the superclass Person are automatically callable in the subclass Student.

Here's an initial definition of the class `Person`.

Example Java Code 1: Person class, starting place

```java
public class Person {
    public String name;
}
```

∎

We have created a `public` class named `Person` that has a public field called `name` of type `String`. The keyword `public` is used to specify what classes have access to this class and this field. This is called specifying the *visibility*. Using `public` visibility means that all other classes have access to this class and field.

That's enough to create an instance (object) of class `Person` and use it. Here's how it will look in DrJava:

```
> Person fred = new Person();
> fred.name
null
> fred.name = "Fred";
> fred.name
"Fred"
```

Public fields can be directly accessed and modified from code in any class using *dot notation*. Just use the variable name followed by a period and then the name of the field. There's an implication of this implementation of `Person`—we can change the name of the person in the Interactions Pane. Should we be able to do this?

```
> fred.name = "Mabel";
> fred.name
"Mabel"
```

If we want to control direct name changes so that they can only happen within the Person class, we should make the field `name` private. *Private visibility* means that only code in the same class has direct access. So, `private` fields can't be directly modified by code in other classes. So, to get to the name in code that is outside the `Person` class, we can use a public *accessor* method (sometimes called a *getter* method because it lets us get the value of a private field. To change the name from outside the class we would use a public *mutator* or *modifier* method (sometimes called a *setter* method because it lets us set the value of a private field. These methods could check whether it's appropriate to get and/or set the variable value and make sure the value is acceptable.

Example Java Code 2: Person, with a private name and public accessor and modifier methods

```java
public class Person {

    private String name;
```

```
public void setName(String someName) {
    this.name = someName;
}

public String getName() {
    return this.name;
}
}
```

■

How It Works.   The field name is now `private`, meaning that it can be directly manipulated only inside the class `Person` (using `this.name`). The mutator method `setName` takes a `String` as input, then sets the name to that input. Since `setName` doesn't return any value, its return value is `void`—literally, nothing. The accessor method `getName` does return the value of the variable name, so it has a return value of `String`. Notice that both of these methods refer to `this.name`. The keyword `this` is a special variable that denotes the object that has been told to `getName` or `setName`. The phrase `this.name` means "The variable name that is in the object `this`, the one that was told to execute this method."

Now, we manipulate the field name using these methods—because we can't access the variable directly anymore. Within `getName` and `setName` in this example, the variable `this` means `fred`—they are two variable names referencing the exact same object.

```
> Person fred = new Person();
> fred.setName("Fred");
> fred.getName()
"Fred"
```

This works well for getting and setting the name. Let's consider what happens when we first create a new `Person` instance.

```
> Person barney = new Person();
> barney.getName()
null
```

Should "barney" have a `null` name? The value `null` means that this variable does not yet reference a `String` object. How do we define an instance of `Person` such that it automatically has a value for its name? That would be the way that the real world works, like baby people get names at birth.

We can make that happen by defining a *constructor*. A constructor gets called when a new object (instance) is created. A constructor has the same name as the class itself. It can take input (parameters), so that we can create an object with certain values. Constructors don't *have* to take input—it's okay to just create an instance and have predefined values for variables.

Example Java Code 3: Person, with constructors

```java
public class Person {

   private String name;

   public Person() {
      this.setName("Not-yet-named");
   }

   public Person(String thename) {
      this.setName(thename);
   }

   public void setName(String someName) {
      this.name = someName;
   }

   public String getName() {
      return this.name;
   }
}
```

∎

How It Works.   This version of class `Person` has two different constructors. One of them takes no inputs, and gives the `name` field a predefined, default value. The other takes one input—a new name to be given to the new object. It's okay to have multiple constructors as long as they can be distinguished by the inputs (this is called *overloading*). Since one of these takes nothing as input, and the other takes a `String`, it's pretty clear which one we're calling when we create `Person` objects. The '//' in the code below is the beginning of a *comment*. A comment is ignored by the computer but helps explain your code to other people.

```java
> Person barney = new Person("Barney")
// Here, we call the constructor that takes a string.
> barney.getName()
"Barney"
> Person wilma = new Person()
// Here, we call the constructor that doesn't take an input
> wilma.getName()
"Not-yet-named"
> wilma.setName("Wilma")
> wilma.getName()
"Wilma"
```

If we specify parameters that don't match the current constructors we will get an error.

```java
> Person agent99 = new Person(99)
NoSuchMethodException: constructor Person(int)
```

This is telling us that there is no constructor in the Person class that takes an integer value.

Discourse Rules for Java

In an American "Western" novel or movie, there are certain expectations. The hero carries a gun and rides a horse. The hero never uses a bazooka, and never flies on a unicorn. Yes, you can make a Western that has a hero with a bazooka or a unicorn, but it's considered a weird Western—you've broken some rules.

Those are *discourse rules*—the rules about how we interact in a certain genre or setting. They are not laws or rules that are enforced by some outside entity. They are about expectations.

There are discourse rules (conventions) in all programming languages. Here are some for Java:

- Class names start with a capital letter and the rest of the first word is lowercase (like String). Variables, fields, parameters, and method names all start with a lowercase word. If a name has more than one word in it the first letter of each new word is capitalized (like FileChooser). This makes it easier to read a variable name that has more than one word in it.
- Class names are never plural. If you want more than one instance of a class, you use an array or a list.
- Class names are typically nouns, not verbs.
- Methods should describe what objects know how to do.
- Accessors and modifiers are typically named "set-" and "get-" followed by the name of the field.

Defining toString

What is an instance (object) of the class Person? What do we get if we try to print its value?

```
> Person barney = new Person("Barney")
> barney
Person@63a721
```

That looks like Barney is a Person followed by some expletive or code. This code is the hashcode, which is a unique identifier for an object. We can make the display of Barney look a little more reasonable by adding the toString method to our Person class. When we try to print an object (by simply displaying its value in the Interactions Pane in DrJava, or when printed from a program using System.out.println), the object is converted to a string and printed. The method toString does that conversion. The Person class inherits the toString method from the class Object. How do we know that, you might ask? Well, if you don't specify what class you are inheriting from when you declare a new class, it automatically inherits from the `Object` class. All classes in Java inherit at some level (parent, grandparent, great-grandparent, etc.) from the `Object` class. The `toString` method in `Object` prints the class name followed by the hashcode of the object. By providing a `toString` method in the `Person` class, we *override* the parent's method with the same name and parameter list. Overriding a parent's method means that the child's method will be called instead of the parent's method. This happens because the method to execute is determined at run-time based on the class that created the object that the method is being called on. This run-time finding of the method to execute based on the class that created the object is a form of *polymorphism*. Polymorphism means many forms, and it allows the same function name to be used for different data types. If the class that created the object that you are calling the method on has the method, it will be called. If the class that created the object doesn't have the method, the parent's method will be executed (if it has the method). If the parent class doesn't have the method, it will keep looking up the inheritance chain to find the method. The method will be found since the code wouldn't have compiled if it didn't exist at some level in the inheritance tree.

Example Java Code 4: toString method for Person

```java
public String toString() {
    return "Person named " + this.name;
}
```

How It Works. The method `toString` returns a `String`, so we declare the return type of `toString` to be `String`. We can stick the words "Person named" before the actual name using the + operator—this is called *string concatenation*.

Now, we can immediately print Barney after creating him, and the output is reasonable and useful.

```
> Person barney = new Person("Barney")
> System.out.println(barney);
Person named Barney
```

Defining Student as Subclass of Person

Now, let's define our class `Student`. A student is a kind of person—we established that earlier. In Java, we say that `Student` extends `Person`—that means that `Student` is a subclass of `Person` (Figure 2.4). It means that a `Student` is everything that a `Person` is. Notice in Figure 2.4 that `Person` is a subclass of `Object` as we mentioned earlier.

How should `Student` instances be different? Let's say that a `Student` has an identifier. That's not particularly insightful, but it is likely true.

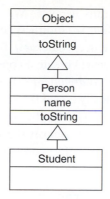

FIGURE 2.4
A UML class diagram for `Person` and `Student`.

Example Java Code 5: Student class, initial version

```java
public class Student extends Person {

    private int id;

    public int getId() {return this.id;}

    public void setId(int theId) {this.id = theId;}
}
```

■

How It Works.   Assuming that the identifier, `id`, will fit within the bounds of an integer `int`, this isn't a bad way to go. If the identifier might be too large, or if we would want to record dashes or spaces within it, using an `int` would be a bad model for the real identifier. Notice that we are also creating a getter and a setter for `id`.

From here, we can create instances of `Student`. We can get and set the name and id.

```
> Student betsy = new Student()
> betsy.getName()
"Not-yet-named"
> betsy.setName("Betsy")
> betsy.getName()
"Betsy"
> betsy.setId(999)
> betsy.getId()
999
```

But, what happens if we try to create a student with a name?

```
> Student betsy = new Student("Betsy")
NoSuchMethodException: constructor Student(java.lang.String)
```

Why did this happen? We were able to create a new student object using `new Student()` but we didn't specify any constructors in the class `Student`. How then were we able to execute `new Student()`? If you don't provide any constructors, the Java compiler will create a constructor for you that doesn't take any parameters. This is called the *no-argument constructor*. But, once you add any constructors, Java will not automatically create the no-argument one for you anymore.

If we print out Betsy, she'll tell us that she's a `Person`, not a `Student`. That's because the class `Student` inherits the `toString` method from `Person`. The method that gets called is the one in `Person`.

```
> betsy
Person named Betsy
```

Let's define the class `Student` with reasonable constructors and with a new `toString` method.

Example Java Code 6: Class Student, with constructors and `toString` method

```java
public class Student extends Person {

    /////////////////// fields //////////////////

    private int id;

    ////////////////// constructors ///////////

    public Student() {
        super(); //Call the parent's constructor
        id = -1;
    }

    public Student(String name) {
        super(name);
        id = -1;
    }

    /////////// methods //////////////////////////

    public int getId() { return this.id;}

    public void setId(int theId) {this.id = theId;}

    public String toString() {
        return "Student named " + this.getName() +
            " with id " + this.id;
    }

}
```

An updated UML diagram for `Person` and `Student` shows that the `Student` class also has the `toString` method now so that it overrides the one in `Person` (Figure 2.5).

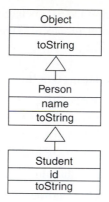

FIGURE 2.5
A modified UML class diagram for `Person` and `Student`.

Notice that we don't show the getter and setter methods in the UML class diagram. If they are not shown, they are implied to exist for each named field.

How It Works. We create a default value for the `id` as −1. We also create an accessor, `getId()` and a mutator or modifier `setId()`, for manipulating the identification. Note that we still want to do whatever the `Person` constructors would do, so we call them with `super`. We added a `toString` method to print out the student's name and id.

```
> Student betsy = new Student("Betsy");
> System.out.println(betsy);
Student named Betsy with id -1
```

Debugging Tip: Make the call to super *first* in a subclass constructor

If a subclass constructor doesn't have a call to `super` as the first statement in the constructor, Java will automatically add a statement that calls the parent's constructor that takes no parameters using `super()`. So, we don't have to have the `super()` call in the constructors above, since it will be added for us if we don't include it, but we wanted to show that it will happen. If you want to call a different constructor than the one that takes no parameters in a subclass constructor, make sure that it is the first statement in the subclass constructor.

Creating a main() Method

How do we test our Java code? For those of us using DrJava,[1] it's easy—we can simply type code in the Interactions Pane. What if you don't *have* an Interactions Pane? Then, you can test code by providing a `main()` method. There can be at most one `main` method in a class. It is often used to try out the class.

---

[1]Or BlueJ, `http://www.bluej.org`.

A main method is declared as public static void main(String[] args), which is a real mouthful. Here is a brief description (there is a better explanation later in the book):

- public means that this method can be accessed by any other class.
- static means that this method is known to the *class*, not just the instances (objects). We can execute it without any objects of the class having been created. This is required because when we first load a class, there aren't any objects that have been created from the class.
- void means that this method does not return anything.
- String[] args means that this method *could* be executed by running it from a command line, and any words on that line (e.g., filenames or options) would be passed on to the main method as elements in an array of strings named args (for "arguments").

Example Java Code 7: main() method for Person

```java
public static void main(String[] args) {
   Person fred = new Person("Fred");
   Person barney = new Person("Barney");

   System.out.println("Fred is a " + fred);
   System.out.println("Barney is a " + barney);
}
```

How It Works.   Add the main method to the Person class and compile the class. You can then run the class (however, your Java environment allows you to do this) or execute it from the command line and this will execute the main method. Two instances (objects) of class Person will be created, and then both are printed to the console (or Interactions Pane, for DrJava) using the toString method.

When we execute the main method by clicking the Run button, we see:

```
Welcome to DrJava.
> java Person
Fred is a Person named Fred
Barney is a Person named Barney
```

Exploring Inheritance

A subclass inherits all the public object methods in the superclass. If the subclass defines its own version of a public method in the superclass, then the subclass version will be executed instead of the version in the parent class. Let's add a method to class Person that allows instances of Person to be friendly and greet people.

Example Java Code 8: greet method for Person

```java
public void greet() {
    System.out.println("Hi! I am " + this.name);
}
```

Executing this method looks like this:

```
> Person bruce = new Person("Bruce")
> bruce.greet()
Hi! I am Bruce
> Student kristal = new Student("Kristal")
> krista.greet()
Hi! I am Kristal
```

Let's imagine that we create a `greet` method for class `Student`, too. We might try something like this:

```java
public void greet() {
    System.out.println("Hi! I'm " + this.name +
                       " but I have to run to class...");
}
```

Unfortunately, that will generate an error when we try to compile `Student`.

```
1 error found:
File: C:\dsBook\java-source-final\Student.java   [line: 26]
Error: name has private access in Person
```

That error occurred because `name` is a `private` variable. The subclass `Student` can't directly access the variable using `this.name`. Only the class that defined it, `Person`, can directly access it, since it is declared `private`. Instances of the class `Student` certainly *have* a name variable—they just can't access it directly. If we want to access the variable `name` in `Student`, we have to use the public accessor method `getName`.

Example Java Code 9: greet method for Student

```java
public void greet() {
    System.out.println("Hi! I'm " + this.getName() +
                       " but I have to run to class...");
}
```

Now we get different results when we ask a `Person` and `Student` to `greet()`.

```
> Person bruce = new Person("Bruce")
> bruce.greet()
Hi! I am Bruce
> Student krista = new Student("Krista")
> krista.greet()
Hi, I'm Krista, but I have to run to class...
```

It's worth thinking this through—what exactly happened when we executed `krista.greet()`?

- Krista knows that she is a Student—an instance of the class `Student`. Krista knows that if she can't greet, she can ask her parent to do it.
- She does know how to `greet()`, so she executes that method.
- But midway, "Uh-oh. I don't know how to `getName()`!" So Krista asks her parent (who might have asked her parent, and so on, as necessary), who does know how to `getName()`.

Let's try one more experiment:

```
> Person fred = new Student("Fred")
> Student mabel = new Person("Mabel")
ClassCastException: mabel
```

Why did the first statement work, but the second one generated an error? Variables in Java always have a particular *type*. They can refer to values that match that type. A `Person` variable `fred` can refer to a `Person` object. A variable of a class type can also refer to instances of any *subclasses*. Thus, the `Person` variable `fred` can refer to an instance of class `Student`. However, a variable of a given type *cannot* refer to objects of any *superclasses*. Thus, the `Student` variable `mabel` cannot refer to an instance of the class `Person`.

There are some subtle implications when referring to an object of one type in a variable of another type. Consider the following example:

```
> fred.greet()
Hi, I'm Fred, but I got to run to class...
> fred.setId(999)
Error: No 'setId' method in 'Person' with arguments: (int)
> ((Student) fred).setId(999)
> ((Student) fred).getId()
999
```

Our `Person` variable `fred` knows how to `greet()`—of course it does, since both `Person` and `Student` classes know how to greet. Note that `fred` executes the *Student* method `greet()`—that also makes sense, since `fred` refers to an instance of the class `Student`.

Here's the tricky part: `fred` can't `setId()`. You may be thinking, "But Fred's a Student! Students know how to set their id!" Yes, that's true. The variable `fred`, though, is declared to be type `Person`. That means that Java is checking that `fred` is only asked to do things that a `Person` might be asked to do. A `Person` does not know how to set its id. We can tell Java, "It's okay—fred contains a Student" by *casting*. When we say `((Student) fred)`, we are telling Java to treat `fred` like a `Student` and let it execute `Student` methods. Then it works.

2.4 MANIPULATING PICTURES IN JAVA

We have created Java classes to make it easy for you to create and manipulate pictures and sounds. These classes are in the `java-source` directory. You also have a `media-source` directory that contains files that contain picture and sound data. You can create a `Picture` object by passing it a full file name. You can get a *full file name* by using the `FileChooser` class and its method `pickAFile()`. The method `pickAFile()` is special in that it's known to the class as well as to objects created from that class (*instances*). It's called a `static` or *class method*. To access a class method, use: *ClassName.methodName()*.

```
> String file = FileChooser.pickAFile();
> System.out.println(file);
"C:\dsBook\media-source\beach-smaller.jpg"
```

In the array example in Section 2.2, we used two class methods: `FileChooser.pickMediaPath` and `FileChooser.getMediapath`. The method `pickMediaPath()` will let you pick a directory that holds your media (media-source) and save that directory path for later use. The method `getMediaPath(filename)` takes a filename, then returns the media directory pathname concatenated in front of it. So `FileChooser.getMediaPath` ("jungle.jpg") actually returns the full file name of "c:/dsbook/media-source/jungle.jpg". *You only need to use pickMediaPath once!* (That is, as long as all your media remain in the same directory.) The pathname for the media gets stored in a file on your computer, so that all your code that uses `getMediaPath` will just work. This makes it easier to move your code around (e.g., for your grader to run your programs).

Recall that just declaring a variable to refer to a picture sets the value of that variable to null to show that it doesn't refer to an object yet.

```
> Picture p;
> p
null
```

Debugging Tip: Did you get an error?

If you got an error as soon as you typed `Picture p;`, there are two main possibilities.

- All the Java files we provide you are in source form. You need to compile them to use them. Open `Picture.java` and click COMPILE ALL. If you get additional errors about classes not found, open those files and compile them, too.

- You might not have your PREFERENCES set up correctly. If Java can't find the `Picture` class, you can't use it. Be sure to add the `java-source` directory to your classpath. ■

Debugging Tip: Semicolons or not?

In the DrJava Interactions Pane, you don't have to end your lines with a semicolon (;). If you don't, you're saying to DrJava, "Evaluate this, and show me the result." If you do, you're saying, "Treat this like a line of code, just as if it were in the Code Pane." Leaving it off is a useful debugging technique—it shows you what Java thinks that variable or expression means. But be careful—you *must* have semicolons in your Code Pane! ∎

To make a new picture, we use the code (you might guess this one) `new Picture (fullFileName)`. Then we'll have the picture show itself by telling it (using dot notation) to `show()` (Figure 2.6).

```
> p = new Picture("c:/dsBook/media-source/beach-smaller.jpg");
> p
Picture, filename c:/dsBook/media-source/beach-smaller.jpg
height 360 width 480
> p.show()
```

The variable p in this example has the type `Picture`. That means that it can only refer to pictures or subclasses of `Picture`. The variable p can't refer to a `Sound` or `int`. We also can't re-declare p.

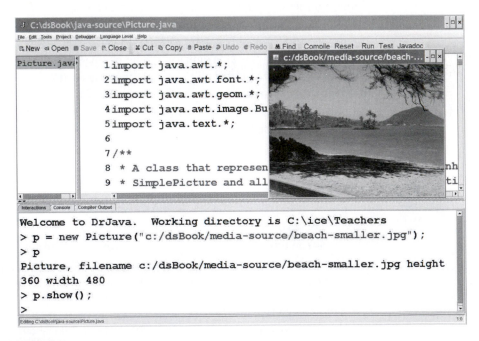

FIGURE 2.6
Showing a picture.

Common Bug: One declaration per scope

Within a given *scope* (e.g., any set of curly braces, such as a single method, or the Interactions Pane in DrJava between compilations or after a reset), a variable can be declared once and only once. Another declaration with the same name is an error. You can change what the variable refers to as you might like after declaration, but you can only *declare* it once.

After the scope in which it was declared, the variable ceases to exist. So, if you declare a variable inside the curly braces of a `for` or `while` loop, it will not be available *after* the end curly brace.

■

Common Bug: Windows may be hidden on Macintosh computers

When you open windows or pop-up file choosers on a Macintosh, they will appear in a separate "Java" application. You may have to find it from the Dock to see it.

■

The downside of types is that, if you need a variable, you need to declare it (with its type) in order to create it. In general, that's not a big deal. You do have to plan ahead when you are programming, to declare the variables you will need before you use them.

When we modify pictures, we will actually change the color of the individual *picture elements*. Picture elements are also called *pixels*. Let's say that you want a variable to refer to a pixel (class `Pixel`) that you're going to assign inside a loop to each pixel in a list of pixels. In that case, the declaration of the variable *should* be *before* the loop. If the declaration was inside the loop, you'd be re-creating the variable each time through the loop, rather than just changing the value of the variable.

To refer to an array of pixels, we use the notation `Pixel[]`. The square brackets are used in Java to index an array. In this notation, the open-close brackets means "an array of indeterminate size." We can use the method `getPixels` to get a one-dimensional array of all the pixels in the picture.

Here's an example of increasing the red for each pixel of a picture by doubling the original red value (Figure 2.7).

```
> Pixel[] pixelArray = p.getPixels();
> for (Pixel pixelObj : pixelArray) {
    pixelObj.setRed(pixelObj.getRed()*2);
  }
> p.show()
```

How would we put this process in a file, something that we could use for *any* picture? If we want *any* picture to be able to double the amount of red, we need to edit the class `Picture` in the file `Picture.java` and add a new `method`, maybe named `doubleRed`.

Here's what we would want to type in. The special variable `this` will represent the Picture instance that is being asked to double red. (In Python or Smalltalk, `this` is typically called `self`.)

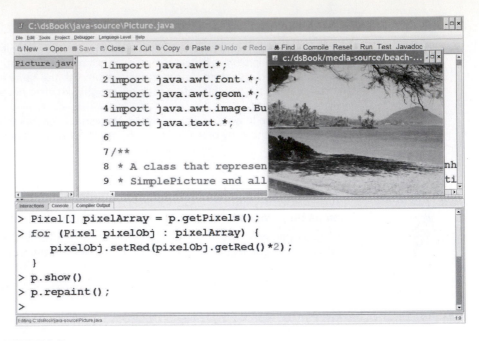

FIGURE 2.7
Doubling the amount of red in a picture.

Example Java Code 10: Method to double the red in a Picture

```
    /**
2    * Method to double the red in a picture.
     */
4   public void doubleRed() {
       // get the array of pixels for this picture
6      Pixel [] pixelArray = this.getPixels();

8      // loop through all the pixels in the array
       for (Pixel pixelObj : pixelArray) {
10
         // set the red at this pixel to twice the original value
12       pixelObj.setRed(pixelObj.getRed()*2);
       }
14   }
```

■

How It Works

- The notation /** begins a Javadoc multi-line comment in Java—stuff that the compiler will ignore. The notation */ ends the comment. Javadoc is a utility that will read our Java source files and create html documentation from the Javadoc comments. Java also has two other types of comments that are ignored by the Javadoc utility. One is a single-line comment using //. This type of comment can be anywhere on a line and comments out the rest of the line. The other is a multi-line comment using /* to start and */ to end. This comments out all lines between the start and end symbols.

- We have to declare methods just as we have to declare variables! The term `public` means that any class can use this method. Why would we want a method to be `private`? Sometimes you want a method to be used only inside the class and not be available to other classes. The term `void` means "this is a method that doesn't return anything—don't expect the return value to have any particular type, then."

Once we type this method into the bottom of class `Picture` (before the closing curly brace), we can press the COMPILE button. If there are no errors, we can test our new method. When you compile your code, the objects and variables you had created in the Interactions Pane disappear. You'll have to re-create the objects you want.

Making It Work Tip: The command history isn't reset!

Though you lose the variables and objects after a compilation, the history of all commands you typed in DrJava is still there. Just hit up-arrow to get to previous commands, then hit return to execute them again.

You can see how this works in Figure 2.8.

```
> Picture p = new Picture(FileChooser.pickAFile());
> p.explore();
> p.doubleRed()
> p.explore();
```

The method `explore` will make a copy of the current picture and open it in a picture explorer. The picture explorer will let you see the red, green, and blue values for any pixel in a picture.

What would happen if the amount of red at a pixel is already near the maximum value of 255 and you try to double it? What do you think should happen? You can call the method `doubleRed` several times on a picture and use the explorer to check what actually happens.

Later on, we're going to want to have characters moving to the left or to the right. We'll probably only want to create one of these (left or right), then flip it for the other side. Let's create the method for doing that. Notice that this method returns a *new* picture, it doesn't modify the original one. Instead of being declared with a return type of `void`, the `flip` method is declared with a return type of `Picture`. This means that it must return a picture. At the bottom of the method, you'll see that it uses `return` to return the `target` picture that we created inside the method. We'll see later that that's pretty useful, to create a new image rather than change the target picture (Figure 2.9).

Example Java Code 11: Method to flip an image

```
/**
2    * Method to flip a picture
   */
4  public Picture flip() {
```

FIGURE 2.8
Doubling the amount of red using our doubleRed method on bigben.jpg.

```
      // declare some local variables
6     Pixel currPixel = null;
      Pixel targetPixel = null;
8     Picture target =
        new Picture(this.getWidth(),this.getHeight());
10
      /* loop through the picture with the source x
12       starting at 0
       * and the target x starting at the width minus one
14     */
      for (int srcX = 0, trgX = getWidth()-1;
16         srcX < getWidth();
           srcX++, trgX--) {
18      for (int srcY = 0, trgY = 0;
             srcY < getHeight();
20           srcY++, trgY++) {

22        // get the current pixel
          currPixel = this.getPixel(srcX,srcY);
24        targetPixel = target.getPixel(trgX,trgY);

26        // copy the color of currPixel into target
          targetPixel.setColor(currPixel.getColor());
28      }
      }
30    return target;
    }
```

FIGURE 2.9
Flipping our guy—original (left) and flipped (right).

```
> Picture p = new Picture(FileChooser.pickAFile());
> p
Picture, filename c:\dsBook\media-source\mLeft1.jpg height 264
width 97
> p.show();
> Picture flipP = p.flip();
> flipP.show();
```

Common Bug: Width is the size, not the index

Why did we subtract one from getWidth() (which defaults to this.getWidth()) to set the target X coordinate (trgX)? getWidth() returns the *number of pixels* across the picture. But the last valid *index* in the row is one less than that, because Java starts all arrays at index *zero*. The method getWidth returns the number of pixels, not the last index.

■

2.5   EXPLORING SOUND IN JAVA

We can create sounds in much the same way we created pictures.

```
> Sound s = new Sound(FileChooser.pickAFile());
> s.play();
> s.explore();
```

How It Works.   Just as with pictures, we can create sounds when we declare them. FileChooser is a class that knows how to pickAFile(). That method puts up a file picker, then returns a string (or null, if the user hits CANCEL). Instances of the class Sound know how to play().

But what if we get it wrong?

```
> s.play()
> s.show()
Error: No 'show' method in 'Sound'
> Picture.play()
Error: No 'play' method in 'Picture'
> anotherpicture.play()
Error: Undefined class 'anotherpicture'
```

You can't ask a Sound object to show(). It doesn't know how to do that. Picture (the class) doesn't know how to play() nor how to show().The *instances* (objects of that type or class) know how to show(). The point of this example isn't to show you Java barking error messages, but to show you that there is no bite there. Typed the wrong object name? Oh well—try again.

2.6   EXPLORING MUSIC IN JAVA

We will be working a lot with *MIDI* (musical information data interchange) in this class. MIDI is a standard representation of musical information. It doesn't record sound. It records notes—when they're pressed, when they're released, how hard they're pressed, and what instrument is being played.

To use MIDI, we have to import some additional libraries. We're going to be using *JMusic* which is a wonderful Java music library that is excellent for manipulating MIDI.

```
> import jm.util.*;
> import jm.music.data.*;
> Note n1;
> n1 = new Note(60,0.5);
> // Create an eighth note at C octave 4
```

How It Works.   First, there are a couple of import statements that allow us to use short names for classes in JMusic. JMusic classes are in packages and the full name for a class in a package is the package name followed by a period followed by the class name. But, if we import all the classes in a package, we can just use the class name to refer to a class in a package. Note is the name of the class that represents a musical note object. We're declaring a note variable named n1. We then create a Note instance (object). We don't need a filename—we're not reading a JPEG or WAV file. Instead, we simply need to know *which* note and for what duration (0.5 is an eighth note). That last line looks surprisingly like English. It is. Any line starting with "//" is considered a *comment* and is ignored by Java. Table 2.1 summarizes the relationships between note numbers and more traditional keys and octaves.

But this isn't actually enough to play our note yet. A note isn't music, at least not to JMusic.

TABLE 2.1 MIDI notes

Octave #						Note Numbers						
	C	**C#**	**D**	**D#**	**E**	**F**	**F#**	**G**	**G#**	**A**	**A#**	**B**
−1	0	1	2	3	4	5	6	7	8	9	10	11
0	12	13	14	15	16	17	18	19	20	21	22	23
1	24	25	26	27	28	29	30	31	32	33	34	35
2	36	37	38	39	40	41	42	43	44	45	46	47
3	48	49	50	51	52	53	54	55	56	57	58	59
4	60	61	62	63	64	65	66	67	68	69	70	71
5	72	73	74	75	76	77	78	79	80	81	82	83
6	84	85	86	87	88	89	90	91	92	93	94	95
7	96	97	98	99	100	101	102	103	104	105	106	107
8	108	109	110	111	112	113	114	115	116	117	118	119
9	120	121	122	123	124	125	126	127				

FIGURE 2.10
Just two notes.

```
> Note n2=new Note(64,1.0);
> View.notate(n1);
Error: No 'notate' method in 'jm.util.View' with arguments:
(jm.music.data.Note)
> Phrase phr = new Phrase();
> phr.addNote(n1);
> phr.addNote(n2);
> View.notate(phr);
-- Constructing MIDI file from'Untitled Score'... Playing with
JavaSound ... Completed MIDI playback --------
```

How It Works.   You just saw that we can't notate() a single note. We can, however, create a phrase that can take two notes (Figure 2.10). A Phrase in JMusic knows how to add a note using the method addNote(). The View class knows how to display a phrase of music in standard Western music notation using the method notate(). Notice that we didn't have to create a View object. We just called the notate method on the class since it is a class method. From the displayed window, we can actually play our music, change parameters (like the speed at which it plays), and shift instruments (e.g., to accordion or wind chimes or steel drums). We'll do more with the display window later.

JMusic is a terrific example of using objects to *model*. JMusic is really modeling music. We can break down the differences between `Note` instances and `Phrase` instances in terms of what they *know* and what they *do*.

- `Note` objects have tones and durations.
- Musical `Phrase` objects are collections of notes.
- The `View` class can display a musical phrase.

	What instances of this class *know*	What instances of this class *do*
Note	A musical pitch and its duration.	(Nothing we've seen yet.)
Phrase	Notes in the phrase.	addNote(aNote)

The entire collection of objects in a JMusic `Score` is a model of Western music, beyond just notes and phrases (Figure 2.11). We can associate instruments with `Part` instances. We could associate them with `Phrase` instances, but that doesn't mesh with how real world parts work. We rarely see the First Violin swapping instruments for a saxophone midway through a piece. `Part` instances are collected into a `Score`. Scores have a tempo. Rarely do different musician's parts have different tempos for the same piece, so it makes sense for the `Score` to have the tempo.

Note that a `Phrase` instance can have any number of `Notes`, a `Part` can have any number of `Phrases`, and a `Score` can have any number of `Parts`. How might that be

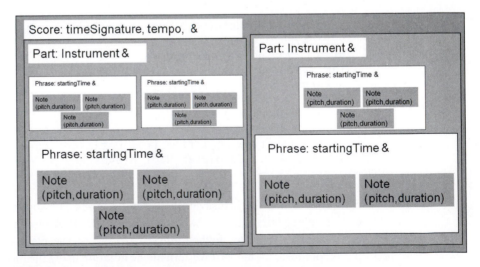

FIGURE 2.11
Structure of a score in terms of JMusic objects.

implemented? Almost certainly, none of these objects contain a pre-sized `Array`. These objects are using dynamic data structures that can expand its size.

EXERCISES

2.1   Define the following:

- inheritance
- polymorphism
- overloading
- overriding
- association
- subclass
- superclass
- instance
- field
- method

2.2   Declare an array of `String` objects and set the array elements to five different strings.

2.3   Declare a variable that will represent if you have eaten. Declare a variable that will represent the score in a soccer game. Declare a variable that will represent the price of an item.

2.4   Declare more than one variable referring to the same object.

2.5   Try to declare two variables with the same name in the same scope. What happens?

2.6   We have been using the type `int` to represent integers. There are other types that you can use to represent integers in Java. What are the other types and what are the differences between them?

2.7   Try to divide 1 by 3 in the Interactions Pane. What result do you get? Is this what you expect? Why do you get this result?

2.8   Try to divide 1.0 by 3.0 in the Interactions Pane. What result do you get? Is this what you expect? Why do you get this result?

2.9   Look up Unicode on the Web. What is it and why does Java use it to represent characters?

2.10   Look up two's complement on the Web. What is it and how does it represent negative numbers?

2.11   Look up IEEE 754 floating point format on the Web. What is it and how does it represent floating point numbers?

2.12   Create a constructor for `Student` that takes a name and an id.

2.13   Add a private field eMail to the Person class. This field will be used to store a person's e-mail address. Add accessor and modifier methods for this private field.

2.14   What happens when you try to directly modify a private field in a child class using dot notation to access the field? Why does this happen?

2.15   Create a class that models a teacher. The Teacher class should also inherit from the Person class. Are there any fields we should add to the Teacher class?

2.16   Create a class that models a credit card. It should contain fields for the person's name, the credit card number, the expiration date, and the security code. Be sure to include constructors, accessors, and modifier methods.

2.17   Create a class that models a car. The Car class should have fields for color, manufacturer, model, and year. Be sure to include constructors, accessors, and modifier methods.

2.18   Create a class that models a class session. Each class session should have an array of students in that class session. Each class session should have a teacher.

2.19   Add a method to the Picture class that sets the red and blue values for each pixel to zero. You can call this keepOnlyGreen. Do you think that you will still be able to tell what is in the picture?

2.20   Add a method zeroBlue to the Picture class that sets the blue value to zero for every pixel in the picture.

3

Methods in Java: Manipulating Pictures

3.1 REVIEWING JAVA BASICS

3.2 CHANGING THE PICTURE CLASS

3.3 METHODS THAT RETURN SOMETHING: COMPOSITING IMAGES

3.4 CREATING CLASSES THAT DO SOMETHING

Chapter Learning Objectives

To make the wildebeests charge over the ridge or the villagers move around in the town square, we need to be able to manipulate pictures. We manipulate pictures using methods, the bits of behavior that classes store for use on their objects. That's the focus of this chapter.

The computer science goals for this chapter are:

- To become more familiar with Java syntax and control statements.
- To create a variety of different kinds of methods, including those that return values.
- To recognize Javadoc comments.
- To chain method calls for compact, powerful expressions.
- To start our discussion of data structures with arrays.

The media learning goals for this chapter are:

- To extend what we can do with pictures.
- To combine methods for powerful picture manipulation.

3.1 REVIEWING JAVA BASICS

Assignment

As we saw in the last chapter, assignments come in the form of

```
TYPE NAME = EXPRESSION;
```

or simply (if the variable has already been declared),

```
NAME = EXPRESSION;
```

As mentioned, we can't declare variables twice in the same scope, and you can't use a variable of one type (or class) with an expression that results in an incompatible type. You can't assign a `String` object to an `int` variable, for example.

Making It Work Tip: DrJava will declare variables for you—maybe not a good thing

If sound is an undeclared variable, DrJava will actually allow you to execute sound = new Sound("D:/myfile.wav"); in the Interactions Pane. DrJava is smart enough to figure out that you must intend that sound to be of type Sound. Our suggestion: don't rely on this. Be explicit in your type declarations. It will be too easy to forget to declare the variables when you're in Java Code Pane and you must declare them there before you use them. ∎

There are rules about *Java programming style* that you should know about. These aren't rules that, if broken, will result in a compiler error (usually). These are rules about how you write your code so that other Java programmers will understand what you're doing. We might call them *discourse rules*—they're the standard style or ways of talking that Java programmers use.

- Always start class names with a capital letter, like `String`.
- Never start variable names, field names, or method names with a capital letter! These names should start with a lowercase word, like `sound`.
- You should capitalize the first letter of each additional word in a name to make it easier to read, like `pixelArray`.

All Java statements end with a semicolon, and indentation doesn't matter at all in Java, unlike in other languages like Python. You can have no indentation at all in Java! Of course, no one, including you, will be able to make out what's going on in your program if you use no indentation at all. You probably should indent as we do here, where the body of a loop is indented deeper than the loop statement itself. DrJava will take care of that for you to make it easier to read, as will some other Java Integrated Development Environments (*IDE*s).

What goes in an expression? We can use +, -, *, and / exactly as you used them in whatever your first programming language was. An expression that you've seen several times already is `new ClassName()`, sometimes with inputs like `new Picture("C:/mypicture.jpg")`. You may have already noted that sometimes you create a new class with inputs, and sometimes you don't. Whether or not you need inputs depends on the *constructors* for the given class—constructors initalize the new object and set the field values to any passed inputs. For example, when we created a new `Note` with a pitch and a duration, we passed the specification of the pitch and duration in as input to the class `Note` and they were used to initialize the new object.

Java has a handful of shortcuts that you will see frequently. Because the phrase x = x + 1 (where x could be any integer variable) occurs so often, we can abbreviate it as x++. Because the phrase y=y-1 occurs so often, it can be abbreviated as y--. There's a general form, too. The phrase x = x + y can be shortened to x += y. There are similar abbreviations x *= y, x /= y, and x -= y.

Arrays

An array is a homogenous (all items are of the same type) linear collection of objects that are together in memory. An array of integers, then, is a whole bunch of numbers (each without a decimal place), one right after another in memory. Being all scrunched together in memory is about as efficient in terms of memory space as they can be, and they can be accessed very quickly—going from one to the other is like leaving your house and going to the house next door.

An array is declared with square brackets []. The square brackets can come before or after the variable name in a declaration, so both of the below are correct Java statements (though clearly you can't use both in the same scope!).

```
Pixel[] myPixels;
Pixel myPixels[];
```

It is important to note that neither of the ways to declare an array actually creates an array. They both just declare a reference to an array of Pixel objects. The value of myPixels will be automatically set to null as shown below.

```
> Pixel[] myPixels;
> System.out.println(myPixels);
null
```

To access an array, we'll use square brackets again, e.g., myPixels[0], which gets the first element in the array. Java begins numbering its indices at zero.

Conditionals

You've seen already that conditionals look like this:

```
if (LOGICAL-EXPRESSION)
    then-statement;
```

As you would expect, the logical expression can be made up of the same logical operators you've used before: <,>,<=,>=,==. Note that == is the test for equivalence—it is not the assignment operator =. Depending on other languages you've learned, you may have used the words and and or for chaining together logical statements, but not in Java. In Java, a logical *and* is &&. A logical *or* is ||.

The then-statement part can be one of two things. It could just be a simple statement ending in a semicolon (e.g., pixel.setRed(0);). Or it could be any number of statements (each separated by semicolons) inside of curly braces, like this:

```
if (pixel.getRed()<25) {
    pixel.setRed(0);
    pixel.setBlue(120);
}
```

Do you need a semicolon after the last curly brace? No, you don't have to, but if you do, it's not wrong. All of the below are correct conditionals in Java.

```
if (thisColor == myColor)
  setColor(thisPixel,newColor);
if (thisColor == myColor) {
  setColor(thisPixel,newColor);
}
if (thisColor == myColor) {
  x = 12;
  setColor(thisPixel,newColor);
}
```

As you recall from the last chapter, we call a set of open and close curly braces a *block*. A block is a single statement to Java. All the statements in the block together are considered just one statement. Thus, we can think of a Java statement ending in a semicolon or a right curly brace (like an English sentence can end in "." or "!" or "?").

After the block for the *then* part (the part that gets executed "if" the logical expression is true, as in "if this, then that") of the if, you can have the keyword else. The else keyword can be followed with another statement (or another block of statements) that will be executed if the logical expression is *false*. You can't use the else statement if you end the *then* block with a semicolon though (like in the last if in the example above). Java gets confused if you do that, and thinks that you're trying to have an else without an if.

Iteration: For each, While, and For

We used the for-each statement in the last chapter to loop through all pixels of a picture.

Example Java Code 12: Method to increase red in Picture

```
 /**
2  * Method to double the red in a picture.
  */
4 public void doubleRed() {
    Pixel [] pixelArray = this.getPixels();
6   for (Pixel pixelObj : pixelArray) {
      pixelObj.setRed(pixelObj.getRed()*2);
8   }
  }
```

A while loop looks like an if:

```
while (LOGICAL-EXPRESSION)
    statement;
```

But they're not at all similar. An if tests the expression *once* and then executes the *then* statement if the expression was true. A while tests the expression, and if true, executes the statement—then tests the expression again, and again executes the statement, and repeats until the expression is no longer true. That is, a while statement *iterates*.

We can use a while for addressing all the pixels in an image and setting all the red values to zero. We just have to walk through the elements of the array ourselves.

```
> p
Picture, filename D:/cs1316/MediaSources/Swan.jpg height 360 width
480
> Pixel [] myPixels = p.getPixels();
> int index = 0;
> while (index < myPixels.length) {
    myPixels[index].setRed(0);
    index++;
}
```

How It Works. Notice the reference to myPixels.length above. This is the standard way of getting an array's length. The expression .length isn't referring to a method. Instead it's referring to a public *instance variable* or *field*. Every array has a field that stores its length. Each length is an instance variable unique to that instance. It's all the same name, but it's the right value for each array.

Here's the same example as the while loop above, but with a for loop:

```
> for (int i=0; i < myPixels.length ; i++) {
    myPixels[i].setRed(0);
}
```

How It Works. Our *initialization* part is declaring an integer (int) variable i and setting it equal to zero. Notice that i will *ONLY* exist within the for loop. On the line afterward, i won't exist—Java will complain about an undeclared variable. The *continuing condition* is i < myPixels.length. We keep going until i is equal to the length, and we *don't* execute when i is equal to the length. The *change area* is i++—increment i by 1. What this does is to make i take on every value from 0 to myPixels.length-1 (minus 1 because we stop when i *IS* the length), and execute the body of the loop—which sets red of the pixel at i equal to zero.

3.2 CHANGING THE PICTURE CLASS

For the Picture object, there is a file named Picture.java that defines the fields and methods that all Picture objects know (Figure 3.1). That file starts out with the line public class Picture. That starts out the definition of the class Picture. Everything inside the open curly brace and matching close curly brace at the end of the file is part of the definition of the class Picture.

Typically, we define at the top of the file the instance variables (fields) that *all* objects of that class know. After that we define the constructors that are used to initialize the fields in new objects. Next we define the methods. The fields, constructors, and methods must be inside the open and close curly braces for the class definition. Each object (e.g., each Picture instance) has the same instance variables, but different values for those variables—e.g., each picture has a filename where it read its file from, but the filenames for different picture objects will be different. All picture objects know the same methods—they *know how to do* the same things.

Picture.java

```
public class Picture  {

/////////// fields ///////////////////////

/////////// constructors ///////////////

/////////// methods ///////////////////////

}
```

FIGURE 3.1
Structure of the `Picture` class defined in Picture.java.

Debugging Tip: You change Picture.java

There should be one and only one `Picture.java` file. This means that you *have to* modify the file that we give you. If you rename it (say, `Picture-v2.java`), Java will just complain about the filename being incorrect. If you save `Picture.java` somewhere else, Java will get confused about two versions. Save a backup copy somewhere, and trust that it will be okay—you won't damage the file too severely. ∎

So what's this `public` statement about the class `Picture`? You might be wondering if there are other options, like `discreet` or `celebrity`. The statement `public` means that the class `Picture` can be used by any other class. This is also called public *visibility*, as in who can see the class. In general, *every* field or method has a visibility which can be `public`, or `protected`, or `private`, or if no visibility is specified, the default is `package` visibility.

- `public` visibility means that the class, field, or method is accessible by anyone. If there was a class with `public` fields, any other object could read those fields or change the values in them. Is that a good thing? Think about it—if objects represent (model) the real world, can you read any value in the world or change it? Not usually.

- `private` visibility means that the field or method can be accessed *only* by the code in the class containing that field or method. That's probably the best option for fields. Some methods might be `private`, but probably most are `public`.

- `protected` visibility is a middle ground that is only really useful for inherited methods. It means that the field or method is accessible by any class or its subclass—or any class belonging to the same *package*. "Package?" you say. "I haven't seen anything about packages!" Exactly—and if you don't deal with packages, `protected` data and methods are essentially `public`. Makes sense? Not to us either.

- `package` visibility means that the class is visible to classes in the same package. Again if you aren't using packages, you can ignore package visibility.

Pictures Are About Arrays and Pixels

A picture has a two-dimensional array of pixels. An array is typically one-dimensional in many programming languages—there's just a collection of values, one right after the other. In a one-dimensional array, each element has a number associated with it called an *index variable*—think of it as the mailbox address for each element. A two-dimensional array is called a *matrix*—it has both height and width. In Java two-dimensional arrays are actually arrays of arrays. We usually number the columns and the rows. With pictures, the upper left hand corner is row number 0 (which we will refer to as the *y* index) and column number 0 (which we will refer to as the *x* index). The *y* values increase going down, and the *x* values increase going to the right.

Each unique pair of a column index and row index of a picture contains a *pixel*. A pixel is a picture element—a small dot of color in the picture or on the screen. Each dot is actually made up of a red component, a green component, and a blue component. Each of those components can have a value between 0 and 255. A red value of 0 is no red at all, and a red value of 255 has the maximum amount of red. All the colors that we can make in a picture are made up of combinations of red, green, and blue values, and each of those pixels sits at a specific (*x*, *y*) location in the picture.

A Method for Decreasing Red

Let's explore a method in the class `Picture` to see how this all works. Here's the method to decrease the red in a picture, which would be inserted in `Picture.java` inside the curly braces defining the class.

Example Java Code 13: decreaseRed in a Picture

```
   /**
2   * Method to decrease the red by half in the current picture
    */
4  public void decreaseRed() {

6    Pixel pixel = null; // the current pixel
     int redValue = 0;   // the amount of red
8
     // get the array of pixels for this picture object
10   Pixel[] pixels = this.getPixels();

12   // start the index at 0
     int index = 0;
14
     // loop while the index is less than the length of the
16   // pixels array
     while (index < pixels.length) {
18
       // get the current pixel at this index
20     pixel = pixels[index];
       // get the red value at the pixel
22     redValue = pixel.getRed();
       // set the red value to half what it was
24     redValue = (int) (redValue * 0.5);
       // set the red for this pixel to the new value
26     pixel.setRed(redValue);
       // increment the index
```

```
28              index++;
          }
30      }
```

We can use this method like this:

```
> Picture myPic =
  new Picture("C:/dsBook/media-source/barbara.jpg");
> myPic.show(); // Show the picture
> myPic.decreaseRed();
> myPic.repaint(); // Update the picture to show the changes
```

The first line creates a picture (new Picture...), declares a variable myPic to be a Picture, and assigns myPic to the new picture (the value at the variable will be a reference to the picture). We then show the picture to get it to appear on the screen. The third line *calls* (or *invokes*) the method decreaseRed on the picture referred to by myPic. The fourth line, myPic.repaint();, tells the picture to update itself on the screen. The method decreaseRed changes the pixels within memory, but repaint tells the window on the screen to update from memory.

How It Works.   Note that this method is declared as returning void—that means that this method doesn't return anything. It simply changes the object that it has been invoked upon. It's public, so anyone (any object) can invoke it.

At the beginning of the method, we typically declare the variables that we will be using. We will be using a variable pixel to hold each and every pixel in the picture. It's okay to have a variable pixel whose class is Pixel—Java is case sensitive so it can figure out the variable names from the case names. We will use a variable named redValue to store the red value for each pixel before we change it (decrease it by 50%). It will be an integer (no decimal part) number, so we declare it to be an int.

Making It Work Tip: Give local variables values as you declare them

It's considered good practice to give initial values to the local variables as you declare them. That way you know what is in there when you start, because you put it in there. Java does not give default values to local variables. Java does assign default initial values to all fields. Fields of type int or double have a default initial value of 0. Fields of type boolean have an initial value of false. Fields of any object type have a default initial value of null.

We give redValue an initial value of zero. We give pixel an initial value of null. null is the value that says, "This variable doesn't refer to any object right now."

The next line in decreaseRed is the statement that both declares the array of pixels and assigns the variable to refer to the array of pixels. The array that we assign it to is what the method getPixels() returns. (That's the method getPixels which takes no inputs, but we still have to type () to tell Java that we want to call the method.) getPixels is a really useful method that returns all those pixels that are in the picture, but as a linear, single-dimensional array. It converts them from the matrix form (array of arrays) to a one-dimensional array form, to make them easier to process. Of course, in the case of a one-dimensional array, we lose the ability to know what row or column a pixel is in, but if we're doing the same thing to all pixels, we really don't care.

Notice that the object that we invoke getPixels() on is this. What's this? The object that we invoked decreaseRed on. In our example, we are calling decreaseRed on the picture referred to by myPic (barbara.jpg). So this is the picture created from the file barbara.jpg.

We are going to use a variable named index to keep track of which pixel we are currently working on in this method. The first index in any array is 0, so we start out index as 0. We next use a while loop to process each pixel in the picture. We want to keep going as long as index is less than the number of pixels in the array. The number of elements in the array pixels is pixels.length.

length is not a method—it's a *field* or an *instance variable*. It's a value, not a behavior. We access it to get the number of elements in an array. Every array has a public field length.

Common Bug: The maximum index is *length* − 1

A common mistake when working with arrays is to make the index go while it is less than or equal to *length*. The length is the *number* of elements in the array. The index numbers (the addresses on the array elements) start at 0, so the maximum index value is *length* − 1. If you try to access the element at index *length* you will get an error that says that you have an OutOfBoundsException—you've gone beyond the bounds of the array.

∎

The body of the while loop in decreaseRed will execute repeatedly as long as index is less than *pixels.length*. Within the loop, we do the following:

- Get the pixel at address index in the array pixels and make variable pixel refer to that pixel.

- Get the redness out of the pixel in variable pixel by calling the method getRed() and store it in redValue.

- Make redValue 50% smaller by setting it to 0.5 times itself. Notice that multiplying redValue by 0.5 could result in a value with a decimal point (think about odd values). But redValue can only be an integer, a value with no decimal point. So, we have to force the return value into an integer. To do that we *cast* the value into an integer; i.e., int. By saying "(int)" before the value we are casting ("(redValue * 0.5))"), we turn it into an integer. There's no rounding involved—any decimal part simply gets hacked off.

- Then store the new redValue back into the pixel with setRed(redValue). That is, we invoke the method setRed on the pixel in the variable pixel with the input redValue: pixel.setRed(redValue);.

- Finally, increment index with index++;. That makes index point toward the next value in the array, all set for the test at the top of the while and the next iteration through the body of the array.

Method with an Input

What if we wanted to decrease red by an *amount*, not always 50%? We could do that by calling decreaseRed with an input value. Now, the code we just walked through doesn't take an input. Here's a method that does.

Example Java Code 14: decreaseRed with an input

```java
/**
 * Method to decrease the red by an amount
 * @param amount the amount to change the red by
 */
public void decreaseRed(double amount) {

  Pixel[] pixels = this.getPixels();
  Pixel p = null;
  int value = 0;

  // loop through all the pixels
  for (int i = 0; i < pixels.length; i++) {

    // get the current pixel
    p = pixels[i];
    // get the value
    value = p.getRed();
    // set the red value the passed amount time what it was
    p.setRed((int) (value * amount));
  }
}
```

How It Works.   This version of decreaseRed has something within the parentheses after the method name—it's the amount to multiply each pixel value by. We have to tell Java the type of the input value. It's the type double, meaning that it's a double-precision value; i.e., it can have a decimal point.

In this method, we use a for loop. A for loop has three parts to it:

- An initialization part, a part that occurs before the loop begins. Here, that's int i = 0. The semicolons indicate the end of a part.
- A test part—what has to be true for the loop to continue. Here, it's that we have more pixels left, i.e., i < pixels.length.
- A change part, something to change each time through the loop. Here, it's i++, which increments the value in variable i by 1.

The rest of this loop is much the same as the other. *It's perfectly okay in Java to have both versions of decreaseRed in the Picture class at once.* Java can tell the difference between the version that takes no inputs and the one that takes one numeric input. We call the name, the number of inputs, and the types of the inputs the *method signature*. As long as two methods have different method signatures, it's okay for them to both have the same name.

Notice the odd comment at the start of the method, the one with the @param notation in it. That is a specialized form of comment that is used to produce HTML documentation for the class using a utility called *Javadoc*. The Javadoc-produced Web pages for the classes provided with this book are in the doc folder inside the java-source folder. These Web pages explain all the methods, their inputs, how they're used, and so on (Figure 3.2). We sometimes refer to this information as the *API* or *Application Program Interface*. The content comes from these specialized comments in the Java files.

Now, if you look at the class Picture, you may be surprised to see that it doesn't know very much at all. Certainly, important methods like show and repaint are missing. Where are they? If you open the class Picture (in the file Picture.java), you'll see that it says:

```
public class Picture extends SimplePicture
```

That means that some of what the class Picture understands is actually defined in the class SimplePicture. Class Picture *extends* class SimplePicture. Picture is a subclass of SimplePicture, which means that class Picture *inherits* everything that SimplePicture has and knows. It's SimplePicture that actually knows about pixels and how pictures are stored, and it's SimplePicture that knows how to show and repaint pictures. Picture inherits all of that by being a *subclass* of SimplePicture.

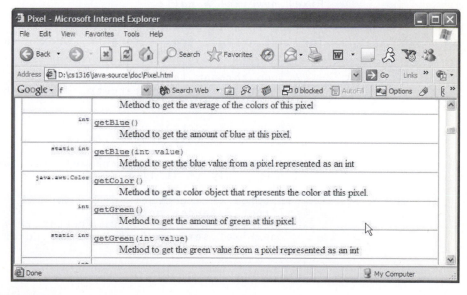

FIGURE 3.2
Part of the JavaDoc page for the Pixel class.

Why do that? Why make `Picture` so relatively dumb? There are lots of reasons for using inheritance. The one we're using here is *information hiding*. Open up `Simple-Picture.java` and take a peek at it. It's pretty technical and sophisticated code, filled with `BufferedImage` objects and references to `Graphics` contexts. We *want* you to edit the `Picture` class, to change methods and add new methods. We want that code to be understandable, so we hide the stuff that is hard to understand in `SimplePicture`.

3.3   METHODS THAT RETURN SOMETHING: COMPOSITING IMAGES

If we're going to make wildebeests or villagers, we need some way of getting those images onto a frame. Here are some methods that can do it. Along the way, we will create methods that return new pictures—a very useful feature for creating more complex pictures.

Example Java Code 15: Method to compose this picture into a target

```
/**
 * Method to compose (copy) this picture onto a target
 * picture at a given point.
 * @param target the picture onto which we copy this picture
 * @param targetX target X position to start at
 * @param targetY target Y position to start at
 */
public void compose(Picture target, int targetX,
int targetY) {

  Pixel currPixel = null;
  Pixel newPixel = null;

  // loop through the columns
  for (int srcX=0, trgX = targetX; srcX < this.getWidth();
      srcX++, trgX++) {

    // loop through the rows
    for (int srcY=0, trgY=targetY; srcY < this.getHeight();
        srcY++, trgY++) {

      // get the current pixel
      currPixel = this.getPixel(srcX,srcY);

      /* copy the color of currPixel into target,
       * but only if it'll fit.
       */
      if (trgX < target.getWidth() &&
          trgY < target.getHeight()) {
        newPixel = target.getPixel(trgX,trgY);
        newPixel.setColor(currPixel.getColor());
      }
    }
  }
}
```

We have been using `FileChooser.pickAFile()` to get the full pathname for a picture file or specifying the full pathname ourselves, but we can simply set the path to the directory that has the media (`media-source`) once and then use `FileChooser.get-MediaPath("name.jpg")` which will add the saved media directory path in front of `name.jpg`. You can use `FileChooser.pickMediaPath()` in the Interactions Pane to pick the directory that has the media in it (media-source) or use `FileChooser.set MediaPath("directory/")` to set it. If you use `FileChooser.setMediaPath ("directory/")` be sure to either double all backslash characters (\\) or use forward slashes ('/'). You do not have to set the media path again unless you change the location of the directory that has the media.

```
> FileChooser.pickMediaPath()
The media directory is now C:\dsBook\media-source/
> String file = FileChooser.getMediaPath("mLeft1.jpg")
> System.out.println(file)
"C:\dsBook\media-source/mLeft1.jpg"
```

Using the `compose` method defined above, we can compose (copy) a guy into the jungle like this (Figure 3.3).

```
> Picture p = new Picture(FileChooser.getMediaPath("mLeft1.jpg"));
> Picture jungle =
  new Picture(FileChooser.getMediaPath("jungle.jpg"));
> p.compose(jungle,65,200);
```

FIGURE 3.3
Composing a guy into the jungle.

```
> jungle.show();
> jungle.write(FileChooser.getMediaPath("jungle-with-guy.jpg"));
```

How It Works.   Basically what happens in this method is that we copy the colors out of the source picture, `this`, and set the pixels in the `target` to those colors. That makes `this` picture (the one you invoked the method on) appear in the target picture.

The `compose` method takes three inputs. The first one is a picture onto which the `this` picture (the one that the method is being invoked upon) will be composed. Think of the input as a canvas onto which we paint this picture. The other two inputs are the *x* and *y* positions where we start painting the picture—the variables `targetX` and `targetY` are integers that define where the upper left hand corner of this picture appears in the target picture.

We don't have the luxury of using `getPixels` this time. We need to know which rows and columns are which, so that we make sure that we copy them all into the right places. We don't want this picture (our source) to show up as one long line of pixels—we want the rows and columns in the source to show up as rows and columns in the target.

We are going to need two `for` loops. One is going to take care of the *x* indices, and the other will take care of the *y* indices. We use two variables for keeping track of the current pixel in `this` picture, our source. Those variables are named `srcX` and `srcY`. We use two other variables for keeping track of the current location in the target, `trgX` and `trgY`. The trick to a composition is to always increment `srcX` and `trgX` together (so that we're talking about columns in the source and the target at the same time), and `srcY` and `trgY` together (so that the rows are also in synch). You don't want to start a new row in the source but not the target, else the picture won't look right when composed.

To keep them in sync, we use a `for` loop where we move a couple of expressions in each part. Let's look at the first one in detail.

```
for (int srcX=0, trgX = targetX; srcX < this.getWidth();
     srcX++, trgX++)
```

- In the initialization part, we declare `srcX` and set it equal to zero, then declare `trgX` and have it start out as the input `targetX`. Notice that declaring variables here is *the same as* (for the `for` loop) declaring them inside the curly braces of the `for` loop's block. This means that those variables exist *only* in this block—you can't access them after the class ends.

- In the testing part, we keep going as long as we have more columns of pixels to process in the source—that is, as long as `srcX` is less than the maximum width of this picture, `this.getWidth()`.

- In the change part, we increment `srcX` and `trgX` together.

Common Bug: Don't try to change the input variables

You might be wondering why we copied targetX into trgX in the compose method. While it's perfectly okay to use methods on input objects (as we do in compose() when we get pixels from the target), and maybe change the object that way, don't try to add or subtract the values passed in. It's complicated why it doesn't work, or how it does work in some ways. It's best just to use them as variables you can *read* and *call methods on*, but not *change*. ∎

The body of the loop essentially gets the pixel from the source picture, gets the pixel from the target picture, and sets the color of the target pixel to the color of the source pixel. There is one other interesting statement to look at:

```
if (trgX < target.getWidth() && trgY < target.getHeight())
```

What happens if you have a really wide source picture and you try to compose it at the far right edge of the target? You can't fit all the pixels, of course. But if you write code that *tries* to access pixels beyond the edge of the target picture, you will get an error about OutOfBoundsException. This statement prevents that.

The conditional says that we get the target pixel and set its color *only* if the *x* and *y* values that we're going to access are less than the maximum width of the target and the the maximum height of the target. We stay well inside the boundary of the picture that way.[1]

So far, we've only seen methods that return void. We get some amazing expressive power by combining methods that return other objects. Below is an example of how we use the methods in class Picture to scale a picture larger (or smaller).

```
> // Make a picture from a file selected by the user
> Picture flower =
  new Picture(FileChooser.getMediaPath("flower1.jpg"))
> Picture bigFlower = flower.scale(2.0);
> bigFlower.show();
> bigFlower.write("bigFlower.jpg"); // write out the changed
  picture
```

Example Java Code 16: Method to scale the Picture by a factor

```
   /**
2   * Method to scale the picture by a factor, and return the
    * result
4   * @param factor to scale by (1.0 stays the same,
    *    0.5 decreases each side by 0.5, 2.0 doubles each side)
6   * @return the scaled picture
    */
8  public Picture scale(double factor) {

10    Pixel sourcePixel, targetPixel;
      Picture canvas = new Picture(
```

[1]Of course, if you try to compose to the *left* of the picture, or *above* it, by using negative starting index values, you will get an exception still.

```
12              (int) (factor*this.getWidth())+1,
                (int) (factor*this.getHeight())+1);
14      // loop through the columns
        for (double sourceX = 0, targetX=0;
16           sourceX < this.getWidth();
             sourceX+=(1/factor), targetX++) {
18
          // loop through the rows
20        for (double sourceY=0, targetY=0;
               sourceY < this.getHeight();
22             sourceY+=(1/factor), targetY++) {

24          sourcePixel = this.getPixel((int) sourceX,
              (int)sourceY);
26          targetPixel = canvas.getPixel((int) targetX,
              (int)targetY);
28          targetPixel.setColor(sourcePixel.getColor());
          }
30      }
        return canvas;
32  }
```

■

How It Works.   The method `scale` takes as input the amount to scale the picture `this`. This method has a return type of `Picture`, instead of `void`—`scale` returns a picture.

The basic process of scaling isn't too complicated. If we have a picture and want it to fit into a smaller space, we have to lose some pixels—we simply can't fit all the pixels in. (All pixels are basically the same size, for our purposes.) One way of doing that is to skip, say, every other pixel, by skipping every other row and column. We do that by adding two to each index instead of incrementing by one each time through the loop. That reduces the size of the picture by 50% in each dimension.

What if we want to scale *up* a picture to fill a large space? Well, we have to duplicate some pixels. Think about what happens if we add 0.5 to the index variable (either for *x* or *y*) each time through the loop. The values that the index variable will take will be 0, 0.5, 1.0, 1.5, 2.0, 2.5, and so on. But the index variable can only be an integer, so we'd chop off the decimal. The result is 0, 0, 1, 1, 2, 2, and so on. By adding 0.5 to the index variable, we end up taking each position twice, thus doubling the size of the picture.

Now, what if we want a different sizing—increase by 30% or decrease by 25%? That's where the `factor` comes in as the input to `scale`. If you want a factor of 0.25, you want the new picture to be 1/4 of the original picture in each dimension. So what do you add to the index variable? It turns out that $1/factor$ works most of the time. For example, 1/0.25 is 4, which is a good index increment to get 0.25 of the size. We said that it works most of the time. Why doesn't it work all of the time? What happens if you try 0.3 as the factor? Does this work?

The `scale` method starts out by *creating* a target picture. The picture is sized to be the scaling factor times the height and width—so the target will be bigger if the scaling factor is over 1.0, and smaller if it is less. As we can see here, new instances of the class `Picture` can be created by filename *or* by specifying the height and width of the picture. The returned picture is blank. We add 1 to deal with off-by-1 errors on oddly sized pictures.

The tricky part of this method is the `for` loops.

```
for (double sourceX = 0, targetX=0;
     sourceX < this.getWidth();
     sourceX+=(1/factor), targetX++)
```

Like in `compose`, we're manipulating two variables at once in this `for` loop. We're using `double` variables to store the indices, so that we can add a $1/factor$ to them and have them work, even if $1/factor$ isn't an integer. Again, we start out at zero, and keep going as long as there are columns (or rows, for the y variable) to process. The increment part has us adding 1 to `targetX` but doing `sourceX += (1/factor)` for the `sourceX` variable. This is a shortcut that is equivalent to `sourceX = sourceX + (1/factor)`.

When we use the index variables, we cast them to integers, which removes the floating point part.

```
sourcePixel = this.getPixel((int) sourceX,(int) sourceY);
```

At the very end of this method, we `return` the newly created picture. The power of returning a new picture is that we can now do a lot of manipulation of pictures by opening only a few pictures and *never changing those original pictures*. Consider the code below which creates a mini-collage by creating a new blank picture (by asking for a `new Picture` with a height and width as inputs to the constructor, instead of a filename) then composing pictures onto it, scaled at various amounts (Figure 3.4).

```
> Picture blank = new Picture(600,600);
> Picture swan = new Picture(FileChooser.getMediaPath("swan.jpg");
> Picture rose = new Picture(FileChooser.getMediaPath("rose.jpg");
> rose.scale(0.5).compose(blank,10,10);
> rose.scale(0.75).compose(blank,300,300);
> swan.scale(1.25).compose(blank,0,400);
> blank.show();
```

What's going on here? How can we *cascade* methods like this? It's because *all* pictures understand the same methods, whether they were created from a file or created from nothing. So, the *scaled* `rose` understands `compose` just as well as the `rose` itself does.

Sometimes you don't want to `show` the result. You may prefer to `explore` it, which allows you to check colors and get exact x and y coordinates for parts of the picture. We can `explore` pictures to figure out their sizes and where we want to compose them (Figure 3.5).

```
> Picture guy =
  new Picture(FileChooser.getMediaPath("mRight.jpg"))
> Picture jungle =
  new Picture(FileChooser.getMediaPath("jungle.jpg"))
```

```
> guy.explore()
> jungle.explore()
```

Composing by Chromakey

Chromakey is the video technique by which a meteorologist on our television screen gestures to show a storm coming in from the east, and we see the meteorologist in front of a map (perhaps moving) where the storm is clearly visible in the east next to the meteorologist's hand. The reality is that the meteorologist is standing in front of a blue or green screen. The chromakey algorithm replaces all the blue or green pixels in the picture with pixels of a different background, effectively changing where it looks

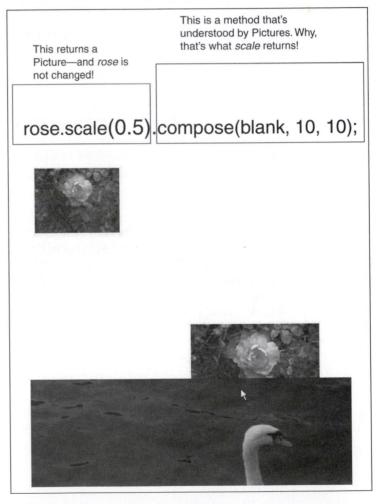

FIGURE 3.4
Mini-collage created with scale and compose.

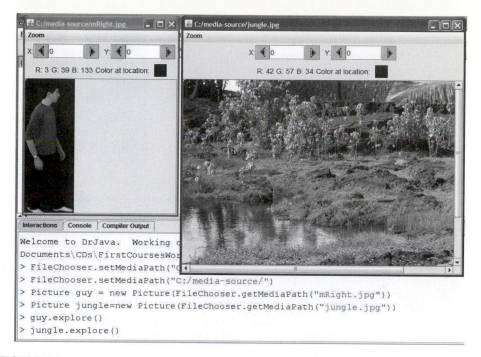

FIGURE 3.5
Using the `explore` method to see the sizes of the guy and the jungle.

like the meteorologist is standing. Since the background pixels won't be all the *exact* same blue or green (due to lighting and other factors), we usually use a *threshold* value. If the blue or green is "close enough" (that is, within a threshold distance from our comparison blue or green color), we swap the background color.

There are a couple of different chromakey methods in `Picture`. The method `chromakey()` lets you input the color for the background and a threshold for how close you want the color to be. The method `blueScreen()` assumes that the background is blue, and looks for more blue than red or green (Figure 3.6). If there's a lot of blue in the character (e.g., the guy's denim slacks in the picture), it's hard to get a threshold to work right. It's the same reason that the meteorologists don't wear blue or green clothes—we'd see right through them!

```
> Picture p = new Picture(FileChooser.getMediaPath("mRight.jpg"))
> Picture back = new Picture(640,480)
> p.bluescreen(back,65,250)
> import java.awt.Color // allows the short name for color
> p.chromakey(back,Color.BLUE,100,165,250)
> p.chromakey(back,Color.BLUE,200,265,250)
> back.show()
```

FIGURE 3.6
Chromakeying the guy onto a blank screen using blueScreen and different thresholds for chromakey.

Example Java Code 17: Methods for general chromakey and blueScreen

```
/**
 * Method to do chromakey using an input color for the
 * background
 * and a point for the upper left corner of where to copy
 * @param target the picture onto which we chromakey this
 * picture
 * @param bgColor the color to make transparent
 * @param threshold within this distance from bgColor, make
 * transparent
 * @param targetX target X position to start at
 * @param targetY target Y position to start at
 */
public void chromakey(Picture target, Color bgColor,
                      int threshold,
                      int targetX, int targetY) {

  Pixel currPixel = null;
  Pixel newPixel = null;

  // loop through the columns
  for (int srcX=0, trgX=targetX;
       srcX<getWidth() && trgX<target.getWidth();
       srcX++, trgX++) {

    // loop through the rows
    for (int srcY=0, trgY=targetY;
         srcY<getHeight() && trgY<target.getHeight();
         srcY++, trgY++) {

      // get the current pixel
      currPixel = this.getPixel(srcX,srcY);

      /* if the color at the current pixel is within
       * threshold of
       * the input color, then don't copy the pixel
       */
      if (currPixel.colorDistance(bgColor)>threshold) {
        target.getPixel(trgX,trgY).setColor(currPixel.
          getColor());
```

```
40            }
           }
42        }
      }

44
      /**
46     * Method to do chromakey assuming a blue background
       * @param target the picture onto which we chromakey this
48     * picture
       * @param targetX target X position to start at
50     * @param targetY target Y position to start at
       */
52    public void blueScreen(Picture target,
                             int targetX, int targetY) {
54
        Pixel currPixel = null;
56      Pixel newPixel = null;

58      // loop through the columns
        for (int srcX=0, trgX=targetX;
60           srcX<getWidth() && trgX<target.getWidth();
             srcX++, trgX++) {
62
          // loop through the rows
64        for (int srcY=0, trgY=targetY;
               srcY<getHeight() && trgY<target.getHeight();
66             srcY++, trgY++) {

68          // get the current pixel
            currPixel = this.getPixel(srcX,srcY);
70
            /* if the color at the current pixel mostly blue
72           * (blue value is
             * greater than red and green combined), then don't
74           * copy pixel
             */
76          if (currPixel.getRed() + currPixel.getGreen() >
                currPixel.getBlue()) {
78            target.getPixel(trgX,trgY).setColor(currPixel.
              getColor());
80          }
          }
82      }
      }
```

■

3.4   CREATING CLASSES THAT DO SOMETHING

So far, we have created methods in the class Picture that know *how* to do something, but we actually *do* things with statements in the Interactions Pane. How do we get a Java class to *do* something? We use a particular method that declares itself to be the main thing that this class *does*. You declare a method like this:

```
public static void main(String[] args) {
  //code goes here
}
```

The code that goes inside a main method is exactly what goes in the Interactions Pane. For example, here's a class where the *only* thing it does is to create a mini-collage.

Example Java Code 18: A public static void main in a class

```
public class MyPicture {

    public static void main(String args[]){

        Picture canvas = new Picture(600,600);
        Picture swan =
          new Picture(FileChooser.getMediaPath("swan.jpg"));
        Picture rose =
          new Picture(FileChooser.getMediaPath("rose.jpg"));
        Picture turtle =
          new Picture(FileChooser.getMediaPath("turtle.jpg"));

        swan.scale(0.5).compose(canvas,10,10);
        swan.scale(0.5).compose(canvas,350,350);
        swan.flip().scale(0.5).compose(canvas,10,350);
        swan.flip().scale(0.5).compose(canvas,350,10);
        rose.scale(0.25).compose(canvas,200,200);
        turtle.scale(2.0).compose(canvas,10,200);
        canvas.show();
    }
}
```

■

The seemingly magical incantation `public static void main(String [] args)` will be explained in detail later, but we can talk about it briefly now.

- `public` means that it's a method that any other class can access.
- `static` means that this is a method accessible from the *class*. We don't need to create instances (objects) of this class in order to run the main method.
- `void` means that the main method doesn't return anything.
- `String[] args` means that the main method can actually take inputs *from the command line*. You can run a main method from the command line by typing the command `java` and the class name, e.g., `java MyPicture` (presuming that you have Java installed!).

To run a main method from within DrJava, use function key F2. That's the same as using RUN DOCUMENT'S MAIN METHOD from the TOOLS menu (Figure 3.7). Or just click on the RUN button.

A main method is not very object-oriented—it's not about defining what an object knows or what it can do. But it is pretty useful.

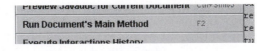

FIGURE 3.7
Run the main method from DrJava.

EXERCISES

3.1 What index would you use to get the 2nd element from an array? What index would you use to get the 10th element from an array?

3.2 What is output of the following code?

```
int[] myArray = {3, 8, 2, 7, 5};
System.out.println(myArray[3]);
System.out.println(myArray[5]);
```

3.3 What is the result of 1 / 3? Can you explain why you get this result?

3.4 What is the result of 4 % 2? What is the result of 5 % 2? What does % do?

3.5 What is the output of the following code?

```
for (int x = 0; x < 5; x++) {
    System.out.println(x);
}
```

3.6 What is the output of the following code?

```
int x = 0;
while (x < 10) {
    System.out.println(x);
    x++;
}
```

3.7 Which loop would you use if you just want to loop through all the pixels in a picture and change each one? Which loop would you use if you want to read all the lines from a file until the method reading lines returns null? Which loop would you use if you want to sum all the numbers from 1 to 100?

3.8 What class does the class Sound inherit from? What class does the class SimplePicture inherit from?

3.9 Look at the documentation in the doc folder of the java-source directory. Find the documentation for the Picture class. How many constructors does it have?

3.10 Look at the documentation in the doc folder of the java-source directory. Find the documentation for the Sound class. How many constructors does it have?

3.11 How many constructors can you find in Picture.java? How many constructors can you find in Sound.java?

3.12 Write a method that creates a black and white picture from a color picture. You can simply set the red, green, and blue values in the picture to the average of the original red, green, and blue values.

3.13 Write a method that creates the negative of the current picture. You can do this by setting the red value to 255 - currPixel.getRed(). Do the same for the green and blue.

3.14   Write a method that flips the pixels in the picture upside down, or 180 degrees.

3.15   Write a method that creates and returns a new picture with the pixels rotated 90 degrees to the left.

3.16   Write a method that creates and returns a new picture with the pixels rotated 90 degrees to the right.

3.17   Write a method that rotates the pixels in a picture 90 degrees to the left.

3.18   Write a method to decrease the red in only the top half of the picture.

3.19   Write a method to increase the red that takes as input a number to use as the amount to multiply the current red value by.

3.20   Write a method to scale only the top half of the picture.

3.21   What happens when you call scale using a factor like one-third? Does it still work correctly?

3.22   Write a method that copies part of the source picture onto the target picture. Specify the region to copy using the x and y values for the top left and bottom right of the region to copy.

3.23   Write a method that does chromakey on only a part of the source picture. Specify the region to do chromakey on using the x and y values for the top left and bottom right of the region to copy.

4

Objects as Agents: Manipulating Turtles

4.1 TURTLES: AN EARLY COMPUTATIONAL OBJECT

4.2 DRAWING WITH TURTLES

4.3 CREATING ANIMATIONS WITH TURTLES AND FRAMES

4.4 MAKING A SLOW MOVING TURTLE WITH SLEEP AND EXCEPTIONS

Chapter Learning Objectives

We are going to model our wildebeests and villagers as *agents*—objects that behave independent of each other, seemingly simultaneously, with a graphical (visible) representation. Turtles are an old computational idea that are useful for understanding agents' behavior. They are also a powerful tool for understanding object-oriented programming. In this chapter, we learn about turtles in order to simplify our later animations and simulations.

The computer science goals for this chapter are:

- To introduce some of the history of object-oriented programming, from Logo (and turtles) to Smalltalk.
- To generalize an understanding of objects, from pictures to turtles.
- To better understand cascading methods.
- To introduce some basic list manipulation ideas, e.g., that nodes are different *objects*.
- To handle *exceptions* in order to use sleep.

The media learning goals for this chapter are:

- To create animations using a FrameSequencer.
- To add another technique for composing pictures.
- To use a simple technique for rotating pictures.

4.1 TURTLES: AN EARLY COMPUTATIONAL OBJECT

In the mid-1960s, Seymour Papert at MIT and Wally Feurzeig and Danny Bobrow at BBN Labs were exploring educational programming by children. That was a radical idea at the time. Computers were large, expensive devices that were shared by multiple people at once. Some found the thought of giving up precious computing time for use by 10- or 11-year-old children to be ludicrous. But Papert, Feurzeig, and Bobrow believed that the activity of programming was a great context for learning all kinds of things, including learning about higher-order thinking skills, like planning and debugging. They created the programming language *Logo* as a simplified tool for children.

The most common interaction with computers in those days was through teletypes—large machines with big clunky keys that printed all output to a roll of paper, like a big cash register receipt paper roll. That worked reasonably well for textual interactions, and much of the early use of Logo was for playing with language (e.g., writing a pig-Latin generator). But the Logo team realized that they really needed some graphical interaction to attract the kids with whom they were working. They created a robot *turtle* with an attached pen to give the students something to control to make drawings.

The simple robot turtle sat on a large piece of paper, and when it moved (and if its pen was "down" and touching the paper) it would draw a line behind it. The Logo team literally invented a new kind of mathematics to make Logo work, where the turtle didn't know Cartesian coordinates ((x, y) points) but instead knew its heading (which direction it was facing), and could turn and go forward. This relative positioning (as opposed to global, Cartesian coordinates) was actually enough to do quite a bit of mathematics, including biological simulations and an exploration of Einstein's Special Theory of Relativity [1].

As we will see in the next section, the Logo turtle is very clearly a computational object. The turtle *knows* some things (like its heading and whether its pen is down) and it can *do* some things (like turn and go forward). But even more directly, the Logo turtle influenced the creation of object-oriented programming. Alan Kay [4] designed his *Smalltalk* programming language using features of Logo. Today, Smalltalk is considered the first object-oriented programming language, and Alan Kay is considered to be the inventor of object-oriented programming.

The Logo turtle still exists in many implementations in many languages. Seymour Papert's student, Mitchel Resnick, developed a version of Logo, *StarLogo*, with thousands of turtles that can interact with one another. Through this interaction, they can simulate scenarios like ants in an anthill, or termites, slime mold, or vehicle traffic [5].

4.2   DRAWING WITH TURTLES

We're going to use turtles to draw on our pictures in interesting and flexible ways, and to simplify animation. Our `Turtle` class instances (objects) can be created on a `Picture` or on a `World`. Think of a `World` as a constantly updating picture that repaints automatically. We create a `World` by simply creating a new one. We create a `Turtle` on this `World` by passing the `World` object in as input to the `Turtle` constructor (Figure 4.1).

Figure 4.2 is an example of opening a turtle on a `Picture` instead. Turtles can be created on blank `Picture` instances (which start out white) in the middle of the picture with pen down and with black ink. When a turtle is told to go forward, it moves forward the input number of *turtle steps* (think "pixels," which isn't *exactly* correct, but is close enough most of the time—the actual unit is computed by Java depending

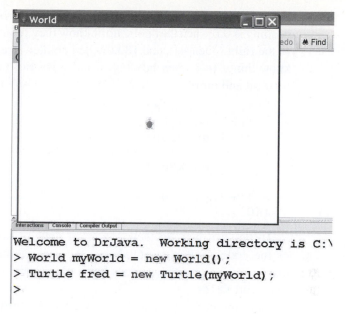

FIGURE 4.1
Starting a Turtle in a new World.

FIGURE 4.2
A drawing on a Picture, made by a turtle.

on your screen resolution) in whatever direction the turtle is currently facing. You can change the direction in which the turtle is facing by using the turn method, which takes as input the number of degrees to turn. Positive degrees are clockwise, and negative ones are counter-clockwise.

```
> Picture blank = new Picture(200,200);
> Turtle fred = new Turtle(blank);
> fred
No name turtle at 100, 100 heading 0.0.
> fred.turn(-45);
> fred.forward(100);
> fred.turn(90);
> fred.forward(200);
> blank.show();
> blank.write("c:/Temp/turtleExample.jpg");
```

Turtles know their position (unlike the original robot turtles) and their heading. The heading is 0.0 when they point north (how they're first created), and 90.0 when pointed to the right (due east), and 180.0 when pointed straight down (south). Clearly, turtles know things (e.g., their heading, *x* and *y* position) and can do things (e.g., like move forward and turn).

```
> fred.forward(100);
> fred.turn(90);
> fred.getHeading()
90
> fred.getXPos()
320
> fred.getYPos()
140
```

Turtles can pick up their pen (stop drawing) using either the method `penUp()` or the code `setPenDown(false)`. We can set the pen down using `penDown()` or `setPenDown(true)`. Java does know about truth, or at least, about *Boolean* values: `true` and `false`.

To draw more complex shapes, we tell the turtle to do its basic steps repeatedly. Telling a turtle to go `forward` a certain number of steps and to `turn` 90 degrees four times draws a square.

```
> for (int sides=0; sides < 4 ; sides++) {
    fred.forward(100); fred.turn(90);
  }
```

When Cascades Don't Work

Here's a thought experiment: will this work?

```
> World earth = new World();
> Turtle turtle = new Turtle(earth);
> turtle.forward(100).right(90);
```

The answer is "no," but can you figure out why? Here's a hint: The error you get in the Interactions Pane is shown below.

```
Error: No
'right' method in 'void' with arguments: (int)
```

The error message is actually telling you exactly what the problem is; it's written in *Javanese*—it presumes that you understand Java and can thus interpret the message.

The problem is that the `forward` method does not return anything, and certainly not a *turtle*. The method `forward` returns `void`. When we cascade methods like this, we are telling Java to invoke `right(90)` on what `turtle.forward(100)` returns. Since `forward` returns `void`, Java checks if instances of class `void` understand `right`. Of course not—`void` is nothing at all. So Java tells us that it checked for us, and the class `void` has no method `right` that takes an integer (`int`) input (e.g., 90 in our example). (Of course, `void` doesn't know anything about `right` with *any* inputs, but just in case we only got the inputs wrong, Java lets us know what it looked for.) Thus: `Error: No 'right' method in 'void' with arguments: (int)`.

You can only use a cascade of method calls if the *previous* method call returns an object that has a method defined for the *next* method call. Since `forward` returns nothing (`void`), you can't cascade anything after it. Sure, we could create `forward` so that it does return the turtle `this`, the one it was invoked on, but does this make any sense? Should `forward` return something?

Making Lots of Turtles

Using Mitchel Resnick's StarLogo as inspiration, we may want to create something with *lots* of turtles. For example, consider what this program draws on the screen.

Example Java Code 19: Creating a hundred turtles

```
public class LotsOfTurtles {

  public static void main(String[] args) {
    // Create a world
    World myWorld = new World();
    // A flotilla of turtles in an array
    Turtle [] myTurtles = new Turtle[100];

    // Make a hundred turtles
    for (int i=0; i < 100; i++) {
      myTurtles[i] = new Turtle(myWorld);
    }

    //Tell them all what to do
    for (int i=0; i < 100; i++) {
      // Turn a random amount between 0 and 360
      myTurtles[i].turn((int) (360 * Math.random()));
      // Go 100 pixels
      myTurtles[i].forward(100);
    }
  }
}
```

■

How It Works. Study the program and think about it before you look at Figure 4.3.

- First we create a `World` and name it `myWorld`.

- Next, we create an array to store 100 `Turtle` instances. Notice that `Turtle [] myTurtles = new Turtle[100];` *creates no turtles!* That 100 is enclosed in square brackets—we're not calling the `Turtle` constructor yet. Instead, we're simply asking for 100 slots in an array `myTurtles` that will each refer to a `Turtle`.

- Inside a `for` loop that goes 100 times, we create each turtle and put a reference to it in the array at the current index using the code: `myTurtles[i] = new Turtle(myWorld);`.

- Finally, we tell each of the turtles to turn a random amount and go forward 100 steps. `Math.random()` returns a number between 0 and 1.0 where all numbers

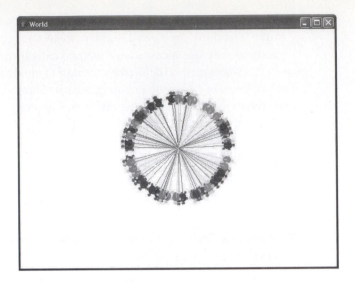

FIGURE 4.3
What you get with a hundred turtles starting from the same point, each turning a random amount from 0 to 360, then moving forward the same amount.

(e.g., 0.2341534) in that range are equally likely. Since that will be a `double`, we have to cast the result to `int` to use it as an input to `forward`.

It makes a circle of radius 100! This is an example from Mitchel Resnick's book that introduced StarLogo [5].

Obviously, we can have more than one `Turtle` in a `World` at once. Instances of class `Turtle` know some methods that allow them to interact with one another. They know how to `turnToFace(anotherTurtle)`, which changes one turtle's heading to point to the other turtle. They also know how to compute `getDistance(x,y)`, which is the distance from this turtle (the one that `getDistance` was invoked upon) to the point *x*, *y*. Thus, in this example, r2d2 goes off someplace random on `tattoine`, but c3po turns to face him and moves forward exactly the right distance to catch r2d2.

```
> World tattoine = new World();
> Turtle r2d2 = new Turtle(tattoine);
> r2d2.turn((int)
      (360 * Math.random()));
> r2d2.forward((int)
      (Math.random() * 100));
> Turtle c3po = new Turtle(tattoine);
> c3po.turnToFace(r2d2);
> c3po.forward((int)
      (c3po.getDistance(
          r2d2.getXPos(),r2d2.getYPos())));
```

FIGURE 4.4
Dropping the monster character.

Composing Pictures with Turtles

We saw earlier that we can place turtles on an instance (object) of class `Picture`, not just instances (objects) of class `World`. We can also use turtles to compose pictures into other pictures, through the use of the `drop` method. Pictures get "dropped" *with the upper left corner of the picture at the center of the turtle and rotated to match the turtle's heading*. If the turtle is facing down (heading of 180.0), then the picture will be upside down (Figure 4.4).

```
> Picture monster =
  new Picture(FileChooser.getMediaPath("mScary.jpg"));
> Picture newBack = new Picture(400,400);
> Turtle myTurtle = new Turtle(newBack);
> myTurtle.drop(monster);
> newBack.show();
```

See the result of the above code in Figure 4.5. Now we'll rotate the turtle and drop the picture again (Figure 4.5).

FIGURE 4.5
Dropping the monster character after a turtle rotation.

FIGURE 4.6
An iterated turtle drop of a monster.

```
> myTurtle.turn(180);
> myTurtle.drop(monster);
> newBack.repaint();
```

We can drop using loops and patterns, too (Figure 4.6). Why don't we see 12 monsters here? Maybe some are blocking the others?

```
> Picture frame = new Picture(600,600);
> Turtle mabel = new Turtle(frame);
> for (int i = 0; i < 12; i++) {
    mabel.drop(monster); mabel.turn(30);
  }
```

We can combine these in a main method to create a more complex image (Figure 4.7).

Example Java Code 20: Making a picture with dropped pictures

```
public class MyTurtlePicture {

  public static void main(String [] args) {
    Picture canvas = new Picture(600,600);
    Turtle jenny = new Turtle(canvas);
    Picture lilTurtle =
        new Picture(
            FileChooser.getMediaPath("Turtle.jpg"));

    for (int i=0; i <=40; i++) {

      if (i < 20) {
        jenny.turn(20);
      }
```

```
16        else {
             jenny.turn(-20);
          }
18
          jenny.forward(40);
20        jenny.drop(lilTurtle.scale(0.5));
       }
22     canvas.show();
     }
24 }
```

■

FIGURE 4.7
Making a more complex pattern of dropped pictures.

4.3   CREATING ANIMATIONS WITH TURTLES AND FRAMES

Our eyes tend to present an image to our brain, even for a few moments after the image has disappeared from sight. That's one of the reasons why we don't panic when we naturally blink (many times a minute without noticing)—the world doesn't go away and we don't see blackness. Rather, our eyes persist in showing the image in the brief interval when we blink—we call that *persistence of vision*.

A movie is a series of images, one shown right after the other. If we can show at least 16 images (*frames*) in a logical sequence in a second, our eye merges them through persistence of vision, and we perceive continuous motion. Fewer frames per second (fps) may be viewed as continuous, but it will probably be choppy. If we show frames that are not in a logical sequence, we perceive a montage, not continuous motion. Typical theater movies present at 24 fps, and video is typically 30 fps.

If we want to create an animation, then, we need to store a bunch of instances of Picture as frames, then play them back faster than 16 fps. We have a class for doing this; it is called FrameSequencer.

- The constructor for FrameSequencer takes a path to a directory where frames will be stored as JPEG images, so that you can reassemble them into a movie using some other tool (e.g., Windows Movie Maker, Apple Quicktime Player, ImageMagick). Or you can write a Quicktime movie or AVI movie from a directory of frames using the class MoviePlayer which is provided in java-source.

- A FrameSequencer knows how to show(). Once shown, a FrameSequencer will show each frame as it is added to the FrameSequencer. When you first tell a FrameSequencer to show, it will warn you that there's nothing to see until a frame is added.

- It knows how to addFrame(aPicture) to add another frame to the Frame-Sequencer.

- It knows how to play(framesPerSecond) to show a sequence of frames back again. The framesPerSecond is the number of frames to show per second. If you specify 16 fps or higher, this will be perceived as continuous motion.

Here's a silly example of how you might use a FrameSequencer. We're adding three (unrelated) pictures to a FrameSequencer via addFrame. We can then play the frame sequence, at 1 fps (or strictly, one frame per 1000 milliseconds).

```
> FrameSequencer f = new FrameSequencer("c:/Temp");
> f.show()
There are no frames to show yet. When you add a frame it will be
shown

> Picture t = new
    Picture(FileChooser.getMediaPath("turtle.jpg"));
> f.addFrame(t);
> Picture barb = new
    Picture(FileChooser.getMediaPath("barbara.jpg"));
> f.addFrame(barb);
> Picture katie = new
    Picture(FileChooser.getMediaPath("kLeft.jpg"));
> f.addFrame(katie);
> f.play(1); // display one frame per second
```

Let's combine turtles and a FrameSequencer to make an animation of frames.

Example Java Code 21: An animation generated by a turtle

```
public class MyTurtleAnimation {

  private Picture canvas;
  private Turtle jenny;
  private FrameSequencer f;

  public MyTurtleAnimation() {

    canvas = new Picture(600,600);
    jenny = new Turtle(canvas);
    f = new FrameSequencer("C:/Temp/");
  }

  public void next() {
    Picture lilTurtle =
      new Picture(FileChooser.getMediaPath("turtle.jpg"));
    jenny.turn(-20);
    jenny.forward(30);
    jenny.turn(30);
    jenny.forward(-5);
    jenny.drop(lilTurtle.scale(0.5));
    f.addFrame(canvas.copy());   // Try this as
                                 // f.addFrame(canvas);
  }

  public void next(int numTimes) {
    for (int i=0; i < numTimes; i++) {
      this.next();
    }
  }

  public void show() {
    f.show();
  }

  public void play(int framesPerSecond) {
    f.show();
    f.play(framesPerSecond);
  }
}
```

■

We run this program like this:

```
> MyTurtleAnimation anim = new MyTurtleAnimation();
> anim.next(20); // Generate 20 frames
> anim.play(2); // Play them back, two per second
```

How It Works.   An instance of MyTurtleAnimation has three instance variables associated with it: a Picture onto which the turtle will draw, named canvas, a Turtle named jenny, and a FrameSequencer. The constructor for MyTurtleAnimation creates the original objects for each of these three names.

Common Bug: Don't declare the instance variables (fields) in methods or constructors

There's a real temptation to put "Picture" in front of that line in the constructor canvas = new Picture(600,600);. But resist it. Will it compile? Absolutely. Will it work? Not at all. If you declare canvas as a Picture inside of the constructor MyTurtleAnimation(), it *only* exists in the constructor. You want to access the field canvas which exists outside that method. If you don't declare it in the constructor, Java figures out that you mean the field (instance variable). It assumes that you mean this.canvas, which is the field canvas in the current object.

∎

There are two different next methods in MyTurtleAnimation. The one that we called in the example (where we told it to go for 20 steps) is this one:

```
public void next(int numTimes) {
  for (int i=0; i < numTimes; i++) {
    this.next();
  }
}
```

All that next(int numTimes) does is to call next() the input numTimes number of times. So the real activity in MyTurtleAnimation occurs in next() with no inputs.

```
public void next() {
    Picture lilTurtle =
      new Picture(FileChooser.getMediaPath("turtle.jpg"));
    jenny.turn(-20);
    jenny.forward(30);
    jenny.turn(30);
    jenny.forward(-5);
    jenny.drop(lilTurtle.scale(0.5));
    f.addFrame(canvas.copy());   // Try this as
                                 // f.addFrame(canvas);

}
```

The method next() does a bit of movement, a drop of a picture, and an addition of a frame to the FrameSequencer. Basically, it generates the next frame in the animation sequence.

The show() and play() methods *delegate* their definition to the FrameSequencer instance. Delegation is where one class accomplishes what it needs to do by asking an instance of another class to do the task. It's perfectly reasonable to ask an animation to show() or play(), but the way that it would accomplish those tasks is by asking the FrameSequencer to show or play.

The Data Structure within FrameSequencer

Did you try this same animation with the last line of next changed to f.addFrame (canvas);? What happened? If you did try it, you may have thought you made a mistake. When you ran the next animation, you saw the animation play out as normal. But when you executed play, you saw only the final frame appear —never any other frame. Go check the temporary directory where the `FrameSequencer` wrote out the frames. You'll find a bunch of JPEG images there: `frame0001.jpg`, `frame0002.jpg`, and so on. So the animation did work and the `FrameSequencer` did write out the frames. But why isn't it replaying correctly?

What we are seeing helps us to understand how `FrameSequencer` works and what its internal data structure is. As you might imagine, a `FrameSequencer` is a series of frames—but that's not correct in the details. The `FrameSequencer` is actually a list of *references* to `Picture` objects. Each element in the `FrameSequencer` refers to some `Picture`.

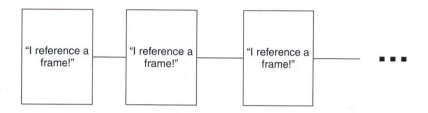

If a `FrameSequencer` does not actually have any frames in it, where do the frames come from? From the `Picture` that you input to `addFrame!` That's what the Frame-Sequencer frame references point to.

Without the `copy()` method call on `canvas`, all the references in the Frame-Sequencer point to *one* `Picture`, `canvas`. There is only *one* picture in the Frame-Sequencer, and since, at the end, the `canvas` is in its final state, then all the references in FrameSeqence point to that same `canvas` `Picture` in its final state.

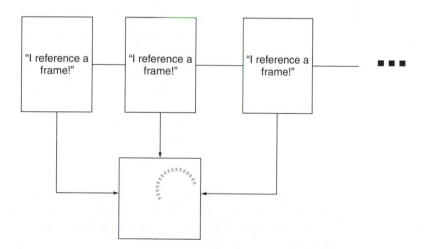

With `canvas.copy()`, you create a copy of the picture in the canvas, a *different* `Picture` for *each* reference in the `FrameSequencer`. When we tell the `FrameSequencer` to `play`, the pictures referenced by the `FrameSequencer` play out on the screen.

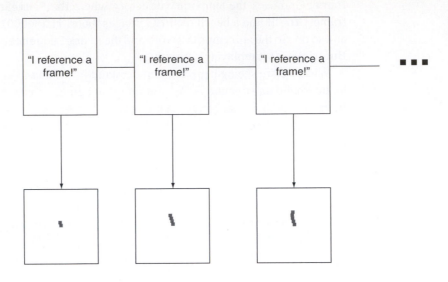

4.4   MAKING A SLOW MOVING TURTLE WITH **SLEEP** AND EXCEPTIONS

Let's say that you wanted a turtle that would move *slowly*, that would pause after moving so that you could more easily watch it move. One way to do that would be to use `blockingPlay` on a sound to pause execution. Fortunately, there's an easier way.

The flow of execution in Java is called a *thread*. The currently executing thread is called `Thread` (capital letter). We can tell the `Thread` to `sleep`, or to pause for a certain number of milliseconds. Executing `Thread.sleep(1000)` would pause execution for one second.

However, we can't just *call* `Thread.sleep`. Java wants you to write code that takes care of bad things that might happen in your code. If you use `Thread.sleep`, you *have* to take care of *exceptions* or else Java won't even compile your code.

Exceptions are disruptions in the normal flow of a program. There is actually a Java class named `Exception` that is used in handling exceptions. In other programming languages, there are ways for programmers to check if something bad has happened—and most programmers don't check. Java *requires* the programmer to handle exceptions. The programmer can be specific (e.g., "If the disk fails, do this. If the filename is bad, do that.") or general (e.g., "If *anything* bad happens, here's how to bail out.").

There is a special Java statement just for handling exceptions. It's called `try-catch`. It looks something like this:

```
try {
\\code that can cause the exceptions
} catch (ExceptionClassName varName) {
    \\code to handle this exception
```

```
} catch (ExceptionClassName varName) {
    \\code to handle that exception
}
```

You can deal with ("catch") several exceptions at once, of different types. If you do try to distinguish between exceptions in a single statement like that, put the most general one last, e.g., catch the general Exception, and maybe one like FileNotFoundException (for trying to open a file for reading that doesn't exist) earlier in the list. All those other exceptions are subclasses of Exception, so catching Exception will handle all others. A general exception handling try-catch might look like this:

```
try {
//code that can throw the exception
} catch (Exception e) {
    System.err.println("Exception: " + e.getMessage());
    System.err.println("Stack Trace is:");
    e.printStackTrace();
}
```

That e in the above code is a variable that will be a reference to the exception object, if an exception occurs. Exceptions know several different methods. One returns (as a String) the error message associated with the exception e.getMessage(). Another prints out the line where the exception occurred in the currently executing method and all the method calls between the beginning of execution and the exception e.printStackTrace().

Since Thread.sleep can throw exceptions, we have to use try-catch around it.

Example Java Code 22: SlowWalkingTurtle

```
/**
 * A class that represents a slow walking turtle
 * @author Mark Guzdial
 * @author Barb Ericson
 */
class SlowWalkingTurtle extends Turtle {

  /** Constructor that takes the model display
    * @param modelDisplay the thing that displays the model
    */
  public SlowWalkingTurtle (ModelDisplay modelDisplay) {
    // let the parent constructor handle it
    super(modelDisplay);
  }

  /**
   * Method to have the turtle go forward then wait a moment
   * and then go on.
   * @param pixels the number of pixels to go forward
   */
  public void forward(int pixels) {
    super.forward(pixels);
    try {
        Thread.sleep(500); // Wait a half sec
```

```
      } catch (Exception e) {
26        System.err.println("Exception: " + e.getMessage());
          System.err.println("Stack Trace is:");
28        e.printStackTrace();
      }
30    }

32 }
```

∎

How It Works.   The SlowWalkingTurtle is a kind of Turtle. We need a constructor
that passes the construction off to the superclass. We override forward so that, after
moving, we pause for a half second. The rest of that method is our try-catch to deal
with anything bad that might happen.

We use our slow-moving turtle like this:

```
> World earth = new World()
> SlowWalkingTurtle mark = new SlowWalkingTurtle(earth)
> mark.forward(100); mark.forward(100);
```

EXERCISES

4.1   What direction will the Turtle be facing after the following code executes?
      What will the *x* and *y* position be?

```
World earth = new World();
Turtle tina = new Turtle(earth);
tina.turn(-90);
```

4.2   What direction will the Turtle be facing after the following code executes?
      What will the *x* and *y* position be?

```
World earth = new World();
Turtle tina = new Turtle(earth);
tina.forward(30);
```

4.3   What direction will the Turtle be facing after the following code executes?
      What will the *x* and *y* position be?

```
World earth = new World();
Turtle tina = new Turtle(earth);
tina.forward(50);
tina.turn(90);
```

4.4   Add a method to the Turtle class to teach all turtles how to draw a square.

4.5   Add a method to the Turtle class to teach all turtles how to draw an equilateral
      triangle.

4.6   Add a method to the Turtle class to teach all turtles how to draw a pentagon.

4.7   Add a method to the Turtle class to teach all turtles how to draw a hexagon.

4.8   Add a method to the Turtle class to teach all turtles how to draw a star.

4.9   Add a method to the Turtle class to teach all turtles how to draw a letter (like T).

4.10   Look at the documentation for the Turtle class. How many constructors does it have? What class does it inherit from? How can you change the color of the pen? How can you make the line the Turtle draws thicker? How do you move the Turtle to a particular position (x and y location)?

4.11   Add a method to the Turtle class that takes the radius of a circle and drops four pictures. It should drop one picture at 0 degrees, one at 90 degrees, one at 180 degrees, and one at 270 degrees on the circle. The pictures should be rotated to match the degrees (so the picture dropped at 90 degrees on the circle should be rotated right 90 degrees).

4.12   Add a method to the Turtle class that takes the radius of a circle and the number of pictures to drop. It should drop the given number of pictures equidistant on the circle.

4.13   Add a method to the Turtle class that takes the picture to drop and drops 12 copies of the picture with the turtle turning 30 degrees after each drop.

4.14   Add a method to the Turtle class that moves the Turtle to a passed x and y location and then drops a passed picture.

4.15   Write a class that creates an image collage using Turtle objects that drop pictures. Each image collage must have the same picture at least four times but the image can be rotated, scaled, flipped, and more.

4.16   Create a movie using the FrameSequencer and a Turtle. In each frame have the Turtle drop a picture and then move forward 5 pixels.

4.17   Create a movie using the FrameSequencer and a Turtle. In the first frame of the movie have a picture in the top left corner, and in each frame move it by 5 pixels in x and y (towards the bottom right corner).

4.18   Create a movie using the FrameSequencer and a Turtle. In the first frame of the movie have a picture in the top right corner, and in each frame move it by -5 pixels in x and 5 pixels in y (towards the bottom left corner).

4.19   Create a movie using the FrameSequencer and a Turtle. For each movie frame create a new blank picture and create a new Turtle on the blank picture at a particular location and then drop a picture. Change the location for each frame by 5 pixels in x.

4.20   Using sampled sounds and turtles, create a musical dance. Play music (sounds at least?) while the turtles move in patterns.

- Your piece must last at least 10 seconds.
- You must have at least five turtles. They can drop pictures, they can leave trails (or not), they can spin slowly, whatever you want them to do. Your turtles must move.
- You must have at least four different sounds.

- There must be some interweaving between turtle motion and sounds. In other words, you can't move the five turtles a little, then play 10 seconds of music. Hint: Use blockingPlay() instead of play() to play the sounds. If you use play(), the turtle movement and the sounds will go in parallel, which is nice, but you'll have no way to synchronize playing and moving. The method blockingPlay() will keep anything else from happening (e.g., turtle movement) during the playing of the sound.

Implement your dance and sounds in a TurtleDance class in a main method. For extra credit, use MIDI (JMusic) instead of sampled sounds. Look up the Play object in the JMusic docs. Play.midi(score,false) will play a score in the background (false keeps it from quitting Java after playing). Play.waitcycle (score) will block (wait) anything else from happening until the score is done playing—essentially, letting you block like blockingPlay().

CHAPTER 5

Arrays: A Static Data Structure for Sounds

5.1   MANIPULATING SAMPLED SOUNDS

5.2   INSERTING AND DELETING IN AN ARRAY

5.3   HOW SLOW DOES IT GET?

Chapter Learning Objectives

The last media type that we will need to create animations like those segments of the wildebeests and villagers is sampled sound. Sampled sound has an advantage for our purposes here—it naturally uses an `array`. Sounds can be thought of as arrays of samples. (Samples are measures of air pressures, as measured by a microphone.) We will use sampled sounds to talk about the strengths and weaknesses of arrays as a data structure.

The computer science goal for this chapter is:

- To use and manipulate arrays, including insertions into the middle (shifting the rest towards the end) and deletions from the middle (shifting the end back and padding).

The media learning goals for this chapter are:

- To understand how sounds are sampled and stored on a computer.
- To learn methods for manipulating sounds.

5.1   MANIPULATING SAMPLED SOUNDS

We can work with sounds that come from WAV files. We sometimes call these *sampled sounds* because they are sounds made up of *samples* (thousands per second), in comparison with *MIDI music*, which encodes music (notes, durations, instrument selections) but not the sounds themselves.

A sampled sound is a series of numbers (samples) that represent the air pressure at a given moment in time. As you may know from physics classes, sound is the result of vibrations in the air molecules around our ears. When the molecules bunch up, there is an increase in air pressure called *compression*; when the molecules spread out, there is a *rarefaction* (a drop in the air pressure). We can plot air pressure over time to see the sound cycles.

Each of these samples is a number that can be both positive (for increases in air pressure) and negative (for decreases in air pressure). Typically, two *bytes* (8 bits each, for a total of 16 bits) are used to store each sample. Given that we have to represent both negative and positive numbers in those 16 bits, we have ±32,000 (roughly) as values in our samples. To capture all the frequencies of a sound that humans can hear, CD-quality sound requires that we capture 44,100 samples every second.

A WAV file stores samples, albeit in a compressed form. MIDI actually stores specifications of music. MIDI files contain encoded commands of the form "Press down on this key now" and later "release that key now." What a "key" sounds like is determined by the MIDI synthesizer when the file is played. A WAV file, though, stores the original samples—the sound itself, as encoded on a computer.

Here's a simple example of creating a Sound instance from a file, and playing it.

```
> Sound s =
  new Sound(FileChooser.getMediaPath("thisisatest.wav"));
> s.play();
> s.increaseVolume(2.0);
> s.play();
```

How It Works.   Here we see us creating a new Sound instance (by saying new Sound). The *constructor* for the Sound class (constructors initialize the fields in a new instance of a class) takes a WAV filename as input, then creates a Sound instance from those samples. We play the sound using the play() method. We then increase the volume by 2.0 and play it again.

Increasing the volume is a matter of increasing the amplitude of the sound. Here's what that method looks like.

Example Java Code 23: Increase the volume of a sound by a factor

```
/**
 * Increase the volume of a sound
 **/
public void increaseVolume(double factor) {

  SoundSample[] samples = this.getSamples();

  for (SoundSample current : samples) {
    current.setValue((int) (factor * current.getValue()));
  }
}
```

How It Works.   The first thing we do is to get all the samples out of the sound. The method getSamples() returns an array of SoundSample objects with all the samples in the sound. We then use a for-each loop to iterate through all the samples in the array. Each time through the loop, we set the variable current to refer to the next sample. We multiply the factor by the integer sample value in the SoundSample object referred to by current. We set the sample value to the product. If the factor is less than 1.0, this reduces the volume, because the amplitude shrinks. If the factor is greater than 1.0, the sound increases in volume because the amplitude grows.

Just like with Picture instances, methods that *return* a new Sound are particularly powerful. Consider the following example:

```
> Sound s =
  new Sound(FileChooser.getMediaPath("thisisatest.wav"));
> s.play();
> s.reverse()
Sound number of samples: 64513
```

Why do you think we see this printout after reverse()? Because reverse doesn't *change* the Sound instance that it's called on—it returns a new one. If you were to execute s.play() right now, the sound would be the same. If you want to hear the reversed sound, you'd need to execute s.reverse().play();.

Here's how we reverse a sound.

Example Java Code 24: Reversing a sound

```
/**
 * Method to reverse a sound.
 **/
public Sound reverse() {
    // create a new sound with the same length
    Sound target = new Sound(getLength());
    int sampleValue;

    /* loop with source index starting at 0 and
     * target index starting at the length - 1 */
    for (int srcIndex=0,trgIndex=getLength()-1;
            srcIndex < getLength();
            srcIndex++,trgIndex--) {
      sampleValue = this.getSampleValueAt(srcIndex);
      target.setSampleValueAt(trgIndex,sampleValue);
    }
    return target;
}
```

How It Works.   The reverse() method first creates a target sound instance. It has the same length as the sound that reverse() is called upon. (Notice that a reference to getLength() without a specified object defaults to being a reference to this.) We use a for loop that manipulates two variables at once. The source index, srcIndex, goes up from 0 (the start of the array). The target index, trgIndex, starts at the end of the list. Each time through the list, we add 1 to the source index and subtract 1 from the target index. The effect is to copy the front of the source to the back of the target, and to keep going until the whole sound is copied—reversing the sound. The methods getSampleValueAt and setSampleValueAt allow you to get and set the number in the sample. Most importantly, the last thing in the method is return target; which lets us meet the requirement of our method `reverse()` declaration, that it returns a Sound.

Debugging Tip: Beware the length as an index

Why did we subtract 1 from getLength to start out the target index (trgIndex)? Because getLength is the *number* of elements (samples) in the array, but the last *index* is getLength()-1. Computer scientists stubbornly insist on starting counting indices from 0, not 1, so the last value is one less than the number of elements there. ∎

Methods that return a new sound can then be used to create all kinds of interesting effects, without modifying the source sound.

```
> Sound s = new Sound(FileChooser.getMediaPath("gonga-2.wav"));
> Sound s2 = new Sound(FileChooser.getMediaPath("gongb-2.wav"));
> s.play(); // create the first sound
> s2.play();  // create the second sound
> s.reverse().play(); // Play first sound in reverse
> s.append(s2).play(); // Play first then second sound
> // Mix in the second sound, so you can hear part of each
> s.mix(s2,0.25).play();
> // Mix in the second sound sped up
> s.mix(s2.scale(0.5),0.25).play();
> s2.scale(0.5).play(); // Play the second sound sped up
> s2.scale(2.0).play(); // Play the second sound slowed down
> s.mix(s2.scale(2.0),0.25).play();
```

Given all of these, we can create a *collage* of sounds pretty easily.

Example Java Code 25: Create an audio collage

```java
public class MySoundCollage {

  public static void main(String [] args){

    Sound snap = new Sound(
        FileChooser.getMediaPath("snap-tenth.wav"));
    Sound drum = new Sound(
        FileChooser.getMediaPath("drumroll-1.wav"));
    Sound clink = new Sound(
        FileChooser.getMediaPath("clink-tenth.wav"));
    Sound clap = new Sound(
        FileChooser.getMediaPath("clap-q.wav"));

    Sound drumRev = drum.reverse().scale(0.5);
    Sound soundA = snap.append(clink).
        append(clink).append(clap).append(drumRev);
    Sound soundB = clink.append(clap).
        append(clap).append(drum).append(snap).append(snap);

    Sound collage = soundA.append(soundB).
        append(soundB).append(soundA).
        append(soundA).append(soundB);
    collage.play();
  }
}
```

Here is how some of these additional methods are coded.

Example Java Code 26: Append one sound with another

```java
/**
 * Return this sound appended with the input sound
 * @param appendSound sound to append to this
 **/
public Sound append(Sound appendSound) {
    Sound target = new Sound(getLength() +
                            appendSound.getLength());
    int sampleValue;

    // Copy this sound in
    for (int srcIndex=0,trgIndex=0;
         srcIndex < getLength();
         srcIndex++,trgIndex++) {
      sampleValue = this.getSampleValueAt(srcIndex);
      target.setSampleValueAt(trgIndex,sampleValue);
    }

    // Copy appendSound in to target
    for (int srcIndex=0,trgIndex=getLength();
         srcIndex < appendSound.getLength();
         srcIndex++,trgIndex++) {
      sampleValue = appendSound.getSampleValueAt(srcIndex);
      target.setSampleValueAt(trgIndex,sampleValue);
    }

    return target;
}
```

Example Java Code 27: Mix in part of one sound with another

```java
/**
 * Mix the input sound with this sound, with percent
 * ratio of input.
 * Use mixIn sound up to length of this sound.
 * Return mixed sound.
 * @param mixIn sound to mix in
 * @param ratio how much of input mixIn to mix in
 **/
public Sound mix(Sound mixIn, double ratio) {

    Sound target = new Sound(getLength());
    int sampleValue, mixValue,newValue;

    // Copy this sound in
    for (int srcIndex=0,trgIndex=0;
         srcIndex < getLength() &&
         srcIndex < mixIn.getLength();
         srcIndex++,trgIndex++) {
      sampleValue = this.getSampleValueAt(srcIndex);
      mixValue = mixIn.getSampleValueAt(srcIndex);
      newValue = (int)(ratio*mixValue) +
         (int)((1.0-ratio)*sampleValue);
      target.setSampleValueAt(trgIndex,newValue);
    }
    return target;
}
```

Example Java Code 28: Scale a sound up or down in frequency

```
   /**
 2  * Scale up or down a sound by the given factor
    * (1.0 returns the same, 2.0 doubles the length,
 4  * and 0.5 halves the length)
    * @param factor ratio to increase or decrease
 6  **/
   public Sound scale(double factor) {
 8    Sound target =
        new Sound((int)(factor *(1 + getLength())));
10    int sampleValue;

12    // Copy this sound in
      for (double srcIndex=0.0,trgIndex=0;
14         srcIndex < getLength();
           srcIndex+=(1/factor),trgIndex++) {
16      sampleValue = getSampleValueAt((int)srcIndex);
        target.setSampleValueAt((int) trgIndex,sampleValue);
18    }
      return target;
20  }
```

How It Works.   There are several tricky things going on in these methods, but not *too* many. Most of them are just copy loops with some tweak.

- The class Sound has a *constructor* that takes the number of *samples*.

- You'll notice in reverse that we can use -- as well as ++. variable-- is the same as variable = variable - 1.

- In scale you'll see another shorthand that Java allows: srcIndex+=(1/factor) is the same as srcIndex = srcIndex + (1/factor).

- A double is a floating point number. These can't be automatically converted to integers. To use the results as integers where we need integers, we *cast* the result. We do that by putting the name of the type to cast to in parentheses before the result, e.g., (int) srcIndex.

5.2   INSERTING AND DELETING IN AN ARRAY

A sampled sound is naturally an array. It's a long list of sample values, one right after the other. Manipulation of sampled sounds gives us a sense of the trade-offs of working with an array.

Imagine that you want to *insert* one sound *into* another—not overwriting parts of the original sound, but pushing the end further down. So if you had "This is a test" and you wanted to insert a *clink* sound after the word "is," you'd want to hear "This is *clink* a test." It might look like this:

```
> Sound test =
  new Sound(FileChooser.getMediaPath("thisisatest.wav"));
```

```
> test.getLength()
64513
> Sound clink =
  new Sound(FileChooser.getMediaPath("clink-tenth.wav"));
> clink.getLength()
2184
> test.insertAfter(clink,40000)
> test.play()
```

How would you do this? Think about doing it physically. If you had a line of objects in particular spots (think about a line of mailboxes in an office) and you had to insert something in the middle, how would you do it? First thing you'd have to do is to make space for the new ones. You'd move the ones from the end of where you are copying further down. You would move the last ones first, and then the ones just before the old last, and then the ones before that—moving backwards towards the front. There are some error conditions to consider, e.g., what if there's not enough mailboxes? Assuming that you *have to* put in the new ones, you have to lose some of the old content. Maybe trim off the end?

In any case, your first step would look something like this:

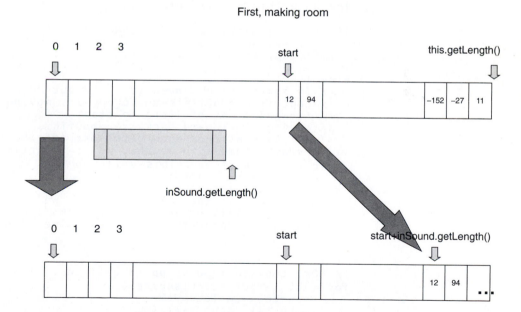

First, making room

And then, you would insert the new things in. That's the easy part.

Second, copying in

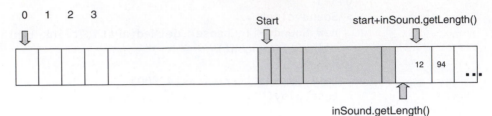

inSound.getLength()

That's essentially what it takes to do it with sounds, too.

Example Java Code 29: Inserting into the middle of sounds

```
   /**
 2  * Insert the input Sound after the specified start
    * Modifies the given sound
 4  * @param inSound Sound to insert
    * @param start index where to start inserting the new sound
 6  */
   public void insertAfter(Sound inSound, int start) {

 8
     SoundSample current=null;

10
     // Find how long inSound is
12   int amtToCopy = inSound.getLength();
     int endOfThis = this.getLength()-1;

14
     if (start + amtToCopy - 1 > endOfThis) {
16     // If too long, copy only as much as will fit
       amtToCopy = endOfThis-start+1;
18   }
     else {
20     // If short enough, need to clear out room.
       // Copy from endOfThis-amtToCopy+1;, moving backwards
22     // (toward front of list) to start,
       // moving UP (toward back) to endOfThis
24     // KEY INSIGHT: How much gets lost off the end of the
       // array?  Same size as what we're inserting -- amtToCopy
26     for (int source=endOfThis-amtToCopy;
            source >= start ;
28          source--) {
         // current is the TARGET -- where we're copying to
30       current = this.getSample(source+amtToCopy);
         current.setValue(this.getSampleValueAt(source));
32     }
     }

34
     // NOW, copy in inSound up to amtToCopy
36   for (int target=start,source=0;
          source < amtToCopy;
38        target++, source++) {
       current = this.getSample(target);
40     current.setValue(inSound.getSampleValueAt(source));
     }
42 }
```

■

Now, imagine that you want to *delete* a portion of a sound. Removing part of a sound has two parts to it:

- First, we have to actually remove the samples you no longer want. Now, we can't actually *remove* elements of an array. We can *copy over* them. We can move the samples *after* the deleted part, *over* the part we want deleted. We copy all the samples that start *right after* the deleted part to the *first* sample in the deleted part.

    We have to be a little careful about how we do that. If the part to be moved is *larger* than the part being deleted, there's going to be an overlap. We don't want to end up overwriting samples that we still need to copy.

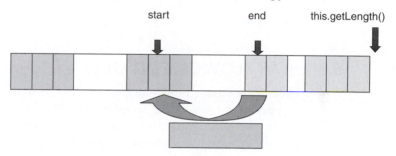

This distance is start-end

- Second, since we're "deleting" some samples, the number of samples will be shorter. However, the sound will be exactly the same length. The extra samples (the same size as the deleted part) are at the end of the sound. When we listen to the sound, we'll hear the ending repeat twice. We don't want that, so we will set those extra samples to *zero* so that the end will be silent.

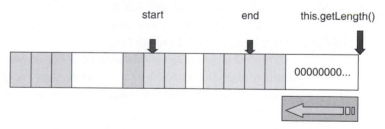

This distance is start-end.

And we'll go from the length backwards.

Example Java Code 30: Deleting from the middle of a sound

```
   /**
 2  * Delete from start to end in this sound
    * @param start where to start deletion
 4  * @param end where to stop deletion
    */
 6 public void delete(int start, int end){

 8     int value = 0;
```

```
10      // Basically, we simply copy from "end" to getLength back
        to start
12      for (int source=end, target=start;
             source < this.getLength();
14           source++, target++)
        {value = this.getSampleValueAt(source);
16        this.setSampleValueAt(target,value);}

18      // Then clear out the rest. Gap is end-start+1 in length
        int gap = end-start+1;
20      for (int i=1; i <= gap ; i++) {
          this.setSampleValueAt(this.getLength()-i,0);}

22    }
```

5.3 HOW SLOW DOES IT GET?

Think for a minute how long each of these methods takes to run, and how that time changes as the size of the sound (or the amount to insert or delete) changes. In the insert method, there are two main loops here, and each one basically involves moving n elements, where n is the number of elements in the inserted array (sound). In the delete method, there are again two main loops, where each involves touching (getting or setting) n elements, where n this time represents the number of array elements to "delete" (i.e., replace with other values, or set to zero).

Computer scientists care about the speed or efficiency of their algorithms. The concern is not so much for the raw amount of time, because that will change with faster (or at least, different) processors. The concern is more about how the time will change as a function of the growth in the amount of data. For each of the insertion or deletion algorithms, we would say that the amount of time needed to run the program grows *linearly* with the growth of n. Inserting or deleting a segment of sound that is twice as long will take twice as much time.

There is a notation for this kind of analysis. It's called *Big-O*. We would say that this algorithm has a complexity $O(2n)$, or since we typically ignore constants in Big-O notation, $O(n)$. The number of operations (the amount of time to execute) grows linearly with the growth of the data.

There are other kinds of notations used to describe complexity. Big-O formally describes the *upper bound* of how long an algorithm will take. It *could* take shorter. There is a *Big-Omega* notation, which describes the lower bound, the fastest an algorithm might execute for a given data size. There is a *Big-Theta* notation, which describes when an algorithm has the *same* upper and lower bound—it will always take the same amount of time.

$O(n)$ (linear) complexity is pretty good for an algorithm. There are better complexities, but there are many far worse.

- In the next chapters, we are going to talk about data structures that allow us to do insertion or deletion in $O(1)$ (constant) time. Finding the right place to do the insertion or deletion might be $O(n)$, but the actual addition or subtraction of the data will always take the *same* amount of time, no matter how big the data segment might be.

- Simple sorting algorithms (where a collection of data is put in order) are $O(n^2)$. Each data item is compared to every other data item, so there are n^2 operations. The best sorting algorithms are smarter about which data elements are compared, so they can actually achieve $O(nlog(n))$ complexity.

- Algorithms that do things *optimally, guaranteeing the best possible outcome*, can have a complexity of $O(n!)$. That's right—the amount of time increases as a *factorial* of the size of the data. That's awful complexity. For even reasonably small n, these types of algorithms can take tens of years to complete even on fast processors.

EXERCISES

5.1   Try playing music over a phone. Does it sound right?

5.2   Use the Internet to find music with hidden messages that you can hear when you play the sounds reversed.

5.3   The values for sounds range from −32768 to 32767. Can you explain why there is one more negative value?

5.4   Create a method that will decrease the volume of a sound.

5.5   Create a method that will increase the volume of a sound only in the given range specified by a start index and a stop index (inclusive).

5.6   Create a method that will find the smallest value in a sound and return it.

5.7   Create a method that counts the number of highest values in a sound (32767) and returns the count.

5.8   Create a method, `clearSound`, that sets all the values in a sound to 0 starting at a given index and ending at a given index (inclusive).

5.9   Create a method that will increase the volume in the first half of the sound and then decrease it in the second half.

5.10   Create a method that will reverse the first half of a sound (the reversed sound will be in the second half of the sound).

5.11   Create a method that will reverse the second half of a sound (the reversed sound will be in the first half of the sound).

5.12   Create a method that will blend (mix) three sounds.

5.13   Create a method that will start with 1/3 the length of one sound, then 1/3 of two sounds blended, and then 1/3 of just the second sound. Start with two sounds of about the same length.

5.14   Does the scale method work for odd factors? Why or why not?

5.15   Write a method that scales just part of a sound.

5.16   Create a method, `createClip`, that creates a clip from the current sound at the passed-in-beginning index and up to the end index (inclusive).

5.17   Create a sentence by appending sound together. You can use the `createClip` method from the previous example to pull out words from other sentences to use in your new sentence.

5.18   Write a method that will add 32768 to the current value, then subtract the result from 65535 and finally subtract 32768. This will cause -32768 to be 32767 and 32767 to be -32768 and 0 to be 0. Try it on speech. Can you still understand the words? This is similar to negating a picture.

5.19   Create your own sound collage. It should have at least three different sounds and do at least two effects to the sounds, such as scale up or reverse.

5.20   Create an array of size 6 with the values 2, 4, and 6 in it at indices 0, 1, and 2. Now move values as needed to add the values 1, 3, and 5 in the correct positions. Loop through the resulting array and print all the values.

5.21   Create an array with the values 1–10 in it. Now remove the value 5 from the array, so that the numbers go from 1 to 4 and then continue from 6 to 10. The last element of the array can be set to -1 to show that it is empty. Loop through the resulting array and print all the values.

PART 2

INTRODUCING LINKED LISTS

CHAPTER 6

Structuring Music Using Linked Lists

6.1 JMUSIC AND IMPORTS

6.2 MAKING A SIMPLE SONG OBJECT

6.3 MAKING A SONG SOMETHING TO EXPLORE AS A LINKED LIST

Chapter Learning Objectives

Media manipulators are often artists and are creative. They need flexibility in manipulating media elements, like inserting some elements here and deleting some there. Arrays, as we saw in the last chapter, are *not* particularly flexible. We will introduce *linked lists* in this chapter as a way of handling data more flexibly. In this chapter, the problem driving our exploration will be, "How do we make it easy for composers to creatively define music?"

The computer science goals for this chapter are:

- To create linked lists of various kinds.
- To understand and use operations on linked lists, including traversals, insertion, deletion, repetition, and weaving.
- To understand the trade-offs between linked lists and arrays.
- To demonstrate a need for tree structures.

The media learning goals for this chapter are:

- To manipulate data flexibly.
- To develop different structures for composing MIDI creatively.
- To use rudimentary forms of automated composition of music.

6.1 JMUSIC AND IMPORTS

The JMusic classes are in several packages. The classes `Note` and `Phrase` are in the package `jm.music.data`. The class `View` is in package `jm.util`. When you use a class that is in a package other than `java.lang`, you must either specify the full name for the class (*packageName.className*) or use an import statement. Import statements tell the compiler where to look for the class definitions for the class names you are using. You can specify an import statement for each class you are using (import *packageName.className*) or just use (import *packageName.**) to indicate all classes in that package.

107

```
Welcome to DrJava.
> import jm.music.data.*;
> import jm.util.*;
> Note n = new Note(60,101);
> n=new Note(60,0.5);
> Phrase phr = new Phrase();
> phr.addNote(n);
> View.notate(phr);
```

Once you have notated a phrase (using View.notate), you can play all the notes in it as shown in Figure 6.1.

The first input (argument) to the *constructor* for class Note is the *MIDI note*. A 60 indicates middle C. Figure 6.2 shows the relation between keys on a piano keyboard, MIDI note values (numbers), and frequencies for the octave starting at middle C.

Here's some more Java code that uses a different Phrase constructor to specify a starting time and an *instrument* to play the notes with. It also uses named constants for musical instruments and note types defined in the class JMC in the jm package. Hit the RESET button in DrJava before trying the following.

```
> import jm.music.data.*;
> import jm.JMC;
> import jm.util.*;
```

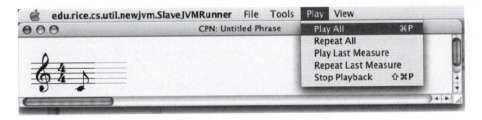

FIGURE 6.1
Playing all the notes in a score.

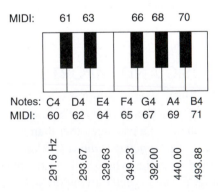

FIGURE 6.2
Keys, MIDI notes (numbers), and frequencies.

```
> Note n = new Note(60,0.5);
> Note n2 = new Note(JMC.C4,JMC.QN);
> Phrase phr = new Phrase(0.0,JMC.FLUTE);
> phr.addNote(n);
> phr.addNote(n2);
> View.notate(phr);
```

How It Works

- We specify the imports that we need for Jmusic.

- We create a note using numeric values, then using named constants. JMC.C4 means "C in the 4th octave." JMC.QN means "quarter note." JMC is the class *Java Music Constants*, and it holds many important constants. The constant JMC.C4 means 60, like in Table 2.1. A sharp would be noted as JMC.CS5 (C-sharp in the 5th octave). The eighth note is JMC.EN and a half note is JMC.HN. A dotted eighth would be JMC.DEN.

- We create a Phrase object that starts at time 0.0 and uses the *instrument* JMC. FLUTE. JMC.FLUTE is a constant that corresponds to a flute sound. There are 128 (numbered 0 to 127) instruments defined in MIDI, as seen in Table 6.1. You can find the defined named constants (like JMC.FLUTE and JMC.PIANO) for all of these by reading the documentation for the JMusic package, available on the Web site.

- We put the notes into the Phrase instance, and then notate and view the whole phrase.

We can create multiple parts with different start times and instruments. We want the different parts to map onto different *MIDI channels* if we want different start times and instruments (Figure 6.3). We'll need to combine the different parts into a Score object, which can then be viewed and notated the same way as phrases and parts.

```
> Note n3 = new Note(JMC.E4,JMC.EN);
> Note n4 = new Note(JMC.G4,JMC.HN);
> Phrase phr2 = new Phrase(0.5,JMC.PIANO);
> phr2.addNote(n3);
> phr2.addNote(n4);
> phr // this will print information about phr like using
  System.out.println(phr);
-------- jMusic PHRASE: 'Untitled Phrase' contains 2 notes.
  Start time: 0.0 --------
jMusic NOTE: [Pitch = 60][RhythmValue = 0.5][Dynamic = 85][Pan =
0.5][Duration = 0.45] jMusic NOTE: [Pitch = 60][RhythmValue =
1.0][Dynamic = 85][Pan = 0.5][Duration = 0.9]
> phr2
-------- jMusic PHRASE: 'Untitled Phrase' contains 2 notes.
  Start time: 0.5 --------
```

TABLE 6.1 MIDI Program numbers

Piano	Bass	Reed
0 — Acoustic Grand Piano	32 — Acoustic Bass	64 — Soprano Sax
1 — Bright Acoustic Piano	33 — Electric Bass (finger)	65 — Alto Sax
2 — Electric Grand Piano	34 — Electric Bass (pick)	66 — Tenor Sax
3 — Honky-tonk Piano	35 — Fretless Bass	67 — Baritone Sax
4 — Rhodes Piano	36 — Slap Bass 1	68 — Oboe
5 — Chorused Piano	37 — Slap Bass 2	69 — English Horn
6 — Harpsichord	38 — Synth Bass 1	70 — Bassoon
7 — Clavinet	39 — Synth Bass 2	71 — Clarinet
Chromatic Percussion	**Strings**	**Pipe**
8 — Celesta	40 — Violin	72 — Piccolo
9 — Glockenspiel	41 — Viola	73 — Flute
10 — Music box	42 — Cello	74 — Recorder
11 — Vibraphone	43 — Contrabass	75 — Pan Flute
12 — Marimba	44 — Tremolo Strings	76 — Bottle Blow
13 — Xylophone	45 — Pizzicato Strings	77 — Shakuhachi
14 — Tubular Bells	46 — Orchestral Harp	78 — Whistle
15 — Dulcimer	47 — Timpani	79 — Ocarina
Organ	**Ensemble**	**Ethnic**
16 — Hammond Organ	48 — String Ensemble 1	104 — Sitar
17 — Percussive Organ	49 — String Ensemble 2	105 — Banjo
18 — Rock Organ	50 — Synth Strings 1	106 — Shamisen
19 — Church Organ	51 — Synth Strings 2	107 — Koto
20 — Reed Organ	52 — Choir Aahs	108 — Kalimba
21 — Accordian	53 — Voice Oohs	109 — Bagpipe
22 — Harmonica	54 — Synth Voice	110 — Fiddle
23 — Tango Accordian	55 — Orchestra Hit	111 — Shanai
Guitar	**Brass**	**Percussive**
24 — Acoustic Guitar (nylon)	56 — Trumpet	112 — Tinkle Bell
25 — Acoustic Guitar (steel)	57 — Trombone	113 — Agogo
26 — Electric Guitar (jazz)	58 — Tuba	114 — Steel Drums
27 — Electric Guitar (clean)	59 — Muted Trumpet	115 — Woodblock
28 — Electric Guitar (muted)	60 — French Horn	116 — Taiko Drum
29 — Overdriven Guitar	61 — Brass Section	117 — Melodic Tom
30 — Distortion Guitar	62 — Synth Brass 1	118 — Synth Drum
31 — Guitar Harmonics	63 — Synth Brass 2	119 — Reverse Cymbal

```
jMusic NOTE: [Pitch = 64][RhythmValue = 0.5][Dynamic = 85][Pan =
0.5][Duration = 0.45] jMusic NOTE: [Pitch = 67][RhythmValue =
2.0][Dynamic = 85][Pan = 0.5][Duration = 1.8]
> Part partA = new Part(phr,"Part A",JMC.FLUTE,1);
> Part partB = new Part(phr2,"Part B",JMC.PIANO,2);
> Phrase phraseAB = new Phrase();
> Score scoreAB = new Score();
```

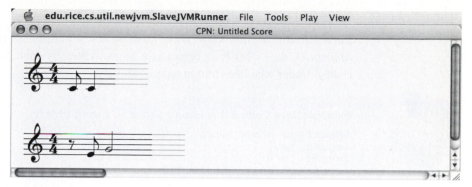

FIGURE 6.3
Viewing a multi-part score.

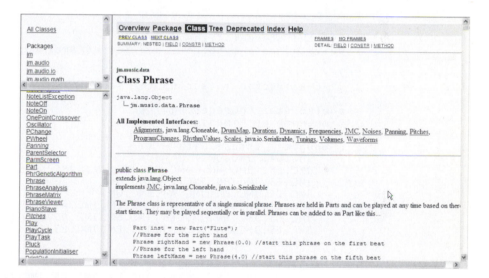

FIGURE 6.4
JMusic documention for the class `Phrase`.

```
> scoreAB.addPart(partA);
> scoreAB.addPart(partB);
> View.notate(scoreAB);
```

How do you figure out what JMusic can do, what the classes are that it provides, and how to use them? There is a standard way of documenting Java classes called *Javadoc comments*, which produces really useful documentation (Figure 6.4) when you run the Javadoc utility. JMusic is documented in this way. You can get to the JMusic documentation produced by Javadoc comments at `http://jmusic.ci.qut.edu.au/jmDocumentation/index.html`, or you can download it onto your own computer from `http://jmusic.ci.qut.edu.au/GetjMusic.html`.

6.2   MAKING A SIMPLE SONG OBJECT

Let's use what we now know about creating notes, phrases, and parts to create the song *Amazing Grace*. This song began as a poem written by John Newton in 1772. He was a slave trader who later fought against slavery.

Example Java Code 31: *Amazing Grace* as a song object

```java
import jm.music.data.*;
import jm.JMC;
import jm.util.*;
import jm.music.tools.*;

/**
 * Class that represents the song Amazing Grace
 * @author Mark Guzdial
 * @author Barb Ericson
 */
public class AmazingGraceSong {

  /** the score for the song */
  private Score myScore = new Score("Amazing Grace");

  /**
   * Constructor to set up the song
   */
  public AmazingGraceSong() {
    myScore.setTimeSignature(3,4);

    double[] phrase1Data = {
       JMC.G4,  JMC.QN,
       JMC.C5, JMC.HN, JMC.E5,JMC.EN, JMC.C5,JMC.EN,
       JMC.E5,JMC.HN,JMC.D5,JMC.QN,
       JMC.C5,JMC.HN,JMC.A4,JMC.QN,
       JMC.G4,JMC.HN,JMC.G4,JMC.EN,JMC.A4,JMC.EN,
       JMC.C5,JMC.HN,JMC.E5,JMC.EN,JMC.C5,JMC.EN,
       JMC.E5,JMC.HN,JMC.D5,JMC.EN,JMC.E5,JMC.EN,
       JMC.G5,JMC.DHN
    };
    double[] phrase2Data = {
       JMC.G5,JMC.HN,JMC.E5,JMC.EN,JMC.G5,JMC.EN,
       JMC.G5,JMC.HN,JMC.E5,JMC.EN,JMC.C5,JMC.EN,
       JMC.E5,JMC.HN,JMC.D5,JMC.QN,
       JMC.C5,JMC.HN,JMC.A4,JMC.QN,
       JMC.G4,JMC.HN,JMC.G4,JMC.EN,JMC.A4,JMC.EN,
       JMC.C5,JMC.HN,JMC.E5,JMC.EN,JMC.C5,JMC.EN,
       JMC.E5,JMC.HN,JMC.D5,JMC.QN,
       JMC.C5,JMC.DHN
    };
    Phrase myPhrase = new Phrase();
    myPhrase.addNoteList(phrase1Data);
    myPhrase.addNoteList(phrase2Data);

    // create a new part and add the phrase to it
    Part aPart = new Part("Parts",
                          JMC.FLUTE, 1);
    aPart.addPhrase(myPhrase);
    // add the part to the score
    myScore.addPart(aPart);

  }
```

```
54
     /**
56
      * Method to show the song
      */
58   public void showMe() {
       View.notate(myScore);
60   }

62 }
```

■

How It Works

- We start with the `import` statements needed to use JMusic classes.
- We're declaring a new `class` whose name is `AmazingGraceSong`. It's `public`, meaning anyone can access it.
- There is a variable named `myScore` which is of type `Score`. This means that the score `myScore` is duplicated in each instance of the class `AmazingGraceSong`. It's `private` because we don't actually want users of `AmazingGraceSong` messing with the score.
- There is a constructor that sets up the song with the right notes and durations (see the phrase data arrays in the constructor with a flute playing the song). There is also a method `showMe` that opens up the song for notation and playing.

    The phrase data arrays are named constants from the JMC class. They're in the order of note, duration, note, duration, and so on. The names actually all correspond to numbers, of the type `double`.

Using the program (Figure 6.5):

```
> AmazingGraceSong song1 = new AmazingGraceSong();
> song1.showMe();
```

6.3   MAKING A SONG SOMETHING TO EXPLORE AS A LINKED LIST

The class `AmazingGraceSong` is not a great rendition of *Amazing Grace*. It also does not help us achieve our goal of providing a tool for composers. We can't really explore much with this version. What does it mean to have a representation of music that we can explore with?

How might one want to explore a song like this?

- How about changing the order of the pieces, or duplicating them? Maybe use a *call and response* structure?
- How about using different instruments?

A great place to start is by thinking about how *composers* think about music. They typically don't think about a piece of music as a single thing. Rather, they think about it

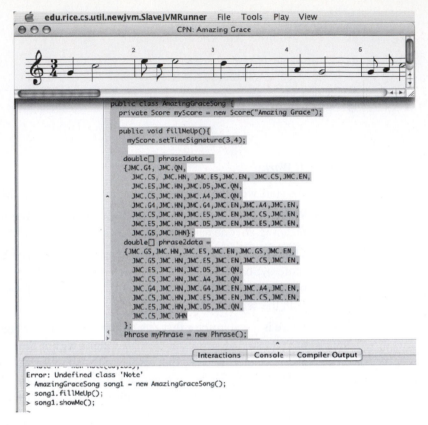

FIGURE 6.5
Trying the Amazing Grace song object.

in terms of a whole (a `Score`), parts (`Part`), and phrases (`Phrase`). They typically think about these things in terms of a *sequence*. One riff or motif (collection of notes) follows another. Each of these parts will have its own notes (its own `Phrase`), though some might be repetitions and others might be modifications of earlier motifs. A common music structure is described as stating a theme (a riff or motif or bit of music) and recapitulating the theme (repeating it, perhaps with modifications).

Most importantly, there is an *ordering* to these parts. To represent music the way that composers think about, we need to be able to describe these motifs or *song elements* and their ordering. We can *model* that ordering by having each element keep track of the next part.

There are really *two* ideas in the above description.

- There's a notion of a song *element*. That's a *something* associated with notes, and with what element comes next.

- There's a notion of a *set of notes*. These notes might be the first four notes of Beethoven's Fifth, or the first half of *Amazing Grace*, or some other little bit of melody. These notes might be used in different ways at different times, even in different songs. They're really quite separate from the ordering in a *particular* song.

We are now going to create *two* classes to implement this structure. Instances of SongNode represent an element of a song. We're going to name our class SongNode to highlight that each element in the song is now a *node* in a *list* of song elements. Computer scientists typically use the term "node" to describe pieces in a list, *tree*, or other data structure. The class SongPhrase will be used to hold sample musical phrases that you can use in your songs. A musical phrase has both notes and the durations to play those notes.

Example Java Code 32: SongNode class

```java
import jm.music.data.*;
import jm.JMC;
import jm.util.*;
import jm.music.tools.*;

/**
 * Represents a node in a flexible song structure
 * @author Mark Guzdial
 * @author Barb Ericson
 */
public class SongNode {

  /** the next SongNode in the list */
  private SongNode next;

  /** the Phrase containing the notes and durations */
  private Phrase myPhrase;

  /**
   * Construct a new song node.
   * The next part is empty, and ours is a
   * blank new part.
   */
  public SongNode() {
    this.next = null;
    this.myPhrase = new Phrase();
  }

  /**
   * setPhrase takes a Phrase and makes it the one for
   * this node
   * @param thisPhrase the phrase for this node
   */
  public void setPhrase(Phrase thisPhrase) {
    this.myPhrase = thisPhrase;
  }

  /**
   * Creates a link between the current node and the
   * input node
   * @param nextOne the node to link to
   */
  public void setNext(SongNode nextOne) {
    this.next = nextOne;
  }

```

```java
    /**
48   * Get the next song node
     * @return the next song node or null if none
50   */
    public SongNode getNext() {
52     return this.next;
    }
54
    /**
56   * Accessor for the node's Phrase
     * @return internal phrase
58   */
    private Phrase getPhrase() {
60     return this.myPhrase;
    }
62
    /**
64   * Accessor for the notes inside the node's phrase
     * @return array of notes and durations inside the phrase
66   */
    private Note[] getNotes() {
68     return this.myPhrase.getNoteArray();
    }
70
    /**
72   * Collect all the notes from this node on
     * in an part (then a score) and open it up for viewing.
74   * @param instrument the MIDI instrument (program) to
     * be used in playing
76   */
    public void showFromMeOn(int instrument) {
78
      // Make the Score that we'll assemble the elements into
80     // We'll set it up with a default time signature and
      // tempo we like
82     // (Should probably make it possible to change these --
      // maybe with inputs?)
84     Score myScore = new Score("My Song");
      myScore.setTimeSignature(3,4);
86     myScore.setTempo(120.0);
88     // Make the Part that we'll assemble things into
      Part myPart = new Part(instrument);
90
      // Make a new Phrase that will contain the notes from
92     // all the phrases
      Phrase collector = new Phrase();
94
      // Start from this element (this)
96     SongNode current = this;
      // While we're not through...
98     while (current != null) {
        collector.addNoteList(current.getNotes());
100
        // Now, move on to the next element
102       current = current.getNext();
      }
104
      // Now, construct the part and the score.
106     myPart.addPhrase(collector);
      myScore.addPart(myPart);
108
```

```
      // At the end, let's see it!
110   View.notate(myScore);
    }
112 }
```

■

We will discuss how SongNode works in a moment. Let's first go through the partner class to SongNode, SongPhrase. A SongPhrase represents a collection of notes that we might use in a song, by associating them with instances of SongNode.

Example Java Code 33: A SongPhrase class

```java
import jm.music.data.*;
import jm.JMC;
import jm.util.*;
import jm.music.tools.*;

/**
 * Class that holds phrases that can be used
 * @author Mark Guzdial
 * @author Barb Ericson
 */
public class SongPhrase {

  /**
   * Class method that returns the first phrase
   * of Amazing Grace
   * @return the first phrase of Amazing Grace
   */
  public static Phrase AG1() {
    double[] phrase1Data = {
      JMC.G4,  JMC.QN,
      JMC.C5,  JMC.HN,  JMC.E5,JMC.EN,  JMC.C5,JMC.EN,
      JMC.E5,JMC.HN,JMC.D5,JMC.QN,
      JMC.C5,JMC.HN,JMC.A4,JMC.QN,
      JMC.G4,JMC.HN,JMC.G4,JMC.EN,JMC.A4,JMC.EN,
      JMC.C5,JMC.HN,JMC.E5,JMC.EN,JMC.C5,JMC.EN,
      JMC.E5,JMC.HN,JMC.D5,JMC.EN,JMC.E5,JMC.EN,
      JMC.G5,JMC.DHN
    };

    Phrase myPhrase = new Phrase();
    myPhrase.addNoteList(phrase1Data);
    return myPhrase;
  }

  /**
   * Class method that returns the second phrase of Amazing
   * Grace
   * @return the second phrase of Amazing Grace
   */
  public static Phrase AG2() {
    double[] phrase2Data = {
      JMC.G5,JMC.HN,JMC.E5,JMC.EN,JMC.G5,JMC.EN,
      JMC.G5,JMC.HN,JMC.E5,JMC.EN,JMC.C5,JMC.EN,
      JMC.E5,JMC.HN,JMC.D5,JMC.QN,
      JMC.C5,JMC.HN,JMC.A4,JMC.QN,
      JMC.G4,JMC.HN,JMC.G4,JMC.EN,JMC.A4,JMC.EN,
```

```
                    JMC.C5,JMC.HN,JMC.E5,JMC.EN,JMC.C5,JMC.EN,
48                  JMC.E5,JMC.HN,JMC.D5,JMC.QN,
                    JMC.C5,JMC.DHN
50              };

52          Phrase myPhrase = new Phrase();
            myPhrase.addNoteList(phrase2Data);
54          return myPhrase;
        }

56
        /**
58       * Class method that returns a phrase from The
         * House of the Rising Sun
60       * @return a phrase from The House of the Rising Sun
         */
62      public static Phrase house() {
            double [] phraseData = {
64              JMC.E4,JMC.EN,JMC.A3,JMC.HN,JMC.B3,JMC.EN,JMC.A3,JMC.EN,
                JMC.C4,JMC.HN,JMC.D4,JMC.EN,JMC.DS4,JMC.EN,
66              JMC.E4,JMC.HN,JMC.C4,JMC.EN,JMC.B3,JMC.EN,
                JMC.A3,JMC.HN,JMC.E4,JMC.QN,
68              JMC.A4,JMC.HN,  JMC.E4,  JMC.QN,
                JMC.G4,JMC.HN,  JMC.E4,JMC.EN,JMC.D4,JMC.EN,JMC.E4,JMC.DHN,
70              JMC.E4,JMC.HN,JMC.GS4,JMC.EN,JMC.G4,JMC.EN,
                JMC.A4,JMC.HN,JMC.A3,JMC.QN,
72              JMC.C4,JMC.EN,JMC.C4,JMC.DQN,JMC.E4,JMC.QN,
                JMC.E4,JMC.EN,JMC.E4,JMC.EN,JMC.E4,JMC.QN,JMC.C4,JMC.EN,
74                JMC.B3,JMC.EN,
                JMC.A3,JMC.HN,JMC.E4,JMC.QN,
76              JMC.E4,JMC.HN,JMC.E4,JMC.EN,
                JMC.E4,JMC.EN,JMC.G3,JMC.QN,JMC.C4,JMC.EN,JMC.B3,JMC.EN,
78              JMC.A3,JMC.DHN
            };
80
            Phrase myPhrase = new Phrase();
82          myPhrase.addNoteList(phraseData);
            return myPhrase;
84      }

86      /**
         * Class method that returns a little riff
88       * @return a phrase with a little riff in it
         */
90      public static Phrase riff1() {
            double[] phraseData = {
92              JMC.G3,JMC.EN,JMC.B3,JMC.EN,JMC.C4,JMC.EN,JMC.D4,JMC.EN
            };
94
            Phrase myPhrase = new Phrase();
96          myPhrase.addNoteList(phraseData);
            return myPhrase;
98      }

100     /**
         * Class method that returns a second little riff
102      * @return a phrase with a second little riff in it
         */
104     public static Phrase riff2() {
            double[] phraseData = {
106             JMC.D4,JMC.EN,JMC.C4,JMC.EN,JMC.E4,JMC.EN,JMC.G4,JMC.EN
            };
108
```

```
        Phrase myPhrase = new Phrase();
110     myPhrase.addNoteList(phraseData);
        return myPhrase;
112   }
}
```

∎

How It Works.   We actually never create instances of `SongPhrase`. Rather, it is filled with `static` methods (methods that can be accessed from the class, without any instances being created) that all return JMusic `Phrases`. Each of these methods has the same structure. An array of doubles is created (`double[]`) for storing pitches and durations. This makes it easier to translate music into JMusic values. We create a `Phrase` instance, then add the note list into the `Phrase` and return it.

Let's try out these classes and use that to motivate our understanding of how they work.

```
> SongNode first = new SongNode();
> first.setPhrase(SongPhrase.riff1());
> import jm.JMC; // To reference instruments by name
> first.showFromMeOn(JMC.FLUTE); // We can play with just one
  node
-- Constructing MIDI file from'My Song'... Playing with
  JavaSound
... Completed MIDI playback --------
```

How It Works.   In this example, we create a `SongNode` instance, and set its phrase to `SongPhrase.riff1()`. We can then view this node in Western music notation (Figure 6.6) and play it (using the PLAY menu in the viewer window). We'll explain how `setPhrase` and `showFromMeOn` work in just a minute. First, we'll add a second node to our list.

FIGURE 6.6
A single SongNode instance.

```
> SongNode second = new SongNode();
> second.setPhrase(SongPhrase.riff2());
> second.showFromMeOn(JMC.PIANO);
> first.setNext(second);
> first.showFromMeOn(JMC.FLUTE);
```

Figure 6.7 shows three windows that we have opened with showFromMeOn. The first node has the notes that appear in the top window, the second node has the notes that appear in the middle window, and the third window shows the first node's notes followed by the second node's notes. Even if you can't read music, you can see that the pattern of notes (which lines they're on, which lines they're between) indicates that the bottom window shows the first node followed by the second node. (Note that the *instrument* associated with the score does not change how the display looks.)

Now let's add one more node to our list.

```
> SongNode third = new SongNode();
> third.setPhrase(SongPhrase.riff3());
> third.showFromMeOn(JMC.PIANO);
> first.setNext(third);
> third.setNext(second);
> first.showFromMeOn(JMC.PIANO);
```

FIGURE 6.7
First score generated from ordered linked list: first node, second node, then first node connected to second node.

FIGURE 6.8
A score made up of three nodes, by inserting the riff (middle window) into the old list (top window), resulting in the bottom window.

The result can be seen in Figure 6.8. The top window shows the two node sequence seen at the bottom of Figure 6.7. The middle window shows the new node `third` with the phrase from `riff3`. In this example, the `third` node is *inserted between* the `first` and `second` nodes. We make node `first` point to `third`, and the node `third` point to node `second`. In the bottom window, we can see the sequence of notes from `first`, then `third`, and finally `second`.

Walking through SongNode

Class SongNode is important to us. It's our first *linked list*, a dynamic data structure that can grow to any size that will fit within memory. Each instance of SongNode knows it's musical phrase and the `next` node in the list.

```java
public class SongNode {
  /**
   * the next SongNode in the list
   */
  private SongNode next;
  /**
   * the Phrase containing the notes and durations
     associated with this node
   */
  private Phrase myPhrase;
```

When a new instance of the class SongNode is created, the *constructor* for the method is called. This method creates the musical Phrase instance, and sets the default next to be null, a special Java variable meaning "not referring to any object yet."

These nodes know how to manipulate their next field.

```
/**
 * Creates a link between the current node and the input node
 * @param nextOne the node to link to
 */
public void setNext(SongNode nextOne){
  this.next = nextOne;
}
/**
 * Provides public access to the next node.
 * @return a SongNode instance (or null)
 */
public SongNode getNext(){
  return this.next;
}
```

The method to setPhrase simply assigns the instance variable for the musical phrase.

```
/**
 * setPhrase takes a Phrase and makes it the one for
 * this node
 * @param thisPhrase the phrase for this node
 */
public void setPhrase(Phrase thisPhrase) {
  this.myPhrase = thisPhrase;
}
```

The really important part of the linked list is its ability to collect all the notes from all the nodes in the list in a process called a *traversal*. The method showFromMeOn visits each node in the list until it reaches the end—the node that has a value of null for its next. When it visits the node, it collects the notes from the node and adds it to a collector.

```
/**
 * Collect all the notes from this node on
 * in an part (then a score) and open it up for viewing.
 * @param instrument MIDI instrument (program) to be used in
   playing this list
 */
public void showFromMeOn(int instrument){
  // Make the Score that we'll assemble the elements into
  // We'll set it up with a default time signature and tempo
  // we like
```

```
Score myScore = new Score("My Song");
myScore.setTimeSignature(3,4);
myScore.setTempo(120.0);

// Make the Part that we'll assemble things into
Part myPart = new Part(instrument);

// Make a new Phrase that will contain the notes from all
// the phrases
Phrase collector = new Phrase();

// Start from this element (this)
SongNode current = this;
// While we're not through...
while (current != null)
{
  collector.addNoteList(current.getNotes());

  // Now, move on to the next element
  current = current.next();
};

// Now, construct the part and the score.
myPart.addPhrase(collector);
myScore.addPart(myPart);

// At the end, let's see it!
View.notate(myScore);

}
```

The heart of this traversal is:

```
// Start from this element (this)
SongNode current = this;
// While we're not through...
while (current != null)
{
  collector.addNoteList(current.getNotes());

  // Now, move on to the next element
  current = current.next();
};
```

Let's consider the scenario which ended in Figure 6.8 and walk through the traversal. When we called, first.showFromMeOn(JMC.PIANO);, here's what happened:

- First, the variable `current` is set to `this`, which is the node we named `first`.

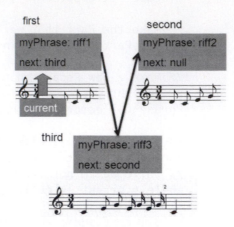

- We then collected the notes from the node at `current` and put them into the phrase variable `collector`.

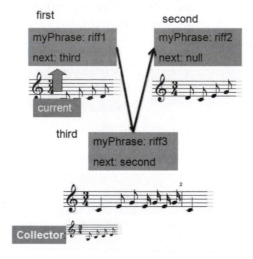

- We set `current = current.getNext();`, which moves the variable `current` to the next node in the list. You might think about traversing a linked list as being like pulling yourself hand-over-hand along a rope or ladder. Your right hand is `current`, and it was holding on to the `first` rung of the ladder. Your left hand reaches out to the `next` rung. You move your right hand up to `second`, too. We collect those notes, too.

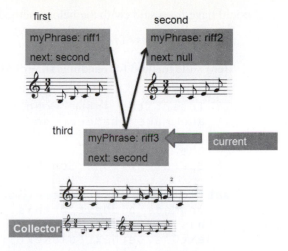

- Again, `current = current.getNext();`, in order to move `current` to the next (and now last) node in the list. We collect those notes, too.

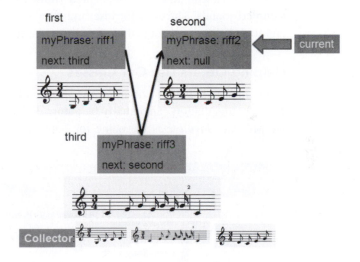

- When we executed `current = current.getNext();` again, `current` points at node `second`'s `next`, which is `null`. `current` is now `null`, so we end the traversal and display the result in Figure 6.8. (In our hand-over-hand metaphor, we've now fallen off the end.)

Improving insertAfter

The process we followed, where we put the node `third` after `first` and before `second`, can be generalized as `insertAfter`. Thus this,

```
> first.setNext(third);
> third.setNext(second);
```

could have been said (with the below method) as:

```
> first.insertAfter(third);
```

Here's the method for handling `insertAfter` with linked lists:

```
/**
 * Insert the input SongNode AFTER this node,
 * and make whatever node comes NEXT become the
   next of
 * the input node.
 * @param nextOne SongNode to insert after this one
 */
public void insertAfter(SongNode nextOne) {
  SongNode oldNext = this.getNext(); // Save its next
  this.setNext(nextOne); // Insert the copy
  nextOne.setNext(oldNext); // Make the copy point
    on to the rest
}
```

You may recall that we implemented `insertAfter` for arrays in the last chapter, for sampled sounds. The code for inserting after a position in an array was more complex and took longer to execute than the code to insert after in a linked list.

Helping Others Use Our Classes

Remember the documentation for the JMusic classes that we saw earlier in the book? That documentation can actually be automatically generated from the comments that we provide. *Javadoc* is the name for both the types of comments and the tool that

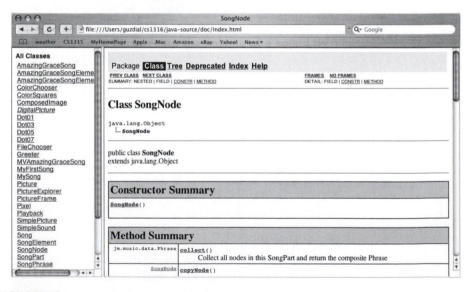

FIGURE 6.9
Javadoc for the class SongNode.

generates HTML documentation from those comments. The commenting structure is to use '/**' to start a Javadoc comment and '*/' to end it. In addition, you can specify tags using '@tagName', which specify things like the author or authors of the class, the parameters passed to methods, and the item returned from a method (Figure 6.9).

Computing Phrases

If we need some repetition, we don't have to type things over and over again—we can ask the computer to do it for us! Our phrases in class SongPhrase don't have to come from constants. It's okay if they are computed phrases.

One way of creating phrases is by taking phrases we have and using while loops to combine them repeatedly. That can make for interesting rhythms.

```
> SongNode steel = new SongNode();
> steel.setPhrase(SongPhrase.pattern1());
> steel.showFromMeOn(JMC.STEEL_DRUM);
```

Example Java Code 34: Computed phrases

```java
/**
 * Class method that returns a pattern
 * @return a phrase with a pattern in it
 */
public static Phrase pattern1() {
  double[] riff1Data = {
    JMC.G3,JMC.EN,JMC.B3,JMC.EN,JMC.C4,JMC.EN,JMC.D4,JMC.EN
  };
  double[] riff2Data = {
    JMC.D4,JMC.EN,JMC.C4,JMC.EN,JMC.E4,JMC.EN,JMC.G4,JMC.EN
  };

  int counter1;
  int counter2;

  Phrase myPhrase = new Phrase();
  // 3 of riff1, 1 of riff2, and repeat all of it 3 times
  for (counter1 = 1; counter1 <= 3; counter1++) {
    for (counter2 = 1; counter2 <= 3; counter2++) {
      myPhrase.addNoteList(riff1Data);
    }
    myPhrase.addNoteList(riff2Data);
  }
  return myPhrase;
}

/**
 * Class method that returns a phrase with a second pattern
 * @return a phrase with a second pattern
 */
public static Phrase pattern2() {
  double[] riff1Data = {
    JMC.G3,JMC.EN,JMC.B3,JMC.EN,JMC.C4,JMC.EN,JMC.D4,JMC.EN
  };
  double[] riff2Data = {
    JMC.D4,JMC.EN,JMC.C4,JMC.EN,JMC.E4,JMC.EN,JMC.G4,JMC.EN
  };
```

```java
    int counter1;
    int counter2;

    Phrase myPhrase = new Phrase();
    // 2 of riff1, 2 of riff2, and repeat all of it 3 times
    for (counter1 = 1; counter1 <= 3; counter1++) {
      for (counter2 = 1; counter2 <= 2; counter2++) {
        myPhrase.addNoteList(riff1Data);
      }
      for (counter2 = 1; counter2 <= 2; counter2++) {
        myPhrase.addNoteList(riff2Data);
      }
    }
    return myPhrase;
  }

/**
  * Class method that returns a phrase with a rhythm in it
  * @return a phrase with a rhythm in it
  */
  public static Phrase rhythm1() {
    double[] riff1Data = {
      JMC.G3,JMC.EN,JMC.REST,JMC.HN,JMC.D4,JMC.EN
    };
    double[] riff2Data = {
      JMC.C3,JMC.QN,JMC.REST,JMC.QN
    };

    int counter1;
    int counter2;

    Phrase myPhrase = new Phrase();
    // 2 of rhythm riff1, 2 of rhythm riff2, and repeat
    // all of it 3 times
    for (counter1 = 1; counter1 <= 3; counter1++) {
      for (counter2 = 1; counter2 <= 2; counter2++) {
        myPhrase.addNoteList(riff1Data);
      }
      for (counter2 = 1; counter2 <= 2; counter2++) {
        myPhrase.addNoteList(riff2Data);
      }
    }
    return myPhrase;
  }
```

■

We can use our ability to compute phrases to do more than simple repetition. For example, let's first create 10 completely random notes. From there, we'll make less-random and more-musical phrases.

Example Java Code 35: 10 random notes SongPhrase

```java
/**
  * Class method that returns a phrase with random notes in it
  * @return a phrase with 10 random notes
  */
  public static Phrase random() {
    Phrase ranPhrase = new Phrase();
    Note n = null;
```

```java
    for (int i=0; i < 10; i++) {
      n = new Note((int) (128*Math.random()),0.1);
      ranPhrase.addNote(n);
    }
    return ranPhrase;
  }
```

∎

How It Works.   `Math.random()` returns a number between 0.0 and 1.0. There are 128 possible notes in MIDI. Multiplying `128*Math.random()` gives us a note between 0 and 127. These are 10 completely random notes.

Complete randomness isn't the most pleasant thing to listen to. We can control the randomness a bit, mathematically. Here, we generate random numbers but *limit* them so that we only generate notes above middle C. Those are less random, and perhaps more interesting notes (depending on what other nodes we're creating).

Example Java Code 36: 10 slightly less-random notes

```java
/**
 * Class method that returns a phrase with random notes
 * in it which are above middle C
 * @return a phrase with 10 random notes above middle C
 */
public static  Phrase randomAboveC() {
  Phrase ranPhrase = new Phrase();
  Note n = null;

  for (int i=0; i < 10; i++) {
    n = new Note((int) (60+(5*Math.random())),0.25);
    ranPhrase.addNote(n);
  }
  return ranPhrase;
}
```

∎

How It Works.   Here, we generate a random number between 0 and 4 by multiplying `Math.random()` by 5. Recall that note 60 is middle C. If we add our random number to 60, we play one of the five notes just above middle C.

We obviously can keep going from there. Perhaps we might generate a random number, then use it to choose (as if flipping a coin) between some different phrases to combine. Or perhaps we choose only among certain notes (not necessarily in a range—perhaps selected from an array) that we want in our composition. It is really possible to have a computer "compose" music driven by random numbers.

Repeating and Weaving to Make Music

Once we have our basic structures, we can play with repetition and weaving in at regular intervals, using patterns like those in Western music. Let's create two new methods: one that repeats an input phrase several times, and one that weaves in a phrase every *n* nodes.

Example Java Code 37: Repeating and weaving methods

```java
/**
 * copyNode returns a copy of this node
 * @return another song node with the same notes
 */
public SongNode copyNode() {
  SongNode returnMe = new SongNode();
  returnMe.setPhrase(this.getPhrase());
  return returnMe;
}

/**
 * Repeat the input phrase for the number of times specified.
 * It always inserts the repeated node after the
 * current node
 * @param nextOne node to be copied in to list
 * @param count number of times to copy it in.
 */
public void repeatNext(SongNode nextOne, int count) {
  SongNode current = this; // Start from here
  SongNode copy; // Where we keep the current copy

  for (int i=1; i <= count; i++) {
    copy = nextOne.copyNode(); // Make a copy
    current.setNext(copy); // Set as next
    current = copy; // Now append to copy
  }
}

/**
 * Weave the input song node count times every skipAmount
 * nodes
 * @param nextOne node to be copied into the list
 * @param count how many times to copy
 * @param skipAmount how many nodes to skip per weave
 */
public void weave(SongNode nextOne, int count,
  int skipAmount) {

  SongNode current = this; // Start from here
  SongNode copy; // Where we keep the one to be weaved in

  // loop count times
  for (int i=0; i < count; i++) {

    //Skip skipAmount nodes (this one is 1)
    for (int j=1; j < skipAmount; j++) {

      // as long as current isn't null move to next
      if (current != null) {
        current = current.getNext();
      }
    }

    // if current isn't null
    if (current != null) {
      // make a new copy
      copy = nextOne.copyNode();

      // insert it after current
      current.insertAfter(copy);
```

```
62          // move current along
            current = copy.getNext();
64      }

66      // else if current is null return (break out early)
        if (current == null) {
68          return;
        }
70      }
    }
```

First, let's make five copies of one pattern (Figure 6.10).

```
> import jm.JMC;
> SongNode riff1Node = new SongNode();
> riff1Node.setPhrase(SongPhrase.riff1());
> riff1Node.repeatNext(riff1Node,4);
> riff1Node.showFromMeOn(JMC.FLUTE);
```

Now, let's create a second pattern from riff2 (Figure 6.11).

```
> SongNode riff2Node = new SongNode();
> riff2Node.setPhrase(SongPhrase.riff2());
> riff2Node.showFromMeOn(JMC.FLUTE);
```

Now, let's weave in a second pattern every other (off by 1) node, for seven times (Figure 6.12).

```
> riff1Node.weave(riff2Node,5,1);
> riff1Node.showFromMeOn(JMC.FLUTE);
```

FIGURE 6.10
Repeating a node five times.

FIGURE 6.11
The new phrase (riff2).

FIGURE 6.12
Weaving in a new node among the old.

And we can keep weaving in more.

```
> SongNode anotherNode = new SongNode();
> anotherNode.setPhrase(SongPhrase.riff4());
> anotherNode.showFromMeOn(JMC.STEEL_DRUMS);
> riff1Node.weave(anotherNode,5,2);
> riff1Node.showFromMeOn(JMC.STEEL_DRUMS);
```

Now, repeatNext is not the most polite method in the world. Consider what happens if we call it on node1 and node1 *already has a next!* The rest of the list simply gets blown away! But now that we have insertAfter, we can produce a more friendly and polite version, repeatNextInserting, which preserves the rest of the list.

Example Java Code 38: RepeatNextInserting

```java
/**
 * Repeat the input phrase for the number of times specified.
 * But do an insertion, to save the rest of the list.
 * @param nextOne node to be copied into the list
 * @param count number of times to copy it in.
 */
public void repeatNextInserting(SongNode nextOne,
  int count) {
  SongNode current = this; // Start from here
  SongNode copy; // Where we keep the current copy

  for (int i=1; i <= count; i++) {
    copy = nextOne.copyNode(); // Make a copy
    current.insertAfter(copy); // INSERT after current
    current = copy; // now move on to the copy
  }
}
```

Linked Lists versus Arrays

What are the advantages of using linked lists here, rather than arrays? Linked lists are better for lots of things, such as being able to create lists that can grow and shrink quickly. However, there are also advantages for arrays. Let's consider them head-to-head.

How complicated is it to traverse a linked list (visit all the elements) versus an array? Here's a linked list traversal:

```
//traversing a list
// Start from this element (this)
  SongNode current = this;
```

```
// While we're not through...
while (current != null) {
  //BLAH BLAH BLAH (Ignore this part for now)

  // Now, move on to the next element
  current = current.next();
}
```

Basically, we're walking hand-over-hand across all the nodes in the list. Think of `current` as your right hand.

- Put your right hand (`current`) on the node referred to by `this`.
- Is your right hand empty? `while (current!= null)`? Assume that it isn't empty this time.
- Process your right hand.
- Then with your left hand feel down the `next` link to the next node—that's what `current.next()` is doing.
- Now, grab with your right hand whatever your left hand was holding—`current = current.next()`.
- Go back to the top of the loop and check if your right hand is empty.
- When we reach the end of the list, your right hand is holding nothing.

Traversing an array is much easier: it's just a `for` loop.

```
> // Now, traverse the array and gather them up.
> Phrase myphrase = new Phrase();
> for (int i=0; i<100; i++) {
    myphrase.addNote( someNotes[i]); }
```

But what if we want to change something in the middle? That's where linked lists shine. Here's inserting something into the middle of a linked list:

```
> part1.setNext(part3);
> part3.setNext(part2);
> part1.showFromMeOn();
```

You know that those `setNext` calls are just a single line of code. We can use *Big-O* notation to talk about these differences. We say that those are $O(1)$ operations, or *constant time* operations. No matter what the size of the data, any `setNext` is only a single statement.

How about inserting into the middle of an array? We saw that in the last chapter with arrays. That code was not only long and complicated, but it was also slow. Insertion into a linked list is $O(1)$, constant time. It always takes the same amount of time, no matter how big the things being inserted are. Insertion into the middle of an array (presuming that you move things over to make room, like the insertion in the linked list does) is $O(n)$, *linear time*. That will always be slower.

Which one is more *memory efficient*, that is, stores the same information in less memory? Arrays are more memory efficient, certainly. For every element in the linked list, there is additional piece of memory needed to keep track of "And here's the next one." It is really quite clear which note follows which other note in an array.

On the other hand, if you do not know the size of the thing that you want before you get started—if maybe you will have dozens of notes one time, and hundreds the next—then linked lists have a distinct advantage. Arrays cannot grow, nor shrink. They simply are the size that they are. Typically, then, you make your arrays larger than you think that you will need—which is a type of inefficiency. Linked lists can grow or shrink as needed.

Creating a Music Tree

Now, let's get back to the problem of having multiple parts, something we lost when we went to the ordered linked list implementation. We'll create a SongPart class that will store the instrument and the start of a SongNode list. Then we'll create a Song class that will store multiple parts—two parts, each a list of nodes. This structure is a start toward a *tree* structure. Trees are similar to linked lists but each node can have more than one next node. Your directory structure on your computer is an example of a tree. Each directory can hold files and other directories. A tree starts with a node called the root. For a windows computer, the root directory is usually "C:".

Example Java Code 39: SongPart class

```java
import jm.music.data.*;
import jm.JMC;
import jm.util.*;
import jm.music.tools.*;

/**
 * Class that represents a part of a song
 * @author Mark Guzdial
 * @author Barb Ericson
 */
public class SongPart {

  /** SongPart has a Part */
  private Part myPart;

  /** the first node in the linked list */
  private SongNode myList;

  /**
   * Construct a SongPart
   * @param instrument MIDI instrument (program)
   * @param startNode where the song list starts from
   */
  public SongPart(int instrument, SongNode startNode) {
    myPart = new Part(instrument);
    myList = startNode;
  }

  /**
   * Method to get the part
   * @ return the part
   */
  public Part getMyPart() {
```

```java
34        return myPart;
      }
36
      /**
38     * Collect parts of this SongPart
       * @return all the notes in a phrase
40     */
      public Phrase collect() {
42       // delegate to SongNode's collect
         return this.myList.collect();
44     }

46     /**
       * Collect all notes in this SongPart and open it up for
48     * viewing.
       */
50    public void show() {

52       // Make the Score that we'll assemble the part into
         // We'll set it up with a default time signature and
54       // tempo we like
         // (Should probably make it possible to change these --
56       // maybe with inputs?)
         Score myScore = new Score("My Song");
58       myScore.setTimeSignature(3,4);
         myScore.setTempo(120.0);
60
         // Now, construct the part and the score.
62       this.myPart.addPhrase(this.collect());
         myScore.addPart(this.myPart);
64
         // At the end, let's see it!
66       View.notate(myScore);
      }
68
    }
```

■

Example Java Code 40: Song class–root of a tree-like music structure

```java
import jm.music.data.*;
2  import jm.JMC;
import jm.util.*;
4  import jm.music.tools.*;

6  /**
    * Class that represents a song
8   * @author Mark Guzdial
    * @author Barb Ericson
10  */
   public class Song {
12
     /** first Channel */
14   private SongPart first;

16   /** second Channel */
     private SongPart second;
18
     /**
20    * Take in a SongPart to make the first channel in the song
      * @param channel1 the first channel in the song
22    */
```

```
       public void setFirst(SongPart channel1) {
24       first = channel1;
         first.getMyPart().setChannel(1);
26     }

28     /**
        * Take in a SongPart to make the second channel in the song
30      * @param channel2 the second channel in the song
        */
32     public void setSecond(SongPart channel2) {
         second = channel2;
34       first.getMyPart().setChannel(2);
       }

36
       /**
38      * Make the score and show it
        */
40     public void show() {

42       // Make the Score that we'll assemble the parts into
         // We'll set it up with a default time signature and tempo
44       // we like
         // (Should probably make it possible to change these --
46       // maybe with inputs?)
         Score myScore = new Score("My Song");
48       myScore.setTimeSignature(3,4);
         myScore.setTempo(120.0);

50
         // Now, construct the part and the score.
52       first.getMyPart().addPhrase(first.collect());
         second.getMyPart().addPhrase(second.collect());
54       myScore.addPart(first.getMyPart());
         myScore.addPart(second.getMyPart());

56
         // At the end, let's see it!
58       View.notate(myScore);
       }

60
     }
```

While our new structure is very flexible, it's not the easiest thing to use. We don't want to have to type everything into the Interactions Pane every time. So, we'll create a class

FIGURE 6.13
Multi-part song using our classes.

that has a `main` method. You can execute the main method using RUN DOCUMENT'S MAIN METHOD (F2) in the TOOLS menu. Using MySong, we can get back to having multi-part music in a single score (Figure 6.13).

Example Java Code 41: MySong class with a main method

```java
import jm.music.data.*;
import jm.JMC;
import jm.util.*;
import jm.JMC;

/**
 * Example class for creating a song
 * @author Mark Guzdial
 * @author Barb Ericson
 */
public class MyFirstSong {
  public static void main(String [] args) {
    Song songroot = new Song();

    SongNode node1 = new SongNode();
    SongNode riff3 = new SongNode();
    riff3.setPhrase(SongPhrase.riff3());
    node1.repeatNext(riff3,16);
    SongNode riff1 = new SongNode();
    riff1.setPhrase(SongPhrase.riff1());
    node1.weave(riff1,7,1);
    SongPart part1 = new SongPart(JMC.PIANO, node1);

    songroot.setFirst(part1);

    SongNode node2 = new SongNode();
    SongNode riff4 = new SongNode();
    riff4.setPhrase(SongPhrase.riff4());
    node2.repeatNext(riff4,20);
    node2.weave(riff1,4,5);
    SongPart part2 = new SongPart(JMC.STEEL_DRUMS, node2);

    songroot.setSecond(part2);
    songroot.show();
  }
}
```

■

The point of all of this is to create a *structure* that enables us to easily explore music compositions. We imagine that most music composition exploration will consist of defining new phrases of notes, then combining them in interesting ways: defining the order the nodes are played, repeating nodes, and weaving nodes into the song. At a later point, we can change the instruments we want to use to play the parts.

EXERCISES

6.1   Create a class that represents another song that is similar to `AmazingGraceSong`.

6.2   Create a version of Amazing Grace that has the first part played with a flute and the second part starting half-way through the first part played by a piano.

6.3   Create a version of Amazing Grace that uses SongNode to play the second part first and then the first part.

6.4   Create a version of Amazing Grace that uses SongNode to make three variations on the song.

6.5   Add three phrases to SongPhrase and use them to make a song.

6.6   Add a new method to SongPhrase that takes a phrase and a number *n* and takes every *n*th note from the passed phrase and puts it in a new phrase to be returned.

6.7   Add a new method to SongPhrase that takes two phrases and returns a new phrase with odd notes from the first phrase followed by even notes from the second phrase.

6.8   The Song structure that we've developed on *top* of JMusic is actually pretty similar to the actual implementation of the classes Score, Part, and Phrase *within* the JMusic system. Take one of the music examples that we've built with our own linked list, and re-implement it using only the JMusic classes.

6.9   Add into Song the ability to set different starting times for the composite SongParts. It's the internal Phrase that remembers the start time, so you'll have to pass it down the structure.

6.10   Add a new method to SongNode that takes a passed-in linked list of nodes. Take the first node from the current linked list and the second node from the passed-in linked list and so on till they are woven together.

6.11   Add a new method to SongNode that takes a SongNode and removes it from the linked list of nodes. Is it possible to remove the first node in the linked list?

6.12   Add a new method to SongNode that returns the number of nodes in the linked list of nodes.

6.13   Add a new method to SongNode that repeats the current node a given number of times before the next node.

6.14   Add a new method to SongNode that removes the last element in the linked list of nodes.

6.15   The current implementation of repeatAfter in SongNode appends the input node, as opposed to inserting it. If you could insert it, then you could repeat a given phrase *between* two other nodes. Create a repeatedInsert method that does an insertion rather than an append.

6.16   The current implementation of Song implements *two* channels. *Channel 9* is the *MIDI Drum Kit* where the notes are different percussion instruments (Table 6.2). Modify the Song class to take a third channel, which gets assigned to MIDI channel 9 and plays a percussion SongPart.

TABLE 6.2 MIDI Drum Kit notes

35	Acoustic Bass Drum	51	Ride Cymbal 1
36	Bass Drum 1	52	Chinese Cymbal
37	Side Stick	53	Ride Bell
38	Acoustic Snare	54	Tambourine
39	Hand Clap	55	Splash Cymbal
40	Electric Snare	56	Cowbell
41	Lo Floor Tom	57	Crash Cymbal 2
42	Closed Hi Hat	58	Vibraslap
43	Hi Floor Tom	59	Ride Cymbal 2
44	Pedal Hi Hat	60	Hi Bongo
45	Lo Tom Tom	61	Low Bongo
46	Open Hi Hat	62	Mute Hi Conga
47	Low -Mid Tom Tom	63	Open Hi Conga
48	Hi Mid Tom Tom	64	Low Conga
49	Crash Cymbal 1	65	Hi Timbale
50	Hi Tom Tom	66	Lo Timbale

6.17   Draw the resulting list. Explain why it looks this way.

```
> import jm.JMC;
> SongNode node1 = new SongNode();
> node1.setPhrase(SongPhrase.riff1());
> node1.repeatNext(node1,3);
> node1.showFromMeOn(JMC.FLUTE);
> SongNode node2 = new SongNode();
> node2.setPhrase(SongPhrase.riff2());
> node1.weave(node2,3,2);
> node1.showFromMeOn(JMC.FLUTE);
```

6.18   Draw the resulting list. Explain why it looks this way.

```
> import jm.JMC;
> SongNode node1 = new SongNode();
> node1.setPhrase(SongPhrase.riff1());
> node1.repeatNext(node1,3);
> node1.showFromMeOn(JMC.FLUTE);
> SongNode node2 = new SongNode();
> node2.setPhrase(SongPhrase.riff2());
> node1.weave(node2,3,3);
> node1.showFromMeOn(JMC.FLUTE);
```

6.19   Draw the resulting list. Explain why it looks this way.

```
> import jm.JMC;
> SongNode node1 = new SongNode();
> node1.setPhrase(SongPhrase.riff1());
> node1.repeatNext(node1,5);
> node1.showFromMeOn(JMC.FLUTE);
> SongNode node2 = new SongNode();
```

```
> node2.setPhrase(SongPhrase.riff2());
> node1.weave(node2,3,1);
> node1.showFromMeOn(JMC.FLUTE);
> SongNode node4 = new SongNode();
> node4.setPhrase(SongPhrase.riff4());
> node4.showFromMeOn(JMC.FLUTE);
> node1.weave(node4,3,3);
> node1.showFromMeOn(JMC.FLUTE);
```

6.20   Using the methods developed here to play with linked lists of music, create a song.

- You must use `weave` and `repeatNext` (or `repeatNextInserting`) to create patterns in your music. You probably would want to use the `SongNode` and `SongPhrase` classes.

- You must use `weave` and either of the repeats *at least five* times in your piece. In other words, repeat a set of nodes, then repeat another set, then repeat another set. Then weave in nodes with one pattern, then weave in nodes with another pattern. That would be five. Or do one repeat to create a basic tempo, then four weaves to bring in other motifs.

- You must use at least four unique riffs from `SongPhrase`. (It's okay for you to make all four of them yourself.)

- You must also create your own riffs in `SongPhrase`. You can simply type in music, or you can compute your riff. Just create at least one phrase (of more than a couple of notes) that is interesting and unique.

- All told, you must have at least 10 nodes in your final song.

You will create a class (with some cunning name like `MyWovenSong`) with a `main` that will assemble your song, then open it with `showFromMeOn` (or `show`; whatever you need to do to open up the notation `View` on your masterpiece). Here's the critical part: Draw a picture of your resultant list structure. Show us where all the nodes are in your final composition. You can do this by drawing with a tool like Paint or Visio or even PowerPoint, or you can draw it on paper and then scan it in. You can turn in JPEG, TIFF, or PPT files.

CHAPTER 7

Structuring Images Using Linked Lists

Chapter Learning Objectives

The villagers and wildebeests scenes are not single images. They are collections of many images—not just the segments of the villagers and wildebeests themselves (like faces and legs), but of the elements of the scene, too. How do we structure these images? We could use arrays, but that doesn't give us enough flexibility to insert new pictures, make things disappear (delete them from the scene), and move elements around. To do that, we will need *linked lists* of images.

The computer science goals for this chapter are:

- To use and manipulate linked lists (of images).
- To use an *abstract superclass* to create a single linked list of multiple kinds of objects.

The media learning goal for this chapter is:

- To use different interpretations of the linearity of linked lists: to represent left-to-right ordering, or to represent front-to-back ordering (or *layering*).

We know a lot about manipulating individual images. We know how to manipulate the pixels of an image to create various effects. We've encapsulated a bunch of these in methods to make them pretty easy to use. The question is how to build up these images into composite images. How do we create *scenes* made up of lots of images?

When computer graphics and animation professionals construct complicated scenes such as in *Toy Story* and *Monsters, Inc.*, they go beyond thinking about individual images. Certainly, at some point, they care about how Woody and Nemo are created, how they look, and how they get inserted into the frame—but all as part of how the *scene* is constructed.

How do we describe the structure of a scene? How do we structure our objects in order to describe scenes that we want to describe, but what's more, how do we describe them in such a way that we can change the scene (e.g., in order to define an animation) in the ways that we'll want to later? Those are the central questions in this chapter.

7.1   SIMPLE ARRAYS OF PICTURES

The simplest thing to do is to simply list all the pictures we want in an array. We can then compose them each onto a background (Figure 7.1).

```
> Picture[] myArray = new Picture[5];
> myArray[0]=new Picture(FileChooser.getMediaPath
  ("katie.jpg"));
> myArray[1]=new Picture(FileChooser.getMediaPath
  ("barbara.jpg"));
> myArray[2]=new Picture(FileChooser.getMediaPath
  ("flower1.jpg"));
> myArray[3]=new Picture(FileChooser.getMediaPath
  ("flower2.jpg"));
> myArray[4]=new Picture(FileChooser.getMediaPath
  ("butterfly.jpg"));
> Picture background = new Picture(400,400);
> for (int i = 0; i < 5; i++) {
  myArray[i].scale(0.5).compose
    (background,i*10,i*10);
  }
> background.show();
```

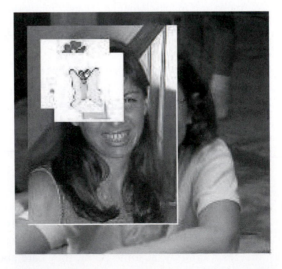

FIGURE 7.1
Array of pictures composed onto a background.

FIGURE 7.2
Elements to be used in our scenes.

7.2 LISTING THE PICTURES, LEFT-TO-RIGHT

We learned about a *linked list* in the last chapter. We can use the same concept for images.

Let's start out by thinking about a scene as a collection of pictures with a left-to-right order to them. Each element of the scene is a picture and knows the next element in the sequence. The elements form a *list* that is *linked* together—that's a *linked list*.

We'll use three little images drawn on a blue background, to make them easier to chromakey onto the image (Figure 7.2).

Example Java Code 42: Elements of a scene in position order

```java
/**
 * Class that represents a positioned scene element
 * @author Mark Guzdial
 * @author Barb Ericson
 */
public class PositionedSceneElement {

  /** the picture that this element holds */
  private Picture myPic;

  /** the next element in the list */
  private PositionedSceneElement next;

  /**
   * Make a new element with a picture as input, and
   * next as null.
   * @param heldPic Picture for element to hold
   */
  public PositionedSceneElement(Picture heldPic) {
    myPic = heldPic;
    next = null;
  }

  /**
   * Method to set the next element
   * @param nextOne next element in list
   */
  public void setNext(PositionedSceneElement nextOne) {
    this.next = nextOne;
  }
```

```
32  /**
     * Method to get the next element
34   * @return the next element in the list
     */
36  public PositionedSceneElement getNext() {
      return this.next;
38  }

40  /**
     * Returns the picture in the node.
42   * @return the picture in the node
     */
44  public Picture getPicture() {
      return this.myPic;
46  }

48  /**
     * Method to draw from this node on in the list, using
50   * blueScreen.
     * Each new element has it's lower-left corner at the
52   * lower-right
     * of the previous node. Starts drawing from left-bottom
54   * @param bg Picture to draw drawing on
     */
56  public void drawFromMeOn(Picture bg) {
      PositionedSceneElement current;
58    int currentX=0, currentY = bg.getHeight()-1;

60    current = this;
      while (current != null) {
62      current.drawMeOn(bg,currentX, currentY);
        currentX = currentX + current.getPicture().getWidth();
64      current = current.getNext();
      }
66  }

68  /**
     * Method to draw from this picture, using blueScreen.
70   * @param bg Picture to draw drawing on
     * @param left x position to draw from
72   * @param bottom y position to draw from
     */
74  private void drawMeOn(Picture bg, int left, int bottom) {
      // Bluescreen takes an upper left corner
76    this.getPicture().blueScreen(bg,left,
                              bottom-this.getPicture().
78                                getHeight());
    }
80  }
```

To construct a scene, we create our `PositionedSceneElement` objects from the
original three pictures. We connect the elements in order, then draw them all onto a
background (Figure 7.3).

```
> PositionedSceneElement tree1 =
  new PositionedSceneElement(new Picture(
    FileChooser.getMediaPath("tree-blue.jpg")));
> PositionedSceneElement tree2 =
```

FIGURE 7.3
Our first scene.

```
    new PositionedSceneElement(new Picture(
      FileChooser.getMediaPath("tree-blue.jpg")));
>   PositionedSceneElement tree3 =
    new PositionedSceneElement(new Picture(
      FileChooser.getMediaPath("tree-blue.jpg")));
>   PositionedSceneElement doggy =
    new PositionedSceneElement(new Picture(
      FileChooser.getMediaPath("dog-blue.jpg")));
>   PositionedSceneElement house =
    new PositionedSceneElement(new Picture(
      FileChooser.getMediaPath("house-blue.jpg")));
>   Picture bg = new Picture(FileChooser.getMediaPath
    ("jungle.jpg"));
>   tree1.setNext(tree2); tree2.setNext(tree3);
>   tree3.setNext(doggy); doggy.setNext(house);
>   tree1.drawFromMeOn(bg);
>   bg.show();
>   bg.write(FileChooser.getMediaPath(
    "first-house-scene.jpg"));
```

This successfully draws a scene, but is it easy to recompose into new scenes? Let's say that we decide that we actually want the dog between trees 2 and 3, instead of tree 3 and the house. To change the list, we need tree2 to point at the doggy element, doggy to point at tree3, and tree3 to point at the house (what the doggy used to point at). Then we will redraw the scene on a new background (Figure 7.4).

FIGURE 7.4
Our second scene.

```
> tree3.setNext(house); tree2.setNext(doggy);
  doggy.setNext(tree3);
> bg = new Picture(
  FileChooser.getMediaPath("jungle.jpg"));
> tree1.drawFromMeOn(bg);
> bg.show();
> bg.write(FileChooser.getMediaPath(
  "second-house-scene.jpg"));
```

Generalizing Moving the Element

Let's consider what happened in this line:

```
> tree3.setNext(house); tree2.setNext(doggy);
  doggy.setNext(tree3);
```

The first statement, `tree3.setNext(house);`, gets the doggy out of the list. `tree3` used to point to (`setNext`) doggy. The next two statements put the doggy after `tree2`. The second statement, `tree2.setNext(doggy);`, puts the doggy after `tree2`. The last statement, `doggy.setNext(tree3);`, makes the doggy point at what `tree2` *used* to point at. All together, the three statements in that line

- remove the item doggy from the list.
- insert the item doggy after `tree2`.

We can write methods to allow us to do this removing and insertion more generally.

Example Java Code 43: Methods to remove and insert elements in a list

```java
/**
 * Method to remove a node from a list, fixing links
 * appropriately.
 * @param node element to remove from list.
 */
public void remove(PositionedSceneElement node) {
  if (node==this) {
    System.out.println("I can't remove the " +
                        "first node from the list.");
    return;
  }

  PositionedSceneElement current = this;

  // While there are more nodes to consider
  while (current.getNext() != null) {

    if (current.getNext() == node) {
      // Simply make node's next be this next
      current.setNext(node.getNext());
      // Make this node point to nothing
      node.setNext(null);
      return;
    }
    current = current.getNext();
  }
}

/**
 * Insert the input node after this node.
 * @param node element to insert after this.
 */
public void insertAfter(PositionedSceneElement node) {

  // Save what "this" currently points at
  PositionedSceneElement oldNext = this.getNext();
  this.setNext(node);
  node.setNext(oldNext);
}
```

The first method allows us to remove an element from a list, like this:

```
> tree1.setNext(tree2); tree2.setNext(tree3);
> tree3.setNext(doggy); doggy.setNext(house);
> tree1.remove(doggy);
> bg = new Picture(FileChooser.getMediaPath
  ("jungle.jpg"));
> tree1.drawFromMeOn(bg);
> bg.show();
```

The result is that doggy is removed entirely (Figure 7.5).

Now we can re-insert the doggy wherever we want, say, after `tree1` (Figure 7.6):

```
> bg = new Picture(FileChooser.getMediaPath
  ("jungle.jpg"));
> tree1.insertAfter(doggy);
> tree1.drawFromMeOn(bg);
> bg.show();
```

FIGURE 7.5
Removing the doggy from the scene.

FIGURE 7.6
Inserting the doggy into the scene.

7.3   LISTING THE PICTURES, LAYERING

In the example from the last section, we used the *order* of the elements in the linked list to determine *position*. We can decide what our representations encode. Let's say that we didn't want to just have our elements be in a linear sequence—we wanted them to each know their positions anywhere on the screen. What, then, would order in the linked list encode? As we'll see, it will encode *layering*.

Example Java Code 44: LayeredSceneElements

```java
/**
 * Class that uses a linked list to indicate
 * the layer a picture is in
 * @author Mark Guzdial
 * @author Barb Ericson
 */
public class LayeredSceneElement {

  /** the picture that this element holds */
  private Picture myPic;

  /** the next element in the list */
  private LayeredSceneElement next;

  /** The coordinates for this element */
  private int x, y;

  /**
   * Make a new element with a picture as input, and
   * next as null, to be drawn at given x,y
   * @param heldPic Picture for element to hold
   * @param xPos x position desired for element
   * @param yPos y position desired for element
   */
  public LayeredSceneElement(Picture heldPic, int xPos,
    int yPos){
    myPic = heldPic;
    next = null;
    x = xPos;
    y = yPos;
  }

  /**
   * Method to set the next element
   * @param nextOne next element in list
   */
  public void setNext(LayeredSceneElement nextOne) {
    this.next = nextOne;
  }

  /**
   * Method to get the next element
   * @return the next element
   */
  public LayeredSceneElement getNext() {
    return this.next;
  }

  /**
   * Returns the picture in the node.
```

```
52        * @return the picture in the node
        */
      public Picture getPicture() {
54        return this.myPic;
      }

56
      /**
58     * Method to draw from this node on in the list, using
       * blueScreen.
60     * Each new element has it's lower-left corner at the
       * lower-right
62     * of the previous node. Starts drawing from left-bottom
       * @param bg Picture to draw drawing on
64     */
      public void drawFromMeOn(Picture bg) {
66       LayeredSceneElement current;

68       current = this;
         while (current != null) {
70         current.drawMeOn(bg);
           current = current.getNext();
72       }
      }

74
      /**
76     * Method to draw from this picture, using blueScreen.
       * @param bg Picture to draw drawing on
78     */
      private void drawMeOn(Picture bg) {
80       this.getPicture().blueScreen(bg,x,y);
      }

82
      /**
84     * Method to remove node from list, fixing links
       * appropriately.
86     * @param node element to remove from list.
       */
88    public void remove(LayeredSceneElement node) {
        if (node==this) {
90        System.out.println("I can't remove the first " +
          "node from the list.");
92        return;
        }

94
        LayeredSceneElement current = this;

96
        // While there are more nodes to consider
98      while (current.getNext() != null) {
          if (current.getNext() == node) {
100         // Simply make node's next be this next
            current.setNext(node.getNext());
102         // Make this node point to nothing
            node.setNext(null);
104         return;
          }
106       current = current.getNext();
        }
108   }

110   /**
       * Return the last element in the list
112    */
```

```
114   public LayeredSceneElement last() {
        LayeredSceneElement current;

116     current = this;
        while (current.getNext() != null) {
118       current = current.getNext();
        }
120     return current;
      }
122
      /**
124    * Reverse the list starting at this,
       * and return the last element of the list.
126    * The last element becomes the FIRST element
       * of the list, and THIS points to null.
128    */
      public LayeredSceneElement reverse() {
130     LayeredSceneElement reversed, temp;

132     // Handle the first node outside the loop
        reversed = this.last();
134     this.remove(reversed);

136     while (this.getNext() != null) {
          temp = this.last();
138       this.remove(temp);
          reversed.add(temp);
140     }

142     // Now put the head of the old list on the end of
        // the reversed list.
144     reversed.add(this);

146     // At this point, reversed
        // is the head of the list
148     return reversed;
      }
150
      /**
152    * Reverse2: Push all the elements on
       * the stack, then pop all the elements
154    * off the stack.
       */
156   public LayeredSceneElement reverse2() {
        LayeredSceneElement reversed, current, popped;
158     Stack stack = new Stack();

160     // Push all the elements on the list
        current=this;
162     while (current != null)
        {
164       stack.push(current);
          current = current.getNext();
166     }

168     // Make the last element (current top of stack) into
        // new first
170     reversed = (LayeredSceneElement) stack.pop();

172     // Now, pop them all onto the list
        current = reversed;
174     while (stack.size()>0) {
```

```
176              popped=(LayeredSceneElement) stack.pop();
                 current.insertAfter(popped);
178              current = popped;
              }
              return reversed;
180          }

182      /**
          * Add the input node after the last node in this list.
184      * @param node element to insert after this.
          */
186      public void add(LayeredSceneElement node) {
            this.last().insertAfter(node);
188      }

190      /**
          * Insert the input node after this node.
192      * @param node element to insert after this.
          */
194      public void insertAfter(LayeredSceneElement node) {
            // Save what "this" currently points at
196         LayeredSceneElement oldNext = this.getNext();
            this.setNext(node);
198         node.setNext(oldNext);
          }
200  }
```

Our use of LayeredSceneElement is much the same as the PositionedScene-
Element, except that when we create a new element, we also specify its position on
the screen.

```
> Picture bg = new Picture(400,400);
> LayeredSceneElement tree1 = new LayeredSceneElement(
new Picture(FileChooser.getMediaPath("tree-blue.jpg")),10,10);
> LayeredSceneElement tree2 = new LayeredSceneElement(
new Picture(FileChooser.getMediaPath("tree-blue.jpg")),100,10);
> LayeredSceneElement tree3 = new LayeredSceneElement(
new Picture(FileChooser.getMediaPath("tree-blue.jpg")),200,100);
> LayeredSceneElement house = new LayeredSceneElement(
new Picture(FileChooser.getMediaPath("house-blue.jpg")),175,175);
> LayeredSceneElement doggy = new LayeredSceneElement(
new Picture(FileChooser.getMediaPath("dog-blue.jpg")),150,325);
> tree1.setNext(tree2); tree2.setNext(tree3);
> tree3.setNext(doggy); doggy.setNext(house);
> tree1.drawFromMeOn(bg);
> bg.show();
> bg.write(FileChooser.getMediaPath("first-layered-scene.jpg"));
```

The result (Figure 7.7) shows the house in front of a tree and the dog. In the upper
left, we can see one tree overlapping the other.

How It Works. Let's talk about how one piece of this class works, the removal of a
node.

FIGURE 7.7
First rendering of the layered scene.

```java
/**
 * Method to remove node from list, fixing links
 * appropriately.
 * @param node element to remove from list.
 */
public void remove(LayeredSceneElement node) {
  if (node==this) {
    System.out.println(
      "I can't remove the " +
      "first node from the list.");
    return;
  }

  LayeredSceneElement current = this;

  // While there are more nodes to consider
  while (current.getNext() != null) {
    if (current.getNext() == node) {
      // Simply make node's next be this next
      current.setNext(node.getNext());
      // Make this node point to nothing
      node.setNext(null);
      return;
    }
    current = current.getNext();
  }
}
```

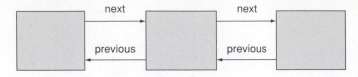

FIGURE 7.8
A doubly-linked list.

You might be wondering what that `param` is about in the comments. This is a note to Javadoc that the method `remove` takes a parameter. What comes after `param` is the parameter name, and then a comment explaining the parameter. This comment will appear in the Javadoc-generated HTML to explain what the `method` does and how to use it.

The first thing we do in `remove` is to check to see if the node to be removed is the same node that we asked to do the `remove`, `this`. Typically, you call `remove` on the first node in the list. Currently, our implementation of a linked list doesn't allow us to remove the first node in the list. If we execute `thisOne.remove(thisOne)`, how could we change `thisOne` to point at anything else? We'll see how to fix that later.

We then traverse the list, checking for `current.getNext() = null`. That's a little unusual—typically, we check for `current = null` when we traverse a list. Why the difference? Because we want to find the node *before* the one we're removing. We need to connect the nodes *around* the node that that's already there. Once we find the node to remove, we want to make the one *before* it point to whatever the removed node *currently* points to. That essentially routes the linked list around the node to be removed—and poof! it's gone. If we stopped when we found the node we were looking for, as opposed to `current.getNext()` being the node we are looking for, we will have gone too far. This is a key idea in linked lists: *there is no link from a node back to the node that is pointing to it*. If you have a pointer to a node, you don't know who points to that node.

That does not have to be true. One can have linked lists where a node points both to its `next` *and* to its `previous` (Figure 7.8). We call those *doubly-linked lists*. They are powerful for finding and replacing nodes, since you can traverse them forwards and backwards. They are more complicated, though—inserting and deleting involves patching up both `next` links and `previous` links. They also waste more space than a *singly-linked list*. With a singly-linked list, each piece of data in a node also has a `next` link associated with it. Compared to an array, a singly-linked list requires an extra reference for every data element. A doubly-linked list gives up *two* references for each data element.

Reordering Elements in a List

Now, let's reorder the elements in the list, without changing the elements—not even their locations. We'll reverse the list so that we start with the house, not the first tree. (Notice that we set the `tree1` element to point to `null`—if we didn't do that, we'd get an infinite loop with `tree1` pointing to itself.)

FIGURE 7.9
Second rendering of the layered scene.

The resultant figure (Figure 7.9) has completely different layering. The trees in the upper left have swapped, and the tree and dog are now in front of the house.

```
> house.setNext(doggy); doggy.setNext(tree3);
> tree3.setNext(tree2); tree2.setNext(tree1);
> tree1.setNext(null);
> bg = new Picture(400,400);
> house.drawFromMeOn(bg);
> bg.show();
> bg.write(FileChooser.getMediaPath(
  "second-layered-scene.jpg"));
```

Have you ever used a drawing program like *Visio* or even *PowerPoint* where you brought an object forward, or sent it to the back? What you were doing is, quite literally, exactly what we're doing when we're changing the order of elements in the list of PositionedSceneElements. In tools such as Visio or PowerPoint, each drawn object is an element in a list. To draw the screen, the program literally walks the list (*traverses* the list) and draws each object. We call the re-creation of the scene through traversing a data structure a *rendering* of the scene. If the list gets reordered (by bringing an object forward or sending it to the back), then the layering changes. "Bringing an object forward" is about moving an element one position further *back* in the list—the things at the end get drawn *last* and thus are on *top*.

One other observation: Did you notice how similar the implementations of both of these elements are?

7.4 REVERSING A LIST

In the last example, we reversed the list "by hand" in a sense. We took each and every node and reset what it pointed to. What if we had a *lot* of elements, though? What if our scene had dozens of elements in it? Reversing the list would take a lot of commands. Could we write down the *process* of reversing the list, so that we can encode it?

There are actually several different ways of reversing a list. Let's do it in two different ways here. The first way we'll do it is by repeatedly getting the last element of the original list, removing it from the list, then adding it to the new reversed list. That will work, but slowly. To find the last element of the list means traversing the whole list. To add an element to the end of the list means walking to the end of the new list and setting the last element there to the new element.

Here's a method that implements that process.

Example Java Code 45: Reverse a list

```java
/**
 * Reverse the list starting at this,
 * and return the last element of the list.
 * The last element becomes the FIRST element
 * of the list, and THIS points to null.
 */
public LayeredSceneElement reverse() {
    LayeredSceneElement reversed, temp;

    // Handle the first node outside the loop
    reversed = this.last();
    this.remove(reversed);

    while (this.getNext() != null) {
        temp = this.last();
        this.remove(temp);
        reversed.add(temp);
    }

    // Now put the head of the old list on the end of
    // the reversed list.
    reversed.add(this);

    // At this point, reversed
    // is the head of the list
    return reversed;
}
```

The core of this program is:

```java
while (this.getNext() != null) {
        temp = this.last();
        this.remove(temp);
        reversed.add(temp);
    }
```

So how expensive is this loop?

- We go through this loop once for each element in the list.
- For each element in the list, we find the `last()` (which requires another complete traversal).
- And when we `add()`, which we know requires another `last()` which is another traversal.

The bottom line is, that for each node in the list, we touch every other node. We call that an $O(n^2)$ algorithm—as the data grows larger (n), the number of steps to execute (the running time) increases as a square of the data size (n^2). For a huge list of lots of images (maybe wildebeests running down a ridge?), that's very expensive.

How would you do it in real life? Imagine that you have a bunch of cards laid out in a row, and you need to reverse them. How would you do it? One way to do it is to *pile* them up, and then set them back out. A pile (also called a *stack* in computer science) has an interesting *property* in that the last thing placed on the pile is the first one to remove from the pile—that's called LIFO, *Last-In-First-Out*. We can use that property to reverse the list. We can define a `Stack` class to represent the abstract notion of a *pile*, then use it to reverse the list. We will see that in the next chapter.

7.5   ANIMATION

Any movie (including animated scenes) consists of a series of images (typically called *frames*) played in a sequence fast enough to trick our eyes into seeing a continuous image. How would you create an animation using data structures? We can come up with a different definition than "a sequence of frames" now. We can think of an animation as "modify the structure describing your scene, then *render* it (turn it into an image), and repeat!"

We can do that even with our simple linked lists. We will create an animation of a doggy at the beginning of a grove of trees, then running between the trees. At the end, he turns around and runs back.

Example Java Code 46: Create a simple animation of a dog running

```java
/**
 * Class that uses modification of a linked
 * data structure to animate a scene
 * @author Mark Guzdial
 * @author Barb Ericson
 */
public class AnimatedPositionedScene {

    /** A FrameSequencer for sequencing the frames */
    private FrameSequencer frames;

    /**
     * We'll need to keep track
     * of the elements of the scene
     */
```

```
16      private PositionedSceneElement tree1, tree2, tree3, house,
            doggy, doggyFlip;
18
        /**
20       * Method to set up the animation
         */
22      public void setUp() {

24        frames = new FrameSequencer("C:/Temp/");

26        Picture p = null; // Use this to fill elements

28        p = new Picture(FileChooser.getMediaPath("tree-blue.jpg"));
          tree1 = new PositionedSceneElement(p);
30
          p = new Picture(FileChooser.getMediaPath("tree-blue.jpg"));
32        tree2 = new PositionedSceneElement(p);

34        p = new Picture(FileChooser.getMediaPath("tree-blue.jpg"));
          tree3 = new PositionedSceneElement(p);
36
          p = new Picture(FileChooser.getMediaPath("house-blue.jpg"));
38        house = new PositionedSceneElement(p);

40        p = new Picture(FileChooser.getMediaPath("dog-blue.jpg"));
          doggy = new PositionedSceneElement(p);
42        doggyFlip = new PositionedSceneElement(p.flip());
        }
44
        /**
46       * Method to do the animation
         */
48      public void make() {
          frames.show();
50
          // First frame
52        Picture bg = new Picture(FileChooser.getMediaPath
            ("jungle.jpg"));
54        tree1.setNext(doggy);  doggy.setNext(tree2);
          tree2.setNext(tree3);
56        tree3.setNext(house);
          tree1.drawFromMeOn(bg);
58        frames.addFrame(bg);

60        // Dog moving right
          bg = new Picture(FileChooser.getMediaPath("jungle.jpg"));
62        tree1.remove(doggy);
          tree2.insertAfter(doggy);
64        tree1.drawFromMeOn(bg);
          frames.addFrame(bg);
66
          bg = new Picture(FileChooser.getMediaPath("jungle.jpg"));
68        tree1.remove(doggy);
          tree3.insertAfter(doggy);
70        tree1.drawFromMeOn(bg);
          frames.addFrame(bg);
72
          bg = new Picture(FileChooser.getMediaPath("jungle.jpg"));
74        tree1.remove(doggy);
          house.insertAfter(doggy);
76        tree1.drawFromMeOn(bg);
          frames.addFrame(bg);
```

```
78      //Dog moving left
80      bg = new Picture(FileChooser.getMediaPath("jungle.jpg"));
        tree1.remove(doggy);
82      house.insertAfter(doggyFlip);
        tree1.drawFromMeOn(bg);
84      frames.addFrame(bg);

86      bg = new Picture(FileChooser.getMediaPath("jungle.jpg"));
        tree1.remove(doggyFlip);
88      tree3.insertAfter(doggyFlip);
        tree1.drawFromMeOn(bg);
90      frames.addFrame(bg);

92      bg = new Picture(FileChooser.getMediaPath("jungle.jpg"));
        tree1.remove(doggyFlip);
94      tree2.insertAfter(doggyFlip);
        tree1.drawFromMeOn(bg);
96      frames.addFrame(bg);

98      bg = new Picture(FileChooser.getMediaPath("jungle.jpg"));
        tree1.remove(doggyFlip);
100     tree1.insertAfter(doggyFlip);
        tree1.drawFromMeOn(bg);
102     frames.addFrame(bg);

104   }

106   /**
       * Method to replay the animation
108    */
      public void replay() {
110     frames.play(100); //3 frames per second
      }
112
      /** main for testing */
114   public static void main(String[] args) {
        AnimatedPositionedScene scene =
116       new AnimatedPositionedScene();
        scene.setUp();
118     scene.make();
      }
120 }
```

When you execute the main method in this class you will see that this is definitely not a great animation (Figure 7.10). It looks more like the trees are hopping out of the way of the dog, like the houses hopping away from the Knight Bus in the Harry Potter novels. But this is our first example of how a real computer-generated animation works: by using a data structure, which gets changed and re-rendered in a loop.

7.6   LISTS WITH TWO KINDS OF ELEMENTS

Why should we have to choose between having elements positioned for us, left-to-right, or layered for us, back-to-front? That doesn't seem like a reasonable limitation for an animation designer—you may want some images just lined up where you don't care so much about the positioning (e.g., trees in a forest, spectators in the audience) and

FIGURE 7.10
A few frames from the `AnimatedPositionedScene`.

other images you want to be in very specific places (e.g., your main characters). We can easily imagine having a list where we have both positioned and layered elements. Some nodes we want to position left-to-right, and other nodes we'd want to go at particular places, and nodes earlier in the list would be understood to be rendered behind other nodes.

That turns out to be a new thing for us to do from a Java perspective. Consider the `PositionedSceneElement`. Its `next` has the type `PositionedSceneElement`. How could the next element be anything *but* a `PositionedSceneElement`? If the next element could be something else, we couldn't use the same code on it. How could we draw some things at their (*x*, *y*) position and *others* left-to-right?

There's another reason to rewrite our existing scene element classes, besides wanting to intermix different kinds of elements. The current implementation has *so much* duplicated code. Check out `last` and `add` in `PositionedSceneElement` and `LayeredSceneElement`. Basically the same thing—why do we have to duplicate this code? Why can't we tell the computer "Here's `last`—always use this definition for all linked lists, please!"?

The way to solve both of these problems (being able to intermix kinds of elements and rewriting to reduce redundancy of code) is with a *superclass*. We will create a superclass called `SceneElement`, then we will create a *subclass* for positioned and layered kinds of scene elements. We'll call these `SceneElementLayered` and `SceneElementPositioned`. This structure solves several of the problems stated above.

- A variable that is declared the type of a superclass can *also* hold objects that have the type of a subclass. So, a variable of type `SceneElement` can also reference a `SceneElementLayered` or `SceneElementPositioned`. That's how we'll define `next` so that each element can point to any other kind of `SceneElement`.

- Any methods in `SceneElement` are *inherited* by its subclasses. So if we define `last` and `add` in `SceneElement`, any instances of `SceneElementLayered` and `SceneElementPositioned` will automatically inherit those methods. Every instance of `SceneElementLayered` and `SceneElementPositioned` will know how to do `add` and `last` because the superclass `SceneElement` knows how to do it.

- Where the subclasses need to be different, they *can* be made different. So `SceneElementPositioned` will have an x and y for positioned, but `SceneElementLayered` will not.

If one of the classes will have an (x, y) and the other one will not, each of the subclasses will have to `drawWith` themselves differently. The `drawWith` method for `SceneElementPositioned` will have to figure out where each element goes left-to-right, and the same method for `SceneElementLayered` will draw the element at its desired x and y.

Since `SceneElement` will not actually know how to draw itself, it is not really a useful object. It is a useful class, though. A class whose main purpose is to hold methods (behavior) and fields (data and structure) that subclasses will inherit is referred to as an *abstract class*. Java even has a keyword `abstract` that is used to identify abstract classes.

An abstract class can have *abstract methods* (also identified with the `abstract` keyword). These are methods in an abstract class that do not actually have implementations—there is no body for the methods. The point of defining an abstract method in an abstract class is to tell Java, "All my subclasses will define this method and provide a real body for this method. I'm just defining it here so that you know that you can expect it—it's okay for a variable declared to be of my type to call this method."

Example Java Code 47: Abstract method drawWith in abstract class SceneElement

```
/*
 * Use the given turtle to draw oneself
 * @param t the Turtle to draw with
 */
public abstract void drawWith(Turtle t);
// No body defined here in the abstract class
```

Okay, now that we know how to declare the abstract class and the abstract method `drawWith`, we can consider how to implement the `drawWith` method for each of the subclasses of `SceneElement`, `SceneElementPositioned`, and `SceneElementLayered`. The challenge of implementing `drawWith` is to keep track of the next *positioned* element when you have to go draw a *layered* element at some particular (x, y). There are lots of ways of doing that, like holding some `nextX` and `nextY` that remembers the next position even when drawing a layered element. Here's the one that we will use here: we will use a turtle to keep track of *where* the element should be drawn. Specifically, each subclass will implement `drawWith`, taking a turtle as input, and they will use that turtle as a *pen* to draw the picture in the node at the right place.

> Abstract Class *SceneElement*
>
> It **knows** its Picture myPic and its next (SceneElement).
>
> It **knows how** to get/set next, to reverse() and insertAfter(), and to drawFromMeOn().
>
> It **defines** drawWith(turtle), but leaves it for its subclasses to complete.

FIGURE 7.11
The abstract class `SceneElement`, in terms of what it knows and can do.

Let's define the `SceneElement` abstract class first. It knows its picture and knows how to do all the basic list manipulations (Figure 7.11)—yet it only knows "abstractly" how to draw. A key part of this class definition is that `next` and all the methods that return an object are declared as class `SceneElement`—which means that they can actually be any instance in the hierarchy.

Example Java Code 48: SceneElement

```java
/**
 * Represents an element that knows how to draw itself in a
 * scene using a Turtle to do the drawing
 *
 * @author Mark Guzdial
 * @author Barb Ericson
 */
public abstract class SceneElement {

  /**
   * the picture that this element holds
   */
  private Picture myPic;

  /**
   * the next element in the list -- any SceneElement
   */
  private SceneElement next;


  /**
   * Method to set the next element
   * @param nextOne next element in list
   */
  public void setNext(SceneElement nextOne) {
    this.next = nextOne;
  }

  /**
   * Method to get the next element
   * @return the next element
   */
  public SceneElement getNext() {
    return this.next;
  }
```

```java
        /**
         * Returns the picture in the node.
         * @return the picture in the node
         */
        public Picture getPicture(){
            return this.myPic;
        }

        /**
         * Method to set the picture in the node
         * @param pict the picture to use
         */
        public void setPicture(Picture pict)
        {
            this.myPic = pict;
        }

        /**
         * Method to draw from this node on in the list.
         * For positioned elements, compute locations.
         * Each new element has it's lower-left corner at the
         * lower-right of the previous node. Starts drawing from
         * left-bottom
         * @param bg Picture to draw drawing on
         */
        public void drawFromMeOn(Picture bg) {

            SceneElement current;

            // Start the X at the left
            // Start the Y along the bottom
            int currentX=0, currentY = bg.getHeight()-1;

            Turtle turtle = new Turtle(bg);
            turtle.setPenDown(false); // Pick the pen up

            current = this;
            while (current != null) {
                // Position the turtle for the next positioned element
                turtle.moveTo(currentX,currentY-current.getPicture().
                    getHeight());
                turtle.setHeading(0);

                current.drawWith(turtle);
                currentX = currentX + current.getPicture().getWidth();

                current = current.getNext();
            }
        }

        /*
         * Use the given turtle to draw oneself
         * @param t the Turtle to draw with
         */
        public abstract void drawWith(Turtle t);
        // No body defined here in the abstract class

        /** Method to remove node from list, fixing links
         * appropriately.
         * @param node element to remove from list.
         */
```

```java
public void remove(SceneElement node) {
    if (node==this) {
        System.out.println("I can't remove the first "
            + "node from the list.");
        return;
    }

    SceneElement current = this;
    // While there are more nodes to consider
    while (current.getNext() != null) {
        if (current.getNext() == node) {
            // Simply make node's next be this next
            current.setNext(node.getNext());
            // Make this node point to nothing
            node.setNext(null);
            return;
        }
        current = current.getNext();
    }
}

/**
 * Insert the input node after this node.
 * @param node element to insert after this.
 */
public void insertAfter(SceneElement node) {

    // Save what "this" currently points at
    SceneElement oldNext = this.getNext();
    this.setNext(node);
    node.setNext(oldNext);
}

/**
 * Return the last element in the list
 */
public SceneElement last() {
    SceneElement current;

    current = this;
    while (current.getNext() != null) {
        current = current.getNext();
    }
    return current;
}

/**
 * Reverse the list starting at this,
 * and return the last element of the list.
 * The last element becomes the FIRST element
 * of the list, and THIS goes to null.
 */
public SceneElement reverse() {
    SceneElement reversed, temp;

    // Handle the first node outside the loop
    reversed = this.last();
    this.remove(reversed);

    while (this.getNext() != null) {
        temp = this.last();
        this.remove(temp);
```

```
160        reversed.add(temp);
        }
162     // At this point, reversed
        // is the head of the list
164     return reversed;
    }
166
    /**
168    * Return the number of elements in the list
       * @return the number of elements in the list
170    */
    public int count() {
172     int numElements = 1;

174     SceneElement current = this;
        while (current.getNext() != null) {
176        current = current.getNext();
           numElements++;
178     }
        return numElements;
180 }

182 /**
       * Add the input node after the last node in this list.
184    * @param node element to insert after this.
       */
186 public void add(SceneElement node) {
      this.last().insertAfter(node);
188 }

190 }
```

The two subclasses, `SceneElementPositioned` and `SceneElementLayered`, are really quite short. They only specify what's *different* from the superclass. The relationship between a superclass and a subclass is often called, by object-oriented designers, a *generalization-specialization relationship* (sometimes shortened to *gen-spec*). The `SceneElement` is the general form of a scene element that describes how scene elements *generally* work. The two subclasses just specify how they are *special*, different from the general case (Figure 7.12).

Example Java Code 49: SceneElementPositioned

```
/**
2  * Class that defines a scene element whose position
   * is defined by its position in the linked list
4  * @author Mark Guzdial
   * @author Barb Ericson
6  */
public class SceneElementPositioned extends SceneElement {
8
   /**
10    * Make a new element with a picture as input, and
      * next as null.
12    * @param heldPic Picture for element to hold
      */
14 public SceneElementPositioned(Picture heldPic) {
     this.setPicture(heldPic);
16   this.setNext(null);
   }
18
```

Abstract Class *SceneElement*

It **knows** its Picture myPic and its next.

It **knows how** to get/set next, to reverse() and insertAfter(), and to drawFromMeOn() and drawWith(turtle)

Class *SceneElementLayered*

It **knows** its position (x,y).

It **knows how** to drawWith(turtle) by moving to (x,y), then dropping.

Class *SceneElementPositioned*

It **knows how** to drawWith(turtle)

FIGURE 7.12
The abstract class `SceneElement` and its two subclasses.

```
    /**
20   * Method to draw from this picture.
     * @param turtle the Turtle to use for drawing
22   */
    public void drawWith(Turtle turtle) {
24     turtle.drop(this.getPicture());
    }
26 }
```

Example Java Code 50: SceneElementLayererd

```
    /**
2    * A scene element that knows its position
     * @author Mark Guzdial
4    * @author Barb Ericson
     */
6  public class SceneElementLayered extends SceneElement {

8    /** The x and y coordinates for this element */
    private int x, y;
10
    /**
12   * Make a new element with a picture as input, and
     * next as null, to be drawn at given x,y
14   * @param heldPic Picture for element to hold
     * @param xpos x position desired for element
16   * @param ypos y position desired for element
     */
18  public SceneElementLayered(Picture heldPic, int xpos,
      int ypos) {
20    setPicture(heldPic);
      setNext(null);
22    this.x = xpos;
      this.y = ypos;
24  }

26   /**
     * Method to draw from this picture on.
```

FIGURE 7.13
A scene rendered from a linked list with different kinds of scene elements.

```
28      * @param turtle the Turtle to draw with
        */
30    public void drawWith(Turtle turtle) {
        // We just ignore the pen's position
32      turtle.moveTo(x,y);
        turtle.drop(this.getPicture());
34    }
    }
```

■

This structure will only make sense when we try it out. Here's a simple example of a picture drawn with both kinds of scene elements in a single linked list (Figure 7.13). Notice that the dog is *under* the flower, both of which are out of the linear sequence across the bottom.

Example Java Code 51: MultiElementScene

```
/**
2     * Demonstration of using both SceneElementPositioned and
      * ScenceElementLayered
```

```
 4    * @author Mark Guzdial
      * @author Barb Ericson
 6    */
     public class MultiElementScene {
 8
       public static void main(String[] args){
10
         // We'll use this for filling the nodes
12       Picture p = null;

14       p = new Picture(FileChooser.getMediaPath("swan.jpg"));
         SceneElement node1 = new SceneElementPositioned
16         (p.scale(0.25));

18       p = new Picture(FileChooser.getMediaPath("horse.jpg"));
         SceneElement node2 = new SceneElementPositioned
20         (p.scale(0.25));

22       p = new Picture(FileChooser.getMediaPath("dog.jpg"));
         SceneElement node3 = new SceneElementLayered(p.scale
24         (0.25),10,50);

26       p = new Picture(FileChooser.getMediaPath("flower1.jpg"));
         SceneElement node4 = new SceneElementLayered(p.scale
28         (0.5),10,30);

30       p = new Picture(FileChooser.getMediaPath("graves.jpg"));
         SceneElement node5 = new SceneElementPositioned
32         (p.scale(0.25));

34       node1.setNext(node2); node2.setNext(node3);
         node3.setNext(node4); node4.setNext(node5);
36
         // Now, let's see it!
38       Picture bg = new Picture(600,600);
         node1.drawFromMeOn(bg);
40       bg.show();
       }
42   }
```

It is easier to see how a single turtle is being used to draw all of these elements if we change how we traverse the list with drawFromMeOn in the SceneElement class. We will simply traverse the list with the turtle's pen *down*.

Example Java Code 52: Modified drawFromMeOn in SceneElement

```
/**
 * Method to draw from this node on in the list.
 * For positioned elements, compute locations.
 * Each new element has it's lower-left corner at the
 * lower-right of the previous node. Starts drawing from
 * left-bottom
 * @param bg Picture to draw drawing on
 */
public void drawFromMeOn(Picture bg) {

  SceneElement current;

  // Start the X at the left
```

```
    // Start the Y along the bottom
    int currentX=0, currentY = bg.getHeight()-1;

    Turtle turtle = new Turtle(bg);
    turtle.setPenDown(true); // SET THE PEN DOWN

    current = this;
    while (current != null) {
      // Position the turtle for the next positioned element
      turtle.moveTo(currentX,currentY-
        current.getPicture().getHeight());
      turtle.setHeading(0);

      current.drawWith(turtle);
      currentX = currentX + current.getPicture().getWidth();

      current = current.getNext();
    }
  }
```

The result is a picture showing the trace of where the turtle moved throughout the traversal (Figure 7.14). The pen gets created in the center, then travels down to the left corner to draw the swan, then moves right (the width of the swan) to draw the horse. The turtle pen moves into position for drawing the flower, but instead moves to the dog's saved position and draws there. The turtle moves back into place to draw the next positioned scene element, but again moves up to draw the flower (on top of a corner of the dog picture). Finally, it moves to the next position and draws the graves there.

Structuring Our Multi-Element Lists

One can imagine using our new kind of multi-element lists to create complicated scenes.

- Imagine creating large sequences of objects next to one another, like trees in a forest, or Orcs about to enter into battle in *The Lord of the Rings*. We could create these by inserting as many nodes as we need with `SceneElementPositioned`. We wouldn't want to position each of these separately—we simply want to add them all into the list and have them drawn at the right place.

- Now, you might want to position some specific characters at specific positions in the scene, such as an elf and a dwarf to battle the Orcs, or a plastic spaceman getting ready to enter the scene.

A linear list is not the best way to present such a scene. You would want to keep track of this band of Orcs here, and that band of Orcs there, with a forest behind, and a few brave heroes getting ready to keep the horde at bay. A linear list doesn't give you an easy way of keeping track of the various pieces. A linear list is just a long list of nodes.

It would be easier to structure and manipulate the scene if one part of the linked list represented the Fifth Army of Orcs, and another part represented the forest, and the heroes were elsewhere—and if all those parts were clearly labeled and manipulatable. To keep track of just that kind of structure, we are going to introduce a *scene graph*, a kind of *tree*. A tree structures a linked list into a hierarchy or clusters. A scene graph is

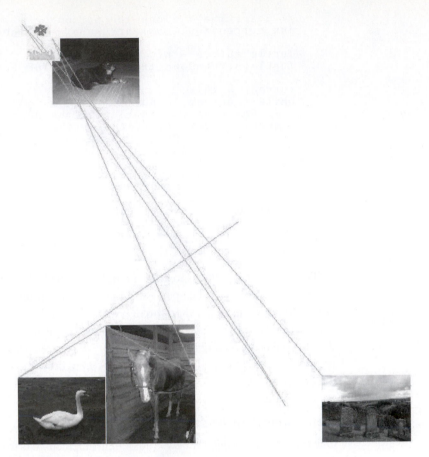

FIGURE 7.14
The same multi-element scene with pen traced.

an important data structure in defining scenes in modern computer animations. That's where we're heading next.

EXERCISES

7.1   Draw the linked list that results from:

```
> PositionedSceneElement tree1 =
  new PositionedSceneElement(
    new Picture(FileChooser.getMediaPath
      ("tree-blue.jpg")));
> PositionedSceneElement tree2 =
  new PositionedSceneElement(
    new Picture(FileChooser.getMediaPath
      ("tree-blue.jpg")));
> PositionedSceneElement tree3 =
  new PositionedSceneElement(
```

```
          new Picture(FileChooser.getMediaPath
            ("tree-blue.jpg")));
    > PositionedSceneElement doggy =
      new PositionedSceneElement(
          new Picture(FileChooser.getMediaPath
            ("dog-blue.jpg")));
    > PositionedSceneElement house =
      new PositionedSceneElement(
          new Picture(FileChooser.getMediaPath
            ("house-blue.jpg")));
    > Picture bg =
      new Picture(FileChooser.getMediaPath
          ("jungle.jpg"));
    > tree1.setNext(tree3); tree3.setNext(doggy);
    > doggy.setNext(tree2); tree2.setNext(house);
```

7.2   Draw the linked list that results from:

```
    > PositionedSceneElement tree1 =
      new PositionedSceneElement(
        new Picture(FileChooser.getMediaPath
          ("tree-blue.jpg")));
    > PositionedSceneElement tree2 =
      new PositionedSceneElement(
        new Picture(FileChooser.getMediaPath
          ("tree-blue.jpg")));
    > PositionedSceneElement tree3 =
      new PositionedSceneElement(
        new Picture(FileChooser.getMediaPath
          ("tree-blue.jpg")));
    > PositionedSceneElement doggy =
      new PositionedSceneElement(
        new Picture(FileChooser.getMediaPath
          ("dog-blue.jpg")));
    > PositionedSceneElement house =
      new PositionedSceneElement(
        new Picture(FileChooser.getMediaPath
          ("house-blue.jpg")));
    > Picture bg = new Picture(FileChooser.
      getMediaPath("jungle.jpg"));
    > tree1.setNext(house); house.setNext(tree2);
    > tree2.setNext(tree3); tree3.setNext(doggy);
```

7.3   Draw the linked list that results from:

```
    > PositionedSceneElement tree1 =
      new PositionedSceneElement(
        new Picture(FileChooser.getMediaPath
          ("tree-blue.jpg")));
    > PositionedSceneElement tree2 =
      new PositionedSceneElement(
        new Picture(FileChooser.getMediaPath
```

```
                         ("tree-blue.jpg")));
    > PositionedSceneElement doggy =
      new PositionedSceneElement(
        new Picture(FileChooser.getMediaPath
          ("dog-blue.jpg")));
    > PositionedSceneElement house =
      new PositionedSceneElement(
        new Picture(FileChooser.getMediaPath
          ("house-blue.jpg")));
    > Picture bg = new Picture(FileChooser.
      getMediaPath("jungle.jpg"));
    > tree1.setNext(house); house.setNext(doggy);
    > doggy.setNext(tree2); tree1.remove(house);
```

7.4   Draw the linked list that results from:

```
    > PositionedSceneElement tree1 =
      new PositionedSceneElement(
        new Picture(FileChooser.getMediaPath
          ("tree-blue.jpg")));
    > PositionedSceneElement tree2 =
      new PositionedSceneElement(
        new Picture(FileChooser.getMediaPath
          ("tree-blue.jpg")));
    > PositionedSceneElement doggy =
      new PositionedSceneElement(
        new Picture(FileChooser.getMediaPath
          ("dog-blue.jpg")));
    > PositionedSceneElement house =
      new PositionedSceneElement(
        new Picture(FileChooser.getMediaPath
          ("house-blue.jpg")));
    > Picture bg = new Picture(FileChooser.
      getMediaPath("jungle.jpg"));
    > tree1.setNext(doggy); doggy.setNext(tree2);
    > tree2.setNext(house); tree1.remove(tree1);
```

7.5   Draw the linked list that results from:

```
    > PositionedSceneElement tree1 =
      new PositionedSceneElement(
        new Picture(FileChooser.getMediaPath
          ("tree-blue.jpg")));
    > PositionedSceneElement doggy =
      new PositionedSceneElement(
        new Picture(FileChooser.getMediaPath
          ("dog-blue.jpg")));
    > PositionedSceneElement house =
      new PositionedSceneElement(
        new Picture(FileChooser.getMediaPath
          ("house-blue.jpg")));
```

```
> Picture bg =
  new Picture(FileChooser.getMediaPath
    ("jungle.jpg"));
> tree1.setNext(house);  house.setNext(doggy);
> doggy.setNext(tree1);
```

7.6   Add a `replaceNext(PositionedSceneElement newNode)` method that replaces the next node with the passed `newNode` in the `PositionedSceneElement` class.

7.7   Add a `replaceOld(PositionedSceneElement oldNode, Positioned-SceneElement newNode)` method that replaces the passed `oldNode` with the passed `newNode` in the `PositionedSceneElement` class.

7.8   Does an abstract class have to have an abstract method? If a class does have an abstract method, does it have to be an abstract class? Can an abstract method be private? What are the differences between interfaces and abstract classes?

7.9   Create a method `copyList` in `SceneElement` that copies the list starting at `this` and returns a new list with the same elements in it.

7.10   Create a method `copyList(int n,m)` in `SceneElement` that starts with `this` as the 0th element in the list and returns a new list from the *n*th to the *m*th element.

7.11   Create a `TimedSceneElement` where each picture is shown before the next one in the linked list. Add a field for how long to show each picture. What class should this inherit from? Create an example using a `TimedSceneElement`.

7.12   Create a `RotatedSceneElement` where each picture is rotated by some amount, but still to the right of the previous picture. Add a field for the amount of rotation. Create an example using a `RotatedSceneElement`.

7.13   Create your own class that uses both types of nodes: `SceneElementPositioned` and `SceneElementLayered`.

7.14   Why does the `remove` method in `SceneElement` not allow you to remove the current node from the list? Is there any way to solve this problem?

7.15   List the situations when it is better to use a linked list than an array. List the situations when it is better to use an array than a linked list.

7.16   You have two kinds of employees, salary and hourly. The salary employees get paid the same each week no matter how many hours they work. The hourly employees get paid depending on how many hours they work. For both types you need to know the employee's name and social security number. For the hourly employees, you also need to know the pay rate. What fields and methods should be in the abstract superclass `Employee`? Should any of the methods be abstract? If so, which one(s)?

7.17   Imagine you have two different kinds of bank accounts: savings and checking. Each account keeps track of the transactions and the balance in the account.

The owner(s) of the account can make deposits and withdrawals on either account. But, if the owner tries to withdraw more than the current balance from the savings account, it isn't allowed. If the owner tries to withdraw more than the current balance from the checking account, then if the savings account has enough money, it is automatically transferred to the checking account. What fields and methods should be in the abstract superclass Account?

7.18   Using any of the linked lists of pictures that we created (where ordering represented linearity, or layering, or using turtles to walk the list), implement three additional methods (where firstNodeInList is a node, not actually a picture):

- firstNodeInList.findAndReplaceRepeat(oldElement, newElement, n): Find oldElement, remove oldElement from the list, and then insert at oldElement's place n copies of the node newElement. Imagine this as implementing the special effect where the witch disappears and gets replaced with three smaller copies of the witch at the same place.

- firstNodeInList.replaceWithModification(findElement, int type): Find the node findElement, then replace it with a node containing a modified picture of the picture in findElement. The type indicates the kind of modification. If 1, negate the picture. If 2, mirror horizontal. If 3, mirror vertical. If 4, sunset. If anything else, insert grayscale. This is about changing the image in some predefined way for any node in the list.

- firstNodeInList.replaceWithModifications(findElement, double[] types): Find the node findElement (a node, not a picture, so you can do an exact match), then replace it with nodes containing a modified picture of the picture in findElement. Insert as many nodes as there are entries in the types array; e.g., if there are three values in the array, insert three copies. The value in the types array indicates the kind of image modification for that element. If 1, negate the picture. If 2, mirror horizontal. If 3, mirror vertical. If 4, sunset. If anything else, insert grayscale. So, if the array was {1,2,5}, you would insert three copies of the picture in findElement, the first negated, the second mirrored horizontal, and the third grayscaled. This is an example of taking a base wildebeest and replacing it with several copies having different colors.

You can be sure that oldElement or findElement will never be equal to the firstNodeInList.

You must also provide a class named PictureTest that has a main() method which utilizes all three of your new methods. When the grader executes the main(), it should show (a) a background with three or more pictures in it, (b) then a new picture after using findAndReplaceRepeat, followed by (c) a third picture after using replaceWithModification, and finally (d) a fourth picture after using replaceWithModifications.

7.19   Create a class with a `main` method that sets up a scene with `LayeredScene-Element`, then change the layering of just a *single* element using `remove` and `insertAfter`—much as we did to make the doggy run in our first animation using `PositionedSceneElement`.

7.20   Take any linked list implementation that we have created thus far, and re-create it as a doubly-linked list. Make sure that `insertAfter` and `remove` work, and implement `insertBefore` as well.

PART 3

TREES: HIERARCHICAL STRUCTURES FOR MEDIA

8

Trees of Images

Chapter Learning Objectives

Having worked with linked lists of images, we are in a position to think about non-linear lists of images. By moving to trees, we can represent structure and hierarchy.

The computer science goals for this chapter are:

• To create and use trees to represent collections of images.
• To construct and traverse trees.

The media learning goals for this chapter are:

• To introduce the structure of a scene graph, which is a common animation data structure.
• To use trees to create an animation.

8.1 REPRESENTING SCENES WITH TREES

A list can really only represent a single dimension—either a linear placement on the screen, or a linear layering front-to-back. A full scene has multiple dimensions. More importantly, a real scene has an organization to it. There's the village over there, and the forest over here, and the squadron of Orcs emerging from the scary cave to the north. Real scenes *cluster*—there is structure and organization to them.

When we left our efforts to create dynamic data structures for representing scenes, we had implemented a special kind of tree where some nodes layered themselves at a particular (x, y), and other nodes just laid themselves out left-to-right. One problem with this structure is that it's linear—none of the structure or organization we would want to model is available in a linear linked list. A second problem is an issue of *responsibility*. Should a picture know where it is going to be drawn? Shouldn't it just

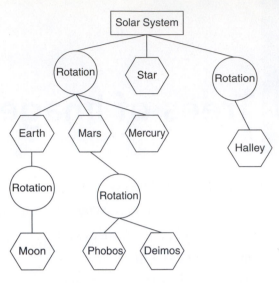

FIGURE 8.1
A simple scene graph.

be drawn wherever it's told to be drawn—whether that's in a long linear list like long lines of Orcs in *The Lord of the Rings* movies,[1] or whether it's particularly positioned like a specific house, tree, or Hobbit.

Computer Science Idea: Distribution of responsibility

A key idea in object-oriented programming is to distribute responsibility throughout the collection of objects in a model. Each object should only know what it needs to know to do its job, and its methods should just be sufficient to implement that job.   ■

We can represent an entire scene with a tree. Computer scientists call the tree that is rendered to generate an entire scene a *scene graph*. Scene graphs are a common data structure representing three-dimensional scenes, examples of which can be found all over the Internet. An interesting aspect of scene graphs is that they typically embed operations within the branches of the tree which effect rendering of their children. Figure 8.1 is a simple scene graph with branches that *rotate* in three dimensions their children elements. The planets have one kind of rotation, the moons have another kind, and a comet has yet another kind. Figure 8.2 is a more sophisticated scene graph based on the *Java 3-D* libraries. This scene graph represents more sophisticated aspects of rendering the scene, like the lighting (both ambient and direct), the graphics platform (e.g., the hardware), and transformations, like *translations* that move the drawing of the children objects to a particular place on the screen.

[1]Do you think someone positioned each of those thousands of Orcs by hand? Or something auto-positioned them?

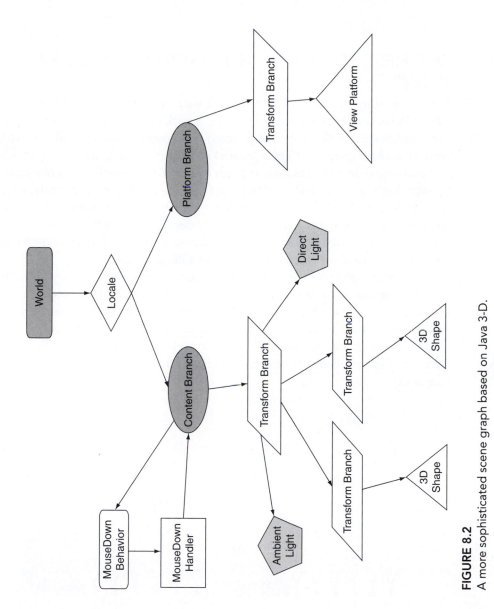

FIGURE 8.2
A more sophisticated scene graph based on Java 3-D.

We are going to use scene graphs to represent a simple two-dimensional movie. A scene graph is a kind of tree. We are going to use our tree to cluster and organize our scene, and we will use operations in the branches of the tree to help define how the scene should be rendered.

8.2   OUR FIRST SCENE GRAPH: ATTACK OF THE KILLER WOLVIES

Here is the story that we will be rendering with our first scene graph. The peaceful village in the forest rests, unsuspecting that a pack of three blood-thirsty doggies, er, fierce wolvies are sneaking up on it (Figure 8.3). Closer they come, until the hero bursts onto the scene (Figure 8.4)! The fear-stricken wolvies scamper away (Figure 8.5).

This scene is described as a scene graph (Figure 8.6). There is a root object, of class `Branch`. Each of the individual pictures are instances of `BlueScreenNode`, which are kinds of `PictNode` (Picture Nodes) that use chromakey ("blue screen") for rendering themselves onto the screen. The position of nodes is done with `MoveBranch` branches. Some of the objects are laid out vertically (like the wolvies) using a `VBranch` instance, and others horizontally (like the forest) using a `HBranch` instance.

The scene graph underlying this scene is quite clearly a tree (Figure 8.7). There is a *root* at the top of the tree that everything is connected to. Each node has at most one *parent node*. There are *branch nodes* that have *children nodes* connected to them. At the ends of each branch, there are *leaf nodes* that have no children. In our scene graph, the leaves are all nodes that draw something. The branches collect the children, and thus, structure the scene. In addition, the branches in the scene graph *do* something.

FIGURE 8.3
The nasty wolvies sneak up on the unsuspecting village in the forest.

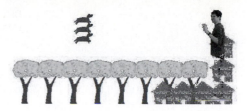

FIGURE 8.4
Then, our hero appears!

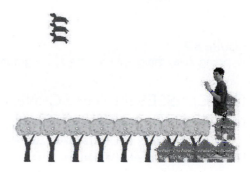

FIGURE 8.5
And the nasty wolvies scamper away.

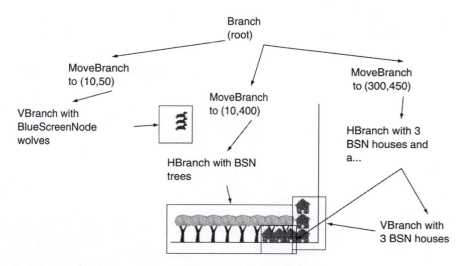

FIGURE 8.6
Mapping the elements of the scene onto the scene graph.

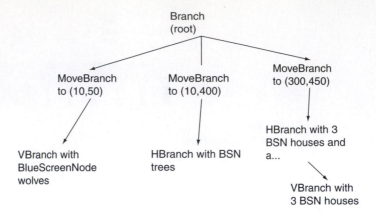

FIGURE 8.7
Stripping away the graphics—the scene graph is a tree.

8.3   THE CLASSES IN THE SCENE GRAPH

The heart of the classes in this scene graph implementation is DrawableNode. All nodes and branches inherit from DrawableNode (Figure 8.8), an abstract superclass. The class DrawableNode defines how to be a node in a linked list—it defines next, and it defines how to add, insertAfter, and the other linked list operations. Most importantly, DrawableNode defines how to *draw* the node—albeit, abstractly.

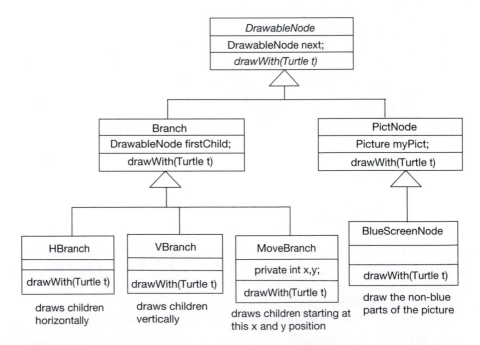

FIGURE 8.8
Unified Modeling Language (UML) class diagram of classes used in our scene graph.

DrawableNode defines how to draw on a given background picture (Example Java Code 53 (page 185)). It simply creates a turtle and draws the node with the turtle (drawWith). The method drawWith is abstract. The definition of how any particular node actually draws itself is left to the subclasses.

Example Java Code 53: The drawing part of DrawableNode

```java
/**
 * Use the given turtle to draw oneself
 * @param t the Turtle to draw with
 */
public abstract void drawWith(Turtle t);
// No body in an abstract method

/**
 * Draw on the given picture
 * @bg the background picture to draw on
 */
public void drawOn(Picture bg) {
  Turtle t = new Turtle(bg);
  t.setPenDown(false);
  this.drawWith(t);
}
```

Common Bug: Class structure ≠ object structure
It's easy to get confused between the tree of classes in Figure 8.8 and the tree of objects in Figure 8.7. The tree of classes describes which classes inherit from which other classes, where DrawableNode is the root of the tree, the superclass or parent class of all the other classes in the hierarchy. *Objects* created from these classes do form a tree (that's why we made those classes), just not the same tree. The trees don't represent the same things. The tree in Figure 8.7 represents a scene—it doesn't say anything about inheritance. A key observation is that there are several instances of the same class in the scene graph (Figure 8.7), though each class appears only once in the class hierarchy (Figure 8.8).

DrawableNode has two children classes—Branch and PictNode. Branch and its subclasses know how to deal with children. A Branch knows how to tell all of its children to draw, and then ask its siblings to draw. PictNode and its subclass, BlueScreenNode, know how to deal with drawing pictures, the leaves of the trees. A PictNode holds a picture, and draws its picture by simply asking the turtle to drop the picture on the background. A BlueScreenNode has a picture, via inheritance from PictNode, but uses chromakey to put the picture onto the background.

Subclasses of Branch are about positioning and ordering the children of the branch.

- A MoveBranch positions the turtle at a particular place before asking the children to draw. The MoveBranch knows the *x* and *y* values for where it should start drawing. An instance of MoveBranch is useful for positioning part of the scene.

- The branches VBranch and HBranch do automatic positioning of the children. A VBranch lays out its children vertically, and a HBranch lays out its children horizontally. Both add a gap variable for how much space to skip between children.

Thus, a MoveBranch with a PictNode or BlueScreenNode essentially does what a SceneElementLayered instance does—draw a particular picture at a particular place on the frame. The first elements that are drawn appear below later elements in the tree. A VBranch or HBranch instance with picture nodes lets you do what a SceneElementPositioned instance does—automatic positioning of a picture. Our scene graph implementation, then, has all the capabilities of our earlier linked list, with the addition of better structuring.

8.4   BUILDING A SCENE GRAPH

Let's walk through the WolfAttackMovie class, to show an example of using these classes to construct a scene graph and then create a movie that is so bad that not even the "Rotten Tomatoes" Web site would review it.

Example Java Code 54: Start of WolfAttackMovie class

```java
public class WolfAttackMovie {

    /** The root of the scene data structure */
    private Branch sceneRoot;

    /** FrameSequencer where the animation is created */
    private FrameSequencer frames;

    /** The nodes we need to track between methods */
    private MoveBranch wolfEntry, wolfRetreat, hero;
```

It makes sense that an instance of WolfAttackMovie will need to know the root of its scene graph, sceneRoot, and that it would be an instance of Branch. It also makes sense that a WolfAttackMovie instance will need to know a FrameSequencer instance for storing and playing back the frames of the movie. What probably does not make sense is why there are three MoveBranch instances defined as instance variables for WolfAttackMovie.

What we are doing is not good object-oriented programming practice. We placed three MoveBranch variables as instance variables to allow for shared data between methods. We are dealing with scope between methods. Within WolfAttackMovie, we have a method, setUp, that creates the scene graph, and a later method, renderAnimation, that creates all the frames. To change the position of some elements in the scene, we will change the (x, y) position of the corresponding MoveBranch instances. How do we find the right MoveBranch instances to, for example, move the wolves closer to the village. Option 1 is to access the right branch through the root: searching the children and next nodes to find it. Option 2 is to store the MoveBranch reference in an instance variable that is then within the scope of *both* setUp and renderAnimation, so that we can create it in setUp and change it in renderAnimation. We're using option 2 here. It's not a great idea to use instance variables to simply solve scoping problems. The advantage of option 2 is that it is simple.

The `setUp` method is a big `private` method in `WolfAttackMovie` that is called by the constructor. It involves creating all the branches that we will need in the tree, which is a larger task than simply creating the first scene. By moving this code out of the constructor we can call it from several constructors as needed (i.e., with different inputs), or have more than one way to set up the movie.

Example Java Code 55: Setting up the movie in `WolfAttackMovie`

```java
/**
 * Constructor that takes no arguments and
 * sets up the movie
 */
public WolfAttackMovie() {
  setUp();
}

/**
 * Set up all the pieces of the tree.
 */
private void setUp(){
  Picture wolf =
    new Picture(FileChooser.getMediaPath("dog-blue.jpg"));
  Picture house =
    new Picture(FileChooser.getMediaPath("house-blue.jpg"));
  Picture tree =
    new Picture(FileChooser.getMediaPath("tree-blue.jpg"));
  Picture monster =
    new Picture(FileChooser.getMediaPath("mScary.jpg"));

  //Make the forest
  MoveBranch forest = new MoveBranch(10,400); // at bottom
  HBranch trees = new HBranch(50); // 50 pixels between
  BlueScreenNode treenode;
  for (int i=0; i < 8; i++) { // insert 8 trees
    treenode = new BlueScreenNode(tree.scale(0.5));
    trees.addChild(treenode);
  }
  forest.addChild(trees);

  // Make the cluster of attacking "wolves"
  wolfEntry = new MoveBranch(10,50); // starting position
  VBranch wolves = new VBranch(20); // space out by 20 pixels
  BlueScreenNode wolf1 = new BlueScreenNode(wolf.scale(0.5));
  BlueScreenNode wolf2 = new BlueScreenNode(wolf.scale(0.5));
  BlueScreenNode wolf3 = new BlueScreenNode(wolf.scale(0.5));
  wolves.addChild(wolf1);
  wolves.addChild(wolf2);
  wolves.addChild(wolf3);
  wolfEntry.addChild(wolves);
```

■

How It Works.   The method `setUp` creates the pictures that we will need in the movie, then defines the forest branch of the tree (Figure 8.9). The code above creates the `MoveBranch` instance stored in the variable `forest`. It creates an `HBranch` named `trees` that will hold all the trees. Each of the `BlueScreenNode` instances for each tree

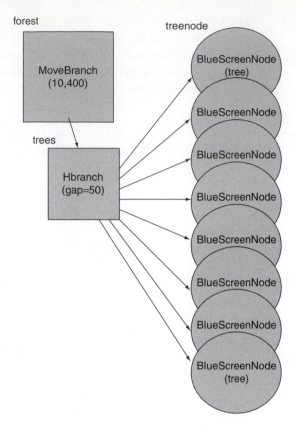

FIGURE 8.9
The forest branch created in setUp—arrows point to children.

is created and named treenode. As the trees are created, they are added as children of the trees branch. Finally, the trees branch is added as a child of the forest.

Next, we create the wolves. There's a critical difference between creating the Move-Branch for the wolfEntry versus the MoveBranch for the forest.

Common Bug: Declaring a variable with the same name as a field hides the field (instance variable)

By declaring the variable forest as a MoveBranch, we make forest a variable local to the method setUp. That means that the variable forest will not exist in renderAnimation. The variable wolfEntry is not declared, so the reference in setUp is actually referencing the instance variable wolfEntry. If we *had* declared wolfEntry as a MoveBranch, the setUp would work still. However, renderAnimation would be referencing the wolfEntry defined as an instance variable, which has a value of null, and so it wouldn't actually do anything. The wolves would never move. Declaring the variable in setUp makes it impossible to reach the instance variable with the same name.

∎

The `wolfEntry` branch is constructed much like the `forest` branch. There is a `MoveBranch` instance for positioning, then a `VBranch` for storing the `wolves`, then three `BlueScreenNode` instances for storing the actual wolves.

Example Java Code 56: Rest of `setUp` for `WolfAttackMovie`

```java
// Make the cluster of retreating "wolves"
wolfRetreat = new MoveBranch(400,50); // starting position
wolves = new VBranch(20); // space them out by 20 pixels
wolf1 = new BlueScreenNode(wolf.scale(0.5).flip());
wolf2 = new BlueScreenNode(wolf.scale(0.5).flip());
wolf3 = new BlueScreenNode(wolf.scale(0.5).flip());
wolves.addChild(wolf1);
wolves.addChild(wolf2);
wolves.addChild(wolf3);
wolfRetreat.addChild(wolves);

// Make the village
MoveBranch village = new MoveBranch(300,450); // on bottom
HBranch hhouses = new HBranch(40); // 40 pixels apart
BlueScreenNode house1 = new BlueScreenNode
  (house.scale(0.25));
BlueScreenNode house2 = new BlueScreenNode
  (house.scale(0.25));
BlueScreenNode house3 = new BlueScreenNode
  (house.scale(0.25));
VBranch vhouses = new VBranch(-50); // move UP 50 pixels
BlueScreenNode house4 = new BlueScreenNode
  (house.scale(0.25));
BlueScreenNode house5 = new BlueScreenNode
  (house.scale(0.25));
BlueScreenNode house6 = new BlueScreenNode
  (house.scale(0.25));
vhouses.addChild(house4);
vhouses.addChild(house5);
vhouses.addChild(house6);
hhouses.addChild(house1);
hhouses.addChild(house2);
hhouses.addChild(house3);
hhouses.addChild(vhouses); // a VBranch can be a child
village.addChild(hhouses);

// Make the monster
hero = new MoveBranch(400,300);
BlueScreenNode heronode =
  new BlueScreenNode(monster.scale(0.75));
hero.addChild(heronode);
//Assemble the base scene
sceneRoot = new Branch();
sceneRoot.addChild(forest);
sceneRoot.addChild(village);
sceneRoot.addChild(wolfEntry);
}
```

■

How It Works.   The rest of `setUp` works similarly. We create a branch for `wolf-Retreat`, which is amazingly similar to `wolfEntry` except that the wolves are flipped—they face away from the village. The `village` is a bit more complicated. There is an `HBranch` that contains three `BlueScreenNode` houses *and* a `VBranch` (with three more houses) as children. When the village is rendered, it will draw one house, then another, then the third, and then, at the spot where a fourth house would go, there is a vertical line of three more houses going straight up.

At the very end of setUp, we add to the sceneRoot the three branches that appear in the first scene: the forest, the village, and the wolfEntry. Where is the wolf-Retreat and the hero branches? They are not in the initial scene. They appear later, when we render the whole thing.

Example Java Code 57: Rendering just the first scene in WolfAttackMovie

```java
/**
 * Render just the first scene
 */
public void renderScene() {
  Picture bg = new Picture(500,500);
  sceneRoot.drawOn(bg);
  bg.show();
}
```

When developing a movie, it's important to see if the basic setUp worked. When we were creating this first movie, we would often create a WolfAttackMovie instance, set it up, then call renderScene to see how the first scene looked. We would then adjust positions of the forest and the village, and repeat until we were happy with the basic set-up.

Now that we have our basic scene graph created, we can render our movie.

Example Java Code 58: renderAnimation in WolfAttackMovie

```java
/**
 * Render the whole animation
 */
public void renderAnimation() {
  frames = new FrameSequencer("C:/Temp/");
  frames.show();
  Picture bg;

  // First, the nasty wolvies come closer to the poor
  // village
  // Cue the scary music
  for (int i=0; i<25; i++) {

    // Render the frame
    bg = new Picture(500,500);
    sceneRoot.drawOn(bg);
    frames.addFrame(bg);

    // Tweak the data structure
    wolfEntry.moveTo(wolfEntry.getXPos()+5,
                     wolfEntry.getYPos()+10);
  }

  // Now, our hero arrives!
  this.getSceneRoot().addChild(hero);
```

```
// Render the frame
bg = new Picture(500,500);
sceneRoot.drawOn(bg);
frames.addFrame(bg);

// Remove the wolves entering, and insert the wolves
// retreating
Branch root = this.getSceneRoot();
root.getFirstChild().remove(wolfEntry);
root.addChild(wolfRetreat);

// Make sure that they retreat from the same place
wolfRetreat.moveTo(wolfEntry.getXPos(),
    wolfEntry.getYPos());

// Render the frame
bg = new Picture(500,500);
root.drawOn(bg);
frames.addFrame(bg);

// Now, the cowardly wolves hightail it out of there!
// Cue the triumphant music
for (int i=0; i<10; i++) {

    // Render the frame
    bg = new Picture(500,500);
    root.drawOn(bg);
    frames.addFrame(bg);

    // Tweak the data structure
    wolfRetreat.moveTo(wolfRetreat.getXPos()-10,
                        wolfRetreat.getYPos()-20);
    }
}
```

How It Works.   Rendering a frame from the scene graph is basically these three lines:

```
// Render the frame
bg = new Picture(500,500);
root.drawOn(bg);
frames.addFrame(bg);
```

The rest of renderAnimation is changing the scene graph around this rendering.

- During the first 25 frames, the evil wolves are sneaking up on the poor, unsuspecting village. Between each frame, the wolves are moved by changing the position of the wolfEntry branch, with a horizontal (x) velocity of 5 pixels per frame and a vertical velocity of 10 pixels per frame.

```
wolfEntry.moveTo(wolfEntry.getXPos()+5,
    wolfEntry.getYPos()+10);
```

- And then, the hero arrives! We insert the hero branch into the code and render.

- Now, we remove the wolfEntry branch and insert the wolfRetreat branch. We carefully make sure that the wolves are retreating from where they last stopped entering, with the line:

```
// Make sure that they retreat from the same place
wolfRetreat.moveTo(wolfEntry.getXPos(),
    wolfEntry.getYPos());
```

- The wolves then scamper away, at a faster rate than when they entered.

We run the movie by using the following main method:

```
public static void main (String[] args) {
  WolfAttackMovie movie = new WolfAttackMovie();
  movie.renderAnimation();
}
```

Common Bug: When you run out of memory, within DrJava

Rendering large movies can easily eat up all the usual amount of memory. You can make DrJava give your Interactions Pane more memory, which would allow you to run large movie code from within DrJava. You can change the maximum heap memory for both the main JVM (Java Virtual Machine) and the Interactions Pane JVM in the MISCELLANEOUS category in the PREFERENCES window (under the EDIT menu) (Figure 8.10).

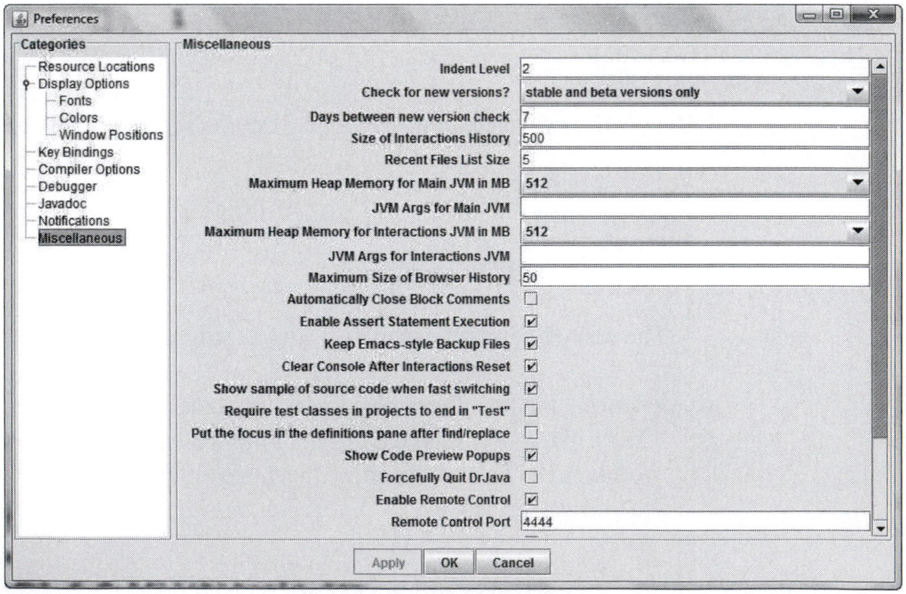

FIGURE 8.10
Reserving more memory for interactions using DrJava's Preferences pane.

Common Bug: Increasing memory at the command line

If you are not running DrJava, or you are so tight on memory that you don't even want DrJava in memory, you still have options if you are running out of memory. You can run your movies from the command line and specify the amount of memory you need.

First, you have to be able to run Java from the command line, which means being able to use the java and javac (*Java compiler*) commands. We have found that some Java installations do not have these set up right. Make sure that your Java JDK bin directory is in your PATH. For Windows, you use the SYSTEM control panel to change environment variables. To use javac to compile your programs, you may need to change the CLASSPATH in system environment variables to point to your java-source directory. If you have javac set up right, you should be able to compile your class files from outside of DrJava—at a command prompt, type javac (YourMovieClassNameHere).java.

To run it, type java -Xms128m -Xmx512m (YourMovieClassNameHere) The option -Xms128m says, "At the very least, give this program 128 megabytes to run." The option -Xmx512m says, "And give it up to 512 megabytes."

Now, when you run java from the command line, you're actually executing the main method.

∎

8.5   IMPLEMENTING THE SCENE GRAPH

One of the lessons from the last chapter is that the way we *think* about a data structure does not have to match the way that it is implemented. While it is useful to think about branches having several children, we do not have to implement multiple references between (say) the forest branch and the tree nodes. Branches must have a way of adding and getting children—that's part of the definition of a tree. How it's implemented is up to us.

Our scene graphs are actually implemented as *lists of lists*. All siblings are connected through next links. Each branch is connected to its *first* child, and only the first child, through its firstChild link. The class Branch defines firstChild, so all branches have the firstChild link by inheritance. But, since firstChild is private, other classes can use the public accessor, getFirstChild(), to access this. Figure 8.11 shows the abstraction of the scene graph tree (as seen in Figure 8.7), overlaid with the actual implementation.

We can think of our notion of parent nodes with children nodes as an abstraction. It is a useful way of thinking about trees. There are many ways of implementing that abstraction, though. Figure 8.12 shows the actual implementation of our scene graph.

The advantage of a list-of-lists implementation is that we are introducing no new data structure implementation ideas. It's all linked lists. There is one *special* kind of link, the firstChild, but other than that, it's all next links and the same methods we've used all along.

Common Bug: Can't remove the first child

There is a bug in our implementation of linked lists up to this point in the book, and that same bug extends to our implementation of children in branches. We cannot remove the first item in a list. We treat the first item as special (i.e., it is referenced by firstChild not

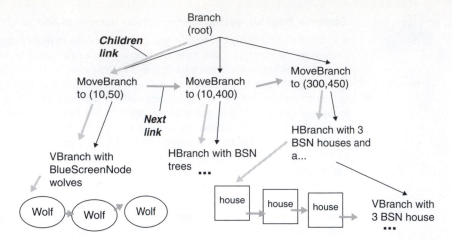

FIGURE 8.11
The implementation of the scene graph overlaid on the tree abstraction.

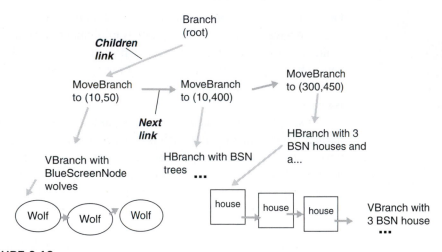

FIGURE 8.12
The actual implementation of the scene graph.

next), and our remove method only works for next links. We will fix this bug in a few chapters, but for now, it dictates the order in which we add children to a branch. Notice that we add the forest as a child of the sceneRoot first. In general, forests don't move (except in *Macbeth*) and don't disappear (except for rain forests). Therefore, we won't have to remove the forest branch from the root, so it's safe to add first. If we had added wolfEntry as the first child of the sceneRoot, we would never have been able to remove it.

Implementing the Abstract Superclass for the Scene Graph: DrawableNode

The heart of our scene graph (literally, the base of the class hierarchy for these classes) is DrawableNode. It's actually not complicated at all. It's mostly the same as SceneElement or any of the other linked lists we've seen so far.

Example Java Code 59: DrawableNode

```java
/**
 * Stuff that all nodes and branches in the
 * scene tree know.
 * @author Mark Guzdial
 * @author Barb Ericson
 */
public abstract class DrawableNode {

  /**
   * The next branch/node/whatever to process
   */
  private DrawableNode next;

  /**
   * Constructor for DrawableNode just sets
   * next to null
   */
  public DrawableNode() {
    next = null;
  }

  /**
   * Method to set the next node
   * @param nextOne next node in list
   */
  public void setNext(DrawableNode nextOne) {
    this.next = nextOne;
  }

  /**
   * Method to get the next node
   * @return the next node
   */
  public DrawableNode getNext() {
    return this.next;
  }

  /**
   * Use the given turtle to draw oneself
   * @param t the Turtle to draw with
   */
  public abstract void drawWith(Turtle t);
  // no body in an abstract method

  /**
   * Draw on the given picture
   * @param bg the background picture to draw on
   */
  public void drawOn(Picture bg) {
    Turtle t = new Turtle(bg);
    t.setPenDown(false);
    this.drawWith(t);
  }
```

```java
/** Method to remove node from list, fixing links
 * appropriately.
 * @param node element to remove from list.
 */
public void remove(DrawableNode node) {
  if (node==this) {
    System.out.println(
      "I can't remove the first node from the list.");
    return;
  }

  // start with this node
  DrawableNode current = this;

  // While there are more nodes to consider
  while (current.getNext() != null) {
    if (current.getNext() == node) {
      // Simply make node's next be this next
      current.setNext(node.getNext());
      // Make this node point to nothing
      node.setNext(null);
      return;
    }
    current = current.getNext();
  }
}

/**
 * Insert the input node after this node.
 * @param node element to insert after this.
 */
public void insertAfter(DrawableNode node) {
  // Save what "this" currently points at
  DrawableNode oldNext = this.getNext();
  this.setNext(node);
  node.setNext(oldNext);
}


/**
 * Return the last element in the list
 * @return the last element in the list
 */
public DrawableNode last() {
  DrawableNode current;

  current = this;
  while (current.getNext() != null) {
    current = current.getNext();
  }
  return current;
}
/**
 * Add the input node after the last node in this list.
 * @param node element to insert after this.
 */
public void add(DrawableNode node) {
  this.last().insertAfter(node);
}


}
```

How It Works.   Class DrawableNode has two main functions:

- The first is to be an abstract superclass for defining linked lists. For that reason, it has a next variable, operations for getting and setting next, and list operations like add and remove.

- The second is to be "drawable." Every DrawableNode subclass instance must know how to drawOn and drawWith.

Implementing the Leaf Nodes: PictNode and BlueScreenNode

Leaf nodes in the scene graphs are the pictures themselves. In WolfAttackMovie, these are the trees, houses, wolves, and hero. The class PictNode simply drops pictures—we don't actually use it in WolfAttackMovie. It is the superclass for BlueScreenNode, the leaf node class that we use in the example movie.

Example Java Code 60: PictNode

```java
/**
 * PictNode is a class representing a drawn picture
 * node in a scene tree.
 * @author Mark Guzdial
 * @author Barb Ericson
 */
public class PictNode extends DrawableNode {

  /**
   * The picture I'm associated with
   */
  private Picture myPict;

  /**
   * Make me with this picture
   * @param pict the Picture to use
   */
  public PictNode(Picture pict) {
    super(); // Call superclass constructor
    myPict = pict;
  }

  /**
   * Method to get the picture
   * @return the picture associated with this node
   */
  public Picture getPicture() { return myPict; }

  /**
   * Method to return a string with information
   * about this node
   * @return the information string
   */
  public String toString() {
    return "PictNode (with picture: " + myPict +
      " and next: " + this.getNext();
  }

  /**
```

```
   * Use the given turtle to draw oneself
   * @param theTurtle the Turtle to draw with
   */
  public void drawWith(Turtle theTurtle) {
    theTurtle.drop(myPict);
  }
}
```

■

How It Works.   Class `PictNode` is really quite simple. It has an instance variable, `myPict`, that represents the picture to be shown for the node. The heart of the class is the `drawWith` method, which only asks the input turtle to `drop` the picture.

The class `BlueScreenNode` inherits from `PictNode` and is only slightly more complicated. Instead of dropping the picture, it uses chromakey to remove the blue background for the image. We could use something other than the all-white background picture, and the background would show through because we use `BlueScreenNode`. (It also explains why the hero's dark slacks disappear in the movie.)

Example Java Code 61: BlueScreenNode

```
/**
 * BlueScreenNode is a PictNode that composes the
 * picture using the blueScreen() method in Picture
 * @author Mark Guzdial
 * @author Barb Ericson
 */
public class BlueScreenNode extends PictNode {

  /**
   * Constructor that sets the picture
   * @param p the Picture to use
   */
  public BlueScreenNode(Picture p){
    super(p); // Call superclass constructor
  }

  /**
   * Method to return a string with information
   * about this node
   * @return the information string
   */
  public String toString()
  {
    return "BlueScreenNode (with picture: "+
      this.getPicture() + " and next: " + this.getNext();
  }

  /**
   * Use the given turtle to draw oneself
   * Get the turtle's picture, then bluescreen onto it
   * @param theTurtle the Turtle to draw with
   */
  public void drawWith(Turtle theTurtle){
    Picture bg = theTurtle.getPicture();
```

```
        Picture myPict = this.getPicture();
        myPict.blueScreen(bg,theTurtle.getXPos(),
                          theTurtle.getYPos());
    }
}
```

∎

How It Works.   The method drawWith in BlueScreenNode is a little tricky. It asks
the turtle that comes in as input, "What's your picture?" by setting Picture bg to
theTurtle.getPicture(). It then calls the Picture method blueScreen to draw the
picture, on the background from the turtle, at the *turtle's x*, *y*, i.e., myPict.blueScreen
(bg, theTurtle.getXPos(), theTurtle.getYPos());.

An interesting side comment to make here is that both of these classes know how
to toString, that is, return a string representation of themselves. Each simply returns
the printable representation of its string and its next. For a brand new node, the next is
simply null.

```
> BlueScreenNode bsn =
new BlueScreenNode(new Picture(
   FileChooser.pickAFile()));
> bsn
BlueScreenNode (with picture: Picture,
filename /home/guzdial/cs1316/MediaSources/
   Student10.jpg
height 333 width 199 and next: null
```

Implementing the Branches: Branch, MoveBranch, VBranch, and HBranch

The branch classes (the class Branch and its subclasses) have a reference to the first
child node called firstChild. Because they inherit from DrawableNode, they also
have a reference to the next node. Thus, branch instances link to both children and
siblings—that's what makes them into branches of trees.

Notice that the type of the firstChild reference is DrawableNode. That means
that *any* other kind of node can be a child of any branch—either leaf nodes or other
branches. Thus, a tree can be of any *depth* (the maximum number of nodes visited to
get from the root to a leaf node) or complexity.

Example Java Code 62: Branch

```
/**
 * A branch of a tree that can have children
 * @author Mark Guzdial
 * @author Barb Ericson
 */
public class Branch extends DrawableNode {

  /**
   * first child in the list of children
   */
```

```java
  private DrawableNode firstChild;

  /**
   * Construct a branch with the first child and
   * next as null
   */
  public Branch() {
    super(); // Call superclass constructor
    firstChild = null;
  }

  /**
   * Method to get the first child in the branch
   * @return the first child in the list
   */
  public DrawableNode getFirstChild()
  { return this.firstChild; }

  /**
   * Method to return a string with information
   * about this branch
   * @returns the information string
   */
  public String toString() {

    String childString = "No children", nextString="No next";
    if (firstChild != null) {
      childString = firstChild.toString();
    }

    if (this.getNext() != null) {
      nextString = this.getNext().toString();
    }

    return "Branch (with child: "+childString+" and next: "+
      nextString+")";
  }

  /**
   * Method to add nodes to children
   * @param child to add
   */
  public void addChild(DrawableNode child) {
    if (firstChild != null) {
      firstChild.add(child);
    }
    else {
      firstChild = child;
    }
  }

  /**
   * Ask all our children to draw,
   * then let next draw.
   * @param turtle the Turtle to draw with
   */
  public void drawWith(Turtle turtle) {
    DrawableNode current = firstChild;

    // Tell the children to draw
    while (current != null) {
      current.drawWith(turtle);
```

```
        current = current.getNext();
      }

      // Tell my next to draw
      if (this.getNext() != null) {
        current = this.getNext();
        current.drawWith(turtle);
      }
    }
  }
}
```

■

How It Works.   The most important responsibility of branches is to manage their children. Instances of Branch (and its subclasses) know their firstChild reference. A branch adds a child (addChild) by first seeing if firstChild is null—if it is, then the new addition is what firstChild is set to; if it is not, then we add the new addition to the end of the firstChild linked list.

Branches also know how to drawWith. Here is the definition of drawWith:

- First, ask all my children to draw.

```
      // Tell the children to draw
      while (current != null) {
        current.drawWith(turtle);
        current = current.getNext();
      }
```

- Next, follow the next links to tell the siblings to draw.

```
      // Tell my next to draw
      if (this.getNext() != null) {
        current = this.getNext();
        current.drawWith(turtle);
      }
```

There is a similar algorithm going on in the definition of toString, to convert a branch to a printable representation. The algorithm is to collect all the string representations of the children, then of the next, and then return all those pieces.

This means that we can actually watch the construction of a branch, by printing it at each step. Below we see a BlueScreenNode, Branch, and PictNode created and connected. The BlueScreenNode shows up first, and when we add the PictNode, it appears as the next of the BlueScreenNode.

```
> BlueScreenNode bsn =
  new BlueScreenNode(new Picture(
    FileChooser.pickAFile()));
> bsn
BlueScreenNode (with picture: Picture,
filename /home/guzdial/cs1316/MediaSources/
  Student10.jpg
height 333 width 199 and next: null
```

```
> Branch b = new Branch();
> b.addChild(bsn);
> b
Branch (with child: BlueScreenNode (with picture:
Picture, filename /home/guzdial/cs1316/MediaSources/
   student1.jpg
height 369 width 213 and next: null and next: No next)
> PictNode pn = new PictNode(new Picture(
   FileChooser.pickAFile()));
> b.addChild(pn);
> b
Branch (with child: BlueScreenNode (with picture:
Picture, filename /home/guzdial/cs1316/MediaSources/
   student1.jpg
height 369 width 213 and next: PictNode (with picture:
Picture, filename /home/guzdial/cs1316/MediaSources/
   Student7.jpg
height 422 width 419 and next: null and next: No next)
```

The two branch subclasses that position their children automatically, HBranch and
VBranch, only provide two methods: a constructor for storing the gap between children, and a new drawWith, which moves the turtle appropriately between drawings of
children.

Example Java Code 63: HBranch

```
/**
 * Class that uses horizontal spacing between
 * children and a gap between them
 * @author Mark Guzdial
 * @author Barb Ericson
 */
public class HBranch extends Branch {

  /** Horizontal gap between children */
  private int gap;

  /**
   * Construct a branch with first child and
   * next as null
   * @param spacing the gap to leave between children
   */
  public HBranch(int spacing) {
    super(); // Call superclass constructor
    gap = spacing;
  }

  /**
   * Method to return a string with information
   * about this branch
   * @return the information string
   */
  public String toString() {
    return "Horizontal "+super.toString();
  }
```

```
/**
 * Ask all our children to draw,
 * then tell the next element to draw
 * @param turtle Turtle to draw with
 */
public void drawWith(Turtle turtle) {

  // start with the first child
  DrawableNode current = this.getFirstChild();

  // Have my children draw
  while (current != null) {
    current.drawWith(turtle);
    turtle.moveTo(turtle.getXPos()+gap,turtle.getYPos());
    current = current.getNext();
  }

  // Have my next draw
  if (this.getNext() != null) {
    current = this.getNext();
    current.drawWith(turtle);
  }
}
}
```

■

Example Java Code 64: VBranch

```
/**
 * Class that uses vertical spacing between
 * children with a gap between children as well
 * @author Mark Guzdial
 * @author Barb Ericson
 */
public class VBranch extends Branch {

  /** Vertical gap between children */
  private int gap;

  /**
   * Construct a branch with children and
   * next as null
   * @param spacing the gap to use
   */
  public VBranch(int spacing) {
    super(); // Call superclass constructor
    gap = spacing;
  }

  /**
   * Method to return a string with information
   * about this branch
   * @return the information string
   */
  public String toString() {
    return "Vertical " + super.toString();
  }

  /**
```

```
 * Ask all our children to draw,
 * then let the next node draw
 * @param turtle the Turtle to draw with
 */
public void drawWith(Turtle turtle) {

  // start with the first child
  DrawableNode current = this.getFirstChild();

  // Have my children draw
  while (current != null) {
    current.drawWith(turtle);
    turtle.moveTo(turtle.getXPos(),turtle.getYPos() + gap);
    current =current.getNext();
  }

  // Have my next draw
  if (this.getNext() != null) {
    current = this.getNext();
    current.drawWith(turtle);
  }
 }
}
```

The class MoveBranch differs in that it keeps track of an *x*, *y* position:

Example Java Code 65: MoveBranch

```
/**
 * Class that represents a change in location
 * @author Mark Guzdial
 * @author Barb Ericson
 */
public class MoveBranch extends Branch {

  /** x position to draw at */
  private int x;

  /** y position to draw at */
  private int y;

  /**
   * Construct a branch with children and
   * next as null
   * @param x the x position to use
   * @param y the y position to use
   */
  public MoveBranch(int x, int y) {
    super(); // Call superclass constructor
    this.x = x;
    this.y = y;
  }

  /**
   * Method to get the x position
   * @return the x position
   */
  public int getXPos() {return this.x;}

  /**
```

```
 * Method to get the Y position
 * @return the y position
 */
public int getYPos() {return this.y;}

/**
 * Method to move to a new x and y
 * @param x the new x
 * @param y the new y
 */
public void moveTo(int x, int y) {
  this.x = x;
  this.y = y;
}

/**
 * Method to return a string with information
 * about this branch
 * @return the information string
 */
public String toString() {
  return "Move ("+ x + "," + y + ") "+ super.toString();
}

/**
 * Set the location, then draw
 * @param t the Turtle to draw with
 */
public void drawWith(Turtle t) {
  t.moveTo(this.x,this.y);
  super.drawWith(t); // Do a normal branch now
}
}
```

■

What would happen if we decided that the moveTo of the turtle in MoveBranch's drawWith should occur *after* processing the children and before processing the next? What would happen if all the branches processed the next before the children? These aren't unreasonable possibilities. They describe different kinds of *traversals* that one can make of the data structure.

The Line between Structure and Behavior

Here's a thought experiment: where is the *program* in our scene graph?

- Is the program the class DrawableNode and its subclasses? That can't be it—by themselves, they don't do anything at all. The DrawableNode class hierarchy defines the *behavior*, but not how that behavior is structured and executed.

- Is the program in the class WolfAttackMovie? It is true that WolfAttackMovie assembles all the pieces from the DrawableNode classes in order to define the movie. The class WolfAttackMovie defines the *structure* of the movie from those classes.

- However, the actual scenes are not defined in WolfAttackMovie. Instead, the scenes emerge from executing that movie. The actual layout of the trees and village houses is not specified in `WolfAttackMovie`. Instead, it's determined by the branches in the tree when the tree is rendered.

As our programs grow more sophisticated, we will find that the behavior is defined in part by the structure of the data in the program. The actual data structure and its use blend structure and behavior. This is a powerful computer science idea, that the line between data and program, between structure and behavior, is blurry.

EXERCISES

8.1   Implement one different traversal of the scene graph, as described at the end of the branch subsection above. Does it change how the scene looks?

8.2   What is the purpose of each class described in this chapter?

8.3   Explain how `HBranch` causes the children to be drawn horizontally.

8.4   Explain how `VBranch` causes the children to be drawn vertically.

8.5   Explain how `MoveBranch` affects the position of the children.

8.6   Create a `ScaleNode` that takes an amount to scale the picture by and draws the picture after scaling it. Create an example using a `ScaleNode`.

8.7   Create a `NegateNode` that draws the picture negated. Create an example using a `NegateNode`.

8.8   Create a `MirrorLeftToRightNode` that draws the picture with the left half mirrored to the right. Create an example using a `MirrorLeftToRightNode`.

8.9   Create a `GrayscaleNode` that draws the picture in shades of gray. Create an example using a `GrayscaleNode`.

8.10   Create a `DiagonalBranch` class that inherits from `Branch`. It should draw the children positioned on a diagonal line from the current position plus the maximum of the width and height of the previous picture. Create an example using a `DiagonalBranch`.

8.11   Create a `RotateBranch` class that inherits from `Branch`. It should have an amount to rotate the children of the branch, which will turn the turtle that number of degrees. Create an example using a `RotateBranch`.

8.12   Create your own movie like the `WolfAttackMovie`. But, make the wolves' attack come from the right edge of the picture and the hero appear near the left edge. What changes do you need to make?

8.13   Most of `renderAnimation` in `WolfAttackMovie` is about changing the location of `MoveBranch` instances. Create a new class, `RelativeMoveBranch`, with a *starting location* (x, y) and a *horizontal velocity* and *vertical velocity*. Each time an instance of a `RelativeMoveBranch` is told to `update`, it automatically updates its current location by its velocity. Rewrite `WolfAttackMovie` to use this new kind of branch.

8.14 Both `PictNode` and `BlueScreenNode` presume that a character is represented by a single image, just a single picture; e.g., if our wolves moved, changed the positions of their head and paws, or even appeared to walk. The animation would be improved considerably if the characters changed. Create a new class, `CharacterNode`, that maintains a list of pictures (you can choose how to represent the list of pictures) for a given character. Each time an instance of `CharacterNode` is asked to `drawWith`, the current character image is incremented (perhaps randomly among the list of pictures), so that the next rendering draws a different image for the character.

8.15 Create an animation of *at least* 20 frames with sounds associated with the frames.

   Here's how you can do it:

- Create a tree of images that describe your scene. I'll refer to this as the scene structure.

- Create another list with the sounds to be played during the animation of this tree. (A rest can be a sound!)

- Here's the key part! When you animate your scene (for at least 20 scenes!) and play your sounds, *you cannot make any new sounds!* You must play your sounds from your list of sounds. In other words, the sounds must be pre-made and assembled in a structure before you start your animation.

You can use and modify any of the data structures that we've described in this chapter. You can create new data structures if you like.

   You will also need to create a class (call it `AnimationRunner`). We should be able to use it by creating an instance of the class
(`AnimationRunner ar = new AnimationRunner()`),
and then . . .

- The method `setUp()` sent to the instance (ar.setUp()) should set up the two data structures.

- The method `play()` sent to the instance should play the movie with sound.

- The method `replay()` should replay the FrameSequencer, but won't do the sound.

There are *several* ways to handle the animation. Here's one:

- Render the first frame to a `FrameSequencer` instance.

- For each frame that you want to generate (there must be at least 20 frames):

   - Make a change in the scene structure. Any change you want is acceptable.

   - Render the scene structure.

   - Play the sound in the frame list element. Use `blockingPlay()` instead of `play()` on your sound to make the processing wait (synchronize) until the sound is done before moving on. (Hint: If your sound is over 1/10 of a second long, you can't get 10 frames per second! These will be short sounds! Want something to play over two frames? Play the first half in one frame, and the second half in the next frame.) Note: You don't *have* to use `blockingPlay()`. You can use a mixture of `play()` and `blockingPlay()` to get better response while still maintaining synchrony.

9

Lists and Trees for Structuring Sounds

9.1 COMPOSING WITH SAMPLED SOUNDS AND LINKED LISTS:
RECURSIVE TRAVERSALS

9.2 USING TREES TO STRUCTURE SAMPLED SOUNDS

Chapter Learning Objectives

In the past chapters, we used linked lists and trees to structure images and music. In this chapter, we'll add a new medium to our repertoire for dynamic data structures: sampled sounds (e.g., .WAV files). But we'll use *recursion* to do the traversals, which provides us a more compact way of describing our traversals.

The computer science goals for this chapter are:

- To iterate across linked lists and trees using recursion.
- To replace elements in a data structure, and to define what the "same" node means.
- To explore different kinds of traversals. We will take an operation embedded in a branch, and choose to apply it to the next branch or to the firstChild branch.

The media learning goal for this chapter is:

- To use our new, dynamic ways of structuring media to describe sound patterns and music.

9.1 COMPOSING WITH SAMPLED SOUNDS AND LINKED LISTS: RECURSIVE TRAVERSALS

We originally started down this path of linked lists and trees in order to create a way to flexibly compose music. Our original efforts started with MIDI. However, one might also want to compose sound using sampled or recorded sound. In this chapter, we use the same data structures that we developed in the previous few chapters in order to support flexible composition of sampled sounds in linked lists.

It's pretty straightforward for us to define a simple linked list structure now. The definition given below of a linked list node, SoundElement, that has a Sound instance within it should look very familiar.

Example Java Code 66: SoundElement

```java
/**
 * Sounds for a linked list
 * @author Mark Guzdial
 * @author Barb Ericson
 */
public class SoundElement {

  /** The sound this element is associated with */
  private Sound mySound;

  /** The next element to process */
  private SoundElement next;

  /**
   * Constructor sets next to null
   * and references the input sound.
   * @param aSound the sound to use
   */
  public SoundElement(Sound aSound){
    next = null;
    mySound = aSound;
  }

  /**
   * The method to get the sound
   * @return the sound associated with this node
   */
  public Sound getSound(){return mySound;}

  /**
   * Play JUST me, blocked.
   */
  public void playSound(){mySound.blockingPlay();}

  /**
   * Play JUST me, blocked.
   */
  public void blockingPlay(){mySound.blockingPlay();}

  /**
   * Provide a printable representation of me
   * @return the information string
   */
  public String toString(){
    return "SoundElement with sound: " + mySound +
           " (and next: " + next + ").";
  }

  /**
   * Method to set the next element
   * @param nextOne next element to add to the list
   */
  public void setNext(SoundElement nextOne) {
    this.next = nextOne;
  }

  /**
   * Method to get the next element
   * @return the next element in the list
   */
  public SoundElement getNext() {
```

```
    return this.next;
  }

  /**
   * Play the list of sound elements
   * after me
   */
  public void playFromMeOn() {
    this.collect().play();
  }

  /**
   * Collect all the sounds from me on,
   * recursively into one sound.
   * @return the resulting sound
   */
  public Sound collect() {
    if (this.getNext() == null) {
      return mySound;
    }
    else {
      return mySound.append(this.getNext().collect());
    }
  }

  /** Method to remove a node from the list, fixing links
   * appropriately.  You can't remove the current node
   * from the head of the list.
   * @param node the element to remove from list.
   */
  public void remove(SoundElement node){

    if (node==this) {
      System.out.println("I can't remove myself from the
        head of the list.");
      return;
    }

    SoundElement current = this;

    // While there are more nodes to consider
    while (current.getNext() != null) {

      if (current.getNext() == node) {
        // Simply make node's next be this next
        current.setNext(node.getNext());
        // Make this node point to nothing
        node.setNext(null);
        return;
      }
      current = current.getNext();
    }
  }

  /**
   * Insert the input node after this node.
   * @param node the element to insert after this.
   */
  public void insertAfter(SoundElement node) {

    // Save what "this" currently points at
    SoundElement oldNext = this.getNext();
```

```
        this.setNext(node);
        node.setNext(oldNext);
    }

    /**
     * Return the last element in the list
     * @return the last element in the list
     */
    public SoundElement last() {
      SoundElement current;

      current = this;
      while (current.getNext() != null) {
        current = current.getNext();
      }
      return current;
    }

    /**
     * Add the input node after the last node in this list.
     * @param node element to insert after this.
     */
    public void add(SoundElement node) {
      this.last().insertAfter(node);
    }

    /**
     * copyNode returns a copy of this element
     * @return another element with the same sound
     */
    public SoundElement copyNode() {
      Sound copySound = new Sound(mySound);
      SoundElement returnMe = new SoundElement(copySound);
      return returnMe;
    }

    /**
     * Repeat the input phrase for the number of times
     * specified.
     * It always appends to the current node, NOT insert.
     * @param nextOne the node to be copied in to list
     * @param count the number of times to copy it in.
     */
    public void repeatNext(SoundElement nextOne, int count) {
      SoundElement current = this; // Start from here
      SoundElement copy; // Where we keep the current copy

      for (int i=1; i <= count; i++) {
        copy = nextOne.copyNode(); // Make a copy
        current.insertAfter(copy); // Set as next
        current = copy; // Now append to copy
      }
    }

    /**
     * Weave the input song node count times every skipAmount
     * nodes
     * @param nextOne node to be copied into the list
     * @param count how many times to copy
     * @param skipAmount how many nodes to skip per weave
     */
    public void weave(SoundElement nextOne, int count,
```

```java
                              int skipAmount) {
    SoundElement current = this; // Start from here
    SoundElement copy; // Where we keep the one to be
    // weaved in

    // loop count times
    for (int i=0; i < count; i++) {

      //Skip skipAmount nodes (this one is 1)
      for (int j=1; j < skipAmount; j++) {

        // as long as current isn't null move to next
        if (current != null) {
          current = current.getNext();
        }
      }

      // if current isn't null
      if (current != null) {
        // make a new copy
        copy = nextOne.copyNode();

        // insert it after current
        current.insertAfter(copy);

        // move current along
        current = copy.getNext();
      }

      // else if current is null return (break out early)
      if (current == null) {
        return;
      }
    }
  }

  /**
   * Replace the one sound with the other sound
   * in all the elements from me on.
   * Two sounds are equal if come from same filename
   * @param oldSound sound to be replaced
   * @param newSound sound to put in its place
   */
  public void replace(Sound oldSound, Sound newSound) {
    if (this.mySound.getFileName() != null) {
      if (this.mySound.getFileName().equals(oldSound.
          getFileName())) {
        this.mySound = newSound;
      }
    }

    if (next != null) {
      next.replace(oldSound,newSound);
    }
  }

}
```

How It Works.   There are two interesting items in this linked list implementation. Both of them involve the use of *recursion* for traversing a data structure.

Look at how we define `toString` for `SoundElement`.

```
return "SoundElement with sound: " + mySound +
       " (and next: " + next + ").";
```

That's really straightforward, isn't it? When we tell a `SoundElement` to display as a string, it:

- Displays "SoundElement with …",
- then the printable representation of the sound in the current node,
- and then the printable representation of the `next`.

Trace through what will happen when `next` is `null`. We call that the *base case*. That makes sense how it would work, as in the below example.

```
> Sound s = new Sound(
  FileChooser.getMediaPath("shh-a-h.wav"));
> Sound t = new Sound(
  FileChooser.getMediaPath("croak-h.wav"));
> Sound u = new Sound(
  FileChooser.getMediaPath("clap-q.wav"));
> SoundElement e1 = new SoundElement(s);
> SoundElement e2 = new SoundElement(t);
> SoundElement e3 = new SoundElement(u);
> e1.playFromMeOn();
> e1 // no next so it will do System.out.println(e1);
SoundElement with sound: Sound file:
c:/dsBook/media-source/shh-a-h.wav
number of samples: 11004 (and next: null).
```

That makes sense. The interesting thing is that this works, still, when we have additional `SoundElement` instances attached to the list.

```
> e1.setNext(e2);
> e1
SoundElement with sound:
Sound file: c:/dsBook/media-source/shh-a-h.wav
number of samples: 11004 (and next:
SoundElement with sound: Sound file:
c:/dsBook/mediasources/croak-h.wav
number of samples: 8808 (and next: null).).
> e2.setNext(e3);
> e1
SoundElement with sound: Sound file: c:/dsBook/
  media-source/shh-a-h.wav
number of samples: 11004 (and next:
SoundElement with sound:
Sound file: c:/dsBook/media-source/croak-h.wav
number of samples: 8808 (and next:
```

```
SoundElement with sound:
Sound file: c:/dsBook/media-source/clap-q.wav
number of samples: 4584 (and next: null).).).
```

Where did all that text come from? When we try to print `next` and it is *not* `null`, then the object that `next` refers to is asked to convert itself to a string (`toString`). If that next object is also a `SoundElement` (as in the examples above), then the *same* `toString` method is executed (the one in `SceneElement`). The difference in the next call is that the object being asked to convert itself (`this`) is different.

In the example above, e1 starts executing `toString`, which then tries to print `next`—which is e2. The node e2 is then asked to execute `toString`, and when it gets to `next`, the node e3 is asked to convert itself (`toString`). When e3 is done (since its `next` is `null`), e3.`toString`() ends, then e2.`toString`() ends, and finally the original call to print e1 ends. This process is called a *recursive traversal* of the linked list— we are *traversing* (walking along, visiting) each node of the linked list, by using the same method, which repeatedly calls itself. In the case of `toString`, the calls are implicit—they happen when we try to print out `next`.

Tracing a Recursive Traversal

In the example above, if we then asked e1.`playFromMeOn`(), another recursive traversal would occur. Let's trace what happens. When we start the execution, the linked list looks like Figure 9.1.

The method `playFromMeOn`() is really short—it only says `this.collect().play();`. The method `collect`() does all the hard work. It collects the sounds from all the individual nodes into one big `Sound` instance, so that the big sound can finally be played. So, the interesting work occurs in `collect`().

So we start out by asking e1 (Figure 9.2), to execute the code below.

```java
public Sound collect() {
  if (this.getNext() == null) {
    return mySound;
  }
```

Otherwise, `getNext`() is not `null`, so we end up making the recursive call.

```java
  else {
    return mySound.append(this.getNext().collect());
  }
```

FIGURE 9.1
The initial `SoundElement` list.

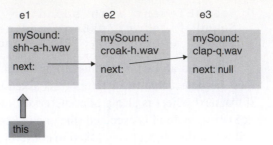

FIGURE 9.2
As we start executing `playFromMeOn()`.

Our call to `e1.collect()` is now *frozen*. It has not ended, but it can't go any further yet. It now has to process `this.getNext().collect()`.

We are now asking `e2` (which is what `this.getNext()` means) to `collect()` (Figure 9.3). The question of "Where is `e1`?" isn't relevant. From `e2`'s perspective, `e1` doesn't exist. We're simply asking for `e2.collect()`.

The node `e2` also has a `next`, so we execute `else return mySound.append(this. getNext().collect());`. Now, we have the execution of `e2.collect()` *frozen*. Neither `e1.collect()` nor `e2.collect()` can end yet—they're waiting in limbo.

Now, we execute `e3.collect()` (Figure 9.4). Finally the first part of `collect()` is true—`next` is `null`. We return the sound in `e3`.

Now we can *unfreeze* `e2.collect()` (Figure 9.5). Now that we have `this. getNext().collect()`, we can append to it the sound of `e2` and return back to `e1.collect()`.

Finally, `e1.collect()` gets the sounds from `e2` and `e3` appended together, from its execution of `this.getNext().collect()`. The sound from `e1` gets appended to the rest, and we finally return from `e1.collect()`. We return "shh-a-h.wav" appended with "croak-h.wav" appended with "clap-q.wav." That's what finally gets played.

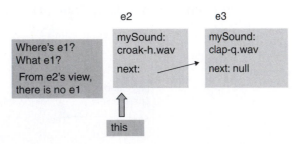

FIGURE 9.3
Calling e2.collect().

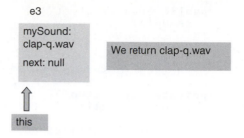

FIGURE 9.4
Finally, we can return a sound.

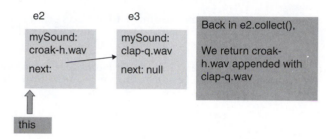

FIGURE 9.5
Ending e2.collect().

Making It Work Tip: Tracing your program

It is very important for you to be able to do what we just did in this section. You should be able to trace through your programs when you need to. You don't always have to be able to trace through your programs at this level of detail, but when something goes wrong, it helps enormously to be able to do this.

Testing and Replacing

Given below is a program that constructs a linked list from the SoundElement class.

Example Java Code 67: SoundListText: Constructing a SoundElement list

```java
/**
 * Class to test a sound list
 * @author Mark Guzdial
 * @author Barb Ericson
 */
public class SoundListTest {

  /** the starting element in the list */
  private SoundElement root;

  /**
   * Constructor that sets up the test
   */
```

```java
public SoundListTest() {
    setUp();
}

/**
 * Method to set up the linked list
 */
private void setUp(){
    Sound s = null;  // For copying in sounds

    s = new Sound(FileChooser.getMediaPath("scratch-h.wav"));
    root = new SoundElement(s);

    s = new Sound(FileChooser.getMediaPath("gonga-2.wav"));
    SoundElement one = new SoundElement(s);
    root.repeatNext(one,5);

    s = new Sound(FileChooser.getMediaPath("scritch-q.wav"));
    SoundElement two = new SoundElement(s.scale(2.0));
    root.weave(two,3,3);

    s = new Sound(FileChooser.getMediaPath("clap-q.wav"));
    SoundElement three = new SoundElement(s);
    root.weave(three,5,2);

    root.playFromMeOn();
}

/**
 * Method to get the root
 * @return the root (start) of the list
 */
public SoundElement getRoot() { return root;}


/** Method to test */
public static void main (String[] args) {
    SoundListTest test = new SoundListTest();
    test.setUp();
}
}
```

■

Go ahead and try it. You'll notice that you hear sounds woven between other listed sounds. The use of repeatNext and weave for SoundElement leads to that mixture of sound. It looks much like the code that we developed for MIDI.

Example Java Code 68: RepeatNext for SoundElement

```java
/**
 * Repeat the input phrase for the number of times
 * specified.
 * It always appends to the current node and loses any
 * next reference.
 * @param nextOne the node to be copied in to list
 * @param count the number of times to copy it in.
 */
public void repeatNext(SoundElement nextOne, int count) {
    SoundElement current = this; // Start from here
    SoundElement copy; // Where we keep the current copy
```

```java
for (int i=1; i <= count; i++) {
    copy = nextOne.copyNode(); // Make a copy
    current.insertAfter(copy); // Set as next
    current = copy; // Now append to copy
  }
}
```

Example Java Code 69: Weave for SoundElement

```java
/**
 * Weave the input song node count times every skipAmount
 * nodes
 * @param nextOne node to be copied into the list
 * @param count how many times to copy
 * @param skipAmount how many nodes to skip per weave
 */
public void weave(SoundElement nextOne, int count,
                  int skipAmount) {

  SoundElement current = this; // Start from here
  SoundElement copy; // Where we keep the one to be
  // weaved in

  // loop count times
  for (int i=0; i < count; i++) {

    //Skip skipAmount nodes (this one is 1)
    for (int j=1; j < skipAmount; j++) {

      // as long as current isn't null move to next
      if (current != null) {
        current = current.getNext();
      }
    }

    // if current isn't null
    if (current != null) {
      // make a new copy
      copy = nextOne.copyNode();

      // insert it after current
      current.insertAfter(copy);

      // move current along
      current = copy.getNext();
    }

    // else if current is null return (break out early)
    if (current == null) {
      return;
    }
  }
}
```

In both of these methods, we create a *copy* of the input node, using the method copyNode. How does that work? What does it mean to copy a SoundElement node?

Example Java Code 70: copyNode for SoundElement

```
/**
 * copyNode returns a copy of this element
 * @return another element with the same sound
 */
public SoundElement copyNode() {
  Sound copySound = new Sound(mySound); // copy the sound
  SoundElement returnMe = new SoundElement(copySound);
  return returnMe;
}
```

A Problem and Its Solution: Removing a node without recreating the list

You should try that example in SoundListTest. It's really annoying. There are 10 gongs in there that seemingly keep going on and on and on. How can we get rid of them?

The obvious thing to do is to modify the SoundListTest class to use fewer (or zero!) gongs, recompile, and re-run it. What if we couldn't? Imagine that you have a long linked list that has been created through many different operations, and it would take too long or be too hard to re-create it.

What we can do is to walk through the list, find the gongs, and replace the sounds in those nodes with some other sound. We'll call it "de-gonging."

Example Java Code 71: De-gonging the list

```
/**
 * Method to test replace one sound with another
 */
public void degong() {
  Sound gong = new Sound(
    FileChooser.getMediaPath("gonga-2.wav"));
  Sound snap = new Sound(
    FileChooser.getMediaPath("snap-tenth.wav"));
  root.replace(gong,snap);
}
```

We know how to write `replace`. We're simply going to iterate through the list, find the nodes that have the gong, and replace it with the snap. However, it's not quite that easy. How do you know which sounds contain the gong sound? That's the trick. The gong sound in the SoundElement is *not* the same object as is input (e.g., it's not == to the sound gong above). We have to figure out what it means for two objects (the input sound and the sound in a node) to be *equivalent* even if they're not the exact same object.

Example Java Code 72: replace for SoundElement

```
/**
 * Replace the one sound with the other sound
 * in all the elements from me on.
 * Two sounds are equal if come from same filename
 * @param oldSound sound to be replaced
```

```
 * @param newSound sound to put in its place
 */
public void replace(Sound oldSound, Sound newSound) {
  if (this.mySound.getFileName() != null) {
    if (this.mySound.getFileName().equals(oldSound.
        getFileName())) {
      this.mySound = newSound;
    }
  }

  if (next != null) {
    next.replace(oldSound,newSound);
  }
}
```

■

How It Works.   For our purposes, we'll use a very simple notion of equivalence. If the sound in the node has the same `fileName` as the input sound, it's the same. This is not a great approach. For example, if you *created* your own sound (i.e., not from a filename), you will not be able to replace that sound using this approach. However, this approach will work for our de-gonging method, though, since we want to find and remove sounds made from the "gong" file.

Notice that, since we're comparing two strings (the filenames), we use the `equals` method. We can't use `==` method because that checks if two objects are *equal*, the exact same object. It's not the case that the two strings are the same object. We need to check if the two strings have the same characters—that's what the `equals` method does. We have to check first that there's a `fileName` string at all. If there isn't (e.g., the `Sound` instance was created via `scale` or some other method that returns a `Sound` instance that was never associated with a file), then the `fileName` is `null`—and `null` does not understand `equals`.

The `replace` method has no explicit loop—no `for`, no `while`. Instead, it traverses the list using *recursion*. We call the method `replace` on each segment of the linked list that we want to check. Let's walk through how that works. Imagine that we execute `e1.replace(croak,clap)` on the list in Figure 9.6.

We start out executing the method `replace` in Figure 9.7:

```
if (this.mySound.getFileName() != null) {
  if (this.mySound.getFileName().equals(oldSound.
      getFileName())) {
    this.mySound = newSound;
  }
}
```

It is clear that the "croak" sound is not the same as the "shh" sound, so we continue on.

```
if (next != null) {
  next.replace(oldSound,newSound);
}
```

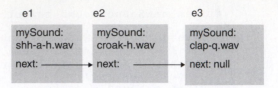

FIGURE 9.6
Starting out with `e1.replace(croak,clap)`.

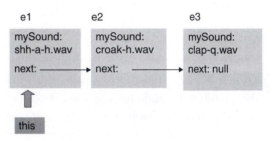

FIGURE 9.7
Checking the first node.

Now, `e2` is asked to `replace(croak,clap)` (Figure 9.8). Node `e2` *does* contain "croak," so we replace it with a "clap." Since the `next` of `e2` is *not* `null`, we go on to call `e3.replace(croak,clap)`.

The node `e3` does not contain the "croak" sound, so we don't replace anything (Figure 9.9). The `next` value on `e3` *is* `null`, so we return.

While it is invisible to us (no additional code is executed), after `e3.replace(croak, clap)` ends, the method execution for `e2.replace(croak,clap)` also ends. Finally, `e1.replace(croak,clap)` ends. Those other method executions were awaiting the completion of the later method executions—they could be thought of as being "frozen" or "in limbo."

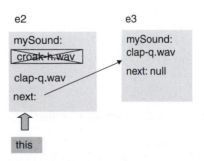

FIGURE 9.8
Replacing from e2 on.

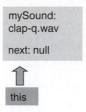

FIGURE 9.9
Finally, replace on node e3.

9.2   USING TREES TO STRUCTURE SAMPLED SOUNDS

Just as with MIDI phrases and images, we may want to structure our sampled sounds in compositions with a sense of clusters or hierarchy. A long, linear list of sampled sounds is hard to manipulate and think about. We naturally think about sound in clusters: motif expositions and recapitulations, or verses and chorus. So, just like with MIDI phrases and images, we can explore the use of trees to structure our sampled sounds.

Just like with our MIDI phrases and images, we might also embed operations in our branches. We might have branches that reverse the sound collected from the children (all appended together), or scale the children's sounds, or normalize the volume of the children's sound. Thus, we can create trees of sampled sounds that combine structure and behavior.

We are going to use an implementation of trees that is similar to the one that we created for images, the structure called a *linked list of lists*. All nodes will have a `next`, and branches will also have a `children` link (Figure 9.10). We will create a normal branch, and a `ScaleBranch` that changes the frequency of the sounds that are children of the branch.

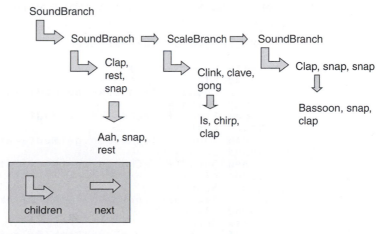

FIGURE 9.10
Our first sampled sound tree.

We would create and play this example sound tree like this:

```
Welcome to DrJava.
> SoundTreeExample tree = new SoundTreeExample();
> tree.play();
```

We might then change the scaling factor in our `ScaleBranch`, then replay the tree:

```
> tree.playScaled(2.0);
> tree.play();
```

Here's what our class `SoundTreeExample` looks like.

Example Java Code 73: SoundTreeExample

```java
/**
 * Class to test the sound tree
 * @author Mark Guzdial
 * @author Barb Ericson
 */
public class SoundTreeExample {

  /** branch that scales the children */
  private ScaleBranch scaledBranch;

  /** the root of the tree */
  private SoundBranch root;

  /**
   * Constructor to set up the example
   */
  public SoundTreeExample() {
    setUp();
  }

  /**
   * Method to get the root of the tree
   * @return the root of the tree
   */
  public SoundBranch getRoot() { return root; }

  /**
   * Method to set up the tree
   */
  private void setUp() {
    Sound clap =
      new Sound(FileChooser.getMediaPath("clap-q.wav"));
    Sound chirp =
      new Sound(FileChooser.getMediaPath("chirp-2.wav"));
    Sound rest =
      new Sound(FileChooser.getMediaPath("rest-1.wav"));
    Sound snap =
      new Sound(FileChooser.getMediaPath("snap-tenth.wav"));
    Sound clink =
      new Sound(
        FileChooser.getMediaPath("clink-tenth.wav"));
    Sound clave =
      new Sound(
        FileChooser.getMediaPath("clave-twentieth.wav"));
    Sound gong =
      new Sound(FileChooser.getMediaPath("gongb-2.wav"));
```

```java
      Sound bassoon =
        new Sound(FileChooser.getMediaPath("bassoon-c4.wav"));
      Sound is = new Sound(
        FileChooser.getMediaPath("is.wav"));
      Sound aah = new Sound(
        FileChooser.getMediaPath("aah.wav"));

      // create the root
      root = new SoundBranch();
      SoundNode sn;

      // create the first branch
      SoundBranch branch1 = new SoundBranch();
      sn = new SoundNode(clap.append(rest).append(snap));
      branch1.addChild(sn);
      sn = new SoundNode(aah.append(snap).append(rest));
      branch1.addChild(sn);

      // create a scaled branch
      scaledBranch = new ScaleBranch(1.0);
      sn = new SoundNode(clink.append(clave).append(gong));
      scaledBranch.addChild(sn);
      sn = new SoundNode(is.append(chirp).append(clap));
      scaledBranch.addChild(sn);

      // create a second sound branch
      SoundBranch branch2 = new SoundBranch();
      sn = new SoundNode(clap.append(snap).append(snap));
      branch2.addChild(sn);
      sn = new SoundNode(bassoon.append(snap).append(clap));
      branch2.addChild(sn);

      // add the children to the tree
      root.addChild(branch1);
      root.addChild(scaledBranch);
      root.addChild(branch2);
    }

  /**
   * Method to play the tree
   */
  public void play() {
    root.playFromMeOn();
  }

  /**
   * Method to test the tree
   */
  public static void main(String[] args) {
    SoundTreeExample tree = new SoundTreeExample();
    tree.getRoot().collect().play();
  }
}
```

■

How It Works.   There are a lot of similarities between this class and the WolfAttack-
Movie class. Each creates a root variable that holds the main branch of the tree. Some
branches that need to be accessed between methods are declared as fields in the class.
The setUp() methods in both classes have a very similar structure. Each creates a

branch, creates the nodes that go in that branch, and then loads the nodes into the branch. SoundTreeExample may be a little confusing, in that each node *only* contains a single Sound, but in this example, each node's Sound is a collection of three appended sounds. It's still one Sound per SoundNode.

Once we create our tree, we can explore the structure of the tree by simply printing it out. All the objects in the sound tree have toString methods. Since we know the implementation of the tree, we can walk the firstChild and next links to explore the whole tree.

```
> tree // Not very useful in itself
SoundTreeExample@92b1a1
> tree.getRoot() // Way useful
SoundBranch (with child:
SoundBranch (with child:
SoundNode (with sound: Sound number of samples: 28568
  and next:
SoundNode (with sound: Sound number of samples: 66993
  and next:
null)) and next:
ScaleBranch (1.0) SoundBranch (with child:
SoundNode (with sound: Sound number of samples: 47392
  and next:
SoundNode (with sound: Sound number of samples: 24478
  and next:
null)) and next:
SoundBranch (with child:
SoundNode (with sound: Sound number of samples: 8452
  and next:
SoundNode (with sound: Sound number of samples: 61643
  and next:
null)) and next:
No next))) and next:
No next)

> tree.getRoot().getFirstChild().getNext() // Second
  branch
tree.getRoot().getFirstChild().getNext()
ScaleBranch (1.0) SoundBranch (with child:
SoundNode (with sound: Sound number of samples: 47392
  and next:
SoundNode (with sound: Sound number of samples: 24478
  and next:
null)) and next:
SoundBranch (with child:
SoundNode (with sound: Sound number of samples: 8452
  and next:
SoundNode (with sound: Sound number of samples: 61643
  and next:
null)) and next:
No next))
```

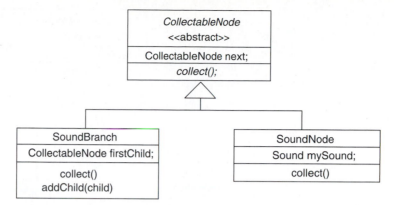

FIGURE 9.11
The core classes in the CollectableNode class hierarchy.

Implementing a Sound Tree

How we build a tree of sounds is very much like how we built a tree of pictures.

- Set up a general *node* abstract superclass that all other node and branch classes inherit from. In our sound tree, this superclass is CollectableNode—a node from which a sound can be collected.

- Create a *leaf* node class that will store our data of interest (sounds). Here, that's a SoundNode.

- Create a *branch* node that will store collections of leaves and references to other branches—a SoundBranch (Figure 9.11).

- Create (as we wish) *branch nodes with operations* that do things to the children of this branch. We have one example of a branch with operations, ScaleBranch (Figure 9.12).

Let's go through these classes in turn. We should note that much of the Collectable-Node class hierarchy looks much like the code in the DisplayableNode class hierarchy.

Example Java Code 74: CollectableNode

```java
/**
 * Node in a sound tree.
 * @author Mark Guzdial
 * @author Barb Ericson
 */
public abstract class CollectableNode {

  /** reference to the next node */
  private CollectableNode next;

  /**
   * No argument constructor that sets
   * next to null
   */
  public CollectableNode() {
    next = null;
  }
```

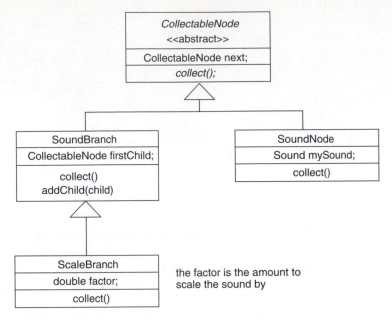

FIGURE 9.12
Extending the class hierarchy with `ScaleBranch`.

```
/**
 * Method to set the next node
 * @param nextOne the next element in list
 */
public void setNext(CollectableNode nextOne) {
  this.next = nextOne;
}

/**
 * Method to get the next node
 * @return the next node in the list
 */
public CollectableNode getNext() {
  return this.next;
}

/**
 * Play the list of sound elements
 * after me
 */
public void playFromMeOn() {
  this.collect().play();
}

/**
 * Collect all the sounds from me on
 * @return the collected sound
 */
public abstract Sound collect();

}
```

How It Works.   For the most part, `CollectableNode` is simply another linked list node class. It has a `next` link and lots of linked list methods. In addition, it defines an abstract method for `collect()`—the method for collecting a `Sound` from the node. No body for the `collect` method is given since it is declared to be an abstract method. The method `playFromMeOn()` is defined here, too. It simply plays what gets collected.

Example Java Code 75: SoundNode

```java
/*
 * SoundNode is a class representing a sound in a sound tree.
 * @author Mark Guzdial
 * @author Barb Ericson
 */
public class SoundNode extends CollectableNode {

  /** The sound I'm associated with */
  private Sound mySound;

  /*
   * Make me with this sound
   * @param sound the Sound I'm associated with
   */
  public SoundNode(Sound sound) {
    super(); // Call superclass constructor
    mySound = sound;
  }

  /**
   * Method to return a string with information
   * about this node
   * @return the information string
   */
  public String toString() {
    return "SoundNode (with sound: " + mySound +
      " and next: " + getNext() + ")";
  }

  /**
   * Collect all the sounds from me on,
   * recursively.
   * @return the collected sound
   */
  public Sound collect() {
    SoundNode nextNode;
    if (this.getNext() == null) {
      return mySound;
    }
    else {
      nextNode = (SoundNode) this.getNext();
      return mySound.append(nextNode.collect());
    }
  }
}
```

■

How It Works.   The class SoundNode models leaf nodes in our sound trees. An instance of the SoundNode class contains a Sound. The most interesting thing about SoundNode is how it defines `toString()` and `collect()`.

- A SoundNode instance converts itself to a String by converting its Sound and its next to a String. That's easy to say, and that's why we define it that way. Tracing it takes some thinking about it.

- A SoundNode collects its sound using the following method: (a) if it has no next node (next is null), by returning its sound; (b) else, by returning its sound appended with whatever its next will return when we ask it to collect(). It's this last part that is recursive. Most powerfully, though, the definition *is* easy to say and easy to understand—"When I'm told to collect, I grab me and whatever my buddy has to return." It's exactly how you collect papers when you're told to hand them to the end of the row: you stick yours on top of what your neighbor returns, then pass the whole stack to the next person.

Example Java Code 76: SoundBranch

```java
/**
 * Class that represents a branch in a tree of
 * sounds
 * @author Mark Guzdial
 * @author Barb Ericson
 */
public class SoundBranch extends CollectableNode {

  /** the first child in the list of children */
  private CollectableNode firstChild;

  /**
   * Construct a branch with the first child and
   * next as null
   */
  public SoundBranch() {
    super(); // Call superclass constructor
    firstChild = null;
  }

  /**
   * Method to return the first child
   * @return the first child
   */
  public CollectableNode getFirstChild()
  { return firstChild; }

  /**
   * Method to return a string with information
   * about this branch
   * @return the information string
   */
  public String toString() {

    String childString = "No firstChild", nextString=
      "No next";

    // if there is a first child get its string
    if (firstChild != null) {
      childString = firstChild.toString();
    }

    // if there is a next node get its string
```

```java
    if (getNext() != null) {
      nextString = getNext().toString();
    }

    return "SoundBranch (with child: "+ childString +
      " and next: "+ nextString + ")";
  }

  /**
   * Method to add a node to the end of the
   * children list
   * @param child the child to add
   */
  public void addChild(CollectableNode child) {
    if (firstChild != null) {
      firstChild.add(child);
    }
    else {
      firstChild = child;
    }
  }

  /**
   * Collect all the sound from our firstChild,
   * then collect from next.
   * @return the combined sound
   */
  public Sound collect() {

    Sound childSound;
    CollectableNode node;

    if (firstChild != null) {
      childSound = firstChild.collect();
    }
    else {
      childSound = new Sound(1);
    }

    // Collect from my next
    if (this.getNext() != null) {
      node=this.getNext();
      childSound=childSound.append(node.collect());
    }

    return childSound;
  }
}
```

How It Works. The class SoundBranch is the generic class for branches in a sound tree. Again, there is a similarity with the Branch class that we used with images.

- The definition for adding a child (addChild) is exactly the same as in Branch—if there's no children link, set it; else, add() to the children.
- The definition of toString() is a little complicated by the fact that we have to traverse both the children and next links to print a branch. We explicitly ask each variable to convert to toString() (being careful never to ask null to convert

itself to a string—though it would be glad to do so). Then we return the string of these pieces concatenated together.

- How a SoundBranch collects all its sounds, in collect(), is straightforward. First, we want to collect all the children's sounds. If the node children is empty (null), we create a very small (1/22,050th of a second) sound to serve as a dummy, empty sound. If there is a first child, collect() from the firstChild. We then return the childSound appended with the collection of sounds from next. In short, a SoundBranch collects sounds by collecting all of its children's sounds (if there are any children) and all of its sibling's sounds, and returns them appended together.

Example Java Code 77: ScaleBranch

```java
/**
 * Class that scales the children
 * @author Mark Guzdial
 * @author Barb Ericson
 */
public class ScaleBranch extends SoundBranch {

  /** Amount to scale the children by */
  private double factor;

  /**
   * Construct a branch with the passed factor
   * @param theFactor the factor to use
   */
  public ScaleBranch(double theFactor) {
    super(); // Call superclass constructor
    this.factor = theFactor;
  }

  /**
   * Method to get the scaling factor
   * @return the scaling factor
   */
  public double getFactor() { return this.factor; }

  /**
   * Method to set the scaling factor
   * @param theFactor the new factor to use
   */
  public void setFactor(double theFactor) {
    this.factor = theFactor;
  }

  /**
   * Method to return a string with information
   * about this branch
   * @return the information string
   */
  public String toString() {
    return "ScaleBranch (" + factor +
      ") "+ super.toString();
  }
```

```
/**
 * Collect all the sound from the children,
 * then collect from next.
 * Scale the getFirstChild()
 * @return the collected sound
 */
public Sound collect() {

  Sound childSound;

  if (getFirstChild() != null) {
    childSound = getFirstChild().collect().scale(factor);
  }
  else {
    childSound = new Sound(1);
  }

  // Collect from my next
  if (this.getNext() != null) {
    Sound nextSound=(this.getNext()).collect();
    childSound = childSound.append(nextSound);
  }

  return childSound;
  }
}
```

■

How It Works.   The class ScaleBranch is a kind of SoundBranch, so it is a branch that knows how to add children and how to collect those children's sounds. In addition, a ScaleBranch has a factor that it uses to scale the sound from its children—scaling it up in frequency or down. This change requires a slightly different constructor (for setting the scaling factor) and accessors. The biggest change is in the collect() method. Now, when children are gathered, they are also scaled:

```
if (getFirstChild() != null) {
  childSound = getFirstChild().collect().
    scale(factor);
}
else {
  childSound = new Sound(1);
}
```

Tracing a Recursive Tree Traversal

We have now seen how we can build and use a tree of sounds, and how that tree of sounds is implemented. In this section, we aim to understand how the tree traversal occurs dynamically. How is it that this simple code in the collect() methods traverses the whole tree?

We start from this code:

```
Welcome to DrJava.
> SoundTreeExample tree = new SoundTreeExample();
> tree.getRoot().collect().play();
```

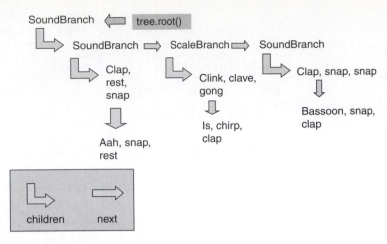

FIGURE 9.13
Starting out with `tree.root().collect()`.

The object in `tree` has a `root` (an instance of the class `SoundBranch`, as we saw earlier), which is created in `setUp()`, which is called by the constructor. We then ask the root to `collect()` all its sounds into one big `Sound`, which we can then `play()`. How does that sound get collected?

When we start executing `tree.getRoot().collect()`, the tree and `this` looks like Figure 9.13. We start executing the following method for `collect()`, with `this` pointing at the root.

```
public Sound collect() {

    Sound childSound;
    CollectableNode node;

    if (firstChild != null) {
        childSound = firstChild.collect();
    }
    else {
        childSound = new Sound(1);
    }
```

Since the root clearly has children, we ask the `firstChild` to `collect()` (Figure 9.14). The call to `getRoot().collect()` is frozen, as we have to wait to get `firstChild.collect()` to return before the call to the root can complete. The same code gets executed as with the root, and since `this` is also a `SoundBranch`, the same code executes.

Again, `this` branch does have children, so we ask the `firstChild.collect()` (Figure 9.15). Now, we're executing a different `collect()` method, because now `this` points at a `SoundNode`. So, we execute this version:

```
public Sound collect() {
    SoundNode nextNode;
```

```
  if (this.getNext() == null) {
    return mySound;
  }
  else {
    nextNode = (SoundNode) this.getNext();
    return mySound.append(nextNode.collect());
  }
}
```

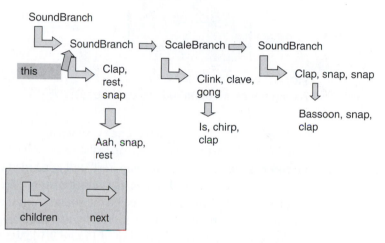

FIGURE 9.14
Asking the root's children to `collect()`.

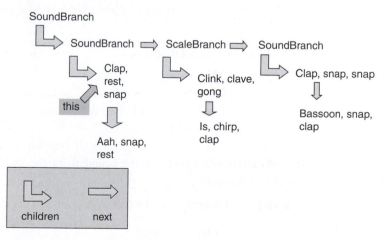

FIGURE 9.15
Asking the first SoundNode to `collect()`.

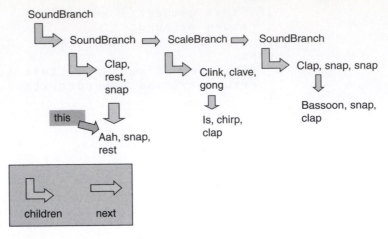

FIGURE 9.16
Asking the next SoundNode to `collect()`.

The current `this` does have a `next`, so we need to `collect()` from there before we can finish this method. We move on to the `next` SoundNode (Figure 9.16). This one has no `next`, so we return "Aah, snap, rest" (all appended together as one Sound object).

At this point, we're back in the position of Figure 9.15, but later in the method `collect()`. We now have collected the sound from the `next`, so we can append `this` sound. We now return "clap, snap, rest" with "aah, snap, rest."

We're now back at the position of Figure 9.14. We now have the children's sound, so we can finish the SoundBranch's `collect()` method.

```
// Collect from my next
if (this.getNext() != null) {
  node=this.getNext();
  childSound=childSound.append(node.collect());
}

return childSound;
}
```

This SoundBranch *does* have a `next`, so we again freeze this method invocation while we ask `node.collect()`. We are now collecting from the `ScaleBranch` that is next to the `SoundBranch` (Figure 9.17).

We know something about what will happen next. The `collect()` method in `ScaleBranch` will gather up the sound from the `children` list. Then that resultant sound will be scaled.

```
public Sound collect() {

Sound childSound;

if (getFirstChild() != null) {
  childSound = getFirstChild().collect().scale
```

```
    (factor);
  }
  else {
    childSound = new Sound(1);
  }
```

We can see from the tree that we will gather "clink, clave, gong" appended to "is, chirp, clap." That will get scaled to whatever factor is in the ScaleBranch. Then the ScaleBranch collect() method will finish:

```
  // Collect from my next
  if (this.getNext() != null) {
    Sound nextSound=(this.getNext()).collect();
    childSound = childSound.append(nextSound);
  }

  return childSound;
}
```

This is the same as in the collect() method of SoundBranch, so we know what's going to happen here. The ScaleBranch invocation of collect() stops executing and waits for this.getNext().collect() to execute. We ask the last SoundBranch to collect() (Figure 9.18).

It's worthwhile to consider just what methods are paused, frozen, or waiting for other methods to finish. We call that list of methods that are currently pending the *stack trace*. These are quite literally in a *stack* like a stack of cups. The last one on must be the first one popped. So, as of Figure 9.18, the methods we have in play are:

- The currently executing method, the call to collect() on the last SoundBranch.

- The call to collect() on the ScaleBranch is waiting for the collection from its next.

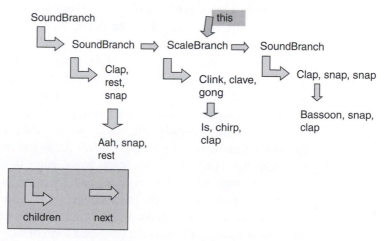

FIGURE 9.17
Collecting from the next of the SoundBranch.

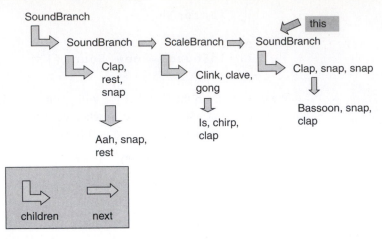

FIGURE 9.18
Collecting from the last `SoundBranch`.

- The call to `collect()` on the first `SoundBranch` is waiting for the collection from the `ScaleBranch`.
- And the call that started it all—the root `SoundBranch`—is waiting for the collection from its `children`.

We know that calling `collect()` on the last `SoundBranch` will result from collecting its children's sounds: "clap, snap, snap" appended with "bassoon, snap, clap" (Figure 9.18). This last `SoundBranch` has no `next`! So this call simply returns the sound "clap, snap, snap, bassoon, snap, clap."

We return to the state of Figure 9.17 and pop the method off the stack. We can now finish the call to `collect()` on the `ScaleBranch`. We return back up "clink, clave, gong, is, chirp, clap" scaled by the factor, appended with "clap, snap, snap, bassoon, snap, clap."

We now pop the next method off the stack, and we're at Figure 9.14. We take the sound from the `next` (the `ScaleBranch` and the rest of the tree), and append the sound from its children. So it returns "clap, rest, snap, aah, snap, rest", plus "clink, clave, gong, is, chirp, clap" scaled by the factor, plus "clap, snap, snap, bassoon, snap, clap."

We pop the last method off the stack—we're at the `collect()` of the root. Obviously, the root has no `next`, so we simply return the sound from the root's `children`: "clap, rest, snap, aah, snap, rest", plus "clink, clave, gong, is, chirp, clap" scaled by the factor, plus "clap, snap, snap, bassoon, snap, clap." And that's the sound that plays.

What we just traced might be called an *in-order traversal*. We visited the children, did whatever the branch needed to do (e.g., scale), then processed the next. There are different orderings of traversals. Imagine a form of `ScaleBranch` that scaled the result from the `next` rather than the children. We will visit more of these traversals in the next chapter.

Where We're Going Next

Take a look at DrawableNode and CollectableNode. Pretty darn similar, aren't they? Duplicated code is a bad idea for several reasons:

- Duplicated code is hard to maintain. Let's say that we figured out a better way to do add() or reverse(). Right now, we have nearly identical code in two different classes, so we would need to fix both of those. What are the odds that we make a mistake at some point and forget to fix one of them when we fix the other?

- Duplicated code is a waste of space. Why should the exact same code be in memory in two different places?

- Duplicated code strains our notion of the *responsibility-driven design* that is important for object-oriented programming. Whose responsibility is it to provide add()? Is it the responsibility of both DrawableNode and CollectableNode? That seems odd. Rather, it should be the responsibility of some third class that both of these classes use. That's where we're going in the next chapter.

In the next chapter, we will correct this problem, and make it easier to create more linked lists and trees in the future. Later, we will find that graphical user interfaces are *also* trees, and that different kinds of traversals of the same graphical user interface tree creates different window appearances.

EXERCISES

9.1   Another option for comparing sounds is to implement the interface Comparable in the package java.lang. To do this you simply need to add the implements Comparable<Sound> after the class definition for Sound. Then also add the public int compareTo(Sound compareSound) method defined in the interface Comparable. In this method you can simply return the result of using the compareTo method on the filenames in both sounds. Modify the replace method in the class SoundElement to use the new compareTo method in Sound.

9.2   Change the replace method in the class SoundElement so that it actually compares the sounds (sample-by-sample) rather than simply comparing the filenames.

9.3   Create your own version of SoundListTest and create a tree using all the branch types in this chapter. Then modify the tree by replacing one of the sounds.

9.4   What is the output from the following code when executed with mystery (1234)? Show each method call.

```java
//precondition:  x >=0
public static void mystery(int x) {
  System.out.print(x % 10);
```

```
      if ((x / 10) != 0) {
        mystery(x / 10);
      }
      System.out.print(x % 10);
    }
```

9.5   What value is returned as the result of the call mystery(5)? Show each method call.

```
public static int mystery(int n) {
  if (n == 0)
    return 1;
  else
    return 10 - mystery (n - 1);
}
```

9.6   What value is returned as the result of mystery(7)? Show each method call.

```
public int mystery(int n) {
  if (n == 0) return 1;
  else return 2 *
        mystery (n - 1);
}
```

9.7   What value is returned as the result of mystery(4)? Show each method call.

```
public int mystery(int n) {
  if (n == 0) return 0;
  else return 2 +
        mystery (n - 1);
}
```

9.8   What value is returned as the result of fibonacci(10)? Show each method call.

```
public int fibonacci(int n) {
  if (n == 0) return 0;
  else if (n == 1) return 1;
  else return (fibonacci(n-1) + fibonacci(n-2));
}
```

9.9   Draw a Unified Modeling Language (UML) class diagram that shows all the classes in this chapter and their relationships to each other.

9.10   Trace the execution of the method renderAnimation in class WolfAttackMovie.

9.11   What is the purpose of each class described in this chapter?

9.12   For each class in this chapter, list the class that is most like it in the previous chapter.

9.13   Implement a subclass of SoundBranch called ReverseBranch that reverses the sound returned from collecting the children's sounds. Build a sound tree example using your new class.

9.14   Implement a subclass of SoundBranch called NormalizeBranch that normalizes the volume in the sound returned from collecting the children's sounds. Build a sound tree example using your new class.

9.15   Implement a subclass of SoundBranch called VolumeChangeBranch that remembers a factor for use in increasing or decreasing the volume returned from collecting the children's sounds. Build a sound tree example using your new class.

9.16   Create a new version of ScaleBranch called ScaleNextBranch that scales its next rather than its children. Build a sound tree example using your new class.

9.17   Record some individual sounds (singing perhaps?) that represent verses and the chorus of some song. Use a SoundTree to organize these sounds into the complete song with the right structure.

10 Generalizing Lists and Trees

Chapter Learning Objectives

In the last two chapters, we used trees to create an animation (the `DrawableNode` class hierarchy) and a complex sound structure (the `CollectableNode` class hierarchy). In this chapter, we create a generalized class that represents any kind of linked list structure. We will then go on to explain how to create generalized tree structures that are particularly efficient for some tasks (like searching).

The computer science goals for this chapter are:

- To *factor* out common functionalities from two classes to create a new abstract superclass.
- To develop strategies for how to respond to Java compiler errors.
- To understand the relative characteristics of arrays, linked lists, and trees for various manipulations.
- To identify some broad applications of trees.
- To use a binary tree structure and understand its value for searching.
- To explore different kinds of traversals on binary trees.

10.1 REFACTORING A GENERAL LINKED LIST NODE CLASS

We are going to remove the duplication between `DrawableNode` and `CollectableNode` by creating a new class, `LLNode`, that has the responsibility of being a linked list node. `LLNode` will be an abstract superclass—we'll never want just an `LLNode` (for one thing, it will have no data—it will just be a `next`). There are several advantages to this structure:

- We remove the duplication of code between `DrawableNode` and `Collectable-Node`.
- We push the responsibility of being a linked list node to a class that bears just that responsibility.

- Once we create an LLNode class, we can create a linked list of anything by simply subclassing LLNode.

Creating an LLNode class is pretty easy. Certainly, LLNode will need a next instance variable. We'll simply copy-paste the linked list code from either of DrawableNode or CollectableNode, then change all the appropriate variable types to LLNode.

Example Java Code 78: LLNode, a generalized linked list node class

```
/**
 * Class that represents a node in a linked list
 * @author Mark Guzdial
 * @author Barb Ericson
 */
public abstract class LLNode {

  /** The next node in the list */
  private LLNode next;

  /**
   * Constructor for LLNode that just sets
   * next to null
   */
  public LLNode() {
    next = null;
  }

  /**
   * Method to set the next element
   * @param nextOne the element to set as next
   */
  public void setNext(LLNode nextOne) {
    this.next = nextOne;
  }

  /**
   * Method to get the next element
   * @return the next element in the linked list
   */
  public LLNode getNext() {
    return this.next;
  }

  /** Method to remove a node from the list, fixing
   * the next links appropriately.
   * @param node the element to remove from the list.
   */
  public void remove(LLNode node) {
    if (node==this) {
      System.out.println("I can't remove myself from " +
                         "the head of the list");
      return;
    }

    LLNode current = this;

    // While there are more nodes to consider
    while (current.getNext() != null) {
      if (current.getNext() == node) {
```

```
52          // Simply make node's next be this next
            current.setNext(node.getNext());
54
            // Make this node point to nothing
56          node.setNext(null);
            return;
58        }
          current = current.getNext();
60      }
    }
62
    /**
64   * Insert the input node after this node.
     * @param node element to insert after this.
66   */
    public void insertAfter(LLNode node) {
68      // Save what "this" currently points at
        LLNode oldNext = this.getNext();
70      this.setNext(node);
        node.setNext(oldNext);
72    }

    /**
74   * Return the last element in the list
     * @return the last element in the list
76   */
    public LLNode last() {
78      LLNode current;

80
        current = this;
82      while (current.getNext() != null) {
          current = current.getNext();
84      }
        return current;
86    }

    /**
88   * Return the number of the elements in the list
     * @return the number of elements in the list
90   */
    public int count() {
92      LLNode current;
        int count = 1;
94
        current = this;
96      while (current.getNext() != null) {
          count++;
98        current = current.getNext();
100     }
        return count;
102   }

104
    /**
106  * Add the passed node after the last node in this list.
     * @param node the element to insert after this.
108  */
    public void add(LLNode node) {
110     this.last().insertAfter(node);
    }
112
```

```
114    /**
        * Reverse the list starting at this,
116     * and return the last element of the list.
        * The last element becomes the FIRST element
118     * of the list, and THIS goes to null.
        * @return the new head of the list
120     */
       public LLNode reverse() {
122      LLNode reversed, temp;

124      // Handle the first node outside the loop
         reversed = this.last();
126      this.remove(reversed);

128      while (this.getNext() != null) {
           temp = this.last();
130        this.remove(temp);
           reversed.add(temp);
132      }

134      // Now put the head of the old list on the end of
         // the reversed list.
136      reversed.add(this);

138      // At this point, reversed
         // is the head of the list
140      return reversed;
       }
142   }
```

Here's where it gets interesting. Can we now make CollectableNode and DrawableNode subclasses of LLNode, rip out all the replicated linked list code from CollectableNode and DrawableNode, *and then* make our WolfAttackMovie animation and sound tree examples work again? The process we're engaging in is called *refactoring*—we are moving replicated code *up* in the class hierarchy, and making sure that everything still works afterward.

Making WolfAttackMovie Work Again

We'll start with the animation. We change DrawableNode in two ways:

- We change the class definition to extend LLNode.

- We remove the linked list code. There's a bit more to do here beyond simply deleting methods like add(). For example, we remove the definition of the next field; we change the constructor to simply call the super.

Example Java Code 79: DrawableNode, with linked list code factored out

```
/**
2    * Stuff that all nodes and branches in the
     * scene tree know.
4    * @author Mark Guzdial
     * @author Barb Ericson
6    */
     public abstract class DrawableNode extends LLNode {
8
```

```
10    /**
       * Constructor for DrawableNode
       */
12    public DrawableNode() {
        super(); // call to parent constructor
14    }

16    /**
       * Use the given turtle to draw oneself
18     * @param t the Turtle to draw with
       */
20    public abstract void drawWith(Turtle t);
      // no body in an abstract method
22
       /**
24     * Draw on the given picture
       * @param bg the background picture to draw on
26     */
      public void drawOn(Picture bg) {
28      Turtle t = new Turtle(bg);
        t.setPenDown(false);
30      this.drawWith(t);
      }
32
    }
```

This new version of DrawableNode is much smaller and seems more appropriate for its responsibility. If the class LLNode now has the responsibility of "Being a linked list node," then class DrawableNode has the responsibility of "Being a linked list node that can be drawn." The amount of code and the methods for that, as seen above, seems appropriate for that responsibility.

When we click COMPILE now, with all the files open, it doesn't work. We get a lot of errors. Refactoring doesn't come for free.

- We get two errors in HBranch. The first error looks like this:

```
File: C:\dsBook\java-source-final\HBranch.java
   [line: 47]
Error: incompatible types
found    : LLNode
required: DrawableNode
```

It turns out that there are two errors in the method drawWith that the above error points at, and they're both really the same thing.

```
/**
 * Ask all our children to draw,
 * then tell the next element to draw
 * @param turtle Turtle to draw with
 */
public void drawWith(Turtle turtle) {

    // start with the first child
    DrawableNode current = this.getFirstChild();
```

```
    // Have my children draw
    while (current != null) {
      current.drawWith(turtle);
      turtle.moveTo(turtle.getXPos()+
        gap, turtle.getYPos());
      current = current.getNext();
    }

    // Have my next draw
    if (this.getNext() != null) {
      current = this.getNext();
      current.drawWith(turtle);
    }
  }
```

The problem is that we are going to try to call drawWith() with the object referenced in current which comes from getNext(). The method getNext() now returns type LLNode, yet current is of type DrawableNode. We *need* current to be a DrawableNode—general linked lists don't know how to drawWith(). That's what's meant by INCOMPATIBLE TYPES: getNext() returns an LLNode, and we're stuffing it into a DrawableNode variable. Now, we know that this will always work—all the nodes linked up to a DrawableNode will, in fact, be kinds of DrawableNodes. We have to tell Java that, by *casting*.

```
/**
 * Ask all our children to draw,
 * then tell the next element to draw
 * @param turtle the Turtle to draw with
 */
public void drawWith(Turtle turtle) {

  // start with the first child
  DrawableNode current = this.getFirstChild();

  // Have my children draw
  while (current != null) {
    current.drawWith(turtle);
    turtle.moveTo(turtle.getXPos()+gap,
      turtle.getYPos());
    current = (DrawableNode) current.getNext();
  }

  // Have my next draw
  if (this.getNext() != null) {
    current = (DrawableNode) this.getNext();
    current.drawWith(turtle);
  }
}
```

• The second set of errors is identical to the first, just now in VBranch rather than in HBranch. (This does suggest that the drawWith code in those two classes is nearly identical, and we could further refactor these two classes.) We similarly have incompatible types in drawWith() because our current variable is an instance of DrawableNode but getNext() returns an LLNode. The fix is the same—we add casting.

Fix the drawWith methods in VBranch, HBranch, and Branch to all cast to DrawableNode.

Recompile the class WolfAttackMovie, and run the main method. We are rewarded with scenes of doggies attacking a village until the brave hero appears. We have successfully refactored the DrawableNode class hierarchy.

Making Sound Trees Work Again

Now, let's shift our attention to sound trees. We start with class CollectableNode. Just like with DrawableNode, we take two steps:

- We change the class definition to extend LLNode.
- We remove the linked list code.

Example Java Code 80: CollectableNode, with linked list code factored out

```java
/**
 * Node in a sound tree.
 * @author Mark Guzdial
 * @author Barb Ericson
 */
public abstract class CollectableNode extends LLNode {

  /**
   * No argument constructor
   */
  public CollectableNode() {
    super(); // call to parent class constructor
  }


  /**
   * Play the list of sound elements
   * after me
   */
  public void playFromMeOn() {
    this.collect().play();
  }

  /**
   * Collect all the sounds from me on
   * @return the collected sound
   */
  public abstract Sound collect();

}
```

■

The new version of CollectableNode is even smaller than the new version of DrawableNode. For the most part, all CollectableNode really does is to define playFromMeOn() (which is only a single line) and declare the abstract method collect().

Perhaps surprisingly, when we compile the new CollectableNode and Sound-TreeExample, no errors arise! The error occurs at run-time, when we try to use it:

```
> SoundTreeExample ste = new SoundTreeExample();
> ste.setUp();
NoSuchMethodError: CollectableNode.add
  (LCollectableNode;)V
  at SoundBranch.addChild(SoundBranch.java:58)
  at SoundTreeExample.setUp(SoundTreeExample.java:44)
...
```

So, we open up SoundBranch and recompile that. Now, we get a compiler error in SoundBranch—one we've seen before.

```
File: C:\dsBook\java-source-final\SoundBranch.java
  [line: 41]
Error: incompatible types
found    : LLNode
required: CollectableNode
```

That line is in the method collect(). The line is node=this.getNext();.

```java
/**
 * Collect all the sound from our firstChild,
 * then collect from next.
 * @return the combined sound
 */
public Sound collect() {

  Sound childSound;
  CollectableNode node;

  if (firstChild != null) {
    childSound = firstChild.collect();
  }
  else {
    childSound = new Sound(1);
  }

  // Collect from my next
  if (this.getNext() != null) {
    node=this.getNext(); // the error is here
    childSound=childSound.append(node.collect());
  }

  return childSound;
}
```

The variable node has type CollectableNode, and getNext() (now) returns an LLNode. We can repair this with a simple cast: node = (CollectableNode) this.getNext().

When we try to run the main method in the class SoundTreeExample, we get the next error, at run-time.

```
NoSuchMethodError: ScaleBranch.getNext()
  LCollectableNode;
  at ScaleBranch.collect(ScaleBranch.java:62)
  at SoundBranch.collect(SoundBranch.java:85)
  at SoundBranch.collect(SoundBranch.java:76)
  at SoundTreeExample.main(SoundTreeExample.java:160)
...
```

The error is in ScaleBranch to be sure, and we can probably guess where the error will be. When we compile ScaleBranch, we get a slightly different error:

```
ScaleBranch.java:63: cannot find symbol
symbol  : method collect()
location: class LLNode
```

What this error says is that our code currently asks an LLNode to collect(). But, CollectableNode instances know how to collect(), not LLNode instances. Here's what the actual line looks like.

```
public Sound collect() {

    Sound childSound;

    if (getFirstChild() != null) {
      childSound = getFirstChild().collect().
        scale(factor);
    }
    else {
      childSound = new Sound(1);
    }

    // Collect from my next
    if (this.getNext() != null) {
      Sound nextSound = (this.getNext()).collect();
      childSound = childSound.append(nextSound);
    }

    return childSound;
}
```

This is actually a similar problem as we had earlier, and this needs a similar fix. this.getNext() returns an LLNode, and LLNode instances don't know how to collect(). We need a cast. Because of the statement, the cast looks a little more complex. Let's break this into two lines. First we will get out the next node and then get the collected sound.

```java
public Sound collect() {

    Sound childSound;

    if (getFirstChild() != null) {
      childSound = getFirstChild().collect().
        scale(factor);
    }
    else {
      childSound = new Sound(1);
    }

    // Collect from my next
    if (this.getNext() != null) {
      CollectableNode next = (CollectableNode) this.
        getNext();
      Sound nextSound = next.collect();
      childSound = childSound.append(nextSound);
    }

    return childSound;
  }
```

Now, finally, we can execute the main in SoundTreeExample

```java
public static void main(String[] args) {
  SoundTreeExample tree = new SoundTreeExample();
  tree.setUp();
  tree.getRoot().collect().play();
}
```

We are rewarded with a gong-ing mess of noise. We have successfully refactored both class hierarchies. We have defined a generalized linked list node, removed the linked list content from both class hierarchies, and made everything work again.

10.2   MAKING A NEW KIND OF LIST

Now that we have a generalized LLNode class, we can create new kinds of linked lists easily. We never have to write add() or remove() again. Instead, we simply subclass LLNode. Our subclasses should define the data that we want to store in the linked list.

As an example, let's use the Student class that we defined back in Chapter 2 and create a linked list of students. We define a StudentNode class that extends LLNode and stores a Student instance for each node.

Example Java Code 81: StudentNode class

```java
/**
 * Class that represents a student node
 * in a linked list
 * @author Mark Guzdial
```

```
 6     * @author Barb Ericson
       */
      public class StudentNode extends LLNode {
 8
      /** the student this node is keeping track off */
10    private Student myStudent;

12    /**
       * Constructor that takes the student
14     * @param someStudent the student to store at this node
       */
16    public StudentNode(Student someStudent) {
        super();
18      myStudent = someStudent;
      }
20
      /**
22     * Method to get the student stored at this node
       * @return the student stored at this node
24     */
      public Student getStudent() {return myStudent;}
26
      /**
28     * Method to get information about this node
       * @return an information string
30     */
      public String toString() {
32      if (this.getNext() == null) {
          return "StudentNode with student: " + myStudent;
34      }
        else {
36        return "StudentNode with student: " + myStudent +
            " and next: " + this.getNext();
38      }
      }
40
      /**
42     * Main method for testing
       */
44    public static void main(String[] args) {
        Student student1 = new Student("Tanya Clark",1);
46      Student student2 = new Student("Tim O'Reilly",2);
        Student student3 = new Student("Tesheika Mosely",3);
48      StudentNode node1 = new StudentNode(student1);
        StudentNode node2 = new StudentNode(student2);
50      StudentNode node3 = new StudentNode(student3);
        node1.setNext(node2);
52      node2.setNext(node3);
        StudentNode node = (StudentNode) node1.getNext();
54      node = (StudentNode) node.getNext();
        System.out.println(node.getStudent());
56    }
    }
```

How It Works. The class declaration was obvious: class StudentNode extends LLNode. We declare a private variable myStudent which has a type of Student. Our constructor for StudentNode sets the instance variable to the input student, using the setter that we also define for manipulating the Student in the node.

The `main()` method simply creates a few nodes (with a few students), then prints the last one. However, the simple code above won't work. When we compile it, we get the error:

```
1 error found:
File: C:\dsBook\java-source-final\StudentNode.java
   [line: 61]
Error: cannot find symbol
symbol  : method getStudent()
location: class LLNode
```

We have seen an error like this previously. It is saying that the class LLNode does not understand getStudent(). That's obvious—the question is, "Where are we asking an LLNode to getStudent()?" The error is in the last line of the `main()` method:

```
System.out.println(node1.getNext().getNext().
   getStudent());
```

While `node1` has type StudentNode, we recall that getNext() is in LLNode. It returns an object of type LLNode. The solution, of course, is to cast. We need to cast the result of node1.getNext().getNext() to StudentNode. Here we have rewritten it into two lines to make the casting clear.

```
StudentNode node = (StudentNode)
   node1.getNext().getNext();
System.out.println(node.getStudent());
```

10.3   THE USES AND CHARACTERISTICS OF ARRAYS, LISTS, AND TREES

At this point, we can start to summarize some of the characteristics of the various data elements that we have been discussing up until now. We have learned about arrays, linked lists, and trees.

Arrays are more compact than linked lists or trees. Arrays are just element after element after element in memory. There is no wasted space. Linked lists use additional memory to hold references to the next elements. Trees are even worse because they contain both next and children links.

If arrays are more compact, why would you ever want to use linked lists or trees? We talked about this before, and we summarize those issues here:

- If you don't know the maximum size of the collection of things *a priori*. A linked list or a tree can grow to any size—that's why they are often called *dynamic data structures*.

- If you want to be able to insert into and delete from the middle of the collection easily. It is complicated and computationally expensive (in other words, it takes a lot of time) to move lots of elements around in an array.

- You don't need to have fast access to any particular element.

There are many applications that need these kinds of characteristics.

- Order of video segments when you do non-linear video editing, as in iMovie or Windows Movie Maker. Think about the amount of memory required to store frames in a video—all those pixels, all that sound. For you to be able to drag and drop groups of frames so easily, it cannot be that all the frames are in a big array. It would take much more time to move frames around if that were true.

- Items in a toolbar. Have you ever re-configured your toolbar in an application? You simply drag and drop these icons into the list of icons. As easily as they are rearranged, inserted, and deleted, it is likely that items in a toolbar are stored in a linked list.

- Slides in a PowerPoint presentation. Just as it's too easy to drag segments of video around, it's too easy to drag around sets of slides in the slide organizer in PowerPoint. If slides were stored as an array, you would expect more of a delay as all those pixels and text are moved around, yet it takes no time at all. It's likely that slides are stored in a linked list.

The last point in that list of strengths of linked lists is particularly important: arrays are fast for accessing any element. Accessing the 105th element of an array is no slower than accessing the 5th. On the other hand, accessing the nth element of a linked list requires $O(n)$ accesses—you have to just walk one element to its next.

How about searching? What if you want to find a particular item in an array? If there is no order to the array or list, it is a linear time, $O(n)$ process to find the element—you simply search one piece after another. However, if the array is in a sorted order, you can use a *binary search*. You probably learned about a binary search in your first computing course.

Searching through a dictionary is a good way to describe a binary search. If you want to find a word ("eggplant" for example), you could simply check one page after the next. That's an $O(n)$ search—you just keep checking element after element for n elements. (On average, the word you are looking for will be halfway through the dictionary.) There's a smarter way.

- Open up the dictionary halfway through. Is the word you want on those pages? If not, is it before or after the halfway point? We can only answer this question because we know that a dictionary is in sorted order—"A" is at the beginning and "Z" is at the end.

- Take the first or second half of the dictionary, whichever way the desired word lies, and split that half in half. Ask the same questions: On this page, before, or after?

In general, a binary search lets you find the word in $O(log_2 n)$ tries. Since you split n in half each time, it's at most $log_2 n$ tries to get all the way down to the page where the word is. That's a lot faster than $O(n)$.

You can't get any real efficiencies in searching a linked list. Even if the linked list is in sorted order, you can't get to the middle one (for example) any faster than just checking each node one-at-a-time from the beginning. Thus, there's no good way to search a linked list.

There is some hope for trees, however. If there is no order to the tree, then searching a tree for some element is just as slow as a linked list. There is a way of structuring trees so that they are as fast to search as a binary search on an array. We say more on that in the next subsection.

Examples of Tree Uses

What are trees good for, if they are less compact than arrays and no faster than linked lists? Trees have two huge benefits:

- Trees represent structure. Whether we consider that structure to be a hierarchy or just clustering, the branching character of a tree allows us to represent something that a linked list doesn't.
- Branches in a tree can represent something apart from data, like the operations in our sound and image trees. That is a powerful ability to encode both structure and behavior in the same computational entity.

Some of the things that we can represent in a tree include:

- Representing how parts of music assemble to form a whole—we saw that earlier.
- Representing the elements of a scene (a *scene graph*)—again, we saw this earlier, and we know that that's how professional 3D animators depict scenes.
- Representing the inheritance relationships among classes (a *class hierarchy*). You may not have thought about that when we were describing our classes. Look again at the descriptions of the `DrawableNode` or `CollectableNode` class hierarchies, and you see a clear tree structure.
- Files and directories on your hard disk—directories are essentially branches, files are leaves.
- Elements in an HTML page. If you know HTML, you know that a whole file splits into `<head>` and `<body>`. A `<head>` can contain (for example), a `<title>`. A `<body>` can have any number of sub-components, such as a `<p>` paragraph which can contain `<b>` bold text or `<i>` italicized text. Thus, a document has two main branches, and sub-branches within those branches. That sounds like a tree.
- An organization chart ("orgchart") is clearly a tree (Figure 10.1)—a manager has some number of employees, and there are levels (hierarchies) of management.

An example that might be surprising is that a tree can represent an equation (Figure 10.2). Operators go in the branches and operands (numbers, variables) are in the leaves. In fact, this is how equations are often represented internally within a computer. The nice thing about representing equations with trees is that a simple *inorder traversal* of the tree re-creates the equations *and* in the order that the operations should be performed. For example, in Figure 10.2, we would do the multiplication before the addition, which laws of mathematics would require us to do.

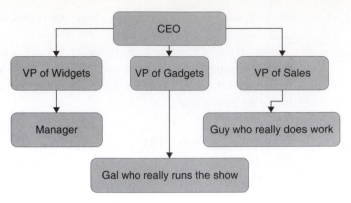

FIGURE 10.1
An example organization chart.

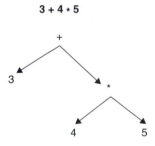

FIGURE 10.2
An equation represented as a tree.

The links in a tree can have meanings. In the examples we have seen already, the links from parent node to child node have different meanings. In a class hierarchy, they indicate that the class represented by the parent node is a superclass of the class represented by the child node. In an organization chart, they indicate the parent is the boss and the children are the employees. In an equation tree, the links indicate that the result from the children will be used in applying the operation in the parent.

We can also use trees to represent *meaning*, where the links represent "the child is similar, but a specific case, of the parent." Consider a tree of words or phrases that represent meaning differences. Figure 10.3 represents a kind of taxonomy, an organization of meanings associated with the concept of "price." The same word "price" might represent what the customer pays versus what another company might pay.

Where might you use such a tree of meanings? Imagine that you want to create a Web site that "*crawls*" (visits and gathers information) various shopping or catalog sites to gather prices, so that you can compare the price of the same product at different sites. Maybe one store calls the price the "price" and the other one calls it the "consumer cost," and you want to avoid the store that talks about "retail price." A tree of meanings

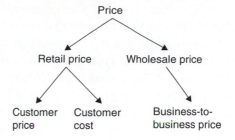

FIGURE 10.3
A tree of meanings.

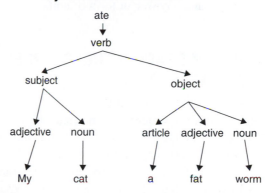

FIGURE 10.4
A sample sentence diagram.

like this can be used to work out how your *Web crawler* program should respond to these different human terms.

For many of you readers, the notion of representing words in trees may be familiar from *sentence diagrams* that you may have used in your primary schooling (Figure 10.4).[1] A sentence diagram explicitly labels the parts of the sentence (e.g., verb, object, subject, predicate phrase, and so on) with the actual words at the leaves or root of the tree—the boundaries.

A sentence diagram actually has computational advantages, too. Imagine that you work for an organization that is concerned with watching for signs of terrorist activity in the United States from captured text messages. Given the amount of captured text messages today, there are probably megabytes and volumes of messages. Do you just search for a phrase like "is going to attack"? How do you deal with synonyms of the word? What you really want to know is if the phrase refers to a location in the United States (and what that location is) as opposed to "is going to attack my homework this evening."

---

[1] There are a wide variety of sentence diagramming techniques and forms. The advantage of this one is that it is certainly unlike any that anyone actually uses.

This problem is actually solvable with trees of the form that we have been talking about in this section. Imagine that you were able to take those enormous text message collections and figure out the meanings of the words so that you could build trees of all the sentences like Figure 10.4. You want to know if "someone" is going to "attack" somewhere in the United States. What if the terrorists use another word for attack? That's where meaning taxonomies as in Figure 10.3 come in. As we find verbs that are similar to attack, we can find them in a taxonomy, and if the other pieces fit (e.g., that the target is somewhere in the United States), we declare a match.

We can do this kind of matching of pieces of various trees with a *unification* algorithm. Unification is very powerful which can match patterns of tree structures and identify where variables in a query match values in other trees. The programming language *Prolog* is actually a language for specifying trees like these, functions as rules on trees, and a powerful form of unification.

10.4 BINARY SEARCH TREES: TREES THAT ARE FAST TO SEARCH

As we said in the previous section, we can structure arrays so that we can search them for something particular (some element) in $O(log_2 n)$. Lists are always $O(n)$ to search. We *can* structure trees in such a way that they are also $O(log_2 n)$ to search. We construct a *binary search tree* out of a *binary tree*.

A binary tree is so named because every branch has at most *two* children (Figure 10.5). We explicitly label the links *left* and *right*. What data is in each of these nodes is left completely open—maybe it's some general string, some objects, some images or sounds, whatever.

The really interesting thing about a binary tree, particularly compared to our trees so far, is that *any* node can be a branch. *Every* node has data associated with it, and a left link, and a right link. That means that any parent node can also be a child node (Figure 10.6). Any branch of a tree, then, is also a tree. It's always the same kinds of objects all the way down. That level of consistency or uniformity can be quite powerful in computation.

Binary trees have a bunch of interesting characteristics that computer scientists have studied over the years. Let's say that you have *n* nodes in a tree. What is the maximum number of levels or generations in that tree? (Think of the number of levels

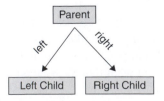

FIGURE 10.5
Simple binary tree.

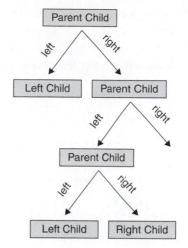

FIGURE 10.6
A more complex binary tree.

or generations as the number of nodes you pass through going from the root of the tree to its farthest away leaf.) Each node could only be linked by the left links, or all by the right links—it's just a linked list. Then the number of levels is n. The *minimum* number of levels, though, is $log_2 n + 1$. Try it—see if you can structure n nodes in fewer levels.

A binary tree is a great example of an Abstract Data Type (ADT). Given what we have seen previously, you can probably imagine much of the definition of a binary tree.

- There is really only one class to define—some kind of `TreeNode`, since we know that all nodes are exactly the same, completely uniform, throughout the tree.

- There must be some way to `getLeft` and `setLeft`, and similarly `getRight` and `setRight`.

- There must be some way to `getData` and `setData`—whatever those data might be. One would probably imagine that the constructor for the node class would take data as input.

- Given that we are going to use this tree for storing data that we can find quickly, we might imagine that there will be a `insert` method that puts a piece of data into the right place in the tree—or maybe we call it an `insertInOrder` method that thus makes it clear that the data inserts in order. We would then (reflectively) expect a `find` method that finds the node that has a particular piece of data.

Given the above, one could start writing programs right now that could use a binary tree—even without seeing the implementation. There actually are several different kinds of implementations of trees. For example, there is an implementation of trees that works in a plain old array by computing indices in a crafty way.[2] The implementation doesn't really matter, as long as the above methods are there and work the way that you expect.

[2]Basically, have an array of strings (for example), and store the left child of index n at $2n$ and the right child at $2n + 1$.

Of course, we are going to implement a binary tree as a `TreeNode` class with object references.

Example Java Code 82: TreeNode, a simple binary tree

```java
/**
 * Class that represents a binary tree node
 * @author Mark Guzdial
 * @author Barb Ericson
 */
public class TreeNode implements BTreeNode {

  /** the data stored at this node */
  private String data;

  /** the left child */
  private TreeNode left;

  /** the right child */
  private TreeNode right;

  /**
   * Constructor that takes the string
   * to store
   * @param something the string to store
   */
  public TreeNode(String something) {
    data = something;
    left = null;
    right = null;
  }

  /**
   * Method to return the data
   * @return the string data at this node
   */
  public String getData() { return data; }

  /**
   * Method to set the data at this node
   * @param something the data to use
   */
  public void setData(String something){data = something;}

  /**
   * Method to get the left child
   * @return the left child (may be null)
   */
  public TreeNode getLeft() {return left;}

  /**
   * Method to get the right child
   * @return the right child (may be null)
   */
  public TreeNode getRight() {return right;}

  /**
   * Method to set the left child
   * @param newLeft the new left child
   */
  public void setLeft(TreeNode newLeft){left = newLeft;}
```

```
58      /**
         * Method to set the right child
60       * @param newRight the new right child
         */
62      public void setRight(TreeNode newRight)
        {right = newRight;}
64
        /**
66       * Method to return a string of information
         * @return the information string
68       */
        public String toString() {
70        return
            "This: " + this.getData()+
72          " Left: " + this.getLeft() +
            " Right: " + this.getRight();
74      }
        }
```

Let's test by building a small tree (just two nodes), and see if it prints correctly.

```
> TreeNode node1 = new TreeNode("George");
> node1 // with no ending ';' it is like a System.
  out.println(node);
This: George Left: null Right: null
> TreeNode node1b = new TreeNode("Alicia");
> node1.setLeft(node1b);
> node1
This: George Left: This: Alicia Left: null Right:
  null Right: null
```

That generally is what we would expect. Now, let's use this binary tree to structure data so that we can search and find things very quickly. The structuring rule for a *binary search tree* is very simple: **The left side data is *less than* the data in the parent node, and the right side data is *greater than or equal to* the data in the parent node**. Structured like that, a binary search tree is like our dictionary—at each branch, we split the dictionary (tree) in half. At least, that's true if the tree is *well-formed*. We say more about a well-formed, *balanced* binary search tree a bit later.

Given the definition of how we want a binary search tree structured, the algorithm for inserting a new piece of data into a binary search tree is about searching for where the data *should* be, if it were there already, then putting it into place. The method insertInOrder is recursive. Because the whole tree is uniform (each parent node is a root of another tree, just a sub-tree of the whole tree's root), we can just pass the buck to the other nodes to do the right thing. The result is that the code is quite short.

How It Works.   First we ask, "Is the value to insert less than the current node's value?" If that's true, we look to see if there is a left branch. If there is, we ask the left branch to insert the data into place—we make a recursive call to insertInOrder. If there is no left branch, we know where to put the data that we want to insert—we insert it on the left. If the value to insert is greater than or equal to the current node's value (which it must be if it's not less-than), then we check to see if there is something on the right branch. If there is, we ask that right branch node to do the `insertInOrder`. If there isn't, bingo! We put the node on the right.

Since we are working on strings here, we are going to have to compare strings in alphabetical order. There is a method on `Strings` to do this: `compareTo()`. The method `compareTo` is sent to a string, and takes a second string as input to the method. The method returns a zero if the two strings are equal (have the same characters), positive if the current string is greater than (alphabetically) the input string, and negative if the current string comes before (is less than) the input string. The value has to do with the number of letters (characters) between the two strings.

```
> "abc".compareTo("abc")
0
> "abc".compareTo("aaa")
1
> "abc".compareTo("bbb")
-1
> "bear".compareTo("bear")
0
> "bear".compareTo("beat")
-2
```

Example Java Code 83: insertInOrder for a binary search tree

```java
/**
 * Method to add a new tree node in the tree
 * @param newOne the node to add
 */
public void insert(TreeNode newOne) {
  /* if the data at this node is greater than the
   * data in the passed node
   */
  if (this.data.compareTo(newOne.data) > 0) {
    // and no left child then add this as the left child
    if (this.getLeft() == null) {
      this.setLeft(newOne);
    }
    // else insert it into the left subtree
    else {
      this.getLeft().insert(newOne);
    }
  }
  // must be great than or equal
  else {
    // if no right child use this as the right child
    if (this.getRight() == null) {
      this.setRight(newOne);
    }
    // else insert into the right subtree
    else {
      this.getRight().insert(newOne);
    }
  }
}
```

Let's try it out:

```
> TreeNode node1 = new TreeNode("Shilpa");
> TreeNode node2 = new TreeNode("Sam");
> TreeNode node3 = new TreeNode("Tina");
> TreeNode node4 = new TreeNode("Zach");
> System.out.println(node1);
This: Shilpa Left: null Right: null
> node1.insert(node2);
> System.out.println(node1);
This: Shilpa Left: This: Sam Left: null Right:
   null Right: null
> node1.insert(node3);
> System.out.println(node1);
This: Shilpa Left: This: Sam Left: null Right:
   null Right: This:
Tina Left: null Right: null
> node1.insert(node4);
> System.out.println(node1);
This: Shilpa Left: This: Sam Left: null Right: null
   Right: This:
Tina Left: null Right: This: Zach Left: null Right:
   null
```

The printing of `node1` at the very end describes the whole tree. It may be hard to understand as such. You might compare it to the drawing of the tree in Figure 10.7.

Now that we have a tree that is formed well for scripting, we can try to write `find()` for this tree. The basic algorithm depends on the same structuring that we talked about earlier: smaller things down the left side, and bigger things down the right. Again, it's recursive because it's working on the uniform structure of the tree.

How It Works.   The method `find()` takes an input string to find. The method asks "Is the input equal to 'me' (`this.getData()`)?" If so, then stop and return this node. If not, then we want to compare the input string to the current data. If it's less, we `find()` down the left branch, and if it is greater than or equal, we search down the right branch.

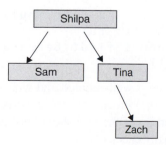

FIGURE 10.7
Tree formed by the names example.

However, if the left or right node isn't there (e.g., we want to `find()` down the left and there is no left node), then we return `null` to indicate that the data was not found.

Example Java Code 84: find, for a binary search tree

```
  /**
2  * Method to find the passed someValue in
   * the tree and return the node or return null
4  * if it isn't found in the tree
   * @param someValue the value to find
6  */
  public TreeNode find(String someValue) {
8    // if we found the value return the node
     if (this.getData().compareTo(someValue) == 0) {
10     return this;
     }
     /* if the data in the current node is greater than
12    * the value */
     if (this.data.compareTo(someValue) > 0) {
14     // if no left child return null (not found)
       if (this.getLeft() == null) {
16       return null;
       }
18     // else look in the left subtree
       else {
20       return this.getLeft().find(someValue);
       }
22   }
     /* the data in the current node is less than the
24    value */
     else {
26     // if no right child then not found
       if (this.getRight() == null) {
28       return null;
       }
30     // look in the right subtree
       else {
32       return this.getRight().find(someValue);
       }
34   }
   }
36 }
```

Let's try it on the tree in Figure 10.7:

```
> node1.find("Tina")
This: Tina Left: null Right: This: Zach Left: null
  Right: null
> node1.find("Barbara")
null
```

If tree is well-ordered and well-structured, then searching in the tree should be an $O(log_2(n))$ process. Each decision splits the amount of data in half. From the top to the bottom of the tree should not take more than $1 + log_2(n)$ steps, so no more than that many checks.

We call that kind of tree *balanced*. A completely valid binary search tree might *not* be balanced—that is, it's *unbalanced*. Figure 10.8 is completely a valid binary

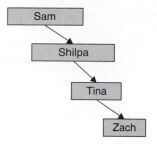

FIGURE 10.8
An unbalanced form of the last binary search tree.

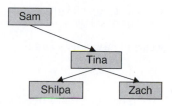

FIGURE 10.9
Rotating the right branch off "Sam."

search tree: no node has more than two children, left is less than the parent, and right is greater than the parent. This is the same tree as in Figure 10.7. How many searches will it take to find "zach" in this tree using `find()`? Just as many nodes as in the tree, n steps (where $n = 4$ here). Since everything is on the right, we just keep checking one node after the other—this is the same as searching a linked list.

What we want is a way of converting an unbalanced tree into a balanced tree, where roughly half of each sub-tree is in the left branch of the sub-tree and the other half is in the right branch of the sub-tree. We are not going to build this algorithm here. The key idea is that we have to *rotate* our nodes. If we were to rotate the right branch off "Sam" in Figure 10.8, we would "rotate up" the node "Tina," moving "Shilpa" to the left and leaving "Zach" on the right. That part isn't hard to understand or even implement. Completely balancing the tree involves rotating left and right to go from Figure 10.8 to Figure 10.7—for example, notice that the node "george" has to become the root of the tree, so another kind of rotation occurs from Figure 10.9 to Figure 10.8.

Traversals of Trees

We can take a binary search tree and print it out in alphabetical order. We use a process called *inorder traversal*—traverse the tree in (alphabetical) order. It's really pretty simple, if we are willing to do it recursively. From each node, the left side has to come before the current (`this`) node, and then the right side should be printed. That would be the order because left is less than `this` data, and right is greater than `this`.

Example Java Code 85: traverse, a binary tree inorder

```
     /**
 2    * Method to do an inorder traversal of the tree
      * @return a string with the data values in it
 4    */
     public String traverse() {
 6     String returnValue = "";

 8     // Visit left
       if (this.getLeft() != null) {
10       returnValue += " " + this.getLeft().traverse();
       }
12     // Visit me
       returnValue += " " + this.getData();

14
       // Visit right
16     if (this.getRight() != null) {
         returnValue += " " + this.getRight().traverse();
18     }
       return returnValue;
20   }
```

Let's try it on our binary tree from Figure 10.7:

```
> node1.traverse()
  Sam Shilpa  Tina   Zach
```

Do we have to do it that way? Of course not! We could visit ourself, then the left and then right. That's called *preorder traversal*. We could also visit the left and then the right, and then ourself. That's called *postorder traversal*. We can think about other orderings as well.

Doing an inorder traversal of a tree makes sense. One can imagine wanting a list of everything in a tree. When we are working with trees of names, doing a preorder or postorder traversal doesn't make much sense. However, it does make sense when there are certain other things in the tree, like the equation tree we saw earlier (Figure 10.2).

Here's an example of the power of different traversals on this kind of tree. If you do an inorder traversal of the equation tree Figure 10.10, you get $(3 * 4) + (x * y)$. That is fine and useful—that is an equation that makes sense. If you do a preorder traversal of the same tree, you get $34 * xy * +$. That may look like gibberish *unless* you have ever used a *reverse Polish notation (RPN)* calculator, like some of Hewlett-Packard's popular calculators. The equation $34 * xy * +$ means "Push a 3 on the *stack*, then a 4,

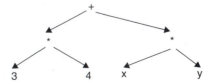

FIGURE 10.10
An equation tree for different kinds of traversals.

multiply two things on the stack and push the result back on the stack. Push the value of x on the stack, then y, multiply the two things on the stack and push the result back. Finally, add the two things on the stack and push the result back on." This turns out to be an efficient way of doing the same computation. A preorder traversal of the same equation tree gives you the RPN form of the equation.

Trees Can Do Anything

We now know a bunch of things that trees can do well:

- It is easy to do useful things with them.
  - Searching is quick.
  - We can use them to evaluate equations.
- Operations on trees are easily written, small, and recursive.
- We know interesting facts about them.

Binary trees can actually do just about anything. A binary tree can represent an n-ary tree, like the ones we used in earlier chapters. A binary tree can even be a list.

Imagine that we want a list (an ordered group of items) where we can add things to the front or end of the list. We can implement that with a linked list, of course. We can also implement this same structure with a binary tree. We make the structuring assumption that *earlier* items are to the left, and *later* items go to the right—a similar assumption to how we made a binary search tree. Here are the methods for doing that, addFirst() and addLast().

Example Java Code 86: addFirst and addLast, treating a tree as a list

```java
/**
 * Method to add the newOne node as
 * the first node in the tree (treating
 * the tree like a list
 * @param newOne the new node to add
 */
public void addFirst(TreeNode newOne) {
  if (this.getLeft() == null) {
    this.setLeft(newOne);
  }
  else {
    this.getLeft().addFirst(newOne);
  }
}

/**
 * Method to add the newNode as the last
 * node in a list (treating the tree like a list)
 * @param newOne the node to add
 */
public void addLast(TreeNode newOne) {
  if (this.getRight() == null) {
    this.setRight(newOne);
  }
```

```
26        else {
            this.getRight().addLast(newOne);
          }
28      }
```

■

```
> TreeNode node1 = new TreeNode("the");
> node1.addFirst(new TreeNode("George of"));
> node1.addLast(new TreeNode("jungle"));
> node1.traverse()
"  George of the  jungle"
```

While binary trees are simple, they are actually quite powerful. There is great power in having a uniform structure—it allows us to write code in short form that actually works. By simply choosing the meaning of our left and right links, we can represent a wide variety of things. This chapter explains some of these.

EXERCISES

10.1   Create an interface to define the ADT binary tree node. Modify the TreeNode class to implement this interface.

10.2   Create a class LinkedList that has in it a reference to the first (head) LLNode in the list. Add methods to insert new nodes at the front of the linked list. Add methods to remove any node in the linked list (including the head).

10.3   Modify the TreeNode class to allow the data to be any object that implements the Comparable interface. Create examples to test this out with different kinds of objects that implement the interface Comparable.

10.4   Modify the LLNode class to store data at the node. Let the data be of any type that implements the Comparable interface. Create examples to test this new functionality.

10.5   How long does it take to insert an object into an array? How long does it take to insert an object into a balanced and sorted binary tree? How long does it take to find an object in an unsorted array? How long does it take to find an object in a balanced and sorted binary tree?

10.6   How would you rewrite VBranch and HBranch so that there is less duplicated code between them? Could you have a general LayoutBranch that calls some method for changing the (x, y) positions, then subclass that to create VBranch and HBranch? Refactor these methods so that there is less duplicated code.

10.7   Use the same approach for rewriting SoundBranch and ScaleBranch so that there is less duplicated code.

10.8   (Advanced) Investigate the Java notion of an interface. Can you come up with a LLBranch interface that all our branches (Branch, VBranch, HBranch,

SoundBranch, and ScaleBranch) might implement so as to reduce the duplication of code? You might also investigate the *design pattern* called "*Visitor*." Can you use that to make tree traversals more common?

10.9   Trace out insert and how it walks through an example tree in order to insert a new piece of data.

10.10   Draw the tree that results from the following code.

```
> TreeNode node1 = new TreeNode("Green");
> TreeNode node2 = new TreeNode("Blue");
> TreeNode node3 = new TreeNode("Yellow");
> TreeNode node4 = new TreeNode("Black");
> TreeNode node5 = new TreeNode("Red");
> node1.insert(node2);
> node1.insert(node3);
> node1.insert(node4);
> node1.insert(node5);
```

10.11   Draw the tree that results from the following code.

```
> TreeNode node1 = new TreeNode("Zebra");
> TreeNode node2 = new TreeNode("Lion");
> TreeNode node3 = new TreeNode("Cow");
> TreeNode node4 = new TreeNode("Chicken");
> TreeNode node5 = new TreeNode("Alligator");
> node1.insert(node2);
> node1.insert(node3);
> node1.insert(node4);
> node1.insert(node5);
```

10.12   Draw the tree that results from the following code.

```
> TreeNode node1 = new TreeNode("Apple");
> TreeNode node2 = new TreeNode("Grape");
> TreeNode node3 = new TreeNode("Pear");
> TreeNode node4 = new TreeNode("Plum");
> TreeNode node5 = new TreeNode("Watermelon");
> node1.insert(node2);
> node1.insert(node3);
> node1.insert(node4);
> node1.insert(node5);
```

10.13   Write a preorder traversal for the binary tree.

10.14   Write a postorder traversal for the binary tree.

10.15   Given the following tree, show the output for each type of traversal.

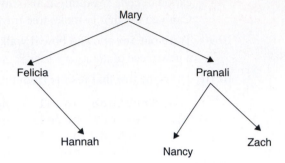

10.16   Write a level-order traversal that does each level of a binary tree before moving on to the next level. Starting with the root, add the children nodes to a list, add the current data to the string, and then process the first item in the list in a recursive fashion.

10.17   Trace out the right calls to `insertInOrder` for a set of eight words that result in (a) an unbalanced tree with all words down the right branch, (b) an unbalanced tree with all words down the left branch, and (c) a balanced tree.

10.18   (Advanced) Write the method `balance()` for a generic binary search tree that produces a balanced tree.

10.19   (Advanced) Read about Red-Black trees. How are these different from binary trees?

10.20   Write `addFirst()` and `addLast()` for `LLNode` so that all our linked lists can add to the front or end.

11

Abstract Data Types: Separating the Meaning from the Implementation

11.1 INTRODUCING STACKS

11.2 INTRODUCING QUEUES

11.3 USING AN ARRAYLIST

11.4 USING A MAP ADT

Chapter Learning Objectives

One of the most powerful ideas in computer science is that the *definition* of a data structure can be entirely separated from the *implementation* of the data structure. This idea is powerful because it allows us to design and write code that uses the given data structure (1) without knowing the implementation of the data structure and (2) even if the implementation of the data structure changes.

The computer science goals for this chapter are:

- To explain the separation of definition and implementation.
- To explain the definition of a queue and offer two implementations of a queue.
- To explain the definition of a stack and offer two implementations of a stack.
- To show an example of using a map.
- To use an `ArrayList`.
- To create and implement an interface. To create an abstract class. To contrast an interface with an abstract class.

The media learning goal for this chapter is:

- To reverse the elements in a list more efficiently using a stack.

11.1 INTRODUCING STACKS

A *stack* is a data structure that corresponds to how a stack (literally!) of plates work. Imagine a stack of plates (Figure 11.1). You only put new plates on a stack from the top. You *can* insert plates in the middle, but not easily, and you risk scraping the plates. You only remove plates from a stack from the top. Removing from the middle or (worse yet) the bottom is dangerous and risks damaging the whole stack.

FIGURE 11.1
A pile of plates—only put on the top, never remove from the bottom.

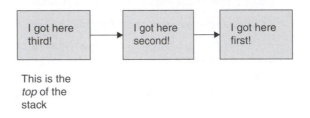

This is the
top of the
stack

FIGURE 11.2
Later items are at the head (top) of stack.

Those basic notions of how a physical stack works corresponds to how the stack data structure works. Think of a stack as a list of elements—just a sequence of items. (Are the items in a linked list? An array? We are *explicitly* not saying at this point.) The first item pushed on the stack stays at the bottom of the stack. Later items are put at the top of the stack (Figure 11.2).

New items are added to the top of the stack (Figure 11.3). When a new item is removed from the stack, it is always the last, newest item in the list which is removed first (Figure 11.4). For that reason, a stack is sometimes also called a *LIFO list*—Last In, First Out. The last item inserted into the stack is the first one back out.

Defining an Abstract Data Type

A stack is an example of an *Abstract Data Type*. An abstract data type (ADT) defines the operations, structure, and behavior of a data structure *without* specifying how those

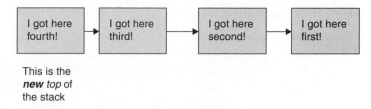

This is the
***new** top* of
the stack

FIGURE 11.3
New items are inserted at the top (head) of the stack.

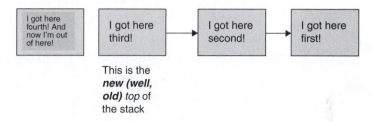

This is the
***new (well,
old)** top* of
the stack

FIGURE 11.4
Items are removed from the top (head) of a stack.

operations, structure, and behavior are actually implemented. By separating the concerns of *what* is supposed to happen from *how* it is supposed to happen, the task of programming with that data type is made easier.

There are formal ways of defining an ADT. These formal methods use symbols and logical equations to define behavior and structure without getting into the implementation. That isn't our focus here. Instead, we will focus on a general notion of how the ADT works.

What should someone be able to do with a stack data structure? Here is a list of basic operations for a stack with a brief description of what each does. If we got these right, these should mesh with the intuitive understanding of stacks described previously.

- push(element): Tack a new element onto the top of the stack.
- pop(): Pull the top (head) element off the stack.
- peek(): Get the top of the stack, but don't remove it from the stack.
- size(): Return the number of elements in the stack.
- isEmpty(): Returns true if the size of the stack is zero—when nothing is in the stack.

Computer Science Idea: Separation of Concerns

By separating the definition of the data structure from the implementation, we can use the new data structure in programs without regard for its implementation. An important implication is that the implementation can be changed (improved, upgraded, whatever) and the programs that use the data structure will only have to change the name of the class that implements the new data structure.

A Stack Interface

Java actually includes a Stack class that uses a Vector to implement a stack. We are going to create a Stack interface in order to separate the description of the data type from the implementation. In Java, one can define an interface. An interface is like an abstract class in that it defines a set of methods and no one can instantiate an object of the interface type. An interface is just the definition of the operations of an ADT, like those we just defined for a stack. A particular class can declare that it implements a given interface. That implementation is then a promise, a contract with programs that use the particular class—that the methods in the interface are implemented and implemented properly so that the operation of the data type works.

Example Java Code 87: A Stack Abstract Data Type (Interface)

```java
/**
 * An abstract definition of a stack
 * @author Barb Ericson
 */
public interface Stack <E> {

  /**
   * Method to add the element to the top of the stack
   * @param element the element to add
   */
  public void push(E element);

  /**
   * Method to return the top element on the
   * stack, but not remove it from the stack
   * @return the top object from the stack
   */
  public E peek();

  /**
   * Method to remove the top element from the
   * stack and return it
   * @return the top element from the stack
   */
  public E pop();

  /**
   * Method to return the number of elements in
   * the stack
   * @return the number of elements in the stack

   */
  public int size();

  /**
   * Method to check if the stack is empty
   * @return true if empty, else false
   */
  public boolean isEmpty();
}
```

An interface defines the methods that classes that implement the interface must have. All of the methods defined in an interface are public and abstract. An abstract method usually has the keyword `abstract` in the method signature, but in an interface, you don't have to specify the `abstract` keyword.

Notice the use of the type E and the generic `Stack<E>`. Starting with Java 1.5 (also called Java 5), generics are used to allow the programmer to specify the type of objects in a collection. So, instead of specifying the type as `Object`, we are using the type E to represent the type given during the creation of the stack. This lets us use the compiler to check that we are putting the correct types into collections and removes the need to downcast from `Object` to a more specific type when returning objects from collections.

Let's implement this interface in a couple of different ways.

Multiple Implementations of a Stack

The two most common implementations of stacks use linked lists and arrays. Let's look at each of those. First, we will implement a stack with a linked list, where we will use Java's provided implementation of a linked list. Yes, Java has a linked list in the `java.util` package! How is it implemented? Is it a singly or doubly linked list? We don't know and we don't care—that's separation of concerns. A bigger question is why we haven't been using Java's linked list all along? We'll explain that when we get to simulations.

Example Java Code 88: Stack implemented with a linked list

```java
import java.util.LinkedList; // Need for LinkedList

/**
 * Class that represents a stack using a linked list
 * of objects
 * @author Mark Guzdial
 * @author Barb Ericson
 */
public class LinkedListStack <E> implements Stack <E> {

    /** Where we store the elements */
    private LinkedList<E> elements;

    /**
     * Constructor that takes no arguments
     */
    public LinkedListStack() {
        elements = new LinkedList<E>();
    }

    //// Methods ///

    /**
     * Method to add an element to the stack
     * @param element the element to add
     */
    public void push(E element) {
        // New elements go at the front
        elements.addFirst(element);
    }

    /**
     * Method to return the top element on the stack
```

```
34      * but leave the element on the stack
        * @return the top element on the stack
36      */
      public E peek() {
38        return elements.getFirst();
      }
40
      /**
42      * Method to remove the top element from a stack
        * and return it
44      * @return the top element from the stack and remove it
        */
46      public E pop() {
        E toReturn = this.peek();
48        elements.removeFirst();
        return toReturn;
50      }

52      /**
        * Method to get the number of elements in the stack
54      * @return the number of elements in the stack
        */
56      public int size(){return elements.size();}

58      /**
        * Method to test if the stack is empty
60      * @return true if the stack is empty, else false
        */
62      public boolean isEmpty() {
        return (size() == 0);
64      }
      }
```

How It Works. The class definition includes the `implements` keyword followed by the name of the interface it implements. In this implementation, we have decided that the head of the stack is the first item in the linked list. Java's linked list implementation provides a `getFirst` and an `addFirst` method—the former is the heart of `peek` and the latter is how we `push`. Since we have `removeFirst` too, that's how we `pop`. It is interesting that the definition of `isEmpty` just uses the `size` method which is part of the `Stack` interface.

Java's linked list implementation can actually store any object. Its implementation works around the class `Object`. Every class (even if it declares no superclass) is a subclass of `Object`. Thus, an `Object` variable can hold anything.

Let's try out our stack.

```
> Stack<String> stack = new LinkedListStack<String>();
> stack.push("This")
> stack.push("is")
> stack.push("a")
> stack.push("test")
> stack.size()
4
```

```
> stack.peek()
"test"
> stack.pop()
"test"
> stack.pop()
"a"
> stack.pop()
"is"
> stack.pop()
"This"
```

In this example, we created a stack of string objects. Since our stack can hold any object, we can create stacks that can hold any kind of objects.

```
> Stack<Picture> stack =
  new LinkedListStack<Picture>();
> stack.push(new Picture
  (FileChooser.getMediaPath("beach.jpg")));
> stack.push(new Picture
  (FileChooser.getMediaPath("arch.jpg")));
> stack.push(new Picture
  (FileChooser.getMediaPath("bridge.jpg")));
> stack.size()
3
> stack.peek()
Picture, filename C:\dsBook\media-source/bridge.jpg
height 640 width 480
> stack.pop()
Picture, filename C:\dsBook\media-source/bridge.jpg
height 640 width 480
> stack.pop()
Picture, filename C:\dsBook\media-source/arch.jpg
height 480 width 360
> stack.pop()
Picture, filename C:\dsBook\media-source/beach.jpg
height 480 width 640
```

This example created a stack of pictures. We can create a stack of any kind of object and we can specify the type of objects that can be placed in the stack using generics.

Notice that you can declare a variable to be of the type Stack<String>, but you must create the stack object using a name of a class that implements the interface LinkedListStack<String>. You cannot create an object using an interface name (new Stack<String>()), just as you cannot create an object of an abstract class. Why would you want to declare a variable to be of the interface type? If you use the interface name everywhere but where you create the actual object, then you only have one thing to change if you later decide to use another class that implements the same interface.

Here's a different implementation, using an array. We will use an array of Object instances, so that we can store anything we want in our stack. In this example, the class ArrayStack has an index in the array for a top.

Example Java Code 89: Stack implemented with an array—declaration, fields, and constructor

```
    /**
2    * Implementation of a stack as an array
     * @author Mark Guzdial
4    * @author Barb Ericson
     */
6   public class ArrayStack<E> implements Stack<E> {

8     /** default size of the array */
      private static final int ARRAY_SIZE = 20;
10
      /** Where we'll store our elements */
12    private Object[] elements;

14    /** Index where the top of the stack is */
      private int top;
16
      /**
18     * No argument constructor
       */
20    public ArrayStack() {
        elements = new Object[ARRAY_SIZE];
22      top = 0;
      }
```

■

Here, the variable `elements` is an array of objects. You can't create an array of a generic type since the generic type isn't known at run-time. This will cause a warning when we compile it, but that can be ignored. We have a constant `static final` variable that declares that our array will have at most 20 elements in it. To create an `ArrayStack`, we create an array of `Objects`, and set the top at element index zero.

Example Java Code 90: Stack implemented with an array—methods

```
    //// Methods ///
2
    /**
4    * Method to add an element to the top of the stack
     * @param element the element to add
6    */
    public void push(E element) {
8
      // New elements go at the top
10    elements[top]=element;
      // then add to the top
12    top++;
      if (top==ARRAY_SIZE) {
14      System.out.println("Stack overflow!");
      }
16  }

    /**
18   * Method to return the top element on the stack
     * but not remove it.
20   * @return the object at the top of the stack
     */
22  public E peek() {
```

```
24      if (top==0) {
          System.out.println("Stack empty!");
26        return null;
        } else {
28        // this will give a warning but it is unavoidable
          return (E) elements[top-1];
30      }
      }

32
      /**
34     * Method to remove and return the top element on the stack
       * @return the element on the top of the stack
36     */
      public E pop() {
38      E toReturn = this.peek();
        top--;
40      return toReturn;
      }

42
      /**
44     * Method to return the number of elements in the stack
       * @return the number of elements in the stack
46     */
      public int size(){return top;}

48
      /**
50     * Method to check if the stack is empty
       * @return true if the stack is empty else false
52     */
      public boolean isEmpty() {return this.size() == 0;}

54
    }
```

How It Works.   In this implementation, the variable `top` is an index to the next *empty* element in the array. The size is then the same as the index. To insert a new element, we set the value at `elements[top]` and increment `top`. The top value is at `elements [top-1]`. To remove an element, we decrement `top`.

We can now test `ArrayStack` and find that it works remarkably like our `LinkedList-Stack`. When we first create an instance of `ArrayStack`, it looks like Figure 11.5. After we push "`Matt`" on the stack, it looks like Figure 11.6—the variable `top` always points

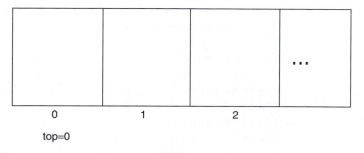

FIGURE 11.5
An empty stack as an array.

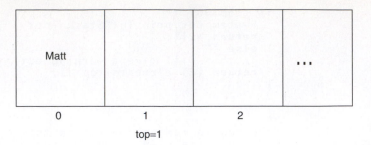

FIGURE 11.6
After pushing Matt onto the stack-as-an-array.

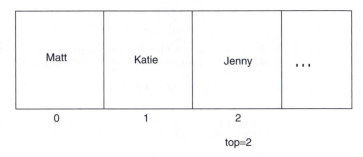

FIGURE 11.7
After pushing Katie and Jenny, then popping Jenny.

at the *next* element on the stack. We then push "Katie" and "Jenny," then pop "Jenny," resulting in Figure 11.7—Jenny is still in the array, but since top points at that element, Jenny will be over-written with the next push().

```
> Stack<String> stack = new ArrayStack<String>();
> stack.push("Matt");
> stack.push("Katie");
> stack.push("Jenny");
> stack.size() // without the ending ';'
  it prints out the result 3
> stack.peek() // without the ending ';'
  it prints out the result
"Jenny"
> stack.pop()
"Jenny"
> stack.pop()
"Katie"
> stack.pop()
"Matt"
```

Again notice that we declared the variable stack to be of type Stack even though we create an object of the class ArrayStack. Again this makes it easier to write code that only requires one change if we choose to use another class that implements the same interface.

There are problems with using `ArrayStack` as an implementation of a stack. For example, what happens if you need more than 20 elements in your stack? And actually, it's 19 elements—`top` always points at an unused cell. However, within the limitations of `ArrayStack` (e.g., as long as you have fewer than 20 elements in the stack), it is a perfectly valid implementation of a stack. Both `LinkedListStack` and `ArrayStack` are implementations of the same stack ADT which is defined in the interface `Stack`.

Uses of a Stack

We haven't seen enough algorithms yet to be able to describe many uses of stacks, though they are quite useful. For example, the process of converting an equation like `4 * sin(x/2)` into operations that a computer can execute uses a stack. Many programs that offer the ability to undo commands use a stack. Programs that simulate card games often have a draw stack of cards and a discard stack. There is one use of a stack that we have already seen a need for—reversing a list. For example, you might keep a list of all the music you play on a radio station and want to print out the list from most recent played to first played on the station's Web site so that people can find information on songs they just heard.

Below is the method that we wrote previously for reversing a list.

Example Java Code 91: Reverse a list—repeated

```java
/**
 * Reverse the list starting at this,
 * and return the last element of the list.
 * The last element becomes the FIRST element
 * of the list, and THIS points to null.
 */
public LayeredSceneElement reverse() {
  LayeredSceneElement reversed, temp;

  // Handle the first node outside the loop
  reversed = this.last();
  this.remove(reversed);

  while (this.getNext() != null) {
    temp = this.last();
    this.remove(temp);
    reversed.add(temp);
  }

  // Now put the head of the old list on the end of
  // the reversed list.
  reversed.add(this);

  // At this point, reversed
  // is the head of the list
  return reversed;
}
```

■

The current `reverse` method is awfully inefficient. To get each item in the list, it goes to the `last()` (which requires touching every element in the list), removes it (which involves touching every node in order to find the one before the one we want to remove), and then adds it to the end of the reversed list (by walking all the elements of the reversed list to get the last). Overall, touching each node of n nodes requires touching every other node at least once, meaning that it's an $O(n^2)$ algorithm.

We can do this much faster with a stack. We simply walk the list pushing everything onto the stack. We pop them off again, and they assemble in reversed order.

Example Java Code 92: Reverse with a stack

```
   /**
2   * Reverse2: Push all the elements on
    * the stack, then pop all the elements
4   * off the stack.
    */
6   public LayeredSceneElement reverse2() {
      LayeredSceneElement reversed, current, popped;
8     Stack<LayeredSceneElement> stack =
        new LinkedListStack<LayeredSceneElement>();
10
      // Push all the elements on the list
12    current=this;
      while (current != null)
14    {
        stack.push(current);
16      current = current.getNext();
      }
18
      // Make the last element (current top of stack)
20    // into new first
      reversed = stack.pop();
22
      // Now, pop them all onto the list
24    current = reversed;
      while (stack.size()>0) {
26      popped = stack.pop();
        current.insertAfter(popped);
28      current = popped;
      }
30    return reversed;
    }
```

There is a big difference in execution time here. Each node is touched exactly twice—once going on the stack, and once coming off. There is no `last` nor `remove` here to cause us extra traversals of the list. This is an $O(n)$ algorithm—much faster than the last one.

Does that really matter? If you really needed to reverse a linked list, does $O(n)$ or $O(n^2)$ matter? Couldn't you just re-create the linked list, even, rather than reverse it? There are situations where the size of the list does matter.

Consider a scene from Pixar's *The Incredibles*, where the monorail enters the bad guy's lair through a waterfall that parts (incredible!) to allow the monorail entry. Each droplet in that scene was modeled as an object that was nearly transparent—it showed up only one-millionth of a bit of color. Thus, everywhere that looks white (which is nearly everywhere in a waterfall scene) is actually over one million objects stacked up at that spot on the screen.

Now, imagine that those droplets are stored in a linked list, and the director says "Ooh! Oooh! Now, let's show the waterfall from the *inside* as the monorail passes through!" At that point, you have to reverse the linked list. You could re-create the list— but that is a big list to re-create. If your algorithm is $O(n)$, that's a million steps per screen element. That's a lot of processing, but not insurmountable. If your algorithm is $O(n^2)$, that's a million-*squared* operations per screen element—one trillion operations per pixel. Computers are fast. But, computers are not infinitely fast.

11.2   INTRODUCING QUEUES

A *queue* is another useful ADT. A queue models what the British call "a queue," and what we in the United States call "a line." A queue is a *FIFO list, First In First Out list*. The first one in the line is the first one served. When someone new comes into the line, the bouncer at the front of the line yells out, "Get in the back of the line!" New elements enter at the end, not at the front, never in the middle (that's called "cutting in the line").

Unlike a stack, which just has a *head* or *top*, a queue has both a *head* and a *tail* (Figure 11.8). Elements are popped from the *head* (Figure 11.9). When a new element comes in, it gets pushed onto the queue at the *tail* (Figure 11.10).

The basic operations of a queue are pretty similar to those of a stack.

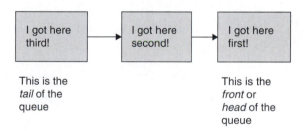

FIGURE 11.8
A basic queue.

FIGURE 11.9
Elements are removed from the top or head of the queue.

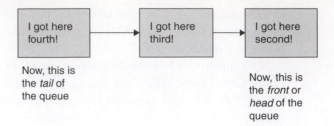

FIGURE 11.10
New elements are pushed onto the tail of the queue.

- push(element): Tack a new element onto the tail (end) of the queue.
- pop(): Pull the top (head) element off the queue.
- peek(): Get the head of the queue, but don't remove it from the queue.
- size(): Return the size of the queue.
- isEmpty(): Return true or false, if the size of the queue is zero.

Java actually defines an interface for a Queue. But, let's define our own interface to represent this ADT.

Example Java Code 93: A Queue Abstract Data Type (Interface)

```
/**
 * Interface to define an abstract queue
 * @author Barb Ericson
 */
public interface Queue<E> {

  /**
   * Push an element onto the tail of the Queue
   * @param element the element to add to the queue
   */
  public void push(E element);

  /**
   * Peek at, but don't remove, the head of the queue
   * @return the head of the queue (top)
   */
  public E peek();

  /**
   * Pop an object from the Queue
   * @return the head (top) of the queue and
   * remove it from the queue
   */
  public E pop();

  /**
   * Return the size of a queue
   * @return the number of elements in the queue
   */
  public int size();
```

```
32      /**
         * Method to see if the queue is empty
34       * @return true if the queue is empty, else false
         */
36      public boolean isEmpty();
    }
```

Implementing a Queue

We can implement a queue using either a linked list, or an array—just like we did
with stack. A linked list implementation of a queue is again made very easy by Java's
LinkedList implementation.

Example Java Code 94: A Queue implemented as a linked list

```
     import java.util.*; // LinkedList representation
2
     /**
4     * Implements a simple queue using a linked list
      * @author Mark Guzdial
6     * @author Barb Ericson
      */
8    public class LinkedListQueue<E> extends AbstractQueue<E> {

10      /** Where we'll store our elements */
        private LinkedList<E> elements;
12
        /**
14       * No argument constructor
         */
16      public LinkedListQueue() {
          elements = new LinkedList<E>();
18      }

20      /// Methods

22      /**
         * Push an element onto the tail of the Queue
24       * @param element the element to add to the queue
         */
26      public void push(E element) {
          elements.addFirst(element);
28      }

30      /**
         * Peek at, but don't remove, top (first) of queue
32       * @return the first object in the queue
         */
34      public E peek() {
          return elements.getLast();
36      }

38      /**
         * Pop an object from the Queue
40       * @return the top object from the queue (and remove it)
         */
42      public E pop() {
          E toReturn = this.peek();
44        elements.removeLast();
          return toReturn;
46      }
```

```
     /**
48    * Return the size of a queue
      * @return the number of elements in the queue
50    */
     public int size() { return elements.size(); }
52
     /**
54    * Method to see if the queue is empty
      * @return true if the queue is empty, else false
56    */
     public boolean isEmpty() { return size() == 0; }
58
     }
```

◾

Let's try this out.

```
> Queue<String> line = new LinkedListQueue<String>();
> line.push("Fred");
> line.push("Mary");
> line.push("Jose");
> line.size()
3
> line.peek() // without ending ';' prints the result
"Fred"
> line.pop()
"Fred"
> line.peek()
"Mary"
> line.pop()
"Mary"
> line.peek()
"Jose"
> line.pop()
"Jose"
```

How It Works.   In this implementation of a queue, the elements are stored in an instance of Java's `LinkedList`. The front of the linked list is the tail of the queue, so that we can add new elements easily to the back of the queue. The last of the linked list is the head, since the first element out of a queue is the first element that you put in. (That may seem backwards, but any arrangement of head/tail to front/back is arbitrary. That one might find an implementation confusing is yet another good reason for separating the concerns.) To pop the stack then requires removing the last (`removeLast`), and to push is adding to the first (`addFirst`).

The critical issue in implementing a queue is that, from the perspective of the use of the queue, the implementation doesn't matter. As long as those same basic operations are available, the implementation of the queue can be swapped out, improved, made faster (or slower, for that matter)—and it just doesn't matter to the program using the queue.

An obvious alternative to the linked list implementation seen above is an implementation based on an array. Implementing a queue using an array to store the elements is much the same as implementing a stack with an array except that, as before, we need both a head and a tail.

Example Java Code 95: A Queue implemented as an array

```java
/**
 * Implements a simple queue using an array
 * @author Mark Guzdial
 * @author Barb Ericson
 */
public class ArrayQueue<E> extends AbstractQueue<E> {

  /** constant for the size of the queue */
  private static final int ARRAY_SIZE = 20;

  /** Where we'll store our elements */
  private Object[] elements;

  /** The index of the head */
  private int head;

  /** The index of the tail */
  private int tail;

  /**
   * No argument constructor
   */
  public ArrayQueue() {
    elements = new Object[ARRAY_SIZE];
    head = 0;
    tail = 0;
  }

  /// Methods

  /**
   * Push an element onto the tail of the Queue
   * @param element the element to add to the queue
   */
  public void push(E element) {
    if ((tail + 1) >= ARRAY_SIZE) {
      System.out.println
        ("Queue underlying implementation failed");
    }
    else {
      // Store at the tail,
      // then increment to a new open position
      elements[tail] = element;
      tail++;
    }
  }

  /**
   * Peek at, but don't remove, the head of the queue
   * @return the head of the queue (top)
   */
  public E peek() {
    // this will give a warning but there is no way around it
    return (E) elements[head];
  }
```

```
58  /**
     * Pop an object from the Queue
     * @return the head (top) of the queue and
60   * remove it from the queue
     */
62  public E pop() {
      E toReturn = this.peek();
64    if (((head + 1) >= ARRAY_SIZE) ||
          (head > tail)) {
66      System.out.println("Queue underlying "+
          "implementation failed.");
68      return toReturn;
      }
70    else {
        // Increment the head forward, too.
72      head++;
        return toReturn;
74    }
    }
76
    /**
78   * Return the size of a queue
     * @return the number of elements in the queue
80   */
    public int size() { return tail-head;}
82
    /**
84   * Method to see if the queue is empty
     * @return true if the queue is empty, else false
86   */
    public boolean isEmpty() { return size() == 0; }
88
  }
```

■

Let's try this out.

```
> Queue<String> line = new ArrayQueue<String>();
> line.push("Fred");
> line.push("Mary");
> line.push("Jose");
> line.size()
3
> line.peek() // without ending ';' prints the result
"Fred"
> line.pop()
"Fred"
> line.peek()
"Mary"
> line.pop()
"Mary"
> line.peek()
"Jose"
> line.pop()
"Jose"
```

How It Works. Each of the `head` and `tail` variables holds an index number on the underlying array. The size of the queue is the difference between the *head* and the *tail*. When the queue is first created, both the *head* and the *tail* are zero, the first cell in the array (Figure 11.11). When we push something on, the *tail* increments to the next empty cell in the array (which has been implemented as the `head` variable in this implementation, Figures 11.12 and 11.13). Popping from the *head* increments it (again, variable `tail` in this implementation, Figure 11.14).

The problems caused by implementing queues as arrays are even greater than the ones caused by implementing stacks as arrays, because now we have both a head and a tail to keep track of. Notice that the head and tail keep moving along the array, so the implementation can't even store 20 elements at once. It can only store 20 elements *ever*—once we get past 20, both head and tail are at the end of the array. There are implementations of queues in arrays that are smarter than this one. For example, there's no reason why we can't wrap around the queue—once we increment past the end, just start re-using cells at the beginning of the array. It's a little trickier to make sure that the head and tail don't overlap one another. Then, the 20 element limitation is just the number of items at once, which isn't unreasonable.

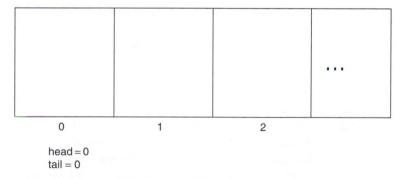

head = 0
tail = 0

FIGURE 11.11
When the queue-as-array starts out, head and tail are both zero.

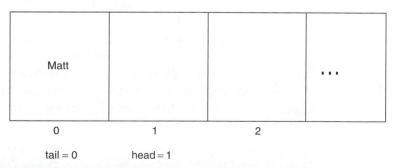

tail = 0   head = 1

FIGURE 11.12
Pushing Matt onto the queue moves up the head to the next empty cell.

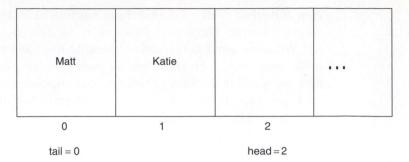

FIGURE 11.13
Pushing Katie on moves the head further right.

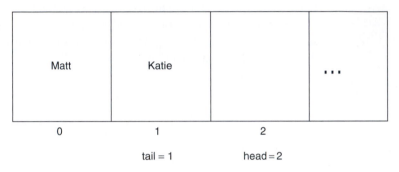

FIGURE 11.14
Popping Matt moves the tail up to Katie.

We haven't seen ways to use a queue yet. Queues will become very important when we create discrete event simulations. When several agents want the same resource (e.g., when customers line up at the cashier station, when movie goers line up at the ticket office), they form a line. We will need queues for modeling those lines.

Creating an Abstract Queue Class

Did you notice that the `isEmpty` method was the same for both the `LinkedListQueue` and the `ArrayQueue`? We should be able to pull out this common method and put it in a parent class. Can we just add it to the `Queue` interface? No, interfaces can only declare method signatures, not method bodies. Let's create a parent class called `AbstractQueue` that implements the `Queue` interface. It will have to be an abstract class since it will still have abstract methods in it. We will need to provide the method signatures for the rest of the methods defined in the `Queue` interface in the class `AbstractQueue`.

Example Java Code 96: Defining an Abstract Queue Class

```
/**
 * Class to define an abstract queue
```

```
 4
 6
 8
10
12
14
16
18
20
22
24
26
28
30
32
34
36
38

40
      * @author Barb Ericson
      */
     public abstract class AbstractQueue<E> implements Queue<E> {

       /**
        * Push an object onto the Queue
        * @param element the element to add to the queue
        */
       public abstract void push(E element);

       /**
        * Peek at, but don't remove, the head of the queue
        * @return the head of the queue (top)
        */
       public abstract E peek();

       /**
        * Pop an object from the Queue
        * @return the head (top) of the queue and
        * remove it from the queue
        */
       public abstract E pop();

       /**
        * Return the size of a queue
        * @return the number of elements in the queue
        */
       public abstract int size();

       /**
        * Method to see if the queue is empty
        * @return true if the queue is empty, else false
        */
       public boolean isEmpty() {
         return (size() == 0);
       }

     }
```

Notice that we did have to use the keyword abstract in the method signature for all the methods from the interface that we didn't add a method body for in the abstract class. And, since there are abstract methods in the class, the class must also be declared abstract.

Now we can modify both LinkedListQueue and ArrayQueue to inherit from AbstractQueue. And we can remove or comment out the isEmpty method from both, since this method will now be inherited from AbstractQueue.

Example Java Code 97: The Revised ArrayQueue Class

```
 2
 4
 6
 8
     /**
      * Implements a simple queue using an array
      * @author Mark Guzdial
      * @author Barb Ericson
      */
     public class ArrayQueue extends AbstractQueue {

       /// ... fields and other methods as before
```

```
10      /**
         * Method to see if the queue is empty
12       * @return true if the queue is empty, else false
         */
14      // commented out since inherited from AbstractQueue
        // public boolean isEmpty() { return size() == 0; }
16
      }
```

Adding "//" before a line of code will comment it out, which means that it will be ignored.

Example Java Code 98: The Revised LinkedListQueue Class

```
import java.util.*; // LinkedList representation
2
    /**
4    * Implements a simple queue using a linked list
     * @author Mark Guzdial
6    * @author Barb Ericson
     */
8   public class LinkedListQueue extends AbstractQueue {

10      // ... fields and other methods as before

12      /**
         * Check if the queue is empty
14       * @return true if no elements in the queue, else false
         */
16      // commented out since inherited from AbstractQueue
        // public boolean isEmpty() {return this.size() == 0;}
18
      }
```

If you look at the interfaces and classes in the package java.util, you will see this pattern repeated many times. An interface defines an ADT, like the interface List. Then an abstract class implements at least one method in the interface and leaves the rest of the methods abstract, like the class AbstractList. Then concrete classes inherit from the abstract class, like ArrayList, LinkedList, and Vector (Figure 11.15). Code that uses any of the implementing classes should declare variables to be of the interface type List rather than the implementing class type. Then if later the user decides to change the implementing class, only the construction of the object changes. Why would you want to use a different implementing class? You might start out with one implementing class and then realize that a different one would be more efficient for the context in which you are using it.

You might start with an ArrayList.

```
> import java.util.*;
> List<String> nameList = new ArrayList<String>();
> nameList.add("Shayna");
> nameList.add("Marcus");
> nameList.add("Jakita");
> nameList
[Shayna, Marcus, Jakita]
```

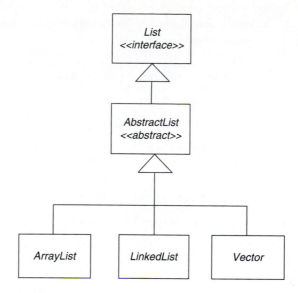

FIGURE 11.15
The inheritance tree for the interface list.

If you realize that you need to do many additions and deletions at specific points in the list, you should probably switch to a linked list.

```
> import java.util.*;
> List<String> nameList = new LinkedList<String>();
> nameList.add("Shayna");
> nameList.add("Marcus");
> nameList.add("Jakita");
> nameList
[Shayna, Marcus, Jakita]
```

Notice that all that changes is which class you create the object from! This is the goal, to limit the number of changes you have to make if you change the implementing class.

11.3 USING AN ARRAYLIST

Our implementation of a stack that uses an array has the problem that we have to specify how big the array is and we will get errors if we try to add more items to the stack than can fit in the array. If we make the array very big, then we will probably have unused space that is wasted. The class `ArrayList` is a list implemented using an array which can grow or shrink as needed. You can use `get(index)` to get the element at the specified index in the list. You can use `remove(index)` to remove and return the element at the specified index. You can use the method `size()` to find out how many elements are in the list.

Let's implement the `Stack` interface using an `ArrayList` object.

Example Java Code 99: The ArrayListStack Class

```java
import java.util.*;

/**
 * Implementation of a stack as an ArrayList
 * @author Mark Guzdial
 * @author Barb Ericson
 */
public class ArrayListStack<E> implements Stack<E> {

  /** Where we'll store our elements */
  private List<E> list = new ArrayList<E>();

  /**
   * No argument constructor
   */
  public ArrayListStack() {
  }

  //// Methods ///

  /**
   * Method to add an element to the top of the stack
   * @param element the element to add
   */
  public void push(E element) {
    list.add(element);
  }

  /**
   * Method to return the top element on the stack
   * but not remove it.
   * @return the object at the top of the stack
   */
  public E peek() {
    return list.get(list.size() - 1);
  }

  /**
   * Method to remove and return the top element on the
     stack
   * @return the element on the top of the stack
   */
  public E pop() {
    return list.remove(list.size() - 1);
  }

  /**
   * Method to return the number of elements in the stack
   * @return the number of elements in the stack
   */
  public int size(){return list.size();}

  /**
   * Method to check if the stack is empty
   * @return true if the stack is empty else false
   */
  public boolean isEmpty() {return this.size() == 0;}

  public static void main(String[] args) {
    Stack<String> stack = new ArrayListStack<String>();
    stack.push("Matt");
```

```
62      stack.push("Katie");
        stack.push("Jenny");
64      System.out.println(stack.size());
        System.out.println(stack.peek());
66      System.out.println(stack.pop());
        System.out.println(stack.pop());
68      System.out.println(stack.pop());
      }
70    }
```

11.4 USING A MAP ADT

A map is an ADT that associates a value with a key. It is similar to a post office box in that you can get the item in the box using the key for that box and you can put an item in the box using the key. But, unlike a real post office box, you can only put one item in the box.

A good example of this is your cell phone contact list. For each name in your contact list, you can store a phone number. So that when you want to call someone, you just find the name and the phone finds the phone number associated with that name.

We will use a map (java.util.Map) to track how often a color appears in a square region of pixels by using the color as the key to the map and saving the count as the value for the key. We will then find the most common (highest count) color in that region of pixels and set the current pixel color to that color. There could be two or more colors with the same count and this program will return the first one it finds with the highest count. This will result in a picture that looks like it was painted.

Example Java Code 100: Oil paint Picture method

```java
/**
2   * Method to do an oil paint effect on a picture
    * @param dist the distance from the current pixel
4   * to use in the range
    * @return the new picture
6   */
    public Picture oilPaint(int dist) {
8
      // create the picture to return
10    Picture retPict = new Picture(this.getWidth(),
        this.getHeight());
12
      // declare pixels
14    Pixel currPixel = null;
      Pixel retPixel = null;
16
      // loop through the pixels
18    for (int x = 0; x < this.getWidth(); x++) {
        for (int y = 0; y < this.getHeight(); y++) {
20        currPixel = this.getPixel(x,y);
          retPixel = retPict.getPixel(x,y);
22        retPixel.setColor(
            currPixel.getMostCommonColorInRange(dist));
24      }
      }
26    return retPict;
    }
```

This method will create a new picture to return and then loop through all the pixels in the current picture and set the color in the return picture to be the most common color found within a square region defined by the given distance from the current pixel. The method creates a new picture so that the search for the most common color in a square region is always operating on the original picture and not the modified one.

The `Pixel` method to find the most common color in the square region is shown below.

Example Java Code 101: Find the most common color method in Pixel

```java
/**
 * Method to return the most common color in the given
 * range from the current pixel in the picture or just
 * return this color.
 * @param dist the distance to use for the range
 * @return the most common color in this range
 */
public Color getMostCommonColorInRange(int dist) {
   Map<Color,Integer> colorMap = new HashMap<Color,Integer>();
   Pixel currPixel = null;
   Integer value = null;
   Color theKey = null;

   // loop through the pixels around this one within the
   // distance
   for (int currY = y - dist; currY <= y + dist; currY++) {
      for (int currX = x - dist; currX <= x + dist; currX++) {
         if (currY >= 0 && currY < picture.getHeight() &&
               currX >= 0 && currX < picture.getWidth()) {
            currPixel = picture.getPixel(currX,currY);
            theKey = currPixel.getColor();
            value = colorMap.get(theKey);
            if (value == null)
               colorMap.put(theKey,1);
            else
               colorMap.put(theKey, value + 1);
         }
      }
   }

   // find the color that is most common
   int maxValue = 1;
   int currValue = 0;
   theKey = this.getColor(); // use current color as default
   Set<Color> keySet = colorMap.keySet();
   for (Color key : keySet) {
      currValue = colorMap.get(key);
      if (currValue > maxValue) {
         theKey = key;
         maxValue = currValue;
      }
   }
   return theKey;
}
```

■

In the Java library `java.util.Map` is an interface and it has several classes that implement this interface. One of the classes that implement the `Map` interface is

FIGURE 11.16
Manipulating a picture to look like it was painted.

java. util.HashMap. Notice that we declare the variable colorMap to be of the type Map, but when we create the map object, we create it using type HashMap. This will allow us to change the implementing class easily.

Also notice that elements that are placed in the map must be objects. In this example, we are using the auto-boxing and unboxing feature added in Java 1.5 (Java 5) to convert between the primitive type integer and the object type Integer. So, we declare the variable value to be of the type Integer. If the color is not in the map yet, the get method will return null. If the color isn't in the map, we will add it with a value of 1, which will be autoboxed into an Integer value. If the color is in the map, we increment the current value of the Integer object. Java will do the conversions for us of the value from Integer to integer and do the increment and then convert back to Integer when the value is put back in the map.

If you try the oilPaint method out on the picture of an arch (arch.jpg) with a distance of 5, you get the result as shown in Figure 11.16.

EXERCISES

11.1 Create an interface Showable that has the method show() in it.

11.2 Create an interface Player that has two methods: planMove() and makeMove().

11.3 Draw the contents of the stack after the following code has executed.

```
> Stack<String> stack =
  new ArrayStack<String>();
> stack.push("Sue");
```

```
> stack.push("Mike");
> stack.peek();
> stack.push("Wanda");
> stack.pop();
> stack.push("Steve");
```

11.4   Draw the contents of the queue after the following code has executed.

```
> Queue<String> queue =
  new ArrayQueue<String>();
> queue.push("Sue");
> queue.push("Mike");
> queue.peek();
> queue.push("Wanda");
> queue.pop();
> queue.push("Steve");
```

11.5   Create an abstract class AbstractStack which implements the Stack interface and put the isEmpty method in it. Remove the isEmpty method from both LinkedListStack and ArrayStack.

11.6   Create a class PhoneContacts that uses a map to associate a name to a phone number.

11.7   How are abstract classes and interfaces alike? How are they different? Which one should you use when you want to create an ADT? Which one should you use when you want to provide the body of a method? Can an abstract class inherit from an abstract class? Can an interface inherit from an interface? Can an abstract class implement an interface? When you compile an interface what gets created?

11.8   How does the Java version of LinkedList in package java.util differ from what we created in the last chapter?

11.9   How does the List interface differ from the Set interface? When would you want to use a set instead of a list? When would you want to use a list instead of a set?

11.10   What does the Map interface define? What classes implement this interface? Describe at least one situation where you would want a map.

11.11   List some other places where stacks and queues are used in your daily life.

11.12   What happens when you execute pop on an empty ArrayStack? What happens when you execute pop on an empty LinkedListStack?

11.13   When should you use an array to implement a stack? When should you use a linked list to implement a stack?

11.14   When should you use an array to implement a queue? When should you use a linked list to implement a queue?

11.15   Java has definitions for stacks and queues as well in package java.util. How are these different from what we have created?

11.16 Add a static (class) method to the `Picture` class that takes a stack of pictures and a number of milliseconds and show each picture one at a time by popping each `Picture` off the stack and showing it, and then waiting the specified number of milliseconds between each. You can use `Thread.sleep(numMilliseconds)` to wait. Do the same with a queue of pictures.

11.17 Create a new class `ArrayListQueue` that uses an `ArrayList` to implement the `Queue` interface. What advantages and disadvantages does this have over an `ArrayQueue`?

11.18 Change the implementation of the queue as an array so that the head and tail variables match the head and tail concepts.

11.19 Change the implementation of the queue as a linked list so that the head is at the front and the tail is at the end.

11.20 Implement a queue in an array with wraparound—when the head or tail gets to the end of the array, it wraps around to the front.

12

Circular Linked Lists and Graphs: Lists and Trees That Loop

12.1 MAKING SPRITE ANIMATION WITH CIRCULAR LINKED LISTS

12.2 GENERALIZING A CIRCULAR LINKED LIST

12.3 GRAPHS: TREES WITH LOOPS

Chapter Learning Objectives

Lists can loop—a latter node can have its next point to an earlier node. We use a *circular linked list* to create lists that loop. You want these, for example, when you are representing the forms of *sprites* in an animation, such as in the Nintendo video game *Mario Brothers*.

Trees can also have loops, with children of different sub-trees linked together. We call those kinds of trees *graphs*. Graphs are useful for modeling many kinds of networks in the real world.

The computer science goals for this chapter are:

- To create linked lists that have loops in them, and to avoid the dangers that can arise from this.
- To explore the use of graphs, and how to traverse them.

The media learning goal for this chapter is:

- To create a looping sprite animation, as used in older video games.

12.1 MAKING SPRITE ANIMATION WITH CIRCULAR LINKED LISTS

The older reader may recall Nintendo's *Super Mario Brothers* (Figure 12.1). The Mario Brothers characters seemed to run and jump under the control of the user in exploring a virtual world. As Mario and Luigi "ran," their arms and legs seemed to move as they moved. The style of animation being used in those style games is called *sprite animation*. A *sprite* is a two-dimensional image or graphic that is composed onto a background. By storing different forms of the sprites and moving between the forms when composing them, the sprites can be made to appear to move.

In a sprite animation, characters are represented by a series of still images. In one image, the right leg might be raised and in front of the body. In the next image, the right leg might be on the ground. In a following image, the left leg might be raised ahead

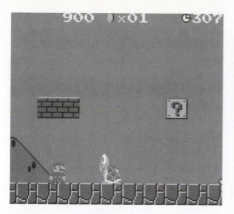
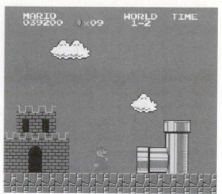

FIGURE 12.1
Scenes from Nintendo's Super Mario Brothers. Images courtesy of Nintendo.

jWalk.jpg   jWalk2.jpg   jSide.jpg

FIGURE 12.2
Three images to be used in a sprite animation.

of the body, and so on. By rapidly showing these images, in sequence, the illusion of moving body parts is created. By moving where the images are displayed, the illusion is created that the moving body parts are actually driving the character. In the end, the character seems to run.

The wildebeests in *The Lion King* and the villagers in *The Hunchback of Notre Dame* are not examples of sprite animation. In those cases, the body parts did move and were controlled at a fine level of detail. However, a sprite animation *could* have been used to represent the characters whose positions are specified by a simulation. It is a particularly easy mechanism to be used in your own animations. Sprite animations were invented for use on lower-powered processors (like the early Nintendo video games), so if you were to do an animation on a computer with little power (e.g., perhaps a cell phone), then sprite animation would be a reasonable choice.

Let's create a version of sprite animation. In your media-source folder on the CD, you will find some pictures of our children in walking positions. These pictures are positioned (as best as we could) to represent different positions in walking (Figure 12.2). We took the pictures against a blue background so that they could be used with chromakey.

We can arrange these images in a sequence to give the appearance of walking, were they to be displayed one right after the other (Figure 12.3). These images are particularly

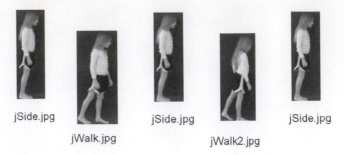

jSide.jpg

jWalk.jpg

jSide.jpg

jWalk2.jpg

jSide.jpg

FIGURE 12.3
A sequence of images arranged to give the appearance of walking.

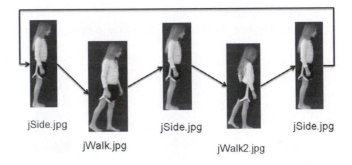

jSide.jpg

jWalk.jpg

jSide.jpg

jWalk2.jpg

jSide.jpg

FIGURE 12.4
A circular linked list of images.

stiff and give more of the impression of Frankenstein's monster walking—hopefully the point is made. Imagine these pictures in a flipbook, so that if you flipped the pages quickly, the images would seem to move.

One structure for arranging these images in the right order for display in a sprite animation is a *circular linked list*. A circular linked list has at least one node (typically, the last node) whose `next` refers to a node earlier in the list (often, the first node). Arranging a series of picture nodes in a circular linked list gives us a simple way of defining the sequence of images for a sprite animation (Figure 12.4).

A circular linked list is really useful for modeling lots of real things in the world. There are many things that contain loops: electrical circuits, pipe systems, maps of roads (e.g., there's always more than one way to go between two spots). The tricky aspect of a circular linked list is *never* to try to traverse the circular linked list to "the end," that is, where `next` is `null`. In a circular linked list, there is no `null` to indicate the end of the list.

Here's the main method we'll use for our walking sprite (Figure 12.5):

```
/** Main for testing */
public static void main(String[] args) {
    WalkingKid j = new WalkingKid();
    j.steps(30);
}
```

FIGURE 12.5
Frames of the walking kid.

How It Works.   To make our `WalkingKid` class work, we keep track of a current node in the circular linked list and where the (*x*, *y*) position should be. To take a step, we display the current node's picture, then set the current equal to its next and update the position instance variables. Now, when the next step comes along, we will be displaying a new picture.

Example Java Code 102: WalkingKid

```
/**
 * Class that represents a walking kid
 * @author Mark Guzdial
 * @author Barb Ericson
 */
public class WalkingKid {

  /** Which character node position are we at? */
  private CharacterNode current;

  /** Starting position for walking */
  private CharacterNode start;

  /** x value for the Position for the character */
  private int x;

  /** y value for the position for the character */
  private int y;

  /** FrameSequence for the display */
  private FrameSequencer frames;

  /**
   * Method to get the x value of the position
   * @return the x value of the position
   */
  public int getX() {return x;}

  /**
   * Method to get the y value of the position
   * @return the y value of the position
   */
  public int getY() {return y;}

  /**
   * Method to set the position to the new x and y
   * @param newX the new x value to use
   * @param newY the new y value to use
```

```
                */
40      public void setLoc(int newX, int newY)
        {
42        x=newX;
          y=newY;
44      }


46      /**
         * We'll do the list setup in the constructor
48       */
        public WalkingKid(){
50        Picture p = null; // For loading up images

52        p = new Picture(FileChooser.getMediaPath("jSide.jpg"));
          start = new CharacterNode(p.flip());
54        p = new Picture(FileChooser.getMediaPath("jWalk.jpg"));
          CharacterNode rightfoot = new CharacterNode(p.flip());
56        p = new Picture(FileChooser.getMediaPath("jSide.jpg"));
          CharacterNode center = new CharacterNode(p.flip());
58        p = new Picture(FileChooser.getMediaPath("jWalk2.jpg"));
          CharacterNode leftfoot = new CharacterNode(p.flip());
60        start.setNext(rightfoot); rightfoot.setNext(center);
          center.setNext(leftfoot);
62        leftfoot.setNext(start);

64        frames = new FrameSequencer("C:/Temp/");
          setUp();
66      }


68      /**
         * Setup to display walking left to right
70       */
        private void setUp(){
72        x = 0; // Left side
          y = 300; // 300 pixels down
74        frames.show();
          this.start();
76      }


78      /**
         * Start a walking sequence
80       */
        public void start() {
82        current = start;
          this.draw();
84      }


86      /**
         * Draw the current character
88       */
        public void draw() {
90        Picture bg = new Picture(400,400);
          Turtle t = new Turtle(bg);
92        t.setPenDown(false);
          t.moveTo(x,y);
94        current.drawWith(t);
          frames.addFrame(bg);
96      }


98      /**
         * Draw the next step
100      */
```

```
102    public void step(){
         current = (CharacterNode) current.getNext();
         x=x+10;  // We'll try this
104      this.draw();
       }

106
       /**
108     * Draw a few steps
        */
110    public void steps(int num){
         for (int i=0; i < num; i++) {this.step();}}
112
       /**
114     * Delegate replay
        */
116    public void replay(int delay){
         frames.replay(delay);
118    }

120    /** Main for testing */
       public static void main(String[] args) {
122      WalkingKid j = new WalkingKid();
         j.steps(30);
124    }

126  }
```

While this works, the walking kid walks stilted. We could fix this problem with better images. We might also remove the image where the legs come together between steps. We can model this by a circular linked list where the loop doesn't go all the way back to the beginning (Figure 12.6). The list starts with a single, standing image, then loops just on the movement of the legs.

12.2 GENERALIZING A CIRCULAR LINKED LIST

Let's create a class like LLNode that makes it easy to create circular linked lists. The trick is never to look for null. This simple version simply refuses to do the things that would normally require a traversal to the null at the end of the list—no last and no remove.

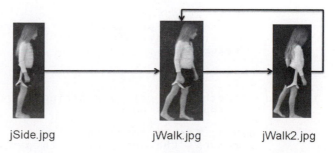

jSide.jpg   jWalk.jpg   jWalk2.jpg

FIGURE 12.6
A partial circular linked list.

```
> CharacterNode ch =
  new CharacterNode(new Picture(20,20));
> ch.last()
Don't try to find last() from a circular list!
CharacterNode with picture:
  Picture, filename null height 20 width 20
> ch.remove(new CharacterNode(new Picture(20,20)))
Very dangerous to try to remove a node from this list!
```

Example Java Code 103: CharacterNode, a class for representing characters in sprite animations

```
   /*
2   * CharacterNode has a picture for a given character.
    * Don't ever try to traverse this one!
4   */
   public class CharacterNode extends LLNode {
6     /**
      * The picture I'm associated with
8     */
     public Picture myPict;

10
     /*
12     * Make me with this picture
      * @param pict the Picture I'm associated with
14     */
     public CharacterNode(Picture pict) {
16       super(); // Call superclass constructor
       myPict = pict;
18     }

20     /**
      * Don't try to remove() from a circular list!
22     */
     public void remove(LLNode node) {
24       System.out.println("Very dangerous to try to remove "+
         "a node from this list!");
26     }

28     /**
      * Don't try to get the last() from a circular list!
30     * @return the current node
      */
32     public LLNode last() {
       System.out.println("Don't try to find last() "+
34         "from a circular list!");
       return this;
36     }

38     /**
      * Method to return a string with information
40     * about this node
      */
42     public String toString() {
       return "CharacterNode with picture: " + myPict;
44     }

46
```

```
48   /*
     * Use the given turtle to draw oneself
     * @param turtle the Turtle to draw with
50   */
   public void drawWith(Turtle turtle) {
52     // Assume that we're at the lower-left corner
     turtle.setHeading(0);
54     turtle.forward(myPict.getHeight());
     Picture bg = turtle.getPicture();
56     myPict.blueScreen(bg,turtle.getXPos(),turtle.getYPos());
   }
58 }
```

■

How It Works.   While CharNode works, it works by taking the easy way out. The methods last(), remove(), and toString in LLNode involve traversing the whole list until next is null. CharNode simply prevents those methods from executing, by overriding them and displaying error messages.

There are better ways of implementing circular linked lists. How can we traverse a circular linked list without going on infinitely, looking for an end to a circle? There are several ways to do it—here are a couple:

- We could add another instance variable, a Boolean named visited. As we visit a node, we mark it true. When we traverse the list, we mark each node that we print or whatever by setting visited to true. Then, rather than looking for next equal to null, we look for visited equal to true. When that's true, we've looped around and can stop. We need a reset method, too, that sets all visited flags to false (and keeps going until it finds a visited flag that is already false).

- We could have *two* next links in each node. One points to the next node created, and the other points to the next node to be traversed when displaying the sprite forms. When we want to traverse all nodes (or add() or remove()), we use the first next. When we want to draw, we use the second next.

12.3   GRAPHS: TREES WITH LOOPS

In the previous sections, we have shown that there are some uses for linked lists with loops in them. How about trees? Is it useful to have nodes that link to previous nodes, e.g., children that point to their grandparents in the tree? With that kind of data structure, we can model all kinds of interesting things that appear in the world.

We call these general structures where loops (or *cycles*) are allowed, *graph*s. A graph is a series of points or *vertices* connected with lines or *edges*. In some graphs, there is a directionality to the line or edge—node1 points to node3, but not vice versa. We call those graphs a *directed* graph. Without that directionality, we call the graph *undirected*.

From this perspective, a tree is an unusual kind of graph. It's a graph without cycles. A tree is a kind of an *acyclic* graph.

Graphs are useful to model structures in the real world that have loops in them.

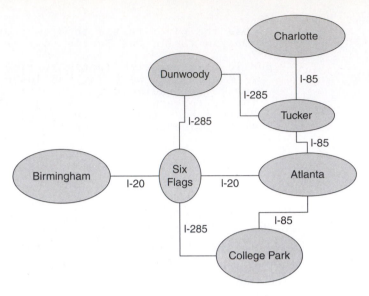

FIGURE 12.7
A map as a graph.

- Think about modeling a human circulatory system. There are clearly cycles in this graph—your blood doesn't flow to the end of your body and then out your fingers and toes. Your blood cycles back to the heart.

- A subway system is another example of a graph that has cycles. Each station is a vertex. Subway lines between stations are edges. Clearly there are cycles—on most subway systems, it's possible to go out one way and come back another way, or to find more than one way to get from one place to another.

- A map is another kind of graph (Figure 12.7). Cities (or even intersections or exits, depending on the detail you want) are vertices, and roads are edges. A map is a good example of a graph that has *costs* associated with edges. For many uses of maps, you care about the distance between any two vertices—that can be the cost of the edge (Figure 12.8).

Traversing graphs (doing something to every node) is particularly hard to do. As you can imagine from these examples, each node or vertex can actually be associated with a number of edges, not just one (as in a linked list) or two (as in a binary tree). This means that a traversal has to make sure that every vertex is included, which may involve traveling down every edge.

The strategies for traversing graphs are similar to the strategies for traversing circular linked lists. We can add a `visited` flag to tell us whether or not we've visited a vertex. Then we can travel down every edge until we are sure that every node has `visited` equal to `true`. We can also keep a separate linked list of all the nodes so that we can check each node, regardless of how it's connected up into the graph.

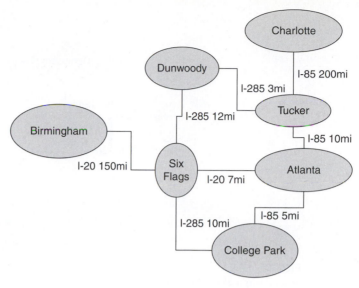

FIGURE 12.8
Apply weights to a graph—distances on a map.

A powerful tool for traversing a graph is to create a *spanning tree*. A spanning tree is the same graph (i.e., includes all the same vertices) without cycles. Once you have a spanning tree, you can visit all nodes using standard tree traversal techniques—you don't have to deal with the cycles.

One approach to computing a spanning tree is to use a *greedy algorithm*. A greedy algorithm, when having to make a choice (say, between which edge to follow from a given vertex) takes the shortest or easiest paths. That's being "greedy." It turns out that a greedy algorithm for creating a spanning tree on a graph actually results in a *minimal spanning tree*—a spanning tree that covers the least ground (has the lowest total cost).

Let's imagine that something bad has happened in the United States—an invasion or an outbreak of an epidemic disease. In Birmingham on our map (Figure 12.7), there are troops or a vaccine. How do we visit all the cities on the map as quickly as possible, traveling the shortest path possible. What we want is a minimal spanning tree.

The first step is obvious. We have to travel from Birmingham to Six Flags (Figure 12.9). From Six Flags we have several choices. We add Atlanta because it's the cheapest (lowest cost, shortest) path out of Six Flags (Figure 12.10). From Atlanta, we move to College Park as the next cheapest edge (Figure 12.11). We then have a problem. The only untraversed link out of College Park goes to Six Flags, where we've already been. We now *backtrack*, re-visiting an earlier node to see if there are more paths from there. We backtrack to Atlanta where we do have a next-cheapest link (after the one to College Park) up to Tucker (Figure 12.12). From Tucker, we add the link to Dunwoody since it's obviously the cheapest (Figure 12.13). Dunwoody has no untraversed nodes (since we can't add Six Flags back in), so we backtrack again to Tucker, and then finish our minimal spanning tree at Charlotte (Figure 12.14).

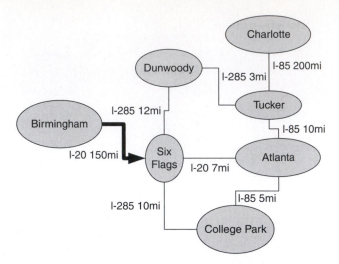

FIGURE 12.9
Traversing a graph to create a spanning tree.

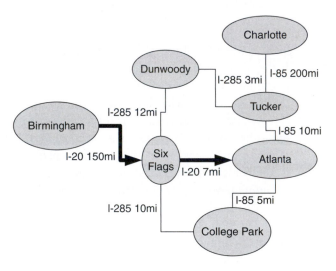

FIGURE 12.10
Choosing the cheapest path out of Six Flags.

You might be wondering how the algorithm figures out to which node to backtrack. It's pretty easy—it's another use for *stack*s. Each node, as it is visited, is pushed onto the stack. If you can't find another edge to follow from the node you're currently at, you pop off the top node from the stack, then see if there are more edges that need exploring from that node. You keep going until the stack is empty. The stack being empty is actually when you know that the algorithm is done.

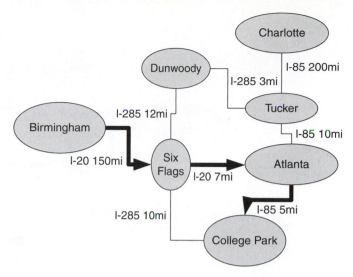

FIGURE 12.11
Going to College Park.

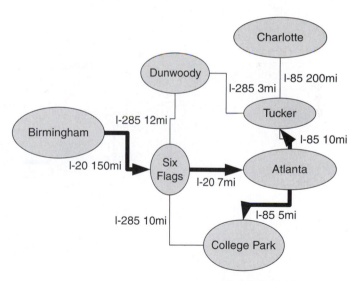

FIGURE 12.12
Backtracking to avoid re-visiting Six Flags.

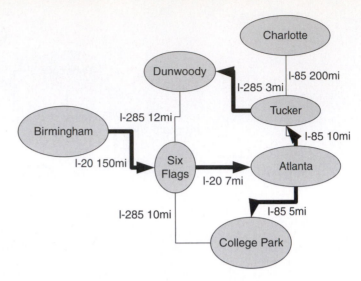

FIGURE 12.13
Adding Dunwoody, the obviously cheaper path.

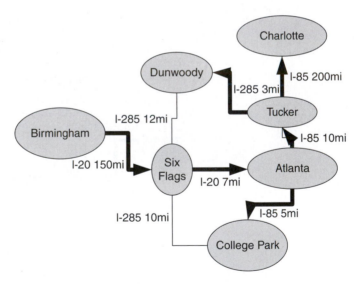

FIGURE 12.14
Finishing up in Charlotte.

EXERCISES

12.1 Create a sample circular linked list where the loop doesn't go all the way back to the front of the loop.

12.2 There are two other sets of blue background images with children in them that could be used for this kind of animation. Modify `WalkingKid` to use those.

12.3 Modify `WalkingKid` to start with the picture of the kid standing still and loop through the walking parts three times.

12.4 Create a class `SpriteAnimation` that takes a list of pictures and has an index to the current picture. Each time a picture is used (drawn or shown), the current picture index is incremented. When you get to the end of the list of pictures, reset the index to the first picture.

12.5 Create a class `SoundLoop` that is a circular list of sounds. The sounds play one after the other for two minutes.

12.6 Create a class `ScreenSaver` that has a circular list of pictures. The pictures show one after the other for two minutes.

12.7 Create a class `RollingCode` that uses a circular list of numbers which are the offsets to add to the current characters to encode a message. So if the current letter is A and the current number is 2, then the output would be C. If the current letter is A and the current number is 5, then the output would be E. Each time a number is used, we move onto the next number.

12.8 Create a class that implements a circular list in an array.

12.9 Create a class `ClosedPolygon` that takes a list of `Point` objects. Draw the closed polygon by drawing lines between all the points and also a line from the last point to the first point.

12.10 Implement `walkBackwards` for the `WalkingKid` class, so that the x position goes right to left, and the order of images swaps.

12.11 Implement `walkToLeft` for the `WalkingKid` class, where the images are flipped and x position goes right-to-left.

12.12 Implement a better `CharacterNode` class that uses one of the strategies described in this method to allow us to traverse a circular linked list without simply blocking dangerous methods.

12.13 Create a method for any of our linked list node classes that checks for a loop. How can you tell if there is a loop in a linked list?

12.14 Create a class that represents a generalized graph node. Each graph node can have any number of edges from it to another graph node. Each edge has a weight on it and links two graph nodes.

12.15   Create a minimal spanning tree for the following graph.

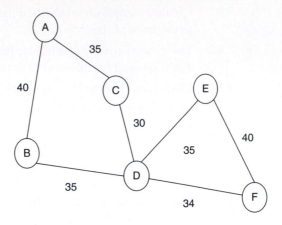

12.16   Create a minimal spanning tree for the following graph.

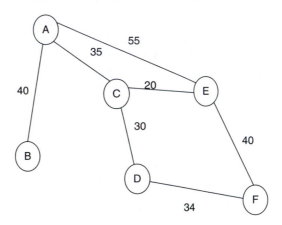

CHAPTER

13

User Interface Structures

13.1 A TOOLKIT FOR BUILDING USER INTERFACES

13.2 BUILDING AND RENDERING USER INTERFACES

13.3 CREATING AN INTERACTIVE USER INTERFACE

13.4 RUNNING FROM THE COMMAND LINE

Chapter Learning Objectives

We are all familiar with the basic pieces of a *graphical user interface (GUI)*: windows, menus, lists, buttons, scrollbars, and the like. As programmers, we can see that these elements are actually constructed using the lists and trees that we've seen in previous chapters. A window contains *panes* that in turn contain components such as *buttons* and *lists*. It's all a hierarchy, as might be represented by a tree. Different *layout managers* are essentially rendering the interface component tree via different traversals.

The computer science goals for this chapter are:

- To learn to construct GUIs using the *Swing* Java library.
- To recognize the structure of a user interface as a tree, and the role of a layout manager as a renderer.
- To use Swing components to construct media tools.
- To use a stack in order to implement *undo*.
- To run Java programs from a command line.

The media learning goals for this chapter are:

- To understand how the interfaces for the applications that media developers use are constructed.
- To use interface components to interact with media.

13.1 A TOOLKIT FOR BUILDING USER INTERFACES

GUIs have many different kinds of components. A modern GUI has buttons (of different kinds, including radio buttons, check boxes, and push buttons), text areas (with or without scrollbars), lists for making selections (some containing text, others with graphics), horizontal and vertical lines separating sections (or *panes*), images, and so on. Programmers typically use libraries to construct user interfaces. (These libraries

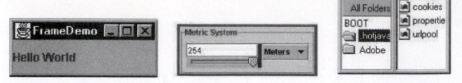

FIGURE 13.1
Examples of Swing components: JFrame, JPanel, and JSplitPane.

are sometimes also called *toolkit*s.) These libraries provide the components, which the programmers can simply create and use.

The first toolkit for Java GUIs was called the *Abstract Window Toolkit* (AWT). AWT provided containers for structuring the components, such as a Frame, which was a main window with a title and a border, a Panel for grouping components, and a Canvas for creating custom components (in case you, as the programmer, really did want to build GUI components for yourself). Components that you would put into these containers included a Label (text that was only displayed, not editable), a Button, a TextField for entry and display of text, a TextArea for entry and display of multiple lines of text, a List for selecting one or more items from a displayed list, and a Choice for selecting a selection from a drop-down list, like a menu.

AWT had many problems. Users did not like the look of AWT user interfaces. AWT made user interfaces look completely different on different platforms (e.g., Microsoft Windows, Apple Macintosh, Linux), since it used native components to represent the Java GUI components (windows, buttons, etc). This made it very hard to design GUIs that could work on all platforms. AWT was also hard to program and fairly inflexible. Still, AWT is available in Java and sometimes (rarely) will be the right toolkit for a given program.

Sun released a new GUI toolkit called *Swing* starting with Java 1.2. The Swing classes are in a package named javax.swing. Swing replaced many of AWT's components, and provided a structure for more flexible and usable user interface components. A Swing main window is called a JFrame (instead of a Frame), a group of components within a JFrame is put in a JPanel, and a button is JButton. Swing provided new components like a JTree for representing hierarchical structures, a JSplitPane for two groups of parallel components, and a JTable, which knows how to display tabular data. (Examples of some of these are in Figure 13.1.) Swing lets the programmer specify how the windows should look, e.g., like those on Microsoft Windows, like those on a Mac, or you can even create your own user interface style.

Building the Simplest Possible Swing User Interface

Here are the steps for simply creating a window with a piece of text in it.

- First, you create the window. The main window is an instance of JFrame. You pass in the desired title to the constructor when you create the instance.

    ```
    JFrame frame = new JFrame("FrameDemo");
    ```

- Next, you add components to the *content pane*. The content pane is the part of the window that holds other pieces of the user interface—the middle of the window, as opposed to the title bar or the close box. For this example, we will create a simple text label (an instance of `JLabel`) that will hold some text, then put that into the window. To make things easier you can also just use the `add` method on `JFrame` directly, which is a convenience method that just gets the content pane and adds the component to it.

  When you add a component to a container, you can tell it *where* you want the component to be. How you tell it where you want the component depends on the *layout manager* that is being used. A layout manager controls the size and position of the components you add and how those properties change when the window is resized. By default a `JFrame` has a `BorderLayout` as the layout manager. We are just going to put our text in the center of the window for now using the constant `BorderLayout.CENTER`. In a `BorderLayout`, the component in the center grows to take all the extra space in the window. So, our label will grow and shrink when the window grows or shrinks.

  ```
  JLabel label = new JLabel("Hello World");
  frame.getContentPane().add(label,
    BorderLayout.CENTER);
  ```

- Now, we need to tell Java that we are done putting components into the window (at least for now). We tell Java to `pack` the window and figure out the minimal size for displaying it on the screen.

  ```
  frame.pack(); // as big as needs to be to display
  //contents
  ```

- Now, we're ready to display the window.

  ```
  frame.setVisible(true);  // display the frame
  ```

When you use Swing to create windows in your programs, you have to decide how to think about and structure your user interface. There are at least three ways to do it.

- Your first option is to think about your application object *as a kind of* `JFrame`. You create your application class as a subclass (`extends`) of `JFrame`. That is probably the easiest way to do it.

- Or, you can think about your application object as something that *has a* `JFrame`. In that case, you typically have an instance variable that will hold the instance of `JFrame`, and you create that instance in the constructor of your application object.

- Or, you can make your application object a kind of `JPanel` that will simply get put into a `JFrame` in some other part of your program. For example, you might build a `StartApplication` class whose constructor method constructs your application object and inserts it into a `JFrame`, and your `main` method might create the `StartApplication` object. The advantage of building your object around a `JPanel` instead of a `JFrame` is that a `JPanel` gives you more flexibility. It can be put into a window, or an applet (a running Java program that runs inside of a Web page in a Web browser, using the class JApplet), or even as part of a larger application.

We are going to stick with the first option for now. We are going to aim for simplicity rather than flexibility right now.

13.2 BUILDING AND RENDERING USER INTERFACES

In this section, we build a very simple user interface. We see how a user interface is a tree, and explore how to render that tree in different ways.

Building a Simple User Interface

Let's build a simple user interface, using the same pattern that we saw before: Making a JFrame and sticking a JLabel in it. Notice that there's more code here, but it is commented out right now.

Example Java Code 104: A Simple GUItree class

```java
import javax.swing.*; // Need this to reach Swing components

/**
 * A GUI that has various components in it, to demonstrate
 * UI components and layout managers (rendering)
 * @author Mark Guzdial
 * @author Barb Ericson
 */
public class GUItree extends JFrame {

  /**
   * Constructor that takes no arguments
   */
  public GUItree() {

    /* create the JFrame with the title */
    super("GUI Tree Example");

    /* Put in a panel with a label in it */
    JPanel panel1 = new JPanel();
    this.getContentPane().add(panel1);
    JLabel label = new JLabel("This is panel 1!");
    panel1.add(label);

    //NOTICE THAT THIS IS COMMENTED OUT!
    /* Put in another panel with two buttons in it
    JPanel panel2 = new JPanel();
    this.getContentPane().add(panel2);
    JButton button1 = new JButton("Make a sound");
    panel2.add(button1);
    JButton button2 = new JButton("Make a picture");
    panel2.add(button2);
    */
```

```
             /* set the size to fit the contents and show it */
36           this.pack();
             this.setVisible(true);
38         }

40         /** test this class */
           public static void main(String[] args){
42           GUItree gt = new GUItree();
           }
44       }
```

■

How It Works.   Our class GUItree is a subclass of JFrame, meaning that creating a GUItree instance creates a window. In our constructor, we explicitly call super("GUI tree example") in order to ask the class JFrame to create a window with the title "GUI tree example." We then create a panel JPanel panel1, and add it into the window's content pane. We create a label saying "This is panel 1!" and put the label into the pane. We commented out a bunch of code between "/*" and "*/," then we set the size of the window to just fit the contents using pack and make the window visible using setVisible(true).

Computer Science Idea: We're building a tree

It might seem backward that we add the panel to the tree, *and then* add the label to the panel. Shouldn't we add the label to the panel, and then the panel to the tree? It really doesn't matter. We're constructing a set of relationships between parts of the GUI tree. The tree is used to make our window visible when we pack it and setVisible(true). The order that the parts are added to the tree does not matter.

■

You can execute the main method to run this program. The window will appear and will look like Figure 13.2.

We hope that you are wondering about that code we commented out. Let's remove the comment characters so that we can run the whole code.

FIGURE 13.2
A simple GUI.

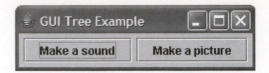

FIGURE 13.3
A slightly more complex GUI, with two buttons.

Example Java Code 105: Slightly more complex GUItree class

```java
public GUItree() {

    /* create the JFrame with the title */
    super("GUI Tree Example");

    /* Put in a panel with a label in it */
    JPanel panel1 = new JPanel();
    this.getContentPane().add(panel1);
    JLabel label = new JLabel("This is panel 1!");
    panel1.add(label);

    //NOTICE THAT THIS IS NO LONGER COMMENTED OUT!
    // Put in another panel with two buttons in it
    JPanel panel2 = new JPanel();
    this.getContentPane().add(panel2);
    JButton button1 = new JButton("Make a sound");
    panel2.add(button1);
    JButton button2 = new JButton("Make a picture");
    panel2.add(button2);
    //

    /* set the size to fit the contents and show it */
    this.pack();
    this.setVisible(true);
}
```

How It Works. This second version simply continues on from where the last one left off. A second panel is created and added to the frame's content pane. Two buttons are created and added to the panel.

We run this version the same way. What we see might be surprising (Figure 13.3). Where did the first panel and its label "This is panel 1!" go? A `BorderLayout` only allows one component in an area so the second `JPanel` replaced the first. But, this doesn't mean that you can only have one component in the `JFrame` as we will see next.

Let's build yet another version of our simple user interface. In this version, we construct the *exact* same components in the exact same way. However, we will use a different *layout manager* that will arrange the panels in a particular way when we *render* the user interface.

Example Java Code 106: A Flowed GUItree

```java
import javax.swing.*; // Need this to reach Swing components
import java.awt.*; // Need this to reach FlowLayout
```

```
 4     /**
        * A GUI that has various components in it, to demonstrate
 6      * UI components and layout managers (rendering)
        * @author Mark Guzdial
 8      * @author Barb Ericson
        */
10     public class GUItreeFlowed extends JFrame {

12       /**
          * Constructor that takes no arguments
14         */
         public GUItreeFlowed() {
16
           /* create the JFrame with the title */
18           super("GUI Tree Flowed Example");

20           /* set the layout to flow layout */
             this.getContentPane().setLayout(new FlowLayout());
22
             /* Put in a panel with a label in it */
24           JPanel panel1 = new JPanel();
             this.getContentPane().add(panel1);
26           JLabel label = new JLabel("This is panel 1!");
             panel1.add(label);
28
             /* Put in another panel with two buttons in it */
30           JPanel panel2 = new JPanel();
             this.getContentPane().add(panel2);
32           JButton button1 = new JButton("Make a sound");
             panel2.add(button1);
34           JButton button2 = new JButton("Make a picture");
             panel2.add(button2);
36
             /* set the size to fit the contents and show it */
38           this.pack();
             this.setVisible(true);
40         }

42     }
```

We can see both panels in this version (Figure 13.4) because of the line:

```
this.getContentPane().setLayout(new FlowLayout());
```

That line creates a new FlowLayout instance and assigns it as the layout manager (via setLayout()) for the frame's content pane.

In both of our last two examples, we were defining a *tree* as in Figure 13.5. A GUI is a tree. The frame is the root of the tree, and it has a child that is a content pane. (It has other children, too, like a title bar, but those will not be visible in our simple examples.)

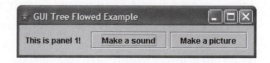

FIGURE 13.4
Our GUItree, using a flowed layout manager.

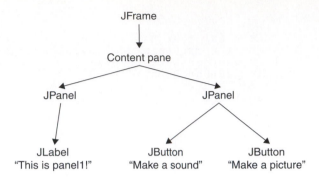

FIGURE 13.5
Diagram of components of GUI tree.

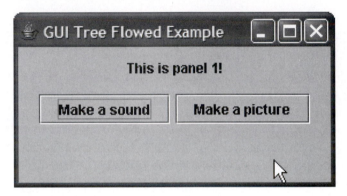

FIGURE 13.6
Resizing the flowed GUItree.

The content pane has two other children—each of the two panels. Those panels contain other children: a label or the two buttons.

The difference between the last two user interfaces, then, is not in the tree, but in how it is rendered. If you do not specify a layout manager for a JFrame, the default one is used (BorderLayout). The default layout manager for a JPanel is a FlowLayout. A flow layout manager makes it easy to lay out one element right after the other, as in Figure 13.4. When we resize the window (Figure 13.6), the components move in a reasonable way—that is also handled by the layout manager.

Java Swing Layout Managers: GUI Tree Renderers

A layout manager figures out how to lay out components within a window. It is possible to specify exactly what position each element should maintain in a window. If you set the layout manager to null, then you must specify the (x, y) position within the window where the component should be drawn, and the height and width of the component. The method for doing that is setBounds(topLeftX, topLeftY, width, height).

However, exact specification can lead to errors, and does not define what should happen if the window is resized.

The layout managers in Swing allow us to arrange components in a logical manner. The layout manager then positions and even sizes the components. The layout manager also handles resizing and repositioning the components (as necessary) when the window is resized. We will see that a layout manager can be assigned to the frame's content pane *or* any panel. Thus, a panel may arrange its components differently than the overall frame (content pane) may arrange its components.

Different layout managers act on the exact same GUI component tree in different ways. Changing the layout manager will change how the elements are positioned and sized. The same window will look differently when the window is resized, depending on the layout manager used.

FlowLayout

We have already seen the `FlowLayout` manager. A FlowLayout manager just places items one after the other, from left-to-right, with no extra space between the components. We can see that in Figures 13.4 and 13.6. That may seem obvious—what else might you want? Turns out that there are *lots* of ways to layout and render a GUI tree.

BorderLayout

A popular layout manager is the `BorderLayout`. Using a BorderLayout manager, you specify the *areas* where you want elements to be placed (Figure 13.7). Elements placed in the "north" appear at the top of the window, and elements placed in the "west" appear at the left. (You do not have to place elements in all the directions—as the programmer, you simply specify the general area in which the elements should be placed.) A BorderLayout manager also resizes elements, besides placing them. It always gives the most space to the "center" element.

A BorderLayout manager lays out elements in a common user interface style. Certainly you have seen user interfaces like this. Word processing and image manipulation

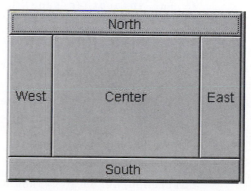

FIGURE 13.7
How a BorderLayout GUI is structured.

programs (as two examples) usually have a large work area with toolbars or menus or lists of options around the edges.

We can change our FlowLayout GUItree into a BorderLayout GUItree pretty simply. Instead of adding a new instance of `FlowLayout` as the layout manager for our content pane, we add an instance of `BorderLayout`.

```java
this.getContentPane().setLayout(new BorderLayout());
```

One more change—as we add elements to our window, now, we specify *where* they are going to go. BorderLayout defines a set of constants, like `BorderLayout.NORTH` that allow us to specify where components should be added.

```java
this.getContentPane().add(panel1,BorderLayout.NORTH);
```

Example Java Code 107: A BorderLayout GUItree

```java
import javax.swing.*; // Need this to reach Swing components
import java.awt.*; // Need this to reach BorderLayout

/**
 * A GUI that has various components in it, to demonstrate
 * UI components and layout managers (rendering)
 * @author Mark Guzdial
 * @author Barb Ericson
 */
public class GUItreeBordered extends JFrame {

  public GUItreeBordered() {

    /* create the JFrame with the title */
    super("GUI Tree Bordered Example");

    /* set the layout manager to BorderLayout */
    this.getContentPane().setLayout(new BorderLayout());

    /* Put in a panel with a label in it */
    JPanel panel1 = new JPanel();
    this.getContentPane().add(panel1,BorderLayout.NORTH);
    JLabel label = new JLabel("This is panel 1!");
    panel1.add(label);

    /* Put in another panel with two buttons in it */
    JPanel panel2 = new JPanel();
    this.getContentPane().add(panel2,BorderLayout.SOUTH);
    JButton button1 = new JButton("Make a sound");
    panel2.add(button1);
    JButton button2 = new JButton("Make a picture");
    panel2.add(button2);

    /* set the size to fit the contents and show it */
    this.pack();
    this.setVisible(true);
  }

  /** test this class */
  public static void main(String[] args){
    GUItreeBordered gt = new GUItreeBordered();
  }
}
```

FIGURE 13.8
A BorderLayout GUItree.

FIGURE 13.9
Resizing the BorderLayout GUItree.

Now, when we create our window, we see Figure 13.8. Since we placed panel1 in the NORTH and panel2 in the SOUTH, one is on top of the other. As we *resize* the window (Figure 13.9), those relationships remain. Compare this with the resizing of the FlowLayout GUItree (Figure 13.6)—the BorderLayout keeps the elements at the top and bottom, whereas the FlowLayout leaves the elements in the middle, one right after the other.

13.3   CREATING AN INTERACTIVE USER INTERFACE

The interfaces we have created thus far have been static. The buttons do not *do* anything. We have not yet seen how to respond to user interactions with these components.

The key to creating interactive user interfaces is dealing with *event*s, that is, *user interface events*. When a user does anything within a user interface, the computer generates an event object. A keystroke on the keyboard, a click of the mouse, or the click and drag on the thumb of a scrollbar are all events. Programs can *listen* for these events—that is, provide a piece of code that will respond to a kind of event and take some action when that event occurs.

Creating a listener is like signing up for the mailing list of your favorite band. By signing up for the mailing list, you are saying to *someone* (in this analogy, the fan club of the band), "Please let me know if the band is doing anything interesting or coming

TABLE 13.1 A selection of events and their listeners

Action Type	Listener Type	Example Event
ActionEvent	ActionListener	A user clicks a button
AdjustmentEvent	AdjustmentListener	Move a scrollbar
FocusEvent	FocusListener	Tab into a text area
ItemEvent	ItemListener	Checkbox checked
KeyEvent	KeyListener	Key stroke
MouseEvent	MouseListener	Mouse button clicked
MouseEvent	MouseMotionListener	Mouse is moved
TextEvent	TextListener	A text is changed
WindowEvent	WindowListener	A window is closed

to my town!" Creating a listener for a given event is saying to *something* (in the user interface case, the user interface event managing program), "I care about this particular event occurring—please let me know if it ever does."

Table 13.1 lists some of the most common user interface events and their listeners. Typically, listeners are associated with (or attached to) particular objects. Thus, the listeners are triggered when the event *associated with that object* occurs. If you have five buttons in your user interface, each will typically have their own `ActionListener` that waits for the user to click on the given button, and each will respond to a click on the associated button.

Notice that there is some ambiguity in these events. The same user interaction could correspond to many different events. Imagine moving a mouse over a button, then clicking on that button. Is that a `MouseEvent` or an `ActionEvent`? The answer is "Yes." You can have listeners for both kinds of events attached to the same button, and then both listeners will be triggered when the corresponding events occur.

In Java terms, a listener is actually an *interface*. It's not an actual class. You cannot create instances of them or subclasses from them. An interface is the definition of a set of methods that perform some specific function or set of functions. A class that claims to `implement` a given interface is agreeing to a contract—the methods of that interface *must* be created in the class.

Swing provides a set of abstract classes called *adapter*s that agree to implement particular listeners. The adapter does provide all the necessary methods, but most of them are just empty—they do nothing at all. You as the programmer then create a subclass of the given adapter and override the methods as you need in order to respond to events appropriately. For example:

```
class MyMouseAdapter extends MouseAdapter {

    /** Method to handle the click of a mouse */
    public void mouseClicked(MouseEvent e) {
    }
}
```

If you think about all the buttons in a given interface, and having to create a new class to listen to each kind of event for each kind of button—you quickly find that there are a lot of classes to create. Java provides a particular structure to use. It's called an *anonymous inner class*. The idea is that you can create a subclass of a given listener class, then instantiate it for use at the moment that you define the class (hence, "inner class," as it is created inside some other class). You do not even have to *name* the class—hence, "anonymous." In the bit of code given below, we are adding an object to listen for a FocusEvent, and we create the class for that object right there—we define the methods focusGained and focusLost in the middle of the method call for addFocusListener.

```
b.addFocusListener(new FocusListener () {
  public void focusGained (FocusEvent evt) {
    // code to handle focus gained
  }
  public void focusLost(FocusEvent evt) {
    // code to handle focus lost
  }
});
```

Common Bug: Anonymous inner classes may not access non-final local variables

Even though anonymous inner classes are created *within* another class's method, the anonymous inner class does not have access to any local non-final variables in the method. A final variable is one that cannot change. Most variables can change and so are not declared final. The restriction that an anonymous inner class can't access non-final local variables turns out to be non-intuitive. You create a variable, and two lines later (in the same method, seemingly) you want to access that variable—but you cannot. You can access any local variables declared final and in this case, the compiler makes a copy of the local variable's value at the time the inner class was created and declares it as a private field in the anonymous inner class. Inner classes *can* access all the fields (instance variables) in the current class, even private ones, since the inner class is part of the outer class.

∎

Making Our GUItree Interactive

After creating many variations on the basic GUItree, it seems reasonable to make our first interactive interface. All we are really doing here is making the "Play" button play some sound, and the "Show" button show some picture. Since we do not plan to do anything fancier with the button than let the user click it (e.g., we won't be playing the sound as soon as the mouse moves over the "Play" button), we will simply create an ActionListener anonymous inner class that will listen for the button's "action"—the typical click on a button.

Example Java Code 108: An interactive GUItree

```
import javax.swing.*; // Need this to reach Swing components
import java.awt.*; // Need this to reach FlowLayout
import java.awt.event.*;
```

2

```
4        // Need this for listeners and events

6    /**
     * A GUI that has various components in it, to demonstrate
8    * UI components and layout managers (rendering).
     * Now with Interactivity!
10   * @author Mark Guzdial
     * @author Barb Ericson
12   */
    public class GUItreeInteractive extends JFrame {

14
     /**
16     * Constructor that takes no arguments
       */
18    public GUItreeInteractive() {

20      /* create the JFrame with the title */
        super("GUI Tree Interactive Example");

22
        /* set the layout to flow layout */
24      this.getContentPane().setLayout(new FlowLayout());

26      /* Put in a panel with a label in it */
        JPanel panel1 = new JPanel();
28      this.getContentPane().add(panel1);
        JLabel label = new JLabel("This is panel 1!");
30      panel1.add(label);

32      /* Put in another panel with two buttons in it */
        JPanel panel2 = new JPanel();
34      this.getContentPane().add(panel2);
        JButton button1 = new JButton("Make a sound");
36      // Here's the listener
        button1.addActionListener(
38                               new ActionListener() {
          // Here's the method we're overriding
40        public void actionPerformed(ActionEvent fred) {
            Sound s =
42          new Sound(FileChooser.getMediaPath("aah.wav"));
            s.play();
44        }
        }
46      );
        panel2.add(button1);

48
        JButton button2 = new JButton("Make a picture");
50      // Here's the listener
        button2.addActionListener(
52                               new ActionListener() {
          // Here's the method we're overriding
54        public void actionPerformed(ActionEvent mabel) {
            Picture p =
56          new Picture(FileChooser.getMediaPath("shops.jpg"));
            p.show();
58        }
        }
60      );
        panel2.add(button2);

62
        /* set the size to fit the contents and show it */
64      this.pack();
```

```
66      this.setVisible(true);
      }
68
      /** test this class */
70    public static void main(String[] args){
        GUItreeInteractive gt = new GUItreeInteractive();
72    }
    }
```

■

How It Works.   Most of the code is identical to our flowed GUItree . The new parts are where we add a listener to each button, using the method addActionListener. The method takes as input an object which will do the listening, that is, provide a method that will take an ActionEvent with the method actionPerformed. We *could* create a subclass of ActionListener, perhaps calling it ShowButtonActionListener and instantiate it here. That is what we are doing, but without the name. Our new subclass of ActionListener has only a single method in it, actionPerformed. That's where we do the showing and playing.

Creating a Picture Tool

How about a picture tool that lets us do some of our image manipulations using a GUI (Figure 13.10). We will start with the ability to pick a picture file to use, save the picture back to the same filename, and save the picture to a different filename. We will also add the ability to negate and flip the picture. By saving a copy of the current picture on a stack of pictures (this time using java.util.Stack) before we change the picture, we can also provide the ability to undo the last command.

Example Java Code 109: Imports and fields for the PictureTool class

```
    import java.awt.*;
2   import javax.swing.*;
    import java.awt.event.*;
4   import java.util.Stack;

6   /**
     * Class that demonstrates creating a graphical
8    * user interface to work with pictures
     * @author Barb Ericson
10   */
    public class PictureTool extends JFrame {
12
      /** picture for the label */
14    Picture picture = new Picture(300,300);

16    /** picture label */
      JLabel pictureLabel = null;
18
      /** stack to hold old pictures for undo */
20    Stack<Picture> pictureStack = new Stack<Picture>();
```

■

This class starts with the imports that are needed to use the short names of the classes in the listed packages. For example, we import javax.swing.* so that we can

FIGURE 13.10
A tool for manipulating pictures.

refer to javax.swing.JFrame and javax.swing.JLabel using the short names of just JFrame and JLabel. Next, we declare the class PictureTool as a subclass of JFrame. The PictureTool class has three fields. One field keeps track of the current picture. One field keeps track of the JLabel that we use to display the picture. And, one field keeps track of the pictures before they were changed on a stack to support the undo feature.

Example Java Code 110: Constructor for the PictureTool class

```
   /**
2   * Constructor that sets up the GUI
    */
4  public PictureTool() {

6    // set title on JFrame
     super("Picture Tool");
8
     // set up the menu
```

```java
        setUpMenu();

        // set the picture in the label
        pictureLabel = new JLabel();
        setPicture(picture);
        this.getContentPane().add(pictureLabel,
          BorderLayout.CENTER);

        // set the frame size and show it
        this.pack();
        this.setVisible(true);
    }
```

The constructor first calls the parent constructor that takes a title for the `JFrame`. Next, it calls the private method `setUpMenu` which sets up the menu bar and menus. Next, it creates a `JLabel` that can set the image in the `JLabel` to be the one from the picture. It also adds the `JLabel` to the center of the border layout so that the picture will take up any additional space if the window is resized. Finally it sets the size of the `JFrame` by packing it to fit the contents of the frame and then showing it.

Example Java Code 111: Start of the setUpMenu method for the PictureTool class

```java
/**
 * Method to set up the menu
 */
private void setUpMenu() {

    // set up the menu bar
    JMenuBar menuBar = new JMenuBar();
    setJMenuBar(menuBar);

    // create the file menu
    JMenu fileMenu = new JMenu("File");
    menuBar.add(fileMenu);
    JMenuItem openItem = new JMenuItem("Open");
    JMenuItem saveItem = new JMenuItem("Save");
    JMenuItem saveAsItem = new JMenuItem("Save As");
    fileMenu.add(openItem);
    fileMenu.add(saveItem);
    fileMenu.add(saveAsItem);
```

This method starts by creating the `JMenuBar` and setting it in the `JFrame`. Then it creates the file menu, adds this menu to the menu bar, and creates three menu items. It then adds the menu items to the file menu.

Example Java Code 112: Handling the file menu items in the PictureTool class

```java
    // handle the open
    openItem.addActionListener(new ActionListener() {
      public void actionPerformed(ActionEvent e) {
        addPictureToStack();
        String file = FileChooser.pickAFile();
        setPicture(new Picture(file));
      }
    });
```

```
10    // handle the save
      saveItem.addActionListener(new ActionListener() {
12      public void actionPerformed(ActionEvent e) {
          String file = picture.getFileName();
14        picture.write(file);
        }
16    });

18    // handle the save as
      saveAsItem.addActionListener(new ActionListener() {
20      public void actionPerformed(ActionEvent e) {
          String file = SimpleInput.getString("Enter filename");
22        picture.write(FileChooser.getMediaPath(file));
        }
24    });
```

For each of the menu items, we add an anonymous inner class to handle the selection of the menu item. If the user selects OPEN, we will ask the user to pick the filename for the picture. If the user selects SAVE, we will write out the current picture using the same filename as it currently has. If the user selects SAVE AS, we will use the `SimpleInput` class to ask for a new filename to use and then write out the current picture using that filename.

Example Java Code 113: Creating the tools menu in the PictureTool class

```
      // create the tools menu
2     JMenu toolsMenu = new JMenu("Tools");
      menuBar.add(toolsMenu);
4     JMenuItem negateItem = new JMenuItem("Negate");
      JMenuItem flipItem = new JMenuItem("Flip");
6     JMenuItem undoItem = new JMenuItem("Undo");
      toolsMenu.add(negateItem);
8     toolsMenu.add(flipItem);
      toolsMenu.add(undoItem);
```

Next, we create the tools menu and add it to the menu bar. We then create the menu items NEGATE, FLIP, and UNDO. We add the menu items to the tool menu.

Example Java Code 114: Handling the tools menu items in the PictureTool class

```
      // handle negate
2     negateItem.addActionListener(new ActionListener() {
        public void actionPerformed(ActionEvent e) {
4         addPictureToStack();
          picture.negate();
6         setPicture(picture);
        }
8     });

10    // handle flip
      flipItem.addActionListener(new ActionListener() {
12      public void actionPerformed(ActionEvent e) {
          addPictureToStack();
14        Picture flippedPict = picture.flip();
          setPicture(flippedPict);
```

```
16        }
      });
18
      // handle undo
20    undoItem.addActionListener(new ActionListener() {
        public void actionPerformed(ActionEvent e) {
22          if (!pictureStack.empty()) {
              Picture pict = pictureStack.pop();
24            setPicture(pict);
            }
26        }
      });
28
    }
```

Next, we create the anonymous inner classes that handle selection of the tools menu items. If the user selects NEGATE, we first save the current picture on the stack of old pictures, negate the picture, and then set the current picture to the negated picture. If the user selects FLIP, we again first save the current picture on the stack of old pictures, flip the picture, and then set the current picture to the flipped picture. If the user selects UNDO, we check that the stack of old pictures isn't empty and if not, we pop off the top one and set the current picture to it.

Example Java Code 115: The rest of the PictureTool class

```
    /**
2     * Method to save the current picture on the stack
     */
4   private void addPictureToStack() {
      pictureStack.push(picture.copy());
6   }

8   /**
     * Method to set the picture to a new picture
10   * @param p the new picture to use
     */
12  public void setPicture(Picture p) {
      picture = p;
14    pictureLabel.setIcon(new ImageIcon(p.getImage()));
      this.pack(); // resize for the new picture
16  }

18  /**
     * Main method for testing
20   */
    public static void main(String[] args) {
22    PictureTool pictTool = new PictureTool();
    }
24  }
```

The rest of the class PictureTool has the private method addPictureToStack that adds a copy of the current picture to the stack of old pictures. It also has the public method setPicture, which handles changing the current picture, changing the icon in the JLabel, and resizing the JFrame to fit the new picture. It also includes a main method that tests this class.

13.4   RUNNING FROM THE COMMAND LINE

What you might want to do with your new interactive programs is to run your tool from the command line. You can do this pretty easily. We can even accept input from the command line, like the name of a filename for the picture to process.

Remember in our `main` methods, we specified `String[] args` as the input? That array of strings actually represents all the words in the command line after the class name when we execute our class from the command line, using the `java` command. Here is a test class for playing with this.

Example Java Code 116: Test program for String[] args

```
/**
 * Class to show using the array of string arguments
 * @author Mark Guzdial
 * @author Barb Ericson
 */
public class TestStringArgs {
  public static void main(String [] args) {
    if (args.length == 0)
      System.out.println("No arguments were entered!");
    for (int i = 0; i < args.length; i++) {
      System.out.println("argument " + i + ": " + args[i]);
    }
  }
}
```

■

You can try this out in the interactions pane of DrJava.

```
> java TestStringArgs
No arguments were entered!
> java TestStringArgs 0 "croak.wav"
argument 0: 0
argument 1: croak.wav
```

How about if we want to execute the `PictureTool` with some file specified as input? We could modify the `main` method to check for input and use the first item in the array of arguments as the filename for the picture. Then, we can pass in the picture name when we execute the `PictureTool` class using the command line as shown in Figure 13.11.

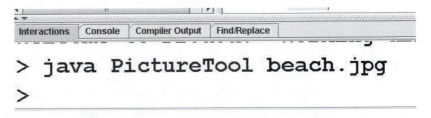

FIGURE 13.11
Executing `PictureTool` from the command line with a filename as input.

Example Java Code 117: The main method in PictureTool

```
public static void main(String[] args) {
2    PictureTool pictTool = new PictureTool();
     if (args.length > 0) {
4       pictTool.setPicture(new Picture(args[0]));
     }
6  }
```

EXERCISES

For these exercises, you will probably need some additional references on Swing, using the concepts introduced in this chapter.

13.1 Which layout manager would you use if you want to exactly position the components and not allow them to automatically resize? Which would you use if you want the components to take up just the amount of space they need and position them from left to right in the center of the screen? Which would you use if you want one component to get all extra space?

13.2 Create a tool to allow a user to specify a rhythm by creating copies of some sound, weaving and repeating the copies into a new sound (Figure 13.12). Here are the parts of this window that we care about.

- Include a text field at the top of the window where the user can specify the filename of a sound to be inserted into our sound sequence. As a simplification, we will assume that all filenames are specified as base names, and they refer to files in other `mediaPath`.

- Add buttons for REPEAT and WEAVE that insert the sound into a sound sequence. These buttons take a numeric input specified in a field below the filename. When the REPEAT button is pressed, that number of copies of the sound are repeated at the end of the sound sequence. When the WEAVE button is pressed, that number of copies of the sound are woven into the sound sequence. We again use a simplification—we assume the weave is skip-one-insert-one.

- Finally, at the bottom, add an a PLAY button to hear the sound sequence that we are creating.

FIGURE 13.12
A tool for generating rhythms.

13.3 Modify the RhythmTool to allow the user to SAVE the newly created sound sequence. Use the write method to write out the final sound.

13.4 Modify the RhythmTool to allow the user to use menu items instead of buttons for play and explore.

13.5 Create another button or a menu item for RhythmTool to create a new sequence—to clear out the current sequence.

13.6 Create a class named Scribbler that lets you draw on a picture using the mouse. Use buttons to select the color to draw with and add a tool for picking the width of the brush.

13.7 Create a class named InteractivePicture that does different things when you move the mouse over five different sections of a picture. For example one section might turn gray when you move the mouse over it.

13.8 Create a class named PlayList that lets the user pick the order of songs to play and move them up and down in the list.

13.9 Create a class named PictureSelect that shows thumbnails of all the pictures in a directory and lets the user select which one to see at full size in the center.

13.10 Create a class named StoryBoard that shows a picture in the middle and a text area underneath. Save out the text that the user enters.

13.11 Create a class named PhotoAlbum that shows thumbnails of all the pictures in a directory with a JTextArea under each picture that allows the user to enter information about the picture. Save the information to a file in the directory. When you start the class, check for the file and read from it if it exists.

13.12 Create a class named RedEyeRemover that allows the user to pick a region and a color and change the red in that region to another color.

13.13 Add more features to the PictureTool class. You get to choose the menu items that you provide, but there must be at least five:

- Provide two menu items for manipulating the color: reduce red, increase red, make it grayscale, darken, or lighten. Your choice. (You can provide more than two if you want.)

- Provide a menu item that takes a numeric input and uses that input to manipulate the picture. Maybe it's a scaling tool and the input is the amount to scale (2.0? 0.5?)? Maybe it's an amount to increase or decrease red?

- Provide a menu item to do some kind of mirroring, either horizontal or vertical.

- One other menu item of any kind you want. Red eye removal? Rotate? Compose another figure scaled down into the bottom of the picture? Chromakey the picture onto a jungle?

The undo feature should continue to work on any new menu items that you add!

13.14   Write a class `TurtleEtchASketch`[1] that will create a version of the classic "Etch-a-sketch" using a `Turtle` and present it visually using a GUI. You will need to have a `Turtle` draw on a `Picture` canvas, with directional buttons to control the movements of the `Turtle`.

Components you need to include:

- Directional buttons to control the `Turtle`.

    1. `upButton` and `downButton` to control vertical movement.

    2. `leftButton` and `rightButton` to control horizontal movement.

- An input area (`JTextArea` and `JTextField` are good choices) to define how many pixels or steps the `Turtle` should move each time a directional button is clicked. (The default number of pixels should be five.)

- A `submitButton` for the input area.

- **Easy option:** Create three buttons to change the color of the line the `Turtle` draws.

- **Harder option:** Have a button to bring up a `JColorChooser` to change the color.

- Use a `JLabel` to hold the `Picture` that will serve as the background for the `Turtle`. The background `Picture` can be blank, but does not have to be.

- Be sure to have a `shakeButton` that clears the whole screen.

13.15   Build a class named `MidiTool` that will create a GUI for creating MIDI (music) sequences.

This GUI will have a string input area where the user can type in a sequence of letters. The letters will define a set of MIDI notes to define a *node*. Only the letters c, d, e, f, g, a, and b are allowed, presumed all in the third octave. Lowercase is an eighth note, uppercase is a quarter note. So cEdEgC would be c3 eighth, e3 quarter, d3 eighth, e3 quarter, g3 eighth, c3 quarter.

There should be buttons that allow users to create notes in a node, then weave nodes into a sequence:

- `MakeNode` converts the current string into a node.

- `PlayNode` plays the node.

- `ClearSequence` clears the current sequence.

- `RepeatInSequence` takes a number in a text area ("3," for example) and repeats the currently made node that number of times onto the end of the sequence.

- `WeaveInSequence` weaves the currently made node into the sequence every other node until the end of the sequence.

- `PlaySequence` plays the sequence.

---

[1]Project created by Dawn Finney and Colin Potts.

Be sure to handle error conditions. What should happen if someone chooses to repeat or weave a node into a sequence when no node has been made? What should happen if illegal characters are entered into the string for a node? These are decisions you can make. A Java run-time error, however, is not an appropriate message to a user.

For extra credit, create a `SaveSequence` button that saves the sequence into a MIDI file.

PART 4

SIMULATIONS: PROBLEM SOLVING WITH DATA STRUCTURES

CHAPTER

14 Using an Existing Simulation Package

14.1 INTRODUCING SIMULATIONS

14.2 OVERVIEW OF GREENFOOT

14.3 GREENFOOT BASICS

14.4 CREATING NEW CLASSES

14.5 BREAKOUT

Chapter Learning Objectives

We're now starting on the third major theme of this book. The first was programming media in Java, and the second was structuring media with dynamic data structures (e.g., linked lists and trees). The third theme is simulations, and here's where we use all of the above to create our villagers and wildebeests.

There are many different existing software packages that can help you create simulations or games (as a *kind* of simulation). In this chapter, we use one existing software package named Greenfoot to create a simulation and a game. In the next chapter, we'll talk about how that works.

The computer science goals for this chapter are:

- To be able to use the basic terminology of simulations: discrete event versus continuous, resources, and queues.
- To create a simulation using an existing software package.
- To create a simple game using an existing software package.

14.1 INTRODUCING SIMULATIONS

A simulation is a representation of a system of objects in a real or fantasy world. The purpose of creating a computer simulation is to provide a framework in which to understand the simulated situation, for example, to understand the behavior of a waiting line, the workload of clerks, or the timeliness of service to customers. A computer simulation makes it possible to collect statistics about these situations, and to test out new ideas about their organization.

The above quote is by Adele Goldberg and Dave Robson from their 1989 book in which they introduced the programming language *Smalltalk* to the world [2]. Smalltalk is important for being the first language explicitly called "object-oriented," and it was the language in which the desktop user interface (overlapping windows, icons, menus, and a mouse pointer) was invented. And Smalltalk was invented, in part, in order to create *simulations*.

Simulations contain representations of the world (models) that are executed (made to behave like things in the world). The idea of objects in Smalltalk was based on a programming language called *Simula*, which was entirely invented to build simulations. Object-oriented programming makes it easier to build simulations, because objects were designed to model real-world objects.

- In the real world, things *know* stuff and they *know how to do* stuff. We don't mean to anthropomorphize the world, but there is a sense in which real-world objects *know* and *know how*. Blood cells *know* the oxygen that they carry, and they *know how* to pass it through to other cells through permeable membranes. Students know the courses they want, and Registrars know the course catalog.

- Objects get things done by *asking* each other to do things, not by demanding or controlling other things. The important point is that there is an *interface* between objects that defines how they interact with each other. Blood cells don't force their oxygen into other cells. Students register for classes by requesting a seat from a Registrar—it's not often that a student gets away with registering by placing themselves on a class roll.

- Objects decide what data they share and what they don't share. The Registrar doesn't know what a student wants to enroll for, and the student won't get the class she wants until the desired course is shared with the Registrar.

Object-oriented programming was invented to make simulations easier, but not *just* to build simulations. Alan Kay, who was one of the key thinkers behind Smalltalk and object-oriented programming, had the insight that simulations were a great way to think about *all* kinds of programs. A course registration system is actually a simulation of a model of how a campus works. A spreadsheet is a simulation of the physical paperbooks in which accountants would do their totals and account tracking.

There are two main kinds of simulations. Continuous simulations represent every moment of the simulated world. Most video games can be thought of as continuous simulations. Weather simulations and simulations of nuclear blasts tend to be continuous because you have to track everything at every moment. Discrete event simulations, on the other hand, do not represent *every* moment of time in a simulation.

Discrete event simulations only simulate the moments when something interesting happens. Discrete event simulations are often the most useful in professional situations. If you want to use a simulation of a factory floor, in order to determine the optimal number of machines and the layout of those machines, then you really don't care about simulating the product when it's in the stamping machine, cutter, or polisher. You only care about noting when material enters and leaves those machines—and having some way to measure how much the material was *probably* in the machine for *about* how long. Similarly, if you wanted to simulate Napoleon's march to Russia (maybe to explore what would have happened if they'd taken a different route, or if the weather was 10 degrees warmer), you care about how many people marched each day, and consider some notion of how many might succumb to the cold each day. But you really don't need to simulate every foot-dragging, miserable moment—just the ones that really matter.

The real trick of a discrete event simulation, then, is to figure out when you should simulate—when something interesting should happen, so that you can jump right to those moments. We're going to find that there are several important parts of a discrete event simulation that will enable us to do that. For example, we will have an *event queue* that will keep track of what are the important points that we know about so far, and when are they supposed to happen.

Discrete event simulations (and sometimes continuous simulations) tend to involve *resources*. Resources are what the active, working beings (or *agents*) in the simulation strive for. A resource might be a book in a library, or a teller in a bank, or a car at a rental agency. We say that some resources are *fixed*—there's only so much of it (like cars in a rental car), and no more is created even if more is needed. Other resources are *produced* and *consumed*, like jelly beans or chips (just keep crunching, we'll make more).

We can also think of resources as points of coordination in a simulation. Imagine that you are simulating a hospital where both doctors and patients are agents being simulated. You want to simulate that, during some procedure (say, an operation), both the doctor and patient have to be at the same place and can't do anything else until the procedure is done. In that case, the operating table might be the *coordinated resource*, and when both the doctor and patient access that resource, they're both stuck until done.

If an agent can't get the resource it wants when it wants it, we say that the agent enters a *queue*. In the United Kingdom, people know that word well—in the United States, we simply call it "a line" and being in a queue is "getting in line." This is the same *queue* that we've been talking about as the data structure `queue`. The real world "queue" that is used as a basic notion of "fairness" (we all wait in line, and first-come-first-served) is the inspiration for and is modeled by the data structure "queue," that we sometimes call a *FIFO list*—a list of items that are first-in-first-out. In simulation terms, if an agent can't get the resource that she wants, she enters a queue waiting for more resource to be produced or for a resource to be returned by some other agent (if it's a fixed resource).

We'll deal with resources and queues when we get into how simulations are built. For now, let's build a simulation using a powerful package designed for that purpose. Then we'll deconstruct the models inside a simulation to understand how they work.

14.2 OVERVIEW OF GREENFOOT

Greenfoot is a framework for creating two-dimensional simulations and games in Java. Greenfoot is built on top of the Java development environment BlueJ, which means that it allows you to visualize the objects and the relationships between the classes.

Greenfoot was developed by a team from the University of Kent in England and Deakin University in Australia. In Greenfoot a set of related classes is called a scenario and Greenfoot comes with predefined scenarios.

Before you can install Greenfoot, you must have the Java Development Kit (jdk) installed on your computer. You should already have this or DrJava wouldn't have worked. You can download Greenfoot from http://www.greenfoot.org. Once you have downloaded and installed Greenfoot, you are ready to start. Click on `greenfoot.exe` to start Greenfoot. To open a scenario, click on Scenario in the menu and then on Open and select a scenario to open. The scenarios are in the scenario directory under the greenfoot directory.

Greenfoot comes with five scenarios. They are ants, balloons, lunarlander, wombats, and wombats2. Open the ants scenario (Figure 14.1) and click the Run button to see the scenario running. The ants will leave the anthill and look for food. Once they find food, they will pick it up and drop pheromones on their way from the food source back to the anthill. Other ants will follow the pheromones. The pheromones fade over time. Click the Scenario Information button to read about the current scenario.

Next, open the balloons scenario (Figure 14.2). This scenario is a game in which you try to pop the balloons using the dart and the bombs before a balloon reaches the top of the window. You can move the dart using the mouse and click to try to pop a

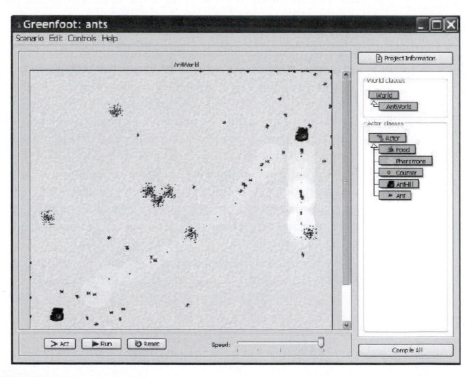

FIGURE 14.1
The ants scenario in Greenfoot.

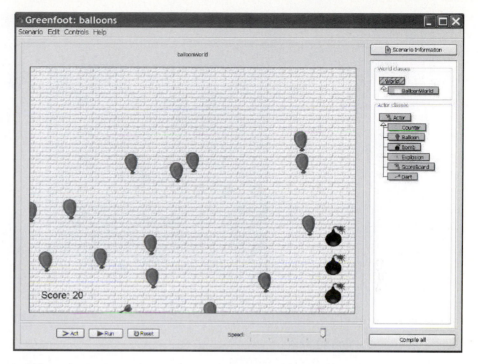

FIGURE 14.2
The balloons scenario.

balloon with the dart. You can drag a bomb onto a balloon to explode it and surrounding balloons. You can click the PAUSE button to pause the action and click on the ACT button to see what happens after each time interval in the simulation.

Next open the lunarlander scenario (Figure 14.3). This scenario is a game in which you try to land the lunar lander by firing a rocket thrust using the down arrow key. If you don't land gently enough, the lunar lander explodes.

Now open the wombats scenario. Notice that this one has a two-dimensional grid. If you click the RUN button nothing happens. This scenario is used in the tutorial that comes with Greenfoot. You can access this tutorial by clicking on HELP in the menu and then on GREENFOOT TUTORIAL. You can also access it from the `tutorial` folder under the `greenfoot` directory.

You can create a wombat object by right-clicking (use control-click on a Mac) on the `Wombat` class in the class hierarchy and then clicking on NEW WOMBAT(). This will create a new wombat object and attach it to the mouse and you can click anywhere in the grid to drop the wombat in that location. Go ahead and try this. Put at least two wombats in the grid. Next, add some leaves. Hold down the SHIFT key when you right-click on the LEAF class and this will allow you to drop multiple leaves in the grid until you release the SHIFT key (Figure 14.4).

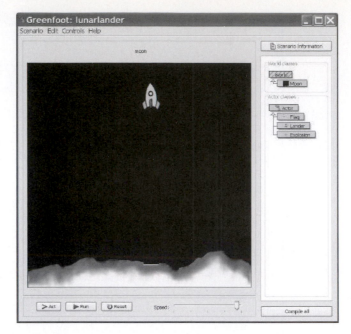

FIGURE 14.3
The lunerlander scenario.

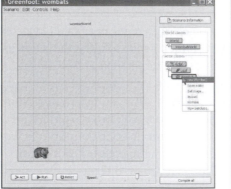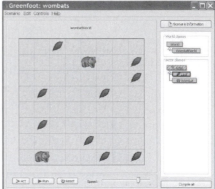

FIGURE 14.4
Creating wombats and leaves in the wombat scenario.

Press the ACT button a few times and you will notice that the wombats move forward and eat any leaves they encounter but they don't necessarily eat all the available leaves. You can right-click on a wombat in the grid and a menu will appear with all the methods that the wombat object knows. You can also double-click on the Wombat class and see the code for that class. See if you can figure out why a wombat won't necessarily find all the available leaves and eat them.

Example Java Code 118: The act method in the Wombat class

```
  /**
2  * Do whatever the wombat likes do to just now.
   */
4 public void act()
  {
6     if(foundLeaf()) {
          eatLeaf();
8     }
      else if(canMove()) {
10        move();
      }
12    else {
          turnLeft();
14    }
  }
```

So, when the ACT button is pushed, the wombat will first see if it found a leaf and if so eat it. Otherwise it will see if it can move and then move. If it didn't find a leaf and can't move, it will turn left. So, this is why it will go in a square pattern eating all the leaves in its path, but not find other leaves.

How can we fix it to find the other leaves? We could allow it to turn in some random direction. How can we do that? We can look at the documentation for the Wombat class by clicking on the down arrow next to the SOURE CODE in the top of the editor window (Figure 14.5).

By looking at the Wombat class documentation, we can see that wombats know how to turn left using the method turnLeft but they don't seem to know how to turn any

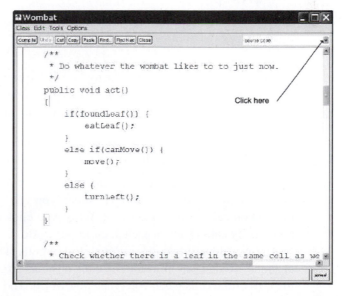

FIGURE 14.5
Switching to the documentation from the editor.

other direction. But, two left turns will point the wombat the opposite way and three left turns results in a right turn. So, we can create a `turnRandom` method that randomly chooses a number of times to turn left.

Example Java Code 119: The turnRandom method in the Wombat class

```java
/**
 * Turn in a random direction
 */
public void turnRandom() {
    // get a random number between 0 and 3 ...
    int numTurns = Greenfoot.getRandomNumber(4);

    // turn left numTurns times
    for (int i = 0; i < numTurns; i++) {
        turnLeft();
    }
}
```

The class method `Greenfoot.getRandomNumber(4)` will return 0, 1, 2, or 3. Now, we can modify the `act` method to turn in a random direction if it can't move.

Example Java Code 120: The act method with a random turn

```java
public void act() {
    if (foundLeaf()) {
        eatLeaf();
    }
    else if (canMove()) {
        move();
    }
    else {
        turnRandom();
    }
}
```

Click the COMPILE button at the top left of the editor window and fix any errors. Run the scenario again and see if the wombats get all the leaves. You can continue with the Greenfoot tutorial by clicking on HELP and then click on GREENFOOT TUTORIAL.

14.3 GREENFOOT BASICS

Greenfoot has two main classes: `World` and `Actor`. A `World` object contains `Actor` objects. Actors know how to act. When you click ACT, the world calls the `act()` method on each actor in the world. When you click on the RUN button, this will loop continually calling act on each actor in the world.

The world has a two-dimensional grid of cells. The size of the cells can be 1 pixel or larger. Actors can fit inside the cells or be as large as they want to be. You can set the size of the cells when you create the world. The width of the world is the number of cells in the horizontal direction. The height of the world is the number of cells in the vertical direction.

The `World` class is an abstract class, so you cannot create a world object. You must create a subclass of `World`. In the wombat scenario you can see that there is a `WombatWorld`, which is a child (subclass) of `World`.

Example Java Code 121: The Start of the WombatWorld Class

```java
import greenfoot.*;  // imports Actor, World, Greenfoot,
// GreenfootImage
import java.util.Random;


/**
 * A world where wombats live.
 *
 * @author Michael Kolling
 * @version 1.0.1
 */
public class WombatWorld extends World
{
    /**
     * Create a new world with 8x8 cells and
     * with a cell size of 60x60 pixels
     */
    public WombatWorld()
    {
        super(8, 8, 60);
        setBackground("cell.jpg");
    }
```

The constructor for the `WombatWorld` calls the `World` constructor using `super(8, 8,60)` which creates a world that has eight cells horizontal and eight cells vertical and each cell is 60 by 60 pixels. Then it sets the image for a cell.

There are two more methods in the `WombatWorld` class. These can be used to populate the `WombatWorld` with wombats and leaves.

Example Java Code 122: The rest of WombatWorld

```java
    /**
     * Populate the world with a fixed scenario of wombats
     * and leaves.
     */
    public void populate()
    {
        Wombat w1 = new Wombat();
        addObject(w1, 3, 3);

        Wombat w2 = new Wombat();
        addObject(w2, 1, 7);

        Leaf l1 = new Leaf();
        addObject(l1, 5, 3);

        Leaf l2 = new Leaf();
        addObject(l2, 0, 2);

        Leaf l3 = new Leaf();
        addObject(l3, 7, 5);
```

```
22          Leaf 14 = new Leaf();
            addObject(14, 2, 6);
24
            Leaf 15 = new Leaf();
26          addObject(15, 5, 0);

28          Leaf 16 = new Leaf();
            addObject(16, 4, 7);
30      }

32      /**
         * Place a number of leaves into the world at random
34       * places.
         * The number of leaves can be specified.
36       */
        public void randomLeaves(int howMany)
38      {
            for(int i=0; i<howMany; i++) {
40              Leaf leaf = new Leaf();
                int x = Greenfoot.getRandomNumber(getWidth());
42              int y = Greenfoot.getRandomNumber(getHeight());
                addObject(leaf, x, y);
44          }
        }
46  }
```

■

You can call the `populate` method in the constructor to add wombats and leaves at specific locations when the world is created. You can use the `randomLeaves` method to randomly place a given number of leaves. Can you write a similar method called `randomWombats` to randomly place a given number of wombats?

14.4   CREATING NEW CLASSES

You can create additional classes that inherit from `Actor`. Just right-click on `Actor` and select NEW SUBCLASS (Figure 14.6).

A window will appear asking for the class name and an image for objects of the class. Enter "Wall" for the name and pick the wall image from the backgrounds category (Figure 14.7).

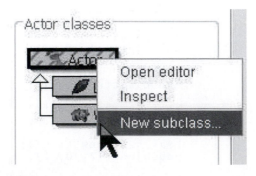

FIGURE 14.6
Creating a subclass of Actor.

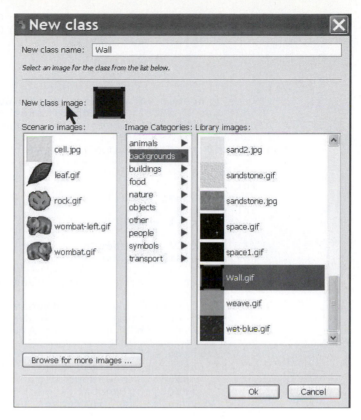

FIGURE 14.7
Creating a `Wall` class.

You can add methods to the `WombatWorld` to also randomly place walls and wombats. We will use the `randomLeaves` method as a starting point but we will make a few changes so that wombats and walls will not be placed in a location that already has an actor in it. We will also change the `randomLeaves` method so that the variables are declared before the loop. This is more efficient since the variables will be created once and then just what they reference will change each time through the loop.

Example Java Code 123: Methods to randomly place leaves, wombats, and walls

```
/**
 * Place a number of leaves into the world at random places.
 * @param howMany the number of leaves to place
 */
public void randomLeaves(int howMany)
{
    Leaf leaf = null;
    int x = 0;
    int y = 0;

    for(int i=0; i<howMany; i++) {
        leaf = new Leaf();
```

```
                             x = Greenfoot.getRandomNumber(getWidth());
14                           y = Greenfoot.getRandomNumber(getHeight());
                             addObject(leaf, x, y);
16           }
         }

18
         /**
20        * Place a number of wombats in the world at random places.
          * Don't put a wombat on top of another actor.
22        * @param howMany the number of wombats to place
          */
24       public void randomWombats(int howMany)
         {
26           int x = 0;
             int y = 0;
28           Wombat wombat = null;
             int count = 0;
30           List objList = null;

32           // loop till put enough
             while (count < howMany) {

34
                 // get a random location and get all wombats at that
36               // location
                 x = Greenfoot.getRandomNumber(getWidth());
38               y = Greenfoot.getRandomNumber(getHeight());
                 objList = this.getObjectsAt(x,y,Actor.class);

40
                 // if no other actors are here then add the wombat
42               if (objList.isEmpty()) {
                     wombat = new Wombat();
44                   addObject(wombat,x,y);
                     count++; // increment count
46               }
             }
48       }

50        /**
          * Place a number of walls in the world at random places.
52        * Don't put a wall on top of another actor.
          * @param howMany the number of walls to place
54        */
         public void randomWalls(int howMany)
56       {
             int x = 0;
58           int y = 0;
             Wall wall = null;
60           int count = 0;
             List objList = null;

62
             // loop till put enough
64           while (count < howMany) {

66               // get a random location and get all wombats at that
                 // location
68               x = Greenfoot.getRandomNumber(getWidth());
                 y = Greenfoot.getRandomNumber(getHeight());
70               objList = this.getObjectsAt(x,y,Actor.class);

72               // if no other actors are here then add the wombat
                 if (objList.isEmpty()) {
74                   wall = new Wall();
```

```
        addObject(wall,x,y);
76        count++; // increment count
      }
78    }
  }
```

We can modify the constructor to randomly place a number of wombats, walls, and leaves.

Example Java Code 124: The modified Wombat constructor

```
/**
2 * Create a new world with 8x8 cells and a cell size of
 * 60x60 pixels
4 * and an amount of randomly placed wombats, walls,
 * and leaves
6 */
public WombatWorld() {
8    super(8, 8, 60);
     setBackground("cell.jpg");
10   randomLeaves(6);
     randomWombats(3);
12   randomWalls(24);
}
```

Now when we compile WombatWorld we will see a world with 3 wombats, 24 walls, and 6 leaves (Figure 14.8). But, there is no guarantee that any wombat will be able to reach any leaf.

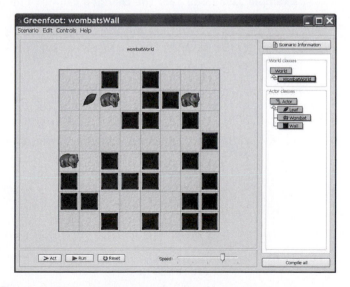

FIGURE 14.8
A new WombatWorld.

Let's change the wombat act method to make it more likely that at least one wombat will reach the leaf. Sometimes even when the wombat can move, let's pick a random direction to turn instead.

Example Java Code 125: The changed act method in Wombat

```java
/**
 * Do whatever the wombat likes to do just now.
 */
public void act()
{
    if(foundLeaf()) {
        eatLeaf();
    }
    // else if can move sometimes (1 of 5 chance) turn
    else if(canMove()) {
        if (Greenfoot.getRandomNumber(5) == 0)
            turnRandom();
        else
            move();
    }
    else {
        turnRandom();
    }
}
```

We will also need to modify the wombat canMove method so that the wombat doesn't walk into the walls.

Example Java Code 126: The changed canMove method in Wombat

```java
/**
 * Test if we can move forward. Return true if we can,
 * false otherwise.
 */
public boolean canMove()
{
    World myWorld = getWorld();
    int x = getX();
    int y = getY();

    // find the next location in the current direction
    switch(direction) {
        case SOUTH :
            y++;
            break;
        case EAST :
            x++;
            break;
        case NORTH :
            y--;
            break;
        case WEST :
            x--;
            break;
    }
```

```
26
         // see if there is a wall in the next location
28       List objList =
           getWorld().getObjectsAt(x,y,Wall.class);
30
         // test for outside border
32       if (x >= myWorld.getWidth()
           || y >= myWorld.getHeight()) {
34         return false;
         }
36       else if (x < 0 || y < 0) {
           return false;
38       }
         else if (!objList.isEmpty()) {
40         return false;
         }
42       return true;
     }
```

■

Run the program. Does at least one wombat find the leaf? How long does it take a wombat to find the leaf? Can you make a smarter wombat? Can you modify the scenario so that wombats can smell leaves that are within a certain radius of their current position? Can you make a wombat that can remember where it has been so that it prefers to check locations it hasn't been yet?

14.5   BREAKOUT

How would we create a breakout game in Greenfoot (Figure 14.9)? In breakout the user hits a ball with a paddle into bricks to try and destroy all the bricks. If the ball gets past the user, you lose that ball and start with a new one. If the user destroys all the bricks before using three balls, then the user wins.

When you do object-oriented analysis you focus on what objects (nouns) are mentioned in the problem description. The description of the breakout game included: game, user, ball, paddle, and brick. Do we need to model the game? Each time we hit RUN we will start a new game, so we can just have the world start the game. Do we need to model the user? If we aren't keeping any information about the user, then we don't have to model the user. But we do need to know where the ball is and if it hit a brick or got past the user. We do need to know where the paddle is and have some way for the user to control it. We do need to know where the brick is and if it has been hit by the ball. So we need to model a ball, a paddle, and a brick. We also need a way to communicate with the user about the state of the game. So we will also include a message class that displays a message to the user like which ball they are on and if they won or lost.

We have to create a BreakoutWorld since the World class is abstract. Here is the class definition, fields, and a constructor.

Example Java Code 127: The beginning of the BreakWorld class

```java
public class BreakoutWorld extends World
{
    /////////////////// constants ////////////////////////////

    /** the width of the bricks in pixels (cells) */
    public static final int BRICK_WIDTH = 36;
    /** the height of the bricks in pixels (cells) */
    public static final int BRICK_HEIGHT = 8;
    /** the distance between bricks in pixels (cells) */
    public static final int BRICK_SEP = 4;
    /** the number of bricks per row */
    public static final int NUM_BRICKS_PER_ROW = 10;
    /** distance from the top edge in pixels (cells) */
    public static final int BRICK_Y_OFFSET = 70;
    /** the number of pixels per cell */
    public static final int RESOLUTION = 1;
    /** world width in pixels (cells) */
    public static final int WIDTH =
        (BRICK_WIDTH + BRICK_SEP) *
        NUM_BRICKS_PER_ROW + BRICK_SEP;
    /** world height in pixels (cells) */
    public static final int HEIGHT = 600;
    /** number of rows of bricks */
    public static final int NUM_ROWS = 10;
    /** the colors to use for each row of bricks */
    public static final Color[] colorArray = {Color.RED,
        Color.RED,
        Color.ORANGE, Color.ORANGE, Color.GREEN,Color.GREEN,
        Color.YELLOW,Color.YELLOW,  Color.CYAN, Color.CYAN};

    /////////////// instance fields //////////////////

    /** the number of balls created in the game so far */
    private int numBalls = 0;

    /** a message displayed for the user */
    private Message message = null;

    /////////// constructors ////////////

    /**
     * No argument constructor
     */
    public BreakoutWorld()
    {
        super (WIDTH, HEIGHT, RESOLUTION);
        setUpBreakout();
    }
```

■

Notice that in the constructor it calls setUpBreakout. This method is shown below.

FIGURE 14.9
The breakout game display.

Example Java Code 128: The method that sets up the breakout game

```java
/**
 * Method to set up the breakout game
 */
public void setUpBreakout()
{
    /* update image */
    updateImage();

    /* set up the message */
    message = new Message("Game starting");
    addObject(message,WIDTH/2, 35);

    /* set up the bricks */
    setUpBricks();

    /* create the paddle */
    addObject(new Paddle(),(WIDTH / 2),HEIGHT - 30);

    /* create a new ball */
    newBall();
}
```

To set up the game, it first sets up the background image by calling the method updateImage. Then it creates a message object, initializes it, and adds it to the world. Then it sets up all the bricks by calling the method setUpBricks. Then it creates a paddle object and adds it to the world. Then it creates a new ball by calling the method newBall.

Example Java Code 129: The method that creates and sets the background image

```
   /**
 2  * Method to create and set the image for the background
    */
 4 public void updateImage()
   {
 6     GreenfootImage image = new GreenfootImage(WIDTH,HEIGHT);
       image.setColor(new Color(200,200,200));
 8     image.fillRect(0,0,WIDTH,HEIGHT);
       setBackground(image);
10 }
```

To create the background image this method creates a new image of the same width and height as the world. Then it sets the color to be used in painting to a gray color. Then it draws a filled rectangle, the size of the world, using the gray color . Finally it sets the background image for the world to this new image.

Next the bricks are created.

Example Java Code 130: The setUpBricks method

```
   /*
 2  * Method to set up the bricks in the world
    */
 4 private void setUpBricks()
   {
 6     int yPos = BRICK_HEIGHT / 2 + BRICK_Y_OFFSET;
       int halfWidth = BRICK_WIDTH / 2;
 8
       // loop through the rows and columns
10     for (int row = 0; row < NUM_ROWS; row++,
           yPos = yPos + BRICK_HEIGHT + BRICK_SEP)
12     {
           for (int col = 0, xPos = BRICK_SEP + halfWidth;
14             col < NUM_BRICKS_PER_ROW;
               col++, xPos = xPos + BRICK_WIDTH + BRICK_SEP)
16         {
               addObject(new Brick(colorArray[row]),xPos,yPos);
18         }
       }
20 }
```

This starts the first row's y position at half the brick height plus the y offset (the amount of space to leave between rows). It loops through all the rows and columns and creates each brick. The color for each row is pulled from an array of colors based on the row index.

The Brick class inherits from the Actor class. It just doesn't do anything when asked to act. It draws itself by creating an image of the same width and height as the brick and then setting the paint color to the brick color and then drawing a filled rectangle. This is the same way that the background image was created in the Breakout World.

Example Java Code 131: The Brick Class

```java
import greenfoot.*;   // (World, Actor, GreenfootImage,
                      // and Greenfoot)
import java.awt.Color;

/**
 * A brick is a filled rectangle that doesn't do
 * anything when it gets the act message.
 *
 * @author Barb Ericson, Georgia Tech
 * @version 1.0, April 6, 2007
 */
public class Brick extends Actor
{
    /** the width of the brick */
    private int width = 36;

    /** the height of the brick */
    private int height = 8;

    /** the color of the brick */
    private Color color;

    ////////// constructor ////////////////

    /**
     * Constructor that takes the color for the brick
     * @param theColor the color to use for this brick
     */
    public Brick(Color theColor)
    {
      color = theColor;
      updateImage();
    }

    /**
     * Constructor that takes the width, height,
     * and color for this brick.
     */
    public Brick(int theWidth, int theHeight,
      Color theColor)
    {
        width = theWidth;
        height = theHeight;
        color = theColor;
        updateImage();
    }

    ///////////// methods //////////////////

    /**
     * Method to act during a time step
     */
```

```
54    public void act()
      {}

56    /**
       * Method to create the image and set it for this brick.
58     * If you change the width, height, or color invoke this
       * method.
60     */
      public void updateImage()
62    {
          GreenfootImage image =
64          new GreenfootImage(width,height);
          image.setColor(this.color);
66        image.fillRect(0,0,width,height);
          setImage(image);
68    }

70    }
```

■

The newBall method increments the number of balls created (the numBalls field) and then checks if more than three balls have been created. If more than three balls have been created, it sets the text of the message to tell the user that the game is over. Otherwise it creates a new ball and adds it to the world. It also sets the message to display the ball number.

The Ball class also inherits from the Actor class.

Example Java Code 132: The beginning of the Ball class

```
      import greenfoot.*;  // (World, Actor, GreenfootImage,
2     // and Greenfoot)
      import java.awt.Color;
4     import java.util.List;

6     /**
       * A ball is an object that can hit other objects and
8      * bounce off the edges of the world (except the bottom edge).
       * It will bounce off of a paddle as well.
10     * @author Barbara Ericson Georgia Tech
       * @version 1.0 April 6, 2007
12     */
      public class Ball extends Actor
14    {

16        /////////// fields /////////////////////////////

18        /** the radius of this ball */
          private int radius = 10;
20
          /** the width of this ball (diameter) */
22        private int width = radius * 2;

24        /** the color of the ball */
          private Color color = Color.BLACK;
26
          /** the amount of change in x during each act */
28        private int velX;

30        /** the amount of change in y during each act */
```

```
32      private int velY = 3;

        /////////////// constructors ////////////////////
34
        /**
36       * Constructor that takes no arguments
         */
38      public Ball()
        {
40          velX = Greenfoot.getRandomNumber(2) + 2;
            if (Greenfoot.getRandomNumber(2) == 0)
42              velX = -1 * velX;
            updateImage();
44      }

46      /**
         * Constructor that takes initial values for all fields
48       * @param theRadius  the radius to use
         * @param theColor   the color to use
50       * @param theVelX    the amount to change in X per act
         * @param theVelY    the amount to change in Y per act
52       */
        public Ball(int theRadius, Color theColor, int theVelX,
54          int theVelY)
        {
56          radius = theRadius;
            color = theColor;
58          velX = theVelX;
            velY = theVelY;
60          updateImage();
        }
```

There are two constructors in the `Ball` class. One constructor takes no arguments and sets the *x* (horizontal) velocity of the ball and then sometimes negates it. A ball is drawn like a brick, but instead of drawing a filled rectangle, it draws a filled oval.

The most important method in the `Ball` class is the `act` method.

Example Java Code 133: The Ball act method

```
        /**
2        * Balls will move and check if they have hit a brick or
         * paddle or one of the edges of the world
4        */
        public void act()
6       {
            BreakoutWorld world = (BreakoutWorld) getWorld();
8
            // move the ball
10          setLocation(getX() + velX, getY() + velY);

12          // check if hit any object and it wasn't the message
            Actor actor = this.getOneIntersectingObject(Actor.class);
14          if (actor != null && !(actor instanceof Message))
            {
16              /* bounce off of the object */
                velY = -(velY + 2);
18
                /* if it was a brick then remove it and check
20                 if won */
```

```
            if (actor instanceof Brick)
22          {
                world.removeObject(actor);
24              world.checkIfWon();
            }
26      }

28      // check if hit walls
        else if (getX() - radius <= 0) // left wall
30          velX = -velX;
        else if (getX() + radius >= BreakoutWorld.WIDTH) //
32        right wall
            velX = -velX;
34      else if (getY() - radius <= 0) // top wall
            velY = -velY;
36      else if (getY() + radius >= BreakoutWorld.HEIGHT) //
          bottom wall
38      {
            world.removeObject(this);
40          world.newBall();
        }
42
    }
```

In this method, it first gets the `BreakoutWorld` object and then moves the ball by adding the *x* and *y* velocities to the current *x* and *y*. Next, it checks if the ball hit any object in the world other than the message (a brick or paddle). It negates the *y* velocity to have the ball bounce off the object and adds 2 to it to speed up the ball a bit. Next, it checks if the ball hit a brick and if so, it removes the brick from the world and asks the world to check if it won. The user wins if there are no more bricks in the world. If we didn't hit any actors in the world, we check if the ball is at the left wall and if so, it bounces off it by negating the *x* velocity. Else if the ball hit the right wall, we also negate the *x* velocity. Else if the ball hit the top wall, we negate the *y* velocity. If the ball hit the bottom wall, we remove the ball from the world and create a new one.

Example Java Code 134: The `newBall` method in `World`

```
    /**
2    * Method to add a new ball
     */
4   public void newBall()
    {
6       /* increment the number of balls created */
        numBalls++;
8
        /* check if used 3 or more */
10      if (numBalls > 3)
        {
12          message.setText("Game over and you lost.");
            Greenfoot.stop();
14      }
        /* create new ball and tell the user the number
16          of balls created */
        else
18      {
            addObject(new Ball(), (WIDTH / 2), 222);
```

```
20          message.setText("Ball " + numBalls);
        }
22    }
```

The method in the `World` class that creates a new ball first increments the number of balls used. Then it checks if the number used is more than three. If it is more than three, it sets the text on the message to tell the user that she or he lost and stops the simulation. Otherwise, it creates a new ball and modifies the ball number message.

Example Java Code 135: The `World` method that checks if the user has won

```
     /**
2     * Method to check if the game is over and if so tell
      * the user
4     * and stop the simulation
      */
6    public void checkIfWon()
     {
8         List brickList = this.getObjects(Brick.class);
          if (brickList.size() == 0)
10        {
              message.setText("You Won!!!!!!");
12            Greenfoot.stop();
          }
14   }
```

The user has won if there are no more bricks in the world. If the user has won, it sets the text of the message to tell the user and stops the simulation.

EXERCISES

14.1   Modify the ants scenario. Add a field to keep track of how much food each ant collects. Add a unique identifier for each ant. When all the food is gone, print out how much food each ant collected.

14.2   Modify the ants scenario. Add a new kind of ant (a scout) that is faster than the normal ants. Does it collect more food than normal ants? How could you test if the scout finds more food than normal ants?

14.3   Modify the ants scenario. Add an object that eats ants. Have the ants try to avoid the actor that eats it.

14.4   Modify the ants scenario. Add a queen ant that produces more ants as long as there is enough food in the anthill.

14.5   Modify the ants scenario. Allow ants to get sick and have them spread illness to other ants.

14.6   Modify the wombats scenario to create a maze with the walls. Modify the wombat to look for a leaf in the maze.

14.7   Modify the wombats scenario so that wombats can detect leaves that are within three cells and choose to move towards the nearest leaf.

14.8   Look up "depth-first search" on the Web. Modify the wombats scenario to use this strategy when looking for a leaf.

14.9   Modify the breakout game scenario. Speed up the ball over time by incrementing the y velocity each time a new ball is created.

14.10   Modify the breakout game scenario. Make the size of the paddle shrink over time.

14.11   Modify the breakout game scenario. Play a sound each time the ball hits something.

14.12   Modify the breakout game scenario to set the color of the ball to the color of the brick when it hits a brick.

14.13   Create a game of pong using Greenfoot. In pong, there is one ball and two paddles and there are two players. Use the up and down arrows to control one paddle and the "q" and "a" keys to control the other.

14.14   Create a word-guessing game. Let the user have 10 chances to guess letters in the word and show the correct letters in their correct positions. Have the user type a letter to guess it.

14.15   Use the Web to find out how to play pacman. Create a version of this game using Greenfoot.

14.16   Create a game of checkers using Greenfoot.

14.17   Why is the `World` an abstract class? What can you do with abstract classes? Do abstract classes have to have an abstract method?

14.18   What are the advantages in using a predefined set of classes for building simulations? What are the disadvantages?

14.19   Does it make sense to call the `act` method on objects that don't do anything in the scenario? Perhaps it would be better to add another class that can have an image and can have a location and be in the world, but doesn't have to act. Draw a UML class diagram that includes this new class.

CHAPTER 15

Introducing UML and Continuous Simulations

Chapter Learning Objectives

In the last chapter, you saw how simulations are built using an existing package. Now, let's go behind the scenes. The problem being addressed in this chapter is how to model dynamic situations, and then, how to simulate those models.

The computer science goals for this chapter are:

- To describe linked lists as a *head* and a *tail* (or *rest*).
- To use generalization and aggregation as two mechanisms for modeling with objects.
- To use *Unified Modeling Language* (*UML*) class diagrams for describing the class structure of increasingly sophisticated object models.
- To implement a simple predator-prey simulation.
- To write numeric data to a file for later manipulation.

The media learning goals for this chapter are:

- To describe (and modify) behavior of agents in order to create different graphical simulations (like the wildebeests and villagers).
- To use spreadsheets (like Excel) for analyzing the results of graphical simulations.

15.1   OUR FIRST MODEL AND SIMULATION: WOLVES AND DEER

The first question of any simulation is, *Is the model right?* Do the agents interact in the way that describes the real world correctly? Do the agents request the right resources in the right way? And then, how do we *implement* those models? To get started, let's build one model and simulate that model.

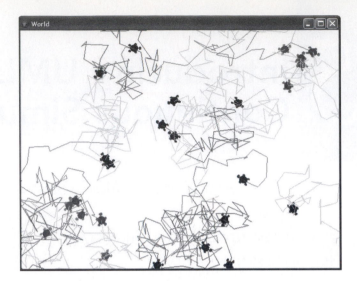

FIGURE 15.1
An execution of our wolves and deer simulation.

We are going to explore a few different kinds of continuous simulations in this chapter. We'll be using our `Turtle` class to represent individuals in our simulated worlds. The first simulation that we're going to build is a simulation of wolves chasing and eating deer (Figure 15.1). Wolves and deer is an instance of a common form of continuous simulation called *predator and prey* simulations.

The name of this class is `WolfDeerSimulation`. We can start an execution like this:

```
Welcome to DrJava.
> WolfDeerSimulation wds = new WolfDeerSimulation();
> wds.run();
>>> Timestep: 0
Wolves left: 5
Deer left: 20
>>> Timestep: 1
Wolves left: 5
Deer left: 20
<SIGH!> A deer died...
>>> Timestep: 2
Wolves left: 5
Deer left: 19
<SIGH!> A deer died...
>>> Timestep: 3
Wolves left: 5
Deer left: 18
>>> Timestep: 4
Wolves left: 5
```

```
Deer left: 18
...
```

What we see is Figure 15.1. Wolves (in gray) move around and (occasionally) catch deer (in brown), at which point the deer turn red to indicate their death (depicted above with a "SIGH!"). This is a very simple model, but we're going to grow it further in the book.

`WolfDeerSimulation` is a continuous simulation. Each moment in time is simulated. There are no resources in this simulation. It is an example of a predator-prey simulation, which is a common real-world (ecological) situation. In these kinds of simulations, there are parameters (variables or rules) to change to explore under what conditions predators and prey survive and in what numbers. You can see in this example that we are showing how many wolves and deer survive at each *time step*—that is, after each moment in the simulation's notion of time. (It's up to the modeler to decide if a moment stands for a nanosecond or a hundred years.)

Modeling the Wolves and Deer

Simulations will require many more classes than the past projects that we have done. Figure 15.2 describes the relationships in the wolves and deer simulation.

- We are going to use our `Turtle` class to model the wolves and deer. The class `Wolf` and the class `Deer` are subclasses of the class `Turtle`. Simulation agents will be told to `act()` once per timestep—it's in that method that wolves and deer will do whatever they are told to do. `Deer` instances also know how to `die()`, and `Wolf` instances also know how to find the closest deer (in order to eat it).

- We will use the handy-dandy `LLNode` class in order to create a linked list of agents (which are in our case kinds of `Turtle`) through the `AgentNode` class. The `AgentNode` class knows how to get and set its agents (`Turtle` instances) and to remove an agent from the list. Removing an agent from the list of agents is a little more complicated than simply removing a node from a linked list—the first thing we have to do is to find the node containing the input turtle and *then* remove the node.

- The overall `WolfDeerSimulation` keeps track of all the wolves and deer. It also knows how to `run()` the simulation. Running a simulation has a few basic parts:

  1. The world must be set up and populated with wolves and deer.

  2. In a loop (often called an *event loop* or *time loop*), time is incremented.

  3. At each moment in time, each agent in the world is told to do whatever it needs to do (e.g., `act()`). Then the world display is updated.

Now, while that may seem complex, the reality is that Figure 15.2 doesn't capture all the relationships between the different classes in this simulation. For example, how does the `WolfDeerSimulation` keep track of the wolves and deer? You can probably figure out that it must have instance variables that hold `AgentNode` instances. But this figure doesn't reflect the entire *object model*. Let's talk about how to describe object

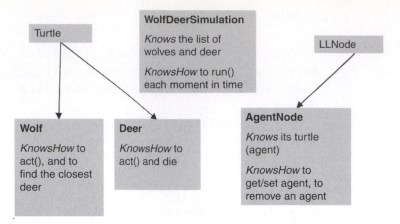

FIGURE 15.2
A diagram of the relationships in the wolves and deer simulation.

models using a software industry standard that captures more of the details in how the classes in the simulation interact.

15.2 MODELING IN OBJECTS

As we said at the beginning of this chapter, object-oriented programming was invented to make simulations easier to build. The individual objects are clearly connected to real-world objects, but there are also techniques for thinking about how classes and objects relate to one another that help to capture how objects in the real world relate to one another. Using these techniques is referred to as *modeling* in terms of objects, or *object modeling*. We call the process of studying a situation and coming up with the appropriate object-oriented model *object-oriented analysis*.

Computer Science Idea: The relationship between objects is meant to model reality
When an object modeler sets up relationships between objects, she is making a statement about how she sees the real world work.   ∎

Two of the kinds of object relationships that we use in modeling are *generalization-specialization* and *association*.

- When we create a *generalization-specialization* relationship, we are saying that one class "is a kind of" the other class. Generalization-specialization relationships occur in the real world. Think of muscle and blood cells as specializations of the general concept of a cell. This relationship is typically implemented as a *subclass-superclass relationship*. When we created the Student class by extending Person, we were saying that a student is a kind of person. A student is a *specialization* of a person. A person is a *generalization* of a student.

- Another common object relationship is *association*. This is simply the idea that objects contain references to other objects. For example, we might need to know all the people on a flight. A `Flight` object might contain a list of `People` objects.

    Another relationship is *aggregation*, where the parts make up the whole. Imagine that you were modeling a human being. You could model the human as two arms and hands, two legs and feet, a torso, and neck and head. In that case, all those parts make up the whole of a human.

We can describe many kinds of object models with just these relationships. But if we were to spell out sentences like, "A Person and a Student have a generalization-specialization relationship" for every relationship in our models, they would go on for pages. Just look at what we wrote in the last section for the wolves and deer simulation, and that wasn't even all the relationships in that model!

Object modelers use graphical notations like the UML for describing their models. The UML has several different kinds of diagrams in it, such as diagrams for describing the order of operations in different objects over time (a *collaboration diagram* or *sequence diagram*) or describing the different states (values of variables) that an object can be in during a particular process (a *state diagram*). The diagram that we're going to use is the *class diagram* that describes the classes in a situation and the relationships between objects of these classes.

Figure 15.3 is a UML class diagram describing the classes in our wolves and deer simulation. There are lots of relationships described in this diagram. While it may look complex, there really are two only kinds of relationships going on here, and the rest are things that you already know a lot about.

The boxes are the individual UML classes (Figure 15.4). They are split into thirds. The top part gives the name of the class. The middle part lists the instance variables (also called *fields*) for the class. Sometimes the type of the field is also listed (e.g., what kind of objects are stored in this variable?). The symbols in front of the names of the fields indicate the accessibility. A "+" indicates a public field, a "−" indicates a private field, and a "#" indicates a protected field. Finally, the bottom part lists the methods or operations for this class. Like the fields, the accessibility is also indicated with a prefix on the method name.

Some fields may not appear in the class box. Instead, they might appear as a name on a reference relationship. Figure 15.5 pulls out just the reference relationship from the overall diagram. Association relationships ("has-a" relationships) can have arrow points, and they indicate that one kind of object contains a reference to the other object. In this example, we see that the class `Wolf` contains a reference to its `WolfDeerSimulation`. The name of this reference is `mySim`. This means that `Wolf` contains an additional field named `mySim` that doesn't have to appear in the class box. You're also seeing a "1" on one end of the reference link, and a "*" on the other end. This means that each `Wolf` references exactly one `WolfDeerSimulation`, but many (that's what "*" means—anywhere from 0 to infinity) wolves might be in one simulation. The arrowhead could actually be on both sides. If a `WolfDeerSimulation` referenced at least one `Wolf`, then the arrows would go both ways.

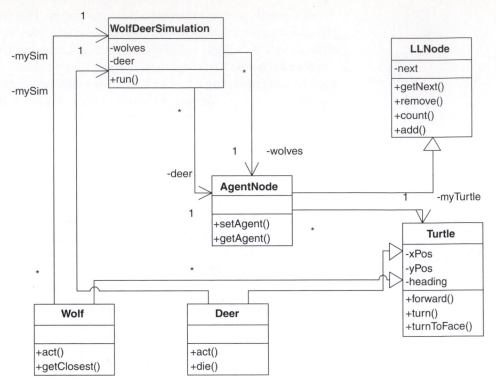

FIGURE 15.3
A UML class diagram for the wolves and deer simulation.

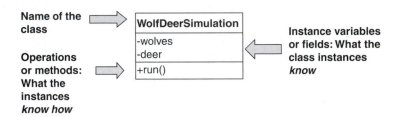

FIGURE 15.4
One UML class.

At this point, you might be wondering, "Huh? I thought that there were wolves in this simulation?" The simulation object does not have a direct association to a wolf object. There are other objects in there. Follow the lines in Figure 15.3. WolfDeerSimulation contains an AgentNode named wolves. (See that "1" in there? Exactly one direct reference.) AgentNode contains a turtle named myTurtle. That's how the simulation contains wolves and deer.

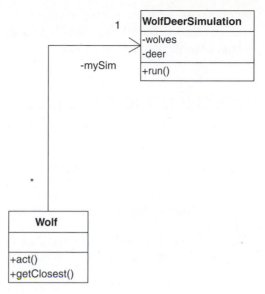

FIGURE 15.5
A reference relationship.

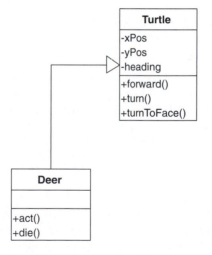

FIGURE 15.6
A gen-spec (generalization-specialization) relationship.

Because, odd as it seems, this diagram claims that wolves and deer are kinds of turtles (Figure 15.6). The lines that have closed arrows (triangles) at their ends are depicting generalization-specialization (*gen-spec*) relationships. The arrow points toward the generalization (superclass). Figure 15.6 says that deers are kinds of turtles. (Are you imagining small turtles with antlers pasted onto their heads? Or maybe with gray or brown fur glued onto the shells?) This is what is sometimes called *implementation inheritance*—we want `Deer` instances to behave like `Turtles` in terms of movement and appearance. But from a modeling perspective, it's pretty silly to say that a deer is a kind of turtle. We'll fix that later.

15.3   IMPLEMENTING THE SIMULATION CLASS

The whole `WolfDeerSimulation` class can be found in the `java-source` directory. Let's walk through the key parts here.

```java
public class WolfDeerSimulation {

  /** a linked list of wolves */
  private AgentNode wolves;

  /** a linked list of deer */
  private AgentNode deer;

   /** A BufferedWriter for writing to */
  private BufferedWriter output;

  /**
   * Constructor to set output to null
   */
  public WolfDeerSimulation() {
    output = null;
  }

  /** Method to get the wolf linked list
    * @return the first wolf in the linked list */
  public AgentNode getWolves(){return wolves;}

  /** Method to get the deer linked list
    * @return the first deer in the linked list */
  public AgentNode getDeer(){return deer;}
```

Why do we declare our `wolves` and `deer` references to be `private`? Because we don't want them to be directly accessible from any other class. They can be accessed through public accessors (getters) that we provide. Just imagine some rogue hacker wolf gaining access to the positions of *all* the deer! No, of course, that's not the idea. But access to data is an important part of the model. Wolves *can* get deer's positions—by seeing them! If that's the only way that wolves find deer in the real world, then we should make sure that that's the only way it happens in our model, and we'll hide information that the wolf shouldn't have access to. If all the data were public, then a programmer might accidentally access data that one part of the model isn't supposed to access.

Now let's start looking at the `run()` method.

```java
  /**
   * Run the simulation
```

```
 */
public void run() {

  World w = new World();
  w.setAutoRepaint(false);

  // Start the lists
  wolves = new AgentNode();
  deer = new AgentNode();

  // create some deer
  int numDeer = 20;
  for (int i = 0; i < numDeer; i++) {
    deer.add(new AgentNode(new Deer(w,this)));
  }

  // create some wolves
  int numWolves = 5;
  for (int i = 0; i < numWolves; i++) {
    wolves.add(new AgentNode(new Wolf(w,this)));
  }
```

The first part of this method is saying that we don't want the World to repaint until we tell it to repaint. Within a single timestep, everything is supposed to be happening at the same moment, but we have to tell each agent to act() separately. We want the World to update during each turtle (er, wolf and deer) movement. So we'll tell it to wait to redraw itself.

The rest of the example above is creating the wolves and deer lists. Notice that the deer variable references an AgentNode that is *empty*—there's no deer in there! Same for wolves. Then in the loops, we create each additional AgentNodes with a Deer or a Wolf. Each Deer and Wolf takes as input the world w and the simulation this. The new AgentNodes get added to the respective linked lists.

Why the empty node at the front? This is actually a much more common linked list structure than the one that we've used up until now. Figure 15.7 describes what the structure looks like. This is sometimes called a *head-tail* or *head-rest* structure. What we're doing is setting up a node for wolves and deer to point at which does *not* itself contain a wolf or deer. Why? Recall our remove() code for removing a node from a list—it can't remove the first node in the list. How could it—we can't change what the variables wolves and deer point at within the method. If the nodes that wolves and deer reference actually contained a wolf and a deer, those would be invulnerable objects—they could never die and thus be removed from the list of living wolves or deer. The first node is immortal! Since it's probably a highly unusual situation to have immortal wolves and deer, we'll use a head-tail structure so that we can remove animals from our list. Or, you could return the new first node in the linked list when you remove the first node in a linked list. But, then the calling method must always reset the reference to the linked list to the returned first linked list node.

FIGURE 15.7
The structure of the `wolves` linked list.

Here's the next part of the `run()` method, where we invite our wolves and deer to act.

```
// declare a wolf and deer
Wolf currentWolf = null;
Deer currentDeer = null;
AgentNode currentNode = null;

// loop for a set number of timesteps (50 here)
for (int t = 0; t < 50; t++) {

  // loop through all the wolves
  currentNode = (AgentNode) wolves.getNext();
  while (currentNode != null) {
    currentWolf = (Wolf) currentNode.getAgent();
    currentWolf.act();
    currentNode = (AgentNode) currentNode.getNext();
  }

  // loop through all the deer
  currentNode = (AgentNode) deer.getNext();
  while (currentNode != null) {
    currentDeer = (Deer) currentNode.getAgent();
    currentDeer.act();
    currentNode = (AgentNode) currentNode.getNext();
  }
```

What's going on in here is that, within a `for` loop that counts up to 50 timesteps, we traverse the `wolves` and then `deer` linked lists, inviting each one to `act()`. But the code probably looks more complicated than that, because of the *casting* going on.

- `currentNode = (AgentNode) wolves.getNext();`—remember that Agent-Node is a subclass of `LLNode`. `getNext()` returns an `LLNode`, so we have to cast it to an `AgentNode` to be able to do `AgentNode`-specific stuff, like getting at the agent.
- `currentWolf = (Wolf) currentNode.getAgent();`—remember that Agent-Nodes contain `Turtles`, but we need a `Wolf` to get it to `act()`. So, we have to cast again.

The same things are going on in the `Deer` part of the loop.

Finally, the end of the `run()` method in `WolfDeerSimulation`.

```
            // repaint the world to show the movement
            w.repaint();

            // Let's figure out where we stand...
            System.out.println(">>> Timestep: "+t);
            System.out.println("Wolves left:
              "+wolves.getNext().count());
            System.out.println("Deer left:
              "+deer.getNext().count());

            // Wait for one second
            //Thread.sleep(1000);
        }
    }
```

First, we tell the world "Everyone's had a chance to update! Repaint the world!" We then print the current statistics about the world—how many deer and wolves are left, by counting. Our `count()` method is very simple and doesn't understand about head-tail structures, so we'll call `count()` on the tail (the `getNext()`) to avoid counting the empty *head* as one wolf or deer. If you have a really fast computer and the world is updating faster than you can really see (one can dream), you might want to uncomment the line `Thread.sleep()`. That causes the execution to pause for 1000 milliseconds—a whole second, so that you can see the screen before it updates again.

15.4 IMPLEMENTING A WOLF

The complete `Wolf` class can be found in the `java-source` directory. Here's how it starts.

```
import java.awt.Color;
import java.util.Random;
import java.util.Iterator;

/**
 * Class that represents a wolf.  The wolf class
 * tracks all the living wolves with a linked list.
 *
 * @author Barb Ericson ericson@cc.gatech.edu
 */
public class Wolf extends Turtle {

    ////////////// fields //////////////////////

    /** class constant for the color */
    public static final Color GRAY = new Color(153,
        153,153);

    /** class constant for probability of NOT
     *   turning */
    public static final double PROB_OF_STAY = 1.0/10;
```

```
/** class constant for top speed (max num steps
  * can move in a timestep) */
public static final int MAX_SPEED = 40;

/** class constant for how far wolf can smell */
public static final double SMELL_RANGE = 50;

/** class constant for how close before wolf
  * can attack */
public static final double ATTACK_RANGE = 30;

/** My simulation */
private WolfDeerSimulation mySim;

/** random number generator */
protected static Random randNumGen = new Random();
```

There's a new term we've never seen here before: `final`. A `final` variable is one that can't actually ever vary—it's value is stuck right from the beginning. It's a *constant*. You never *have* to say `final`, but there are advantages to using it. Java can be more efficient in its use of memory and generate even a little faster code if you declare things that will never change `final`.

We are also using `protected` visibility here on the `randNumGen` field. Protected means that all subclasses and all classes in the same package have direct access to this field. We are using `protected` here to make it easy for subclasses to use the random number generator. If this field was `private`, we would have to provide a public accessor (getter) for access to this field. Most fields should be `private`, but constants are usually `public`, and occasionally you can allow `protected` access. But, only use `protected` if you aren't worried about allowing direct access to subclasses and all classes in the same package. We haven't declared a package here, so all of our classes are in the unnamed package. This means that all of our classes have direct access to the random number generated in `Wolf`, but unless they set it to `null`, they won't cause any problems.

Making It Work Tip: Names of constants are capitalized

Java discourse rules say that you capitalize values that are `final` in order to highlight them and set them apart. If the name contains more than one word, add a "_" between the words. ∎

We're using `final` values here to set the value of the wolves and the probability that they will *not* turn in any given timestep. We really only need one copy of these variables for the whole class (e.g., we don't need another copy of the color `gray` for each and every wolf), so we're declaring them `static`, too.

In the past, when we needed a random value, we simply accessed the method `Math.random()`. That method returns a `double` between 0 and 1, where all values are equally likely. That all numbers are "equally likely" is called a *uniform distribution*. That's a problem because relatively few things are uniformly distributed. Think about heights in your room or in your school. Let's say that you have someone who is 6 foot 10 inches tall and someone else 4 foot 11 inches tall. Does that mean that there are just as many people 6-10 as there are 4-11, and 5-0, 5-1, 5-2, and so on? We know that that's not how heights work. Most of the people are near the average height, and only a few people are at the maximum or minimum. That's a *normal distribution*, so named because it is so, well, *normal*!

Instances of the class Random know how to generate random values on a normal distribution, as well as on a uniform distribution. We'll see those methods later, but we'll get started creating instances of Random now to get ready for that.

The next part of Wolf are the constructors. The constructors for Wolf are fairly complicated. They have to match Turtle's constructors which have to do with things like ModelDisplay, which is an interface that World obeys. We will also have them call init() in order to *initialize* the agent. Here's what they look like.

```
/////////////////// Constructors ///////////////////

  /**
   * Constructor that takes the model display
   * (the original
   * position will be randomly assigned)
   * @param modelDisplayer thing that displays
   * the model
   * @param thisSim my simulation
   */
  public Wolf (ModelDisplay modelDisplayer,
               WolfDeerSimulation thisSim) {
    super(randNumGen.nextInt(
        modelDisplayer.getWidth()),
        randNumGen.nextInt(
        modelDisplayer.getHeight()),
        modelDisplayer);
    init(thisSim);
  }

  /** Constructor that takes the x and y and a model
   * display to draw it on
   * @param x the starting x position
   * @param y the starting y position
   * @param modelDisplayer the thing that displays
   * the model
   * @param thisSim my simulation
   */
  public Wolf (int x, int y,
    ModelDisplay modelDisplayer,
    WolfDeerSimulation thisSim) {
    // let the parent constructor handle it
    super(x,y,modelDisplayer);
    init(thisSim);
  }
```

Initializing a `Wolf` is fairly simple.

```
/////////////////// methods ///////////////////

/**
 * Method to initialize the new wolf object
 * @param thisSim the simulation
 */
public void init(WolfDeerSimulation thisSim) {

  // set the color of this wolf
  setColor(GRAY);

  // turn some random direction
  this.turn(randNumGen.nextInt(360));

  // set my simulation
  mySim = thisSim;
}
```

Here, we are setting the wolf's color to gray, making it point in some random direction, and setting its reference `mySim` back up to the simulation that was passed in via the constructor. The method `nextInt` on `Random` returns a random integer between 0 and one less than the number provided as input. So `randNumGen.nextInt(360)` then returns a random number between 0 and 359.

Next comes a very important method, especially if you are a wolf. How do we figure out if there's a deer near enough to eat?

```
/**
 * Method to get the closest deer within the passed
 * distance to this wolf. We'll search the input
 * list of the kind of objects to compare to.
 * @param distance the distance to look within
 * @param list the list of agents to look at
 * @return the closest agent in the given distance
 * or null
 */
public AgentNode getClosest(double distance,
                            AgentNode list) {
  // get the head of the deer linked list
  AgentNode head = list;
  AgentNode curr = head;
  AgentNode closest = null;
  Deer thisDeer;
  double closestDistance = 999;
  double currDistance = 0;

  // loop through the linked list looking
  // for the closest deer
  while (curr != null) {
    thisDeer = (Deer) curr.getAgent();
    currDistance =
```

```
          thisDeer.getDistance(this.getXPos(),
                               this.getYPos());
      if (currDistance < distance) {
        if (closest == null ||
            currDistance < closestDistance) {
          closest = curr;
          closestDistance = currDistance;
        }
      }
      curr = (AgentNode) curr.getNext();
    }
    return closest;
}
```

The method getClosest() searches through the given list to see if there's a deer-agent in the list that is within the specified distance (the input parameter) of this wolf. Wolves can only see or hear or smell within some range or distance, according to our model. So, we'll look for the closest deer within the range. If the closest deer is outside the range, this method will just return null.

For the most part, this is just a traversal of the linked list. We walk the list of AgentNodes, and grab thisDeer out of the current node curr. We then compute the distance between thisDeer and this wolf's position (*x* and *y* location). If the distance to this deer is within our range distance, then we consider if it's the closest. The two vertical bars (||) mean logical "or." If we have no closest deer yet (closest == null) or if this is closer than our current closest deer (currDistance < closestDistance), then we say that the current AgentNode is the closest, and that this currDistance is the new closestDistance. At the end, we return the closest AgentNode.

Now that we know how wolves will go about finding something to eat, we can see how they will actually behave when told to act().

```
/**
 * Method to act during a time step
 * pick a random direction and move some random
 * amount up to top speed
 */
public void act() {

  // get the closest deer within some specified
  // distance
  AgentNode closeDeer =
    getClosest(30,
               (AgentNode)
               mySim.getDeer().getNext());

  if (closeDeer != null) {
    Deer thisDeer = (Deer) closeDeer.getAgent();
    this.moveTo(thisDeer.getXPos(),
                thisDeer.getYPos());
    thisDeer.die();
  }
```

```
    else {
      // if the random number is > prob of NOT turning
      // then turn
      if (randNumGen.nextFloat() > PROB_OF_STAY) {
        this.turn(randNumGen.nextInt(360));
      }

      // go forward some random amount
      forward(randNumGen.nextInt(MAX_SPEED));
    }
  }
```

Here's what our `Wolf` does:

- The very first thing a wolf does is to see if there's something to eat! It checks to see if there's a close deer within its sensing range (30). If there is, the wolf gets the deer out of the agent (via `getAgent`), moves to the position of that deer, and eats the deer (tell it to `die`).

- If the wolf can't eat, it moves. It generates a random number (with `nextFloat()` which returns a uniform number between 0 and 1), and if that random number is greater than the probability of just keeping our current heading (PROB_OF_STAY), then we turn some random amount. We then move forward at some random value less than a wolf's maximum speed.

15.5 IMPLEMENTING DEER

The `Deer` class is in the `java-source` directory. There's not much that is new in the declarations of `Deer` (e.g., we declare a `public static final` value for BROWN instead of GRAY). The constructors are the same as well. When `Deer` instances `act()`, they don't eat anything in this model, so they don't have to hunt for a closest anything. Instead, they just run around randomly. Note that they don't even look for wolves and try to get away from them yet.

```
/**
 * Method to act during a time step
 * pick a random direction and move some
 * random amount up to top speed
 */
public void act() {
  if (randNumGen.nextFloat() > PROB_OF_STAY) {
    this.turn(randNumGen.nextInt(360));
  }

  // go forward some random amount
  forward(randNumGen.nextInt(MAX_SPEED));

}
```

The interesting thing that `Deer` instances do in contrast to `Wolf` instances is to die.

```java
/**
 * Method that handles when a deer dies
 */
public void die() {

  // Leave a mark on the world where I died...
  this.setBodyColor(Color.RED);

  // Remove me from the "live" list
  mySim.getDeer().remove(this);

  // say that the deer died
  System.out.println("SIGH!  A deer died...");
}
```

When a `Deer` instance dies, we set its body color to `Color.RED`. We then remove the deer from the list of living deer. We could, if we wished, remove the body of the dead deer from the screen, by removing the turtle from the list of turtles in the world. That's what `this.getModelDisplay().remove(this);` does. Finally, we print the deer's obituary to the screen.

15.6 IMPLEMENTING AGENTNODE

The full class `AgentNode` is in the `java-source` directory. As we know from our earlier use of `LLNode`, there's not much to `AgentNode`—it's fairly easy to create a linked list of agents (`Turtle` instances) by subclassing `LLNode`.

The interesting part of `AgentNode` is the removal method that takes a `Deer` as input and removes the `AgentNode` that contains the input `Deer` instance.

```java
/**
 * Remove the node where the passed turtle is found.
 * @param myTurtle the turtle to remove
 */
public void remove(Turtle myTurtle) {

  // Assume we're calling on the head
  AgentNode head = this;
  AgentNode current = (AgentNode) this.getNext();

  while (current != null) {
    if (current.getAgent() == myTurtle) {
      // If found the turtle, remove that node
      head.remove(current);
    }

    current = (AgentNode) current.getNext();
  }
}
```

In this method, we have a linked list traversal where we're looking for the node whose agent is the input Turtle—current.getAgent() == myTurtle. Once we find the right node, we call the normal linked list remove() on that node.

This is a generally useful method—it removes a node based on the *content* of the node. Could we add this method to LLNode? Do we have to subclass and create AgentNode in order to make this work? Actually we could create a general linked list class that could hold anything. There is a class named Object that is the superclass of everything—even if you don't say extends, you are implicitly subclassing Object in Java. If you had an instance variable that was declared Object, it could hold any kind of content: a Picture, a Turtle, a Student—anything.

15.7   EXTENDING THE SIMULATION

There are lots of things that we might change in the simulation. We might have wolves that are hungry sometimes and not hungry other times. We could have wolves chase deer, and have deer run from wolves. We'll implement these variations to see how we change simulations and implement different models. That is how people use simulations to answer questions. But to get answers, we need to do more than simply run the simulation and watch the pictures go by. We need to be able to get data out of it. We'll do that by generating files that can be read into Excel and analyzed, e.g., with graphs.

Making Hungry Wolves

Let's start out by creating a subclass of Wolf whose instances are sometimes hungry and sometimes satisfied. What's involved in making that happen? The whole class is in the java-source directory.

```
/**
 * A class that extends the Wolf to have a
 * hunger level.
 * Wolves only eat when they're hungry
 * @author Mark Guzdial
 * @author Barb Ericson
 */
public class HungryWolf extends Wolf {

  /** Number of cycles before I'll eat again */
  private int satisfied;

  /** class constant for number of turns before
   *   hungry */
  public static final int MAX_SATISFIED = 3;
```

Obviously, we need to subclass Wolf. We will also need to add another field, satisfied, that will model how hungry or satisfied the HungryWolf is. We will have a new constant that indicates just how satisfied the HungryWolf instance is.

Here's how we will model satisfaction, which means how full the wolf is. When a HungryWolf eats, we will set the satisfied state to the MAX_SATISFIED. But each time that a timestep passes, we decrement the `satisfied` state—making the wolf less satisfied. The wolf will only eat, then, if the wolf's satisfaction drops to zero.

The constructors for `HungryWolf` look just like `Wolf`'s.

```
//////////////////////// Constructors ////////////

/**
 * Constructor that takes the model display (the
 * original position will be randomly assigned) and
 * the simulation
 * @param modelDisplayer thing that displays
 * the model
 * @param thisSim my simulation
 */
public HungryWolf (ModelDisplay modelDisplayer,
                   WolfDeerSimulation thisSim) {
  super(modelDisplayer,thisSim);
}

/** Constructor that takes the x and y position,
 * a model display to draw it on, and a simulation
 * @param x the starting x position
 * @param y the starting y position
 * @param modelDisplayer the thing that displays the
 * model
 * @param thisSim my simulation
 */
public HungryWolf (int x, int y,
                   ModelDisplay modelDisplayer,
                   WolfDeerSimulation thisSim) {
  // let the parent constructor handle it
  super(x,y,modelDisplayer,thisSim);
}
```

The initialization method for `HungryWolf` does not do much, nor does it need to. By simply calling upon its superclass, the `HungryWolf` only has to do what it must do as a specialization—start out satisfied.

```
/**
 * Method to initialize the hungry wolf object
 * @param thisSim the simulation
 */
public void init(WolfDeerSimulation thisSim) {
  super.init(thisSim);
  satisfied = MAX_SATISFIED;
}
```

How a `HungryWolf` acts must also change slightly compared with how a `Wolf` acts. The differences require us to rewrite `act()`—we can't simply inherit and specialize as we did with `init()`.

```
/**
 * Method to act during a time step
 * pick a random direction and move some
 * random amount up to top speed
 */
public void act() {

  // Decrease satisfied time, until hungry again
  satisfied--;

  // get the closest deer within some specified
  // distance
  WolfDeerSimulation sim = getSimulation();
  AgentNode closeDeer =
    getClosest(30,
    (AgentNode) sim.getDeer().getNext());

  // check if there was a close deer
  if (closeDeer != null) {
    // Even if deer close, only eat it if you're
    // hungry.
    if (satisfied <= 0) {
      Deer thisDeer = (Deer) closeDeer.getAgent();
      this.moveTo(thisDeer.getXPos(),
                  thisDeer.getYPos());
      thisDeer.die();
      satisfied = MAX_SATISFIED;
    }
  }

  else {

    // if the random number is > prob of NOT turning
    // then turn
    if (randNumGen.nextFloat() > PROB_OF_STAY) {
      this.turn(randNumGen.nextInt(360));
    }

    // go forward some random amount
    forward(randNumGen.nextInt(MAX_SPEED));
  }
}
```

The difference between HungryWolf and Wolf instances is that hungry wolves will eat, but satisfied ones will not. So after the HungryWolf finds a close deer, it considers whether it's hungry. If so, it eats the deer. If not, that's the end of act() for the HungryWolf. The HungryWolf only wanders aimlessly if it finds no deer.

How do we make the simulation work with HungryWolf? We only have to change the code in the run() method, so that hungry wolves are created instead of normal wolves. *Everything else just works!* Because a HungryWolf is a kind of Wolf, all references to wolves work for hungry wolves.

```
// create some wolves
int numWolves = 5;
for (int i = 0; i < numWolves; i++)
{
  wolves.add(new AgentNode(new HungryWolf(w, this)));
}
```

Writing Results to a File

As we start making changes to our simulations, we would like to get a sense of what effects our changes are making. Certainly, we can see the number of wolves and deer left at the end of the simulation, but what if we care about more subtle changes than that. What if we want to know, for example, how *quickly* the deer die? Is it all at once, or over time? Is it all at first, or all at the end?

But even more important than being able to compare different runs of our simulation, we may care about the results of any given simulation. Maybe we are ecologists who are trying to understand a particular setting for wolves and deer. Maybe we are trying to make predictions about what will happen in a given situation. If your simulation is a video game, you just want to watch it go by. But if your simulation is answering a question for you, you probably want to get the answers to your questions.

There are three parts to creating a file of data that we can open up and analyze in Excel.

1. We need to open a *stream* to a file. A stream is a data structure that efficiently handles data that flows—goes in only one direction.

2. We need to be able to write strings to that stream.

3. We need to be able to handle exceptional events, like the disk becoming full or the filename being wrong.

Java handles all file input and output as a stream. It turns out that streams are useful for more than just files. For example, you can create large, sophisticated strings, say, of HTML, by assembling the string using output streams. An input stream might be coming from a file, but might also be coming from a network connection, for example.

It turns out that you've been using streams already. There is a stream associated with where you can print, known as `System.out`. Thus, when you use the method `System.out.println()`, you are actually sending a string to `System.out` to print it using `println`. There is also a stream that you might have used called `System.err`, where errors are expected to be printed. And as you might expect, there is a stream called `System.in` for taking in input from the keyboard. All of this suggests one way of handling the second task: we can get strings to our stream simply by using `println`. We can also use a method named `write()`.

To get a stream on a file, we use a technique called *chaining*. Basically, it's wrapping one object in another so that you get the kind of access you want. To get a stream for reading from a file, you'll need a `BufferedReader` to buffer the input for more efficient reading, and a `FileReader` for accessing the file and turning it into a stream. It would look something like `new BufferedReader(new FileReader(fileName));`.

Thus, there are three parts to writing to a file.

1. Open up the stream. `writer = new BufferedWriter(new FileWriter(file-Name));`

2. We write to the stream. `writer.write(data);`

3. When done, we close the stream (and the file). `writer.close();`

Now, it's not enough to have a stream. Java requires you to deal with the *exceptions* that might arise when dealing with input and output (I/O). Things can go wrong when dealing with output to a stream. What happens if the disk fills while you are still writing data? What if the filename is bad? We'll use the `try-catch` structure that we saw with Java back in the turtles chapter. It looks something like this:

```
try {
\\code that can cause the exceptions
} catch (ExceptionClassName varName) {
    \\code to handle this exception
} catch (ExceptionClassName varName) {
    \\code to handle that exception
}
```

There's an interesting variant on the `try-catch` that you should know about. You can specify a `finally` clause, that will always be executed *whether or not* any exceptions occur.

```
try {
\\code that can cause the exception
} catch (FileNotFoundException ex) {
    \\code to handle when the file isn't found
} finally {
    \\code to always be executed
}
```

Putting it all together, here's how you would *read* from a file in Java.

```
BufferedReader reader = null;
String line = null;

// try to read the file
try {

  // create the buffered reader
  reader =
    new BufferedReader(new FileReader(fileName));

  // loop reading lines till the line is null
  // (end of file)
  while ((line = reader.readLine()) != null) {
    // do something with the line
  }

  // close the buffered reader
```

```
    reader.close();

} catch (Exception ex) {
  // handle exception
}
```

Now let's add a file output capability to our simulation. We want to be able to do this:

```
Welcome to DrJava.
> WolfDeerSimulation wds = new WolfDeerSimulation();
> wds.openFile("c:/dsbook/wds-run1.txt");
> wds.run();
```

The idea is that the simulation instance (named wds above) should be able to run with or without an open file. If there is a file open, then text lines should be written to the text file—one per each timestep. And after running the simulation timing loop, the file should be closed.

The first step is to create a new instance variable for WolfDeerSimulation that knows a BufferedWriter instance. By default (in the constructor), the output file should be null.

```
/** A BufferedWriter for writing to */
private BufferedWriter output;

/**
 * Constructor to set output to null
 */
public WolfDeerSimulation() {
  output = null;
}
```

We're going to use the idea of the output file being null to *mean something*. If the file is null, we'll presume that there is no file to be written to. While that may be obvious, it's important to consider with respect to those pesky exceptions discussed earlier in this section. What happens if we *try* to write to the file but something bad happens? If anything untoward happens to the file processing, we'll simply set output to null. Then, the rest of the code will simply presume that there is no file to write—even though there *was* one once.

For example, we'll give WDSimulation instances the knowledge of how to open-File()—but if anything bad happens, output goes back to null.

```
/**
 * Open the input file and set the BufferedWriter
 * to speak to it.
 * @param filename the name of the file to write to
 */
public void openFile(String filename) {
  // Try to open the file
  try {
```

```
      // create a writer
      output =
        new BufferedWriter(new FileWriter(filename));

  } catch (Exception ex) {
    System.out.println("Trouble opening the file " +
      filename);
    // If any problem, make it null again
    output = null;
  }
}
```

We need to change the bottom of the timing loop, too. We need to write to the file. But we *only* write to the file if output is not null. If an exception gets thrown, we set output back to null.

```
// If we have an open file, write the counts to it
if (output != null) {
  // Try it
  try {
    output.write(wolves.getNext().count()+
        "\t"+deer.getNext().count());
    output.newLine();
  } catch (Exception ex) {
    System.out.println("Couldn't write the data!");
    System.out.println(ex.getMessage());
    // Make output null so that we don't keep trying
    output = null;
  }
}
```

Check out the above for just a moment: Why are we saying wolves.getNext(). count()? Why aren't we just saying wolves.count()? Remember that our count method counts every node from this. We haven't updated it yet for our head-rest list structure. Since the head of the list is empty, we don't want to include it in our count, so we start from its *next*.

After the timing loop, we need to close the file (if output is not null).

```
// If we have an open file, close it and null
// the variable
if (output != null) {
  try {
    output.close();
  } catch (Exception ex) {
    System.out.println("Something went wrong " +
      "closing the file");}
  finally {
    // No matter what, mark the file as not-there
    output = null;
  }
}
```

Getting Results from a Simulation

We can use our newly developed ability to write out results of a simulation to a text file in order to analyze the results of the simulation. From DrJava, using our new methods, we can write out a text file like this.

```
> WolfDeerSimulation wds = new WolfDeerSimulation();
> wds.openFile("c:/dsbook/wds-run1.txt")
> wds.run();
```

Our file is made up of lines with a number, a tab, and another number. Excel can interpret that as two columns in a spreadsheet.

EXERCISES

15.1   Change the Deer so that it always zips around at maximum speed. Do you think that that would make more Deer survive, since they'll be moving so fast? Try it! Can you figure out why it works the way that it does? Here's a hint (that gives away what you can expect): notice where the dead deer bodies pile up.

15.2   There is an inefficiency to this simulation, in that we return the closest Agent-Node, but then we just pull the Wolf or Deer out of it. And then when a Deer dies, we get the Deer out of the AgentNode and call remove()—but the first thing that AgentNode's remove() does is to figure out the node containing the input Deer! These kinds of inefficiencies can arise when designing programs, but once you take a global perspective (considering what all the methods are and when they're getting called), we can improve the methods and make them more efficient. Try fixing both of these problems in this simulation.

15.3   Build the LinkedListNode class that can contain any kind of object. Make sure that AgentNode's remove works in that class.

15.4   The HungryWolf checks to see if there's a close deer *and then* decides whether or not it's hungry. Doesn't that seem silly? Change the HungryWolf act() method so that it checks if it's hungry *first*.

15.5   Add a SmartDeer class that inherits from the Deer class. When it acts, it checks for the closest wolf and turns in a direction away from the wolf and moves forward the maximum amount. Does this change cause more smart deer to survive?

15.6   Add a StupidDeer class that inherits from the Deer class. When it acts, it checks for the closest wolf and turns toward the wolf and moves forward the maximum amount. Does this change cause more stupid deer to die?

15.7   Add a LazyWolf class that inherits from the Wolf class. When it acts, it just checks if a deer is close to it and if there is one, it kills it. It doesn't bother to move. Does this wolf kill more or less deer than a regular wolf?

15.8   Add a SickDeer class that inherits from Deer. Add a boolean field that indicates if the deer is sick or not. If the deer is sick, it can only move at up to half the maximum speed when it acts. When it acts it has a 10% chance of getting sick. Do sick deer die more often than healthy deer?

15.9   Add an age field to `Wolf` and `Deer` that counts how long the animal has been alive. Add 1 to this field at each timestep. Add another field that is the maximum age before the animal will die. In `act` check if the animal has reached this MAXIMUM_AGE and if so, have it die.

15.10   Add a `BabyDeer` class that inherits from the `Deer` class. A baby deer can move only half as fast as a normal deer and tries to stay with its parent. Create about 10% of the deer to be babies. Do more babies die than adults?

16 Abstracting Simulations: Creating a Simulation Package

Chapter Learning Objectives

It has finally become time to make those wildebeests and villagers. We're going to do it in two steps:

- First, we create a set of classes to make it easier to build simulations. We don't want to go to all the effort of the last chapter for every simulation we want to build. We'll build a few simulations using our new set of classes, to show both how easy it is to do and to show how we can use simulations to explore a model.
- Then, we'll map our turtles to characters in order to create simulations, like the wildebeests charging over the ridge in Disney's *The Lion King* or the villagers in the square in Disney's *The Hunchback of Notre Dame*.

The computer science goals for this chapter are:

- To create a set of classes that make it easier to make new applications, through subclassing.
- To make a different simulation by re-using a simulation framework.
- To use pre-existing collection classes, rather than always building our own.
- To use an `Iterator` to loop through a linked list.
- To use the Java `switch` statement.

The media learning goal for this chapter is:

- To make animations from simulations by creating a mapping from turtle positions to animation images.

16.1 CREATING A GENERALIZED SIMULATION PACKAGE

While the wolf and deer simulation was fun and interesting to explore, it was not easy to build. You might imagine that, if you wanted to build a variety of simulations to explore different models for a particular phenomenon, the effort to build simulations could dissuade you. You would be less likely to explore simulations if each one took the same amount of effort as the one in the last chapter.

We can make it easier by providing a set of classes that define a basic, default simulation. We can construct these classes such that we *subclass* existing classes to create new, differentiated components. We *override* methods in order to define new, differentiated behavior.

Packages of functionality are often defined in object-oriented languages as a set of classes to be subclassed, extended, and differentiated. Object-oriented programmers spend much of their development effort finding appropriate classes and extending them in just this way—subclassing the provided class, and overriding methods to define the specific functionality that they need. In this chapter, we see both—how a set of classes like that work, and how to extend a set of classes.

First, we have to tell the truth about data structures.

Real Programmers Rarely Build Data Structures

Thank you for willingly suspending your beliefs about data structures up until now. You may have been manipulating these linked lists and constructing these trees wondering, "I know lots of programmers, and they don't talk about doing things like this. Why am I doing this?"

The reality is that real programmers[1] rarely build data structures from basic objects and references as we have up until now. Very few programmers build arrays ever. Most programmers do not build lists, trees, hashtables, heaps, stacks, or queues.

These basic data structures are typically provided in the programming language. In the case of languages like Smalltalk and Python, some of these data structures, such as a map or *hashtables*, are so important that they are a built-in feature of the language. A hashtable (also called a *dictionary* in Python, or an *associative array*) can be thought of as an array where the index can be something other than a number, often a string.

Hashtables are a key feature of Python and Smalltalk. The lists of methods that classes know and the lists of variables that objects know are all implemented in the form of a hashtable. Python also builds in lists as a pre-defined structure. Smalltalk requires users to use a particular class (like `OrderedCollection`) for manipulating lists.

In other languages, such as Java, all the basic data structures are provided in a set of data structures called the *Collection Classes*. The various data structures (such as *HashMap* which is a Java hashtable, and *ArrayList* which is a kind of list) are defined in classes that you then instantiate like any other object in Java. These are particularly good implementations that are designed to be as fast as possible and use as little memory as possible.

```
> import java.util.*
> ArrayList v = new ArrayList()
> v.add(1)
```

---

[1]Where "real programmers" can mean "professional programmers" or "people who program often" or even "people who already got through this class."

```
true
> v.add(2)
true
> v
[1, 2]
> HashMap dict = new HashMap()
> dict.put("name","Mark")
null
> dict.get("name")
"Mark"
```

The bottom line is that few programmers, in any object-oriented language, ever write data structures on their own. There are several good reasons for this. First, it is difficult to implement these data structures to make them as fast and efficient as possible. It serves everyone well to use a single implementation that is very well constructed. Second, the critical issues with which most programmers deal are about applications and features that users need, not the low-level issues of how to make the hashtable look up keys particularly fast.

Now, there *are* times when programmers build data structures. Sometimes, a programmer may need a particular data structure that is not defined. Sometimes, a programmer may think of a data structure with particular features that would be appropriate for a given application. However, these times rarely happen.

Real Programmers Make Models and Choices

What real programmers[2] do *all* the time is define models. For example, what is the best way to represent the relationship between a hospital and its rooms? Maybe this hospital is really defined in terms of clinics, and the rooms are related to the clinics. How many of each are there? Are all rooms the same, or are there types (classes?) of rooms? How about clinics—all the same, or different types/classes? Figuring out how the real world is constructed, in terms that allow us to construct models that we can implement and manipulate on the computer, is what system analysts do all the time.

Real programmers use the same modeling techniques that we saw in the last chapter. We use *association* when we connect a hospital to its rooms or its clinics. We use *generalization-specialization* when we define types of rooms and clinics, then specialize them for particular kinds of rooms or clinics.

While real programmers do not implement data structures from scratch often, they are *always* deciding which data structures would be the best ones to use for implementing their models. For this reason, it is important for a programmer to understand data structures, down to the level of how they are implemented, in order to make these choices.

- Some of these choices are made on the basis of functionality. The line of patients waiting for a particular test or treatment is probably best modeled as a queue. Are

---

[2]There is some difference in nomenclature here. Some might call the job we are describing here "systems analysis," or "software engineering," or simply "being a computer scientist." Any of those are fine with us.

the rooms in the hospital best modeled as a long array or list of rooms? Or are they better clustered in terms of floors or clinics? That sounds more like a tree. Or maybe they are better listed by their room number that encodes floor, clinic, and room like "2A-350," and perhaps a hashtable is the best data structure to model the structure.

- Some of these choices are made on the basis of speed. Those decisions are typically made based on what we want to *do* with the model. We could use an array or list to track all of the patients in our hospital, perhaps sorted by last name or patient identification number. Imagine, though, that we need to match patients for possible blood or tissue transportation. Matching may take place based on factors such as blood type, tissue type, allergies, or illnesses. Searching the array or list based on all those factors may take too long. If we clustered the patients using a tree, where branches represent different blood types, then tissue types, and then other factors, we could find similar patients quickly.

While you will rarely do *exactly* what we have been doing in these chapters, you will often make *decisions* based on this knowledge. That is why we went through the process of constructing the data structures ourselves. From here on, we will be using the data structures provided by Java in order to create models for our simulations.

The Structure of the Simulation Package

To provide a goal for our simulation package, let's work on defining three different simulations:

- We will re-create our wolves and deer predator-prey simulation. If you are moving from an existing implementation to a more generalized implementation, it's a useful exercise to make sure that you can still create the original application.
- We will build a simulation of *disease propagation* (Figure 16.1). In our simple form, one person is ill, and all the 60 people in the simulation walk around aimlessly. If the sick person gets close to a healthy person, the healthy person gets sick, too.

The general structure of the simulation package is described by the *Unified Modeling Language(UML)* diagram in Figure 16.2.

- All of the actors in our simulations will be subclasses of the class Agent, which is a subclass of Turtle. Instances of Agent will then track their (x, y) position and heading within the world, as instances of Turtle do. In addition, Agent instances know which simulation they are part of.
- Simulations are an instance of the class Simulation. Each simulation defines the general way that simulations work; e.g., how many actors and of what types enter the simulation, and when. An instance of Simulation also knows a FrameSequencer in order to create an animation from the simulation sequence of Turtle/Agent motions.

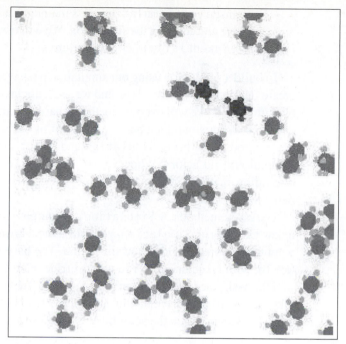

FIGURE 16.1
Sample of disease propagation simulation.

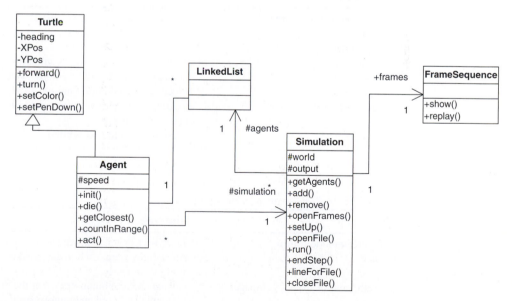

FIGURE 16.2
UML diagram of the base simulation package.

- Each instance of Simulation class maintains a list of all the Agent instances that are alive and active in the simulation. We will use an instance of the Java collection class LinkedList to track these agents.

To build a simulation using our simulation package, we will subclass Simulation to create our own simulation class, and we will subclass Agent for each class of actors in our simulation. We will override methods that are in the superclass in order to define the specifics of our simulation and the behavior of our actors. We do not *have to* override the methods. The basic Simulation and Agent classes define perfectly reasonable simulations and actors. Whenever we want to use that pre-defined behavior in our overriding methods, we can call super (e.g., super.die()) to ask for the default behavior to occur.

The basic methods of Simulation are summarized in Table 16.1. When you create a new subclass of Simulation, you will almost always override setUp since you will want to put some agents in the simulation. The base setUp method simply opens up a World, with no actors in it. You will override other methods as needed.

The basic methods of Agent are listed in Table 16.2. The constructor for Agent takes the World instance in which the turtle should be created and the instance of the Simulation in which the actor lives. Often, a subclass of Agent will override init in

TABLE 16.1 Basic methods of Simulation class

Method	Meaning
getAgents(), add(), remove()	Returns or manipulates the list of valid agents.
setUp()	Define the simulation, e.g., the number of agents.
openFile()	Starts to write data to a file.
openFrames()	Starts to write frames of an animation.
run()	For a given number of timesteps, ask each living agent to act.
endStep()	Processes the end of a timestep.
lineForFile()	Returns a string to write to a data file. By default, write out the number of agents.
closeFile()	Close the data file for writing.

TABLE 16.2 Basic methods of Agent class

Method	Meaning
init(Simulation sim)	Initialize a new agent, e.g., add it to the live agents list.
act()	At each timestep, each agent is asked to act(). By default, wander aimlessly.
setSpeed(int speed), getSpeed()	Change the maximum speed of the agent in the World.
die()	Make the body red and remove from the agents list.
getClosest(LinkedList agents)	Return the agent from the list of agents closest to this agent.
countInRange(double range, LinkedList agents)	Count the number of agents within range of me.

order to do something special with the creation of the actor. Almost always, the subclass will override `act` in order to do something specific in the simulation.

Note that `getClosest` and `countInRange` expect a `LinkedList` of `Agents` to search. If an actor needs to search all the agents, then each instance can use the `simulation` field and ask for `simulation.getAgents()` to get the list of all agents. If, however, the simulation calls for checking just *some* agents, then a `LinkedList` of *just those* agents needs to be maintained. We'll see that in two of our three example simulations.

Using a `LinkedList` from the Java Collection Classes

The Java *API* (Application Programmer Interface) documentation describes what `LinkedList` instances know. Some of these methods are summarized in Table 16.3. You will notice that these methods look like they could be provided for just about any data structure, including arrays and `ArrayList` instances. In fact, these methods *do* work for just about every collection.

So how does one pick one collection versus another? You choose a collection class based on what you expect to be doing with the collection, and how fast you want the method to be. Will you be doing a lot of insertions into the middle of the list, like with `add(int index, Object element)`? If so, then a `LinkedList` would make

TABLE 16.3 Methods understood by instances of `LinkedList`

Method	Meaning
add(int index, Object element)	Adds the `element` into the list at position index—all other elements are pushed down to make room.
add(Object element)	Adds `element` to the end of the list.
addAll(Collection c)	Adds each element from the input collection to the end of the list.
addAll(int index, Collection c)	Adds each element from the collection, starting at the `index`.
addFirst(Object element)	Adds the `element` at the start of the list.
addLast(Object element)	Adds the `element` at the end of the list.
clear()	Removes all elements from the list.
clone()	Returns a copy of the list.
contains(Object element)	Returns true if `element` is in the list.
get(int index)	Returns the element at position `index`.
getFirst(), getLast()	Returns the element at the front, or end (respectively), of the list.
indexOf(Object element)	Returns the index value where the (first, if there are duplicates) `element` is in the list.
lastIndexOf(Object element)	Returns the last index where the `element` is found in the list.
remove(int index)	Removes the element at `index`.
removeFirst(), removeLast()	Removes the first or last element.
set(int index, Object element)	Puts the `element` into position `index`, replacing if something else is there.
size()	Returns the number of elements in the list.

an excellent choice. Will you be mostly getting a value from a given index, as with `get(int index)`? Then you know that an array would be much faster.

Do also notice that some of the methods that we have come to know and love in our linked list implementations, like `insertAfter` are *not* in Java's `LinkedList` class. The Java Collection Classes, to the extent possible, have exactly the same methods for each class. The reason is to enable the programmer to swap between different collection classes with minimal changes required to your code. Not sure whether to use a `LinkedList` or an `ArrayList`? Each of these implements the `List` interface, so if you declare them to be of type `List`, you can easily try them both and the majority of your code will stay the same.

On the other hand, there are some things that you might want to do where you want to take advantage of the structure of the linked list. You might *want* to do `insertAfter`. In those cases, you may want to use your own linked list implementation. As a programmer, you have to consider the trade-off between using a pre-existing, well-debugged, and efficient collection class and thus saving yourself the development time, versus the effort of developing your own version and being able to take advantage of the special functionality or speed optimizations that you can implement for yourself.

16.2   RE-MAKING THE WOLVES AND DEER WITH OUR SIMULATION PACKAGE

A good test of our simulation framework is making the wolves and deer simulation again, this time with the simulation package. If it is much easier this time, while still getting the same functionality as we had before, then that is a good indication that we are on the right path in our framework.

A UML diagram of the simulation classes with the classes needed for the wolves and deer simulation appears in Figure 16.3. All that gets added here are the three classes at the bottom.

- `WDSimulation` is the subclass of `Simulation` that sets up the wolves and deer. Notice that it has no instance variables and only two methods. `WDSimulation` needs to `setUp` the wolves and deer, and it overrides `lineForFile` in order to write out the number of wolves and deer separately.

- `WolfAgent` redefines `init` in order to set up wolf-specific behavior and fields (e.g., making them gray). One new static field is a `LinkedList` of `allWolves`. `WolfAgent` also overrides `act` in order to define the wolf-specific behavior of chasing and eating deer.

- `DeerAgent` redefines `init` and `act` in just the same ways; e.g., a static field named `allDeer` keeps track of deer agents. `DeerAgent` also overrides `die`, in order to remove the dead deer from the `allDeer` list, as well as the overall agents list.

Let's see how `WDSimulation` is defined. Remember that we only need two methods.

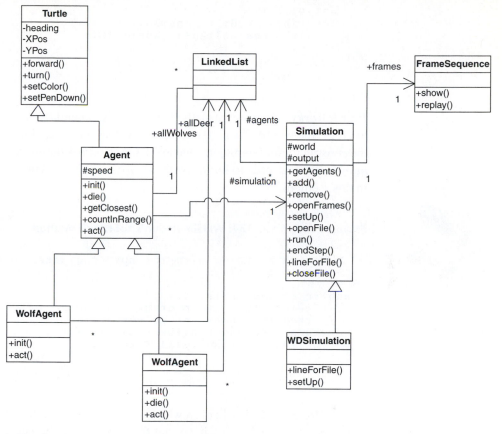

FIGURE 16.3
UML class diagram for wolves and deer with the simulation package.

Example Java Code 136: WDSimulation's setUp() method

```
   /**
2   * Fill the world with wolves and deer
    */
4  public void setUp() {

6    // Let the simulation be set up
     super.setUp();
8
     // Just for storing the new deer and wolves
10   DeerAgent deer;
     WolfAgent wolf;
12   World world = getWorld();

14   // create some deer
     int numDeer = 20;
16   for (int i = 0; i < numDeer; i++) {
       deer = new DeerAgent(world,this);
18   }

20   // create some wolves
```

```
        int numWolves = 5;
22      for (int i = 0; i < numWolves; i++) {
          wolf = new WolfAgent(world,this);
24      }
      }
```

How It Works. The `setUp` method first calls the superclass (`super.setUp()`) in order to create the `World`. Then 20 deer and 5 wolves are created in the world. Notice that the constructor for `DeerAgent` and `WolfAgent` echoes the constructor for `Agent`. Each `Agent` instance needs to know its `World` instance and its `Simulation` instance (`this` in this method).

Example Java Code 137: WDSimulation's toString() method

```
   /**
 2  * return a string with the number of deer and the
    * number of wolves
 4  */
   public String toString() {
 6    // return the number of deer followed by a tab and
      // then the number of wolves
 8    return (DeerAgent.allDeer.size() + "/t" +
        WolfAgent.getWolves().size());
10  }
```

How It Works. `WDSimulation` wants to write out the number of deer and the number of wolves, separated by a tab, so that the numbers can be put in Excel and graphed. What we see here is that each of the classes `DeerAgent` and `WolfAgent` is asked for its list of live members, `allDeer` and `allWolves` respectively. The `size()` of these lists is automatically converted to a string, since we are appending it to a string. A tab character is inserted using "/t," and the pieces are concatenated using "+."

Next, we'll tour each of `WolfAgent` and `DeerAgent`. From the UML class diagram, we are only expecting to see five methods.

Example Java Code 138: The start of DeerAgent including the init method

```
   import java.awt.Color; // Color for colorizing
 2 import java.util.LinkedList;

 4 /**
    * DeerAgent -- Deer as a subclass of Agent
 6  * @author Mark Guzdial
    * @author Barb Ericson
 8  */
   public class DeerAgent extends Agent {

10   /** class constant for the color */
12   public static final Color BROWN = new Color(116,64,35);

14   /** class constant for how far deer can smell */
```

```
16      public static final double SMELL_RANGE = 50;

        /** Collection of all Deer */
18      public static LinkedList<DeerAgent> allDeer =
          new LinkedList<DeerAgent>();
20
        /**
22       * Method to get the linked list of deer
         * @return the linked list of deer
24       */
        public static LinkedList<DeerAgent> getDeer() {
26        return allDeer;
        }
28
        /**
30       * Initialize, by adding to Deer list
         * @param thisSim the simulation
32       */
        public void init(Simulation thisSim) {
34
          // Do the normal initializations
36        super.init(thisSim);

          // Make it brown
38        setColor(BROWN);
40
          // Add to list of Deer
42        allDeer.add(this);
        }
```

◼

How It Works.   We see many of the same variables that we saw in our previous `Deer` class. A new static field is `allDeer`. We need this field to be `static` because we want to make *one* list that is shared by all the deer agents. We do *not* want each deer agent object to have an instance variable `allDeer`—we do not want to maintain the list (e.g., adding new deer, removing old deer) in each and every `DeerAgent` instance. The method `init` does the initialization of agents (`super.init(thisSim)`), which adds the agent to the list of all agents. Then deer are made BROWN and added to the `allDeer` list.

Example Java Code 139: DeerAgent's die() method

```
        /**
2        * To die, do normal stuff, but
         * also remove from deer list
4        */
        public void die() {
6         super.die();
          allDeer.remove(this);
8         System.out.println("Deer left: " + allDeer.size());
        }
```

◼

How It Works.   When deer die, they do the normal things (e.g., turn red, and be removed from the agents list so that they stop moving) via `super.die()`. Then, they get removed from the `allDeer` list. For interest's sake, we're printing out the number of deer still alive whenever one dies.

Common Bug: Removing from only one list

What would happen if you forgot the `super.die()` in the above code? Then the deer would still be removed from the `allDeer` list, but it would still be in the simulation agents list. The deer would still be told to act, so the deer would run around and flee from wolves. But since the deer wouldn't be on the `allDeer` list, the deer would never be found or eaten by wolves, since that's the list that wolves look at.

What would happen if you forgot the `allDeer.remove(this)` instead? Now, the deer are not on the agents list, so they never are told to act and they never move. However, wolves can still find them and eat them.

This is the trouble with maintaining multiple lists—you have to synchronize adding and removing from them. ∎

Example Java Code 140: DeerAgent's act() method

```java
/**
 * How a DeerAgent acts
 */
public void act()
{
  // get the closest wolf within the smell range
  WolfAgent closeWolf =
    (WolfAgent) getClosest(SMELL_RANGE,
                            WolfAgent.getWolves());

  if (closeWolf != null) {
    // Turn to face the wolf
    this.turnToFace(closeWolf);
    // Now turn in the opposite direction
    this.turn(180);
    // How far to run? How about half of current speed??
    this.forward((int) (getSpeed()/2));
  }
  else {
    // Run the normal act() -- wander aimlessly
    super.act();
  }
}
```

How It Works. We know how deer are supposed to act, so we can compare the above to our expectations. When a `DeerAgent` is told to act, it checks to see if it can smell a wolf, by looking for the closest agent in `WolfAgent.allWolves` (casted to a `WolfAgent`) within the `SMELL_RANGE`. If there is one, the deer faces the closest wolf, turns around, and runs away. If there isn't one, we simply do the default `super.act()` which involves wandering aimlessly.

Example Java Code 141: DeerAgent's constructors

```
//////////////////////////// Constructors //////////////////////
// Copy this section AS-IS into subclasses, but rename

/**
 * Constructor that takes the model display (the original
 * position will be randomly assigned) and the simulation
 * @param modelDisplayer thing that displays the model
 * @param thisSim my simulation
 */
public DeerAgent (ModelDisplay modelDisplayer,
  Simulation thisSim)
{
  super(randNumGen.nextInt(modelDisplayer.getWidth()),
        randNumGen.nextInt(modelDisplayer.getHeight()),
        modelDisplayer, thisSim);
}

/** Constructor that takes the x and y, a model
 * display to draw it on, and a simulation
 * @param x the starting x position
 * @param y the starting y position
 * @param modelDisplayer the thing that displays the model
 * @param thisSim my simulation
 */
public DeerAgent (int x, int y, ModelDisplay modelDisplayer,
                  Simulation thisSim) {
  // let the parent constructor handle it
  super(x,y,modelDisplayer,thisSim);
}
```

■

How It Works.   These constructors must be in the DeerAgent class because Agent has them, and because Turtle needs a form of them. ModelDisplay is an interface that World implements. The first constructor, then, is the one we normally call when creating an Agent. The first form computes a random horizontal and vertical location, based on the width and height of the World, then calls the second one which places the agent at that (x, y) in the World for the thisSim instance of Simulation.

In general, constructors of this form need to be in every subclass of Agent. There is not much, if anything, to change with these. We will not show these in other agents—you will need to have them, still; just copy-paste them and change the name of the class in the constructor to the current class name.

Example Java Code 142: WolfAgent's fields, getWolves, and init method

```
public class WolfAgent extends Agent {

  /** class constant for how far a wolf can smell */
  public static final double SMELL_RANGE = 50;

  /** class constant for the attack range */
  public static final double ATTACK_RANGE = 30;

  /** Collection of all Wolf Agents */
  private static LinkedList<WolfAgent> allWolves =
```

```
                              new LinkedList<WolfAgent>();
12
       /** My x position */
14     private int myX;

16     /** My y position */
       private int myY;
18
       //////////////////////// Constructors //////////////////
20     // not shown here

22     /**
        * Get the linked list of Wolf Agent
24      * @return the linked list of wolves
        */
26     public static LinkedList<WolfAgent> getWolves()
       { return allWolves; }
28
       /**
30      * Initialize, by adding to Wolf list
        * @param thisSim the simulation
32      */
       public void init(Simulation thisSim) {
34
         // Do the normal initializations
36       super.init(thisSim);

38       // Make it Gray
         setColor(Color.GRAY);
40
         // Add to list of Wolves
42       allWolves.add(this);

44       /* set the x and y position */
         myX = this.getXPos();
46       myY = this.getYPos();
       }
```

How It Works.   There really is not anything new here. Like the class Wolf, our WolfAgent has an ATTACK_RANGE. The rest of the code is identical to our DeerAgent— except, of course, that wolves are gray rather than brown.

Example Java Code 143: WolfAgent's act() method

```
      /**
2      * Chase and eat the deer
       */
4     public void act() {

6       // get the closest deer within the attack distance
        DeerAgent closeDeer = (DeerAgent)
8         getClosest(ATTACK_RANGE, DeerAgent.getDeer());

10      if (closeDeer != null) {
          this.moveTo(closeDeer.getXPos(),
12                    closeDeer.getYPos());
          closeDeer.die();
14      }
```

```
16      // otherwise
        else {
18
          // get the closest deer within smelling range
20        closeDeer = (DeerAgent)
            getClosest(SMELL_RANGE, DeerAgent.allDeer);
22
          // if there is a close deer
24        if (closeDeer != null) {
            // Turn toward the deer
26          this.turnToFace(closeDeer);
            // How much to move?  How about minimum of maxSpeed
28          // or distance to deer?
            this.forward((int) Math.min(getSpeed(),
30                  closeDeer.getDistance(this.getXPos(),
                                    this.getYPos())));
32        }

34        else { // Otherwise, wander aimlessly
            super.act();
36        } // end else
      } // end else
38  } // end act()
```

■

How It Works.   Instances of the class WolfAgent act like the ones in Wolf. First, the wolf sees if there is a deer within the attack range.

```
// get the closest deer within the attack distance
DeerAgent closeDeer = (DeerAgent)
   getClosest(ATTACK_RANGE,DeerAgent.getDeer());
```

If there is a deer within the attack range, the wolf moves to the deer position and the deer dies. If there isn't a deer in the attack range, then we check if there is a deer in the smell range.

```
// otherwise
else {

  // get the closest deer within smelling range
  closeDeer = (DeerAgent)
    getClosest(SMELL_RANGE,  DeerAgent.allDeer);
```

If there is a deer in the smell range, then the wolf turns toward the deer, and moves the *minimum* (Math.min) of the wolf's maximum speed and the distance to the deer. Why the minimum? It may be obvious to you now, but it was not to us when we first built this class. We had the wolf move full-speed toward the closest smelled deer—and we noticed that few deer were getting eaten. Then we noticed that the wolves would run toward the deer *and run past them!* That was when we realized that we need the minimum of the full-speed leap and the distance to the deer.

If there is no deer within the smell range, the wolf wanders aimlessly via super.act().

We could run this simulation with a `main` method in `WDSimulation`, or we might just do it from the INTERACTIONS PANE:

```
Welcome to DrJava.
> WDSimulation wd = new WDSimulation();
> wd.openFrames("C:/temp/");
  // If you want an animation
> wd.openFile("C:/dsBook/wds-data1.txt");
  // If you want an output file.
> wd.run();  // By default, run for 50 steps
```

If you simply want to run the simulation, without frames or data written out, use:

```
WDSimulation wd = new WDSimulation();
wd.run(); // By default, run for 50 steps
```

16.3   MAKING A DISEASE PROPAGATION SIMULATION

Next, let us see how hard it is to implement a new simulation using our package. Figure 16.4 describes the UML class diagram for the disease propagation simulation. Notice that we need to create only two new classes to implement the disease propagation simulation: `DiseaseSimulation` and `PersonAgent`.

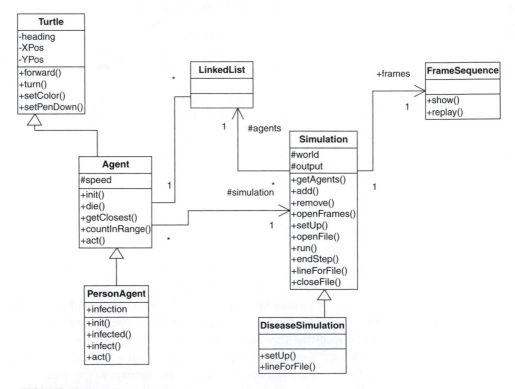

FIGURE 16.4
UML Class diagram of disease propagation simulation.

- `DiseaseSimulation` overrides the same two methods as `WDSimulation`. It overrides `setUp` in order to create the simulation structure—here, a bunch of people where one of them is sick. It overrides `toString` to separately list healthy and sick people. You will see that we get these counts *without* separate lists for this simulation.

- `PersonAgent` overrides `init` and `act`, just like the wolf and deer agents. `PersonAgent` has two other methods, that deal with `infecting` a person and counting the number of `infected` persons. The instances of `PersonAgent` have one additional field, a `boolean` (a variable that is only `true` or `false`) indicating whether the person is `infected`.

Example Java Code 144: DiseaseSimulation's setUp method

```java
/**
 * Initialize the world for the simulation.
 * Fill the world with 60 persons, one sick
 */
public void setUp() {

    // Let the world be set up
    super.setUp();
    // or Set it up with a smaller world
    //world = new World(300,300);
    //world.setAutoRepaint(false);

    PersonAgent moi;

    // 60 people
    for (int num = 0; num < 60; num++) {
        moi = new PersonAgent(getWorld(),this);
    }

    // Infect the first one
    moi = (PersonAgent) getAgents().get(0);
    moi.infect();
}
```

How It Works.   Basically, the `setUp` method makes 60 instances of `PersonAgent`. It picks the first one (which could be anywhere in the `World`, since agents are placed at random positions) via `getAgents().get(0)` and infects it. Notice that we first set up the world with `super.setUp()`, but we also have code there to create the `World` ourselves, but smaller than the default (640, 480) world. We will play around with that later.

Example Java Code 145: WDSimulation's toString method

```java
/**
 * create an information string with the number infected
 * @return the number infected as a string
 */
public String toString() {
    PersonAgent first;
    first = (PersonAgent) getAgents().get(0);
    return (new Integer(first.getNumInfected()).toString());
}
```

Notice that in the `toString` method, we convert the `integer` value to a string by first creating a new `Integer` object with the same value and then asking it to convert to string using `toString`. This is what happens automatically if we append an integer and a string.

How It Works.   Unlike the wolf and deer simulation, our `PersonAgent` class *computes* the number of different kinds of agents. In contrast, the wolf and deer simulations keep *track* of the wolves versus deer agents in two separate lists. The `getNumInfected` method in `PersonAgent` gets the list of agents in the simulation and then determines the number of infected people by checking if the `infected` field is true, so we can just grab any agent and ask it for the number of infected, then write it to a file.

Example Java Code 146: PersonAgent's init method

```java
/**
 * Initialize, by setting color and making the person
 * move fast
 */
public void init(Simulation thisSim) {

    // Do the normal initializations
    super.init(thisSim);

    // Make it lightGray
    setColor(Color.LIGHT_GRAY);

    // Don't need to see the trail
    setPenDown(false);

    // Start out uninfected
    infected = false;

    // Make the speed large
    setSpeed(100);
}
```

How It Works.   `PersonAgent` defines the `infected` variable as a `boolean`—it is either `true` or `false`. By default, people are `Color.LIGHT_GRAY` and uninfected, with a fairly fast speed. They also do not have their pens set down—while that is the default condition for `Agents`, putting it in explicitly makes it explicit that we can turn it on, too. Sometimes, it's useful to see where the infected people wander and who comes in touch with them.

Example Java Code 147: PersonAgent's act method

```java
/**
 * How a Person acts
 */
public void act() {

    // Is there a person within infection range of me?
```

```
       Simulation sim = getSimulation();
 8     PersonAgent closePerson =
         (PersonAgent) getClosest(20,
10                               sim.getAgents());

12     if (closePerson != null) {
         // If this person is infected, and I'm not infected
14       if (closePerson.infected && !this.infected) {
           // I become infected
16         this.infect();
         }
18     }

20     // Run the normal act() -- wander aimlessly
       super.act();
22   }
```

How It Works.   PersonAgent's act method is the heart of the disease propagation simulation. This method describes what each person does, once per timestep. In this method, the infection range is 20. If there is a person within 20 steps (`closePerson != null`), and this close person *is* infected (`codePerson.infected`) and I am *not* infected (`!this.infected`), then I become infected (`this.infect()`).

Example Java Code 148: PersonAgent's infect method

```
     /**
 2    * Become infected - set infected to true
      */
 4   public void infect() {
       this.infected = true;
 6     this.setColor(Color.RED);

 8     // Print out count of number infected
       System.out.println("Number infected: " +
10       getNumInfected());
     }
```

How It Works.   This is the method called when a person becomes infected. The `boolean` field `infected` is set to `true`—the person now has an infection. The person's color becomes `Color.RED`. Purely for the fun of tracking, we print out the number infected.

Example Java Code 149: PersonAgent's getNumInfected method

```
     /**
 2    * Count the number infected
      * @return the number of people infected
 4    */
     public int getNumInfected() {
 6     int count = 0;
       LinkedList agents = getSimulation().getAgents();
 8     PersonAgent check;
```

```
      Iterator itr = agents.iterator();
10
      while (itr.hasNext()) {
12      check = (PersonAgent) itr.next();
        if (check.infected) {count++;}
14    }
      return count;
16  }
```

How It Works.   This is a straightforward count (also called an "*enumeration*") of elements meeting a particular criteria. We start with our `count` variable set to zero. We get the list of all agents, and then create an iterator (`java.util.Iterator`) to loop through all the elements in the list. We have been using a `for` loop to loop through the items in our linked lists and using `get` to get the item at a particular index. But, this isn't very efficient since the linked lists keep a reference to the first and last elements only. This means that each time we get the next element we start from the front or back of the list and walk through all the elements till we get the one that matches the index. But, an iterator can keep track of the last element and we can use it to find the next element. `Iterator` is actually an interface that defines two methods: `boolean hasNext()` and `Object next`. We loop as long as the iterator has more elements (`hasNext()` will be true) and get the next element using `next()`. We check if the `PersonAgent` is infected and if it is, we increment the count. We return the count of infected `PersonAgent` objects.

A Problem and Its Solution: Enumerating elements of a particular type

We have now seen two ways of counting a particular kind of agent. With the wolves and deer, we kept two separate lists, and when needed, took the `size` of the lists. With persons who are infected or not, we instead have a *flag* (the `boolean` variable) in each person agent indicating if s/he is infected, and keep just a single list of all the person agents. When we need to count (enumerate) the sick persons, we go through the list of all persons and count up those for whom the flag is true. Which is better? It depends on what you need to do. If you just want to count, then keeping the single list is easiest. Maintaining separate lists is more complex, as we saw in how we added to the lists and removed (in the case of deer dying). In the wolves and deer case, we needed separate lists of each (for looking for near members), so it was worthwhile to make the extra effort.

Now, we can run our disease propagation simulation, with code like this:

```
DiseaseSimulation ds2 = new DiseaseSimulation();
ds2.openFile("C:/dsBook/disease-fullsize.txt");
ds2.run();
```

Exploring Scenarios in Disease Propagation

There are lots of interesting scenarios to explore in disease propagation simulations. One of them is already set up in the code. When we run our simulation using some

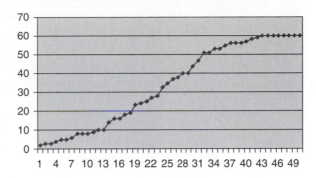

FIGURE 16.5
A graph of infection in the large world.

code like the above, we get a file with the number of infected people written out, one number per line, one line for each timestep. That is perfect for reading into Microsoft Excel, Open Office Spreadsheet, or just about any other graphing tool.

First, we should look at what a typical run of our simulation looks like. Figure 16.5 shows a graph of one run of the simulation, set up exactly as described in this chapter. We see a steady increase in the number of infected people until we reach about timestep 43, at which point everyone is infected.

A Problem and Its Solution: How do we determine *typical* behavior?

No two runs of any of our simulations should ever be identical, not if Java's random number generator is working well. Since the decision for each agent to turn (or not) and how much to travel is driven by the random number generator, and the initial positions are all chosen randomly, and all other decisions in our simulations are based on agent locations, then our simulation results should be quite different for each run. How do we know, then, if a given result (e.g., of so many people infected in such an amount of time) is *typical*? If we ran the last scenario again, could it be that not everyone gets infected, or that everyone gets infected much sooner. This is exactly where *statistics* enter the picture. The goal of a hypothesis test (like a *t-test* or *chi-square test*) is exactly to enter the question, "Did our study get a reasonable number of subjects? What are the odds that we happen to pick n oddball samples to study, and these are not at all typical?" We are not going to answer that question here. Instead, we point you to your next classes and to the connections between computer science, simulations, and probability and statistics. ∎

Now, in `DiseaseSimulation` method `setUp()`, let us change how the world is set up. Change the commenting at the start so that it looks like this:

```
// Let the world be set up
//super.setUp();
// or Set it up with a smaller world
world = new World(300,300);
world.setAutoRepaint(false);
```

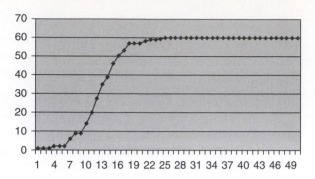

FIGURE 16.6
A graph of infection in a smaller world.

The two uncommented lines do the same thing as super.setUp(), but with a much smaller world—300 × 300 instead of 640 × 480. Does that matter? Figure 16.6 is a graph of a run with the smaller world. It looks like it matters very much. In the smaller world, everyone is infected by timestep 25. Perhaps this is why diseases tend to spread much more quickly in tight-knit groups or in urban settings. If there are as many people, but everyone travels in a smaller area, people are more likely to bump into one another.

When we explore this simulation in class, we often run experiments like this exploration of greater or smaller space in the simulation. Sometimes we vary the number of people in the space, sometimes we have agents avoid visibly infected agents, and other times we change aspects of the disease. One semester, a student suggested a change to the disease where it kills infected people after three days, but their bodies would still lie around infecting others. (We might note that this was a particularly morbid student.) What was the impact on the infection rate? Surprisingly to all of us in the class, the infection rate *dropped* dramatically. When we mentioned this result to mathematical biologists, they were not at all surprised. That finding has been well known by mathematical biologists. That is why the *Ebola virus* has not reached the general populace, we were told. When a disease agent kills rapidly, it also eliminates the opportunity for the infected people to spread the disease further.

16.4 WALKING THROUGH THE SIMULATION PACKAGE

We are not going to walk through *all* of the simulation package in this chapter. For the most part, it looks like the wolves and deer simulation of the last chapter. What is useful to understand is how the *overriding* works. When do methods get called in Simulation, Agent, a particular Simulation subclass, and a particular Agent subclass?

Let's *trace* the execution of the disease propagation simulation from:

```
DiseaseSimulation ds = new DiseaseSimulation();
ds.run();
```

The first line executes the *constructor* for the class. Since DiseaseSimulation does not have its own constructor, we will call the one in **Simulation**:

```java
/**
 * Constructor to set output to null
 */
public Simulation() {
  // By default, don't write to a file.
  output = null;
  // By default, don't have an animation
  frames = null;
}
```

The method run is in the **Simulation** package. Note that there is a run() that accepts no inputs, and a run(int timeRange) that defines the number of steps to execute. Executing ds.run() calls the first method:

```java
/**
 * Run for a default of 50 steps
 */
public void run(){
  this.run(50);
  this.closeFile();
}
```

And it in turn executes the second version. Here are the first few lines of that method.

```java
/**
 * Ask all agents to run for the number of input
 * steps
 * @param numSteps the number of timesteps to run
 */
public void run(int numSteps) {

  // For storing the current agent
  Agent current = null;

  // Set up the simulation
  this.setUp();
```

When we get to this step in Simulation's run method, we ask this (which is our DiseaseSimulation instance in variable ds) to setUp(). **DiseaseSimulation** does have a setUp() method, so we will call that.

```java
public void setUp() {

  // Let the world be set up
  super.setUp();
  // or Set it up with a smaller world
  //world = new World(300,300);
  //world.setAutoRepaint(false);

  PersonAgent moi;

  // 60 people
  for (int num = 0; num < 60; num++) {
```

```
      moi = new PersonAgent(getWorld(),this);
    }

    // Infect the first one
    moi = (PersonAgent) getAgents().get(0);
    moi.infect();
  }
```

The *very first* line in this method, though, calls super.setUp(), which executes **Simulation**'s setUp() method.

```
  /**
   * setUp the simulation.
   * Subclasses should call this (via super)
   * and create agents.
   */
  public void setUp() {
    // Set up the World
    world = new World();
    if (background != null)
      world.setPicture(background);
    world.setAutoRepaint(false);
  }
```

After executing this method, we return to the rest of DiseaseSimulation's setUp() method, which creates the 60 people, one ill. We are now back in **Simulation**'s run(int timeRange) method. We just finished the setUp() method, so we go on to the time loop:

```
  // Set up the simulation
  this.setUp();

  // loop for a set number of timesteps
  for (int t = 0; t < numSteps; t++) {

    // loop through all the agents, and have them
    // act()
    for (int index=0; index < agents.size(); index++) {
      current = (Agent) agents.get(index);
      current.act();
    }
```

Each of current in this loop is a PersonAgent. Does **PersonAgent** have an act() method? Sure it does!

```
  /**
   * How a Person acts
   */
  public void act() {

    // Is there a person within infection range of me?
    Simulation sim = getSimulation();
```

```
    PersonAgent closePerson =
      (PersonAgent) getClosest(20,
                                sim.getAgents());

    if (closePerson != null) {
      // If this person is infected,
      // and I'm not infected
      if (closePerson.infected && !this.infected) {
        // I become infected
        this.infect();
      }
    }
  }
```

Note that at the end of this method, we call super.act(). This means that **Agent**'s act() method will then execute. This is the method that implements wandering aimlessly.

```
/**
 * Method to act during a timestep.  The
 * default is to pick a random direction and
 * move some random amount up to the top speed.
 */
public void act() {

  /* if the random number is > prob of NOT
   * turning then turn */
  if (randNumGen.nextFloat() > PROB_OF_STAY) {
    this.turn(randNumGen.nextInt(360));
  }

  // go forward some random amount
  forward(randNumGen.nextInt(speed));
} // end act()
```

We then return to **Simulation**'s run(int timeRange) method. After each agent is asked to act(), the world gets updated (world.repaint()). If there is a simulation, a frame gets written out.

```
    // repaint the world to show the movement
    // IF there is a world
    if (world != null) {
      world.repaint();
    }

    // Do the end of step processing
    this.endStep(t);

    // Wait for one second
    //Thread.sleep(1000);
  }
}
```

We then execute the endStep method. Since DiseaseSimulation does not have one, we call **Simulation**'s endStep method.

```
/**
 * End of step processing
 * @param t the current timestep number
 */
public void endStep(int t) {

  // Let's figure out where we stand...
  System.out.println(">>> Timestep: " + t);

  // If we have an open FrameSequencer,
  // write world to it.
  if (frames != null) {
    Picture copyPict = null;
    if (background != null) {
      copyPict = new Picture(background);
    }
    else {
      copyPict =
        new Picture(world.getWidth(),
                              world.getHeight());
    }
    world.setPicture(copyPict);
    frames.addFrame(copyPict);
  }

  // If we have an open file, write the counts to it
  if (output != null) {
    // Try it
    try {
      output.write(this.toString());
      output.newLine();
    } catch (Exception ex) {
      System.out.println("Couldn't write the data!");
      System.out.println(ex.getMessage());
      // Make output null so that we don't keep trying
      output = null;
    }
  }
}  // endStep()
```

But wait! In the middle of that method is a call to this.toString(). **DiseaseSimulation** *does* have a toString() method!

```
/**
 * create an information string with the number
 * infected
 * @return the number infected as a string
 */
public String toString() {
```

```
    PersonAgent first;
    first = (PersonAgent) getAgents().get(0);
    return (new Integer(first.getNumInfected()).
      toString());
}
```

That ends the execution for *one* call to an `act()` method for *one* agent in *one* timestep. This process of calling between the different classes and methods happen for *every* agent for *every* timestep. Fortunately, processors are really fast.

You do not really have to know what is inside of `Simulation` nor `Agent` to use the package. The important thing to know is what methods to override, and how (and when) your methods will be called. This walk through should give you a better sense of how the code in your subclasses gets called, and when the methods in the superclass gets used.

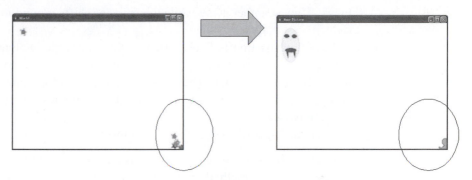

FIGURE 16.7
Mapping from agent (turtle) positions on the left to character positions on the right.

16.5   FINALLY! MAKING WILDEBEESTS AND VILLAGERS

After hundreds of pages, we can *finally* create an animation that is generated from a simulation! This is a similar method to what is used in Disney's *The Lion King*, when the wildebeests charged over the ridge, or in *The Hunchback of Notre Dame*, when the villagers milled about in the square.

The basic process is quite simple. We write a simulation, using the same approach seen previously in the chapter. Each agent should represent one character in our simulation. At each timestep, we create a *new* frame and draw our character images in the frame. We will use exactly this approach in creating our movie about the birdlike beings investigating the mysterious egg (Figure 16.7).

Here is the story of this movie. The turtle-like curious bird-things[3] wander, slowly, toward the mysterious egg. As they get up close to it—it opens its eyes and shows its

---

[3]We made these quickly, unsure whether we wanted turtles or birds. Since then, we have left them in their quasimodo state because they serve as a low bar for future movie makers. Certainly, *anyone* can make better-looking characters than these!

FIGURE 16.8
Frames from the egg–bird movie.

fangs! They scamper away while the monster shifts around and looks to the left and right.

Your first reaction is likely, "How is this unlike the wolvies attacking the village movie?" Yes, it is quite similar. However, in this version, the positions of the investigating birds are not scripted. They emerge from the random number generator. We could easily run the simulation again to get a different movie—we can have as many "takes" as we may like.

There are three classes in this simulation:

- `BirdSimulation` sets up the birds and the egg. The real work of the *mapping* occurs in the method `endStep()`.

- `BirdAgent` defines the behavior of the birds.

- `EggAgent` defines the behavior of the egg.

We are going to make a couple of changes to `Agent` and `Simulation` as we go along, in order to make the mapping work more easily to the animation. These changes do not interfere with the previous simulations in this chapter. In fact, the Java class files that you have been using (assuming you have been experimenting all along here) already have all of these changes. One change creates a character image for mapping to the agent, and another change allows us to get a timestep number in `act()` in case we want to do something in a particular frame.

Example Java Code 150: BirdSimulation's class declaration, fields, and setUp method

```
   /**
2   * BirdSimulation
    * A flock of 10 birds investigate a mysterious egg,
4   * which suddenly shows itself to be a monster!
    * @author Mark Guzdial
6   * @author Barb Ericson
    */
8  public class BirdSimulation extends Simulation {

10    /** the egg to investigate */
```

```
12    private EggAgent egg;
         // We'll need to get this later in BirdAgent

14    /** to make the animation */
      private FrameSequencer myFrames;
16       // Need a separate one from Simulations

18    /**
       * Set up the world with 10 birds and the mysterious egg
20     */
      public void setUp() {
22
         // Set up the world
24       super.setUp();

26       // We'll need frames for the animation
         myFrames = new FrameSequencer("C:/Temp/");
28       myFrames.show();

30       // create 10 birds
         BirdAgent tweetie;
32       World world = getWorld();
         for (int num = 0; num < 10; num++) {
34         tweetie = new BirdAgent(world,this);}

36       // And the egg
         egg = new EggAgent(world,this);
38    }
```

How It Works.   After seeing three simulations previous to this one, it's pretty clear what's going on here. We create 10 birds and one egg. One difference is the creation of a FrameSequencer for storing our simulation frames.

Example Java Code 151: BirdSimulation's endStep method

```
    /**
2    * What to do at the last timestep
     * t the current timestep
4    */
  public void endStep(int t) {
6
     // Do the normal file processing (if any)
8    super.endStep(t);

10   // But now, make a 640x480 frame, and copy
     // in pictures from all the agents
12   Picture frame = new Picture(640,480);
     Agent drawMe = null;
14   for (int index=0; index<this.getAgents().size();
        index++) {
16     drawMe = (Agent) this.getAgents().get(index);
       drawMe.getPicture().blueScreen(frame,drawMe.getXPos(),
18                                     drawMe.getYPos());
     }
20   myFrames.addFrame(frame);
   }
```

How It Works.   This method does the mapping process. At the end of each timestep, we create a picture to store our frame. For each agent, we get its picture (`drawMe.myPict`) and then use `blueScreen` to draw the picture at the position `drawMe.getXPos()`, `drawMe.getYPos()` of the turtle/agent. We then add the frame to the `frame` Frame-Sequencer.

We modified `Agent` to have this new field:

```
public class Agent extends Turtle {

/////////////// fields ////////////////////

/** the picture of the agent */
private Picture myPict;
```

The other change we need is to get the frame number passed into `act`, if the agent wants it. This is a fairly tricky change. We want the `Agent` subclasses to get the frame number (timestep number—same thing) if it wants it, but we do not want to require an input to `act()`. Here's how we solve it: We change the `run` method in `Simulation` to pass a timestep number, but we also provide an implementation in `Agent` that accepts a timestep number and calls `act()` without an input. In this way, if the timestep is not needed, the other version of `act()` gets called.

Example Java Code 152: Changing Simuation's run() method for a timestep input to act()
```
  // loop through all the agents, and have them
2 // act()
  for (int index=0; index < agents.size(); index++) {
4   current = (Agent) agents.get(index);
    current.act(t); // NEW -- pass in timestep
6 }
```

Example Java Code 153: Changing Agent to make time step inputs optional
```
  /**
2  * act() with a timestep
   **/
4 public void act(int t){
    // By default, don't act on it
6   this.act();
  }
```

Now we can build our agents.

Example Java Code 154: BirdAgent's class declaration, fields, and init method
```
  /**
2  * BirdAgents use the bird character JPEGs
   * @author Mark Guzdial
4  * @author Barb Ericson
   */
6 public class BirdAgent extends Agent {
```

```
8   /** the pictures to use */
    private static Picture bird1, bird2,
10      bird3, bird4, bird5, bird6;

12  //////////////////////// Constructors ///////////////////
    // not shown here
14
    /**
16   * Set up the birds
     * @param thisSim the simulation to use
18   */
    public void init(Simulation thisSim) {
20
      if (bird1 == null) {
22      // Do we have the bird characters defined yet?
        bird1 =
24        new Picture(FileChooser.getMediaPath("bird1.jpg"));
        bird2 =
26        new Picture(FileChooser.getMediaPath("bird2.jpg"));
        bird3 =
28        new Picture(FileChooser.getMediaPath("bird3.jpg"));
        bird4 =
30        new Picture(FileChooser.getMediaPath("bird4.jpg"));
        bird5 =
32        new Picture(FileChooser.getMediaPath("bird5.jpg"));
        bird6 =
34        new Picture(FileChooser.getMediaPath("bird6.jpg"));
      }
36    // Start out with myPict as bird1
      this.setPicture(bird1);
38
      // Do the normal initializations
40    super.init(thisSim);

42    // Move all the birds to the far right corner
      this.setPenDown(false);
44    this.moveTo(600,400);

46    // Set speed to relatively slow
      this.setSpeed(40);
48
    }
```

FIGURE 16.9
The individual images for the bird characters.

How It Works. Since all our bird characters will look the same (Figure 16.9)[4], we simply load them all into a set of `static` variables. No, they do not *have* to be static,

[4]See previous explanation for the birds' look-and-feel.

but we also do not need to waste the space since they will all look the same. We use a trick here to load the six images. When the first bird is created, bird1 will be null. We then load all six images. The rest of the birds will check if bird1 is null, but of course, it won't be. All birds will start out with the first image, and down in the lower right-hand corner of the world.

Example Java Code 155: BirdAgent's act method

```java
/**
 * act(t) For first 20 steps, walk toward the egg,
 * +/- 30 degrees.
 * Then walk AWAY from the egg,
 * and with MORE wandering (panic).
 */
public void act(int t) {

    // First, handle motion
    int speed = getSpeed();
    if (t <= 20) {
        // Tell it that this really is a BirdSimulation
        BirdSimulation mySim = (BirdSimulation) getSimulation();
        // which has an egg
        this.turnToFace(mySim.getEgg());
        this.turn(randNumGen.nextInt(60)-30);
        forward(randNumGen.nextInt(speed));
    } else {
        // Run away!!
        this.turnToFace(640,480); // Far right corner
        this.turn(randNumGen.nextInt(80)-40);
        forward(randNumGen.nextInt(speed));
    }

    // Next, set a new character
    int cell = randNumGen.nextInt(6)+1; // 0 to 5, +
    // 1 => 1 to 6
    switch (cell) {
        case 1:
            this.setPicture(bird1);
            break;
        case 2:
            this.setPicture(bird2);
            break;
        case 3:
            this.setPicture(bird3);
            break;
        case 4:
            this.setPicture(bird4);
            break;
        case 5:
            this.setPicture(bird5);
            break;
        case 6:
            this.setPicture(bird6);
            break;
    } // end switch
} // end act
```

How It Works.   This is an `act` method that takes a timestep as an input, `t`. The birds act different in the first 20 frames than they do in the rest of the movie. During the first 20 frames, the birds always head toward the egg (which we will see is in the upper left-hand corner). They turn a bit while heading there. The formula `randNumGen.nextInt(60)-30` means that a random number between 0 and 59 will be generated, then 30 will be subtracted from that. The result is a value between -30 and 29. The birds will generally be meandering toward the egg. The birds then move forward at a random value based on their speed.

Once the egg becomes scary in frame 20, the birds face the opposite corner. The range of variance is larger for turning, from -40 to 39—they are more chaotic running away.

No matter what the frame is, the birds consider changing their look with every frame. A die is thrown, using `randNumGen.nextInt(6)+1` to store a value between 1 and 6 in the variable `cell`. A `switch` statement is used to make a choice.

Think of a `switch` statement as a shortcut for a bunch of `if` statements. Read:

```
switch (cell) {
    case 1:
        this.setPicture(bird1);
        break;
    case 2:
        this.setPicture(bird2);
        break;
```

as:

```
if (cell == 1) {
    this.setPicture(bird1);
    }
else if (cell == 2) {
    this.setPicture(bird2);
    }
```

The `break` says "Only one `case` is going to match, so skip to the end of the `switch` statement now."

Example Java Code 156: EggAgent's declaration and fields

```
   /**
2   * EggAgent -- big scary egg that sits there until t=20,
    * then emerges as a monster!
4   * @author Mark Guzdial
    * @author Barb Ericson
6   */
   public class EggAgent extends Agent {
8
    /** the pictures to use */
10   private static Picture egg1, egg2, egg3, egg4;
```

FIGURE 16.10
The various egg images.

Example Java Code 157: EggAgent's init method

```
   /**
2   * To initialize, set it up as the Egg in the upper
    * lefthand corner
4   * @param thisSim the simulation
    */
6   public void init(Simulation thisSim) {
     if (egg1 == null) { //Initialize
8       egg1 =
          new Picture(FileChooser.getMediaPath("egg1.jpg"));
10      egg2 =
          new Picture(FileChooser.getMediaPath("egg2.jpg"));
12      egg3 =
          new Picture(FileChooser.getMediaPath("egg3.jpg"));
14      egg4 =
          new Picture(FileChooser.getMediaPath("egg4.jpg"));
16    }

18    // Start out as egg1
     this.setPicture(egg1);
20
     // Normal initialization
22    super.init(thisSim);

24    // Make the turtle disappear
     this.hide();
26    this.setPenDown(false);

28    // Move the egg up to the lefthand corner
     this.moveTo(10,10);
30   }
```

How It Works. The EggAgent init method works much as the BirdAgent's does. First, the four egg images are loaded into static methods. The egg starts looking like the first one—just a plain ordinary egg (Figure 16.10). The egg (remember that only one instance of EggAgent is created) is in the upper left-hand corner.

Example Java Code 158: EggAgent's act method

```
   /**
2   * To act, just drop the Egg for 19 steps,
    * then be the eyes opened for five steps,
```

```
 4    * then be the eyes switching back-and-forth
      * @param t the timestep
 6    */
     public void act(int t) {
 8     if (t < 19) {
         this.setPicture(egg1);
10     }

12     if (t > 19 && t < 24) {
         this.setPicture(egg2);
14     }

16     if (t > 23) {
         int choose=randNumGen.nextInt(2);
18       if (choose == 1) {
           this.setPicture(egg3);
20       }

22       else {
           this.setPicture(egg4);
24       }
       }
26   } // end act()
```

■

How It Works.   The EggAgent is the only agent we have seen that never moves at all—not aimlessly, not toward an object. For the first 19 frames, the egg just sits there. Then, the eyes open at frame 20—that's the egg2 image in Figure 16.10. After frame 23, the egg randomly shifts between the final two images, where the eyes shift left and right.

Going Beyond the Wildebeests

And that's it! We've now figured out the basic computer science behind the wildebeests and the villagers!

There are lots of interesting things to do with even this simple bird animation.

- Birds could start out all over the screen, and slowly move themselves toward the egg—then all run away in the same direction. That might have more visual impact.

- Rather than use frame numbers in the BirdAgent act(), the egg could have a method like looksScary(). Then, instead of checking for the frame number, the BirdAgent could ask if (egg.looksScary()) in order to decide to run away. The code would be less complex and read more easily.

- The birds could respond to one another, like avoiding crowds.

Perhaps the biggest idea here is that mapping a simulation to an animation is just *one* kind of mapping that one could create. An animation is only one kind of representation to make from a simulation. How about playing certain sounds or MIDI phrases from different characters when they act at different times? Music could be a result of a simulation as well as an animation is.

Despite the interestingness of continuous simulations, they are not the most common kinds of simulations. The most common kinds of simulations, and perhaps the most useful for answering people's questions, are *discrete event simulations*. So even though we have finished our journey to the wildebeests here, we are going to have one more chapter to finish our exploration of the usefulness of simulations.

EXERCISES

16.1 Look for other places where we use a `for` loop and the `get` method to loop through all the elements in a linked list. Modify this code to use an `Iterator` instead.

16.2 Do the first exercise from the last chapter, with this new `WDSimulation`: "Change the `Deer` so that there is no random amount that it moves—it always zips around at maximum speed." How much harder or easier is it?

16.3 `PersonAgent`'s `act` method is not quite right. Rather than asking if there's an infected person within range of me, it asks who the closest person is to me and if that person is infected. Fix the `act` method so that it does the right thing.

16.4 Using the simulation package developed in this chapter, create a simulation of an ecology. Use classes `WolfAgent`, `DeerAgent`, and a new `CornAgent` (that you will write), and your simulation should extend the `Simulation` class. Set up your simulation like this:

- Create a dozen deer and three wolves to start with.
- Create three dozen pieces of corn.

When running your simulation, let's consider a timestep to be about a week. Run the simulation for two years (104 timesteps). Here are the basic rules for the simulation.

- Deer can smell wolves within 20 steps and will move away from them. (Initial max speed is 20.)
- Wolves can smell deer within 15 steps and will move to the deer, kill it, and eat it. (Initial max speed is 25.)
- Deer can smell corn within five steps and can move to it within a single step. If a deer lands on a corn, it eats the corn.
- If a deer goes two weeks without corn, its speed drops by half. Once it eats corn, its speed goes back to maximum.
- If a deer goes four weeks without corn, it dies.
- If wolves go five weeks without a deer, their speed drops by half. Once a wolf eats a deer, its speed goes back to maximum.
- If a wolf goes 10 weeks without a deer, it dies.
- If corn survives for 12 weeks, it grows two more corn plants next to itself (any direction). *Every* 12 weeks, it can have two more children.
- Store to a file the number of wolves, deer, and corn at each timestep.

An important part of this exercise is to do *experimentation*. Run this simulation with these rules three times. Then try two other sets of rules and run each of those three times also. Your goal is to reach equilibrium—that there are roughly as many deer, corn, and wolves as you start out with at the end of the simulation. Things that you might want to try changing in your rules:

- *Initial counts.* Should there be more corn, or fewer deer? Would culling the herd help more survive? Would more wolves create better equilibrium?

- *Ranges.* Should deer or wolves smell only closer, or farther? Should they not be able to jump to corn or deer in a single timestep?

For extra credit, implement male and female deer. Every 12 weeks, the female deer can become pregnant if there is a male deer within smell range. (You decide if the female jumps to the male, or the male jumps to the female.) Pregnancy lasts for six weeks, during which time the female will die if she doesn't get corn every *three* timesteps. At the end of six weeks, a new deer is produced (randomly selected gender).

In addition to your program, you are to produce a report with graphs of all *nine* of your runs—that's three runs of each of three sets of variables. Show all three variables: wolves, deer, and corn per timestep for all three of the scenarios that you explored. Explain what you changed in each scenario and why you think the results differed from the other scenarios.

16.5   Using the simulation package developed in this chapter, create a simulation of immigration behavior.

Here's the initial set-up:

- Create a world that is 400 × 400. (If your world gets crowded, you're welcome to make it bigger.)

- The rightmost 200 pixels represent Europe. The leftmost 100 pixels represent America.

- Create 150 people scattered across Europe.

When running the simulation, let's consider a timestep to be about a month. Run the simulation for 10 years (120 timesteps). Here are the starting (overly simplistic and not historically accurate) rules.

- If a person has over five neighbors within 20 pixels for three consecutive timesteps, then that person feels overcrowded and decides to emigrate to America.

- There is a 10% probability for each person in Europe that they experience crop failure each timestep. If a person experiences crop failure, they decide to emigrate to America.

- There is only a 5% chance that someone moves somewhere else in Europe in a timestep, and if they do, they only move between 1 and 16 steps away. (And always within Europe—not into the Atlantic.)

- It takes three timesteps to cross the Atlantic. 10% of those that start the journey don't make it across. (That's not 10% per timestep—it's 10% of the number of people.) Be sure to show the people making the journey, about

33 steps per timestep. (Note that it is easier to compute a 1/10 chance of dying each emigration timestep. That is a reasonable simplification, but it's not really the same thing.)

- Once a person moves to America, they move more often (20% chance of moving each timestep, in a range of 1 to 100 pixels, but always within America), but disease is common there. About 2% of the population in America becomes diseased (maybe changes color?) each timestep (they don't move when sick). About 50% of those ill get healthy again each timestep. If someone is ill for four timesteps in success, they die.
- Store to a file the number of people in Europe, in transit, and in America each timestep.

Again, *experiment*—use these initial rules to start, and try two other scenarios. Here are some issues that you might want to try changing in your rules:

- *Overcrowding.* Maybe there are more people to start with, or it takes more too-close neighbors to convince someone that they're overcrowded, or more timesteps of crowded conditions to convince them to move.
- *Crop failures.* What if crop failures were more common, or it took multiple consecutive crop failures to convince someone to emigrate.
- *Travel.* What if people didn't die on the trip over, or if it took longer.
- *Movement.* What if people moved more often, or further, in either America or Europe.
- *Disease.* In America, more crowded conditions would lead to higher probabilities of disease. What if people moved like they do in Europe, or if they all came ashore at the same two or three spots (e.g., *Ellis Island*), and then the incidence of disease was dependent on the number of people around you.
- *Wealth.* Add the additional variables of wealth and cost to the simulation and come up with reasonable rules for how this wealth is used in the simulation. Europeans may have a normal distribution of wealth, but perhaps with a wide variance. The least wealthy are more likely to get sick, more likely to have crop failure, and are more likely to want to emigrate. The most wealthy are the least likely to want to emigrate, are less likely to have crop failure, and are less likely to get sick. Once in America, wealth still is a factor (most of the *Founding Fathers* were quite wealthy)—an interesting question is what kind of distribution of wealth appears in America given the rules that you set out and which Europeans emigrate. Wealth plays less of a role in movement, but still plays a role in whether you get sick and die.

Produce a report with graphs of all *nine* of your runs—that's three runs of each of three sets of variables. Show all three variables—Europeans, in-transit, and Americans per timestep for all three of the scenarios that you explored. Explain what you changed in each scenario and why you think the results differed from the other scenarios.

Note: It is particularly fun to generate this simulation as a series of JPEG frames, then create a movie from them!

16.6   Using the simulation package developed in this chapter, and replacing the turtle with character images, create a crowd scene simulation. Start out with 100 villagers scattered around the world.

During the simulation, let's imagine that a timestep is a minute. Run the simulation for 90 minutes.

- If there is no one around a villager (say, within 50 steps), the villager will set a heading for the closest person and take a couple of steps that way.

- If there are three or more people too close (say within 10 steps), a villager will get out of there (pick a random direction and move speed distance away—not a random speed, but actual speed.) (It's pretty hard to set a heading toward open space, but if you can do it, go ahead!)

- In general, people are milling about. They take 1–5 steps per timestep. They have only a 10% chance of changing direction of movement. They change physical position regularly—25% chance each timestep of changing the direction they're facing, 5% chance each timestep of waving (i.e., putting hand up, putting it down next timestep). Implement any other milling-about rules (e.g., more position changes) you'd like.

- Ten minutes into the simulation, the Nasty Bad Dude (or *Dudess*, as you wish), walks into the world. The NBD doesn't change direction, and just walks 2–5 steps per timestep. But the villagers don't want to be anywhere near the NBD! If the NBD is near (say, within 30), they walk exactly away (turn toward, then turn 180, and move). Nobody ever sets a heading *toward* the NBD anymore. They quietly just start milling away from the NBD as s/he walks across the world.

This simulation aches for generating JPEG movies in order to see the resultant movie! (You may notice some similarities between this situation and the crowd scenes in Disney's *The Hunchback of Notre Dame*.)

16.7   Using the simulation package developed in class, and replacing the turtle with character images, create a stampeding crowd scene simulation.

At the beginning of the simulation, have 100 crowd members (wildebeests?) on the left edge of the world (within 100 pixels of the left edge). All headings are initially set to the right edge. Have 10 "obstacle" agents scattered in the middle 200 pixels of the world.

During the simulation, let's imagine that a timestep is a minute. Run the simulation for 30 minutes.

- The crowd moves relentlessly from the left edge to the right, with a minimum movement each step being 3 pixels, and a maximum of 10 steps.

- The crowd doesn't want to be bumping into others. If there are three or more people too close (say within 10 steps), a person will get out of there (pick a random direction and move speed distance away—not a random speed, but maximum speed). (It's pretty hard to set a heading toward open space, but if you can do it, go ahead!)

- Nobody in the crowd wants to be within 10 steps of an obstacle. If someone is heading for an obstacle, and they're within 20 steps of the obstacle, they're going to turn 45 degrees to the left or right (randomly). (What if they're NOW heading for an obstacle, after turning? Better turn again! Find some direction where you're NOT facing an obstacle!)

- People change physical position regularly—25% chance each timestep of changing the direction they're facing, 5% chance each timestep of doing something else (waving? i.e., putting hand up, putting it down next timestep). Implement any other milling-about rules (e.g., more position changes) you'd like.

- If at the start of a timestep, you're not facing the right edge, start heading back that way. Change your heading by 10 degrees each timestep to head toward the right edge (e.g., if your heading is 5, and you want to be 90, change to 15).

This might sound like the charging of the wildebeests in Disney's *The Lion King*.

16.8   Simulations can also be used to explore social science questions. In this simulation, we explore ways in which political influence might spread among members of different political affiliations. Build a simulation of *political influence*. Create a simple model where there are people with one kind of political conviction ("Reds") and others with another conviction ("Blues"). Each has a region of their own—to the left and to the right. Each moves around, and there is an overlap area. If a Red gets surrounded by more Blues than Reds, then the Red is argued down and converts to Blue. If a Blue gets surrounded by more Reds than Blues, then the Blue is converted to Red.

16.9   Using the simulation package developed in this chapter, and replacing the turtle with character images, create a simulation of the *Running of the Bulls in Pamplona*.

Set up the simulation with a world that is 800 pixels long, but only 75 wide. Create 25 runners at $x = 50$ in the world. Create five bulls at the left edge, $x = 0$.

During the simulation, let's imagine that a timestep is a minute, and run the simulation for 30 minutes. You decide on the parameters like max speed and ranges to create a good-looking simulation.

- The runners move from the left edge to the right, but they do wander a bit top to bottom sometimes, but always within the lane.

- Bulls also move relentlessly from the left edge to the right, but if a bull gets close to a runner, it moves toward that runner.

- The runners don't want to be bumping into other runners. If there are three or more people too close (say within 10 steps), a person will get out of there (pick a random direction and move at maximum speed).

- If a runner gets close to a bull, the runner will double their max speed for one timestep just to get ahead of the bull.

- If a bull catches a runner, the runner is then injured (maybe dead?) and stops. All of the bulls and the rest of the runners keep going.

- Runners change physical position regularly, sometimes they're watching over their left, sometimes over their right, and sometimes they're running straight ahead. You must have at least three different positions for runners that your animations move through.

- If at the start of a timestep, you're not facing the right edge, start heading back that way. Change your heading by 10 degrees each timestep to head toward the right edge (e.g., if your heading is 5, and you want it to be 90, change to 15).

16.10 Enhance the disease propagation simulation into something much more fiendish now.

- People, once infected (come within 10 steps of an infected person), don't turn red for two days, though they do spread the disease. There is a 0.05 possibility that an infected person NEVER becomes red, but does spread the disease. Call those the "*Typhoid Mary*" carriers.

- Healthy people, if they get within 20 steps of a *visibly* infected person (someone red), turn away. But, of course, some people are not visibly carrying the disease, but are infected.

- After five days of becoming infected, 25% of the people die. Their bodies remain infected and spread the disease, but they are red so that people will avoid them. The rest of the infected people become non-red at day 6 and become un-infected at day 7. (Yes, there is one day at the end when they are not visibly infected, but they are still infected.)

Implement these rules and note the average number of people infected (normal size world, start with 100 people and one infected) and the average number of dead over three runs. Run your simulation for 100 timesteps.

The goal is to *increase* the number that survive and decrease the number of people who become infected. Implement *two* of the below public health policies. Implement one of the policies, try out three runs and compute the average infected and dead, then implement the second policy and compute the average infected and dead. Produce a report with graphs of the number of healthy, infected, and dead people for each of the 100 days of each run. Your report should have three graphs for the original rules, then three graphs after the first policy implementation and a description of what happened (including average counts of diseased and dead) and why, then three graphs after both policies are implemented with a description of what happened with counts and why.

POLICIES:

- Reduce the mobility of the sick: When someone becomes visibly infected (red), their speed drops by half.

- Reduce mobility of the healthy: Decrease from the start the speed of all people (so they don't bump into the infected as much).

- Voluntary quarantine of the sick: When someone is visibly infected, at the beginning of each step, they turn to face (640, 480). That way, sick people will tend to move toward the lower right.

- Voluntary segregation of the sick and healthy. Visibly infected people turn to face (640, 480), and healthy (or presumably healthy such as those that are non-red) people turn to face (0, 0).

- Mandatory quarantine of the sick: At the beginning of the step for visibly infected, they *immediately move* to (640, 480). They can move some from there, but they always go back to their quarantine spot.

- Mandatory quarantine of the sick and healthy: All visibly infected move to (640, 480), and all visibly healthy people move to (0, 0).

- Removal of the dead (the *Monty Python's Holy Grail's* "bring out your dead!" policy): All dead bodies immediately go to (640, 0). (Presume that people in bioprotection suits are moving the dead without becoming infected themselves.)

- Scarce vaccine (the chosen few policy): Five people (probably national leaders or doctors or police) are given vaccines when first created. They never become infected.

- The paranoid policy: Everyone stays away from everyone else.

16.11 Use the simulation package and any of your disease simulations (including the enhanced one from the previous exercise), and create an animation from it. Implement:

- Three different types of people: they can be different genders, different looks, etc.

- A difference between healthy people and sick people (but not all people show the sickness, if you are using an enhanced disease). That means that each of the three different types of people must have a different look in sickness and health.

- There must be at least three different positions for each type of people, for example one might be facing left, another facing right, moving left, moving right, etc. You must rotate among these positions, perhaps with a probability of 0.3 of changing position with each timestep.

- Dead people should look different from healthy or sick people.

That is a total of 3 positions × 3 types × 2 (sick or healthy) = 18 images that you need to have for the living people, plus one more image for dead people.

16.12   (*Advanced.*) All of our simulations are flawed in that activity (death, political change, and infection) occurs *within* the timestep. That means that the *order* in which agents are processed will change the simulation, e.g., if a person goes from Red to Blue, then that changes the number of Blue for his or her neighbor, or a wolf may move toward a deer that gets eaten in the same timestep by another wolf. A better way to do this is to consider all changes *before* making *any* changes. This is called a *transaction model*—all transactions occur at once. Change the `Simulation` and `Agent` classes so that all our simulations work, but are based on a single transaction.

CHAPTER 17

Discrete Event Simulation

Chapter Learning Objectives

The difference between continuous and *discrete event simulations* is that the latter only represent *some* moments of time—the ones where something important happens. Discrete event simulations are powerful for describing (and allowing us to make predictions about) a wide variety of situations including supermarkets, factory floors, hospitals, and economies. In order to create these simulations, we will use *random distributions* to describe behaviors when we do not know all the relevant factors. There are many kinds of random distributions, not just the simple `random number generator` that we have used so far. Once we make things happen randomly, we have to make sure that we keep *time order* true—first things come first, and next things come next. We will use a couple of different ways to maintain order, by sorting events into the right order, and by inserting events in order.

The computer science goals for this chapter are:

- To use queues to maintain order in a simulation.
- To use normal and uniform random distributions.
- To use both sorting and insertion into a sorted sequence to maintain a monotonically increasing notion of time.
- To introduce a min-heap (priority queue).

17.1 DESCRIBING A MARKETPLACE

Imagine this scenario:

- You are in charge of a small business that you would like to optimize.

- You have three trucks that bring your product from the factory to the warehouse. On average, they take three days to arrive, but it could take two days (if traffic and police are light) or four or more (if weather acts up or there is engine trouble). Each truck brings somewhere between 10 and 20 units (all values in the range are equally likely, depending on production issues).

- You have five distributors who pick up the product from the warehouse with orders. Usually they have orders ranging from 5 to 25 units, all equally likely.

- It takes the distributors an average of two days to get back to the market, and an average of five days to meet with customers, deliver the product, and take new orders.

There are lots of things that you might wonder about in this situation.

- How much product gets delivered like this?

- Do distributors have to wait for the product? How long do they have to wait? How long does the line get?

- How much product sits in the warehouse?

- What would help us move more product? Having more trucks or larger trucks? Moving the warehouse closer to the factory? Moving the warehouse closer to the market? Having more distributors?

You do *not* want a continuous simulation to explore this situation. You do not care about every moment. There will be days in this simulation where nothing happens at all. You want specific answers to specific questions—you want to know the exact times that events occur. The animation of distributors and trucks moving between the factory, warehouse, and market is not important to answering these questions. You don't care, for example, how close the trucks and distributors are to one another.

What you *do* need is a *discrete event simulation*. You want to represent the *specific* events that you are interested in. You want to skip all the rest of them. You want to control the random distributions and the interactions between components of the simulation.

17.2   DIFFERENCES BETWEEN CONTINUOUS AND DISCRETE EVENT SIMULATIONS

Discrete event simulations are quite different from continuous simulations. Now that you understand continuous simulations well, we can describe these differences in terms of how we construct the simulation.

There is no time loop in discrete event simulations. In continuous simulations, we wanted to represent all time values from 1 to the number of timesteps that we want to simulate. In a discrete event simulation, we run until we *pass* a given time. Time values do not come from a loop. Instead, events (like a distributor arriving at the warehouse, or a truck arriving at the factory) lead to computation of when the *next* event will occur. We run the simulation from one event time to the next event time. If nothing ever happens on day two of the simulation, that means that no event occurs on day two, and we simply skip it. It never occurs in our simulation.

The key here is that we must keep a list of events to occur *in the order that they should occur*. Imagine that a distributor arrives at the marketplace, and schedules an event to occur to leave the marketplace five days later. A second later, a truck leaves the factory, and it schedules the event to arrive at the warehouse two days later. In reality, the truck would arrive at the warehouse before the distributor leaves the marketplace. However, we generated the events in the reverse order. We have to make sure that we *simulate* the events in the correct, realistic order.

Time travel is really easy in a discrete event simulation, and the same dangers of creating contradictions exist. Imagine that the distributor arrives at the warehouse, and there's no product, so the distributor starts waiting for a truck. The truck then arrives—three days earlier. Did the distributor just wait for a negative three days?

Agents do not *act()* in a discrete event simulation. If there is no timing loop, there is no loop in which we say to each agent, "It's your turn to do something!" The notion of only executing *events* means that the whole idea of giving every agent a "turn" is wrong.

Agents only do something when their event occurs. When an event occurs, the agent gets the chance to handle the event. Unless the agent dies in the event, the agent should then schedule the *next* event to occur. The agents do that using the random distributions relevant to their activities.

Introducing Resources

A big difference between continuous and discrete event simulations is the use of *resources*. Agents in a discrete event simulation cannot do everything they want all the time. What is interesting about the scenarios in which you use discrete event simulations is the interaction between agents and the struggle for resources.

Resources in our scenario are *products*. Trucks deliver them, and distributors distribute them. Distributors cannot distribute the product until it arrives at the warehouse. The products, then, are the *synchronization* between the actors (trucks and distributors).

If the resources are not available when the agents need them, the agents become *blocked*. The agents cannot schedule any events until they become unblocked. If there are several agents awaiting a resource, we can implement whatever policy we want for who gets the resource next. Typically, we implement a "first-come, first-served" policy. That is where a *queue* enters the situation. Blocked agents awaiting a resource wait in a queue, and when a resource becomes available, the first agent in the queue gets the resource.

17.3   DIFFERENT KINDS OF RANDOM

> Anyone who considers arithmetical methods of producing random digits is, of course, in a state of sin.
>
> — JOHN VON NEUMANN (1903–1957)

When you first start using `Math.random()`, you probably just think of getting a *random* number. What you might not think about is that there are different *kinds* of random.

- Are the numbers real (with a decimal point) or integer?
- From what range are the numbers drawn? For `Math.random()`, the range is 0.0–1.0. For lottery tickets, the random numbers are usually in a much more well-defined range, like from 0 to 42, with no real numbers allowed.
- Are all numbers in that range equally likely?

Random Distributions in the World

That last issue is quite important. `Math.random()` uses a *uniform random distribution*. All values between 0.0 and 1.0 are equally likely. Actually, few things that you might want to measure in the real world have a uniform distribution.

- Imagine that you made a list of all the heights of any randomly selected group of people, such as the heights of people in your class. The smallest might be five foot tall, and the largest might be six foot four inches. A uniform distribution would suggest that there are just as many people at five foot, as at five foot one inch, as at five foot two inches, as at six foot three inches, and six foot four inches. In reality, we know that there are few people at either end of a range, and most of the people will be around the average height of the group. We call this a *normal distribution* or a *Gaussian distribution* (after the person who first described it).

  A *normal probability distribution* describes what happens if you put all these people in a room, then asked them to come out, one-at-a-time, in any order. The heights of the people coming out of that room would range between five foot and six foot four. Most of them will be around average. If you knew the average height of people in that room, and then a bunch of six foot four people came out of the door, you would think that something was strange. You would expect that the height of the people emerging from the room would fill in a normal distribution.

- Let us consider a different distribution. From any random group of people, consider the number of people with some disease (like tuberculosis or lung cancer) and the amount of exposure to some disease-causing agent (like radiation or cigarette smoking). You would expect that very few people who have never smoked have lung cancer. (In fact, lung cancer was virtually unknown, except among miners, before smoking became widespread.) The number of lung cancer cases as the amount of smoking increases only increases—it never drops (Figure 17.1). It is not the case that one's doctor ever says, "Okay, your risk for lung cancer is really high now, but if you only smoke *a little bit more*, your risk of lung cancer will drop."

  Our cigarette-to-cancer relationship might be an example of a *Poisson distribution* (again, after the person who first described it). It depends on how the cigarettes and lung cancer relationship progresses. If it's a *linear* relationship, then the difference in number of cancer cases between two and four packs of cigarettes per day should be about the same as four and six packs of cigarettes per day. However,

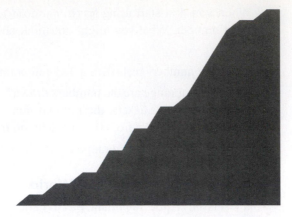

FIGURE 17.1
A distribution where there is only an increase.

if the relationship between the variables changes much more quickly than that (e.g., on an exponential curve), then it may be a Poisson distribution.

Imagine that we have a hat, on which we have thrown pieces of paper, each with two numbers written on it: the number of cigarettes smoked (on average) per day, and the number of people who have lung cancer (from the group we randomly selected) who smoked that much. As we pull numbers out of the hat, we expect that a larger first number will also have a correspondingly large second number. If all the second numbers were the same, that would be a uniform distribution, and we would find that odd. If we found that the second numbers seem to cluster around an average value, then start to *decrease* while the first number gets even larger, that would be a normal distribution, and we would not expect that either.

Generating Different Random Distributions

There are lots of different kinds of relationships between two different variables: increasing, decreasing, uniform, curved increasing, curved decreasing, S-shaped, and so on. The most common distributions that one deals with in a simulation are normal and uniform. Those two are built-in to the Random class that we have been using in this book.

- When we ask an instance of Random to provide a nextFloat(), we will get a random number between 0.0 and 1.0 drawn from a uniform probability distribution—all values are equally likely.

- When we ask an instance of Random to provide a nextGaussian(), we will get a random float number drawn from a normal probability distribution. The average value is 0.0 and a *standard deviation* of 1.0. The standard deviation describes the *spread* of the normal distribution "hill." If the standard deviation is small, then the hill is tall and spikey. If the standard deviation is large, then the values spread out more, and the hill is more like a rise along a flat plane. In any case, the majority of values in the hill fall between the mean value *minus* the standard deviation (-1.0 in the nextGaussian() distribution) and the mean value *plus* the standard deviation (1.0 for nextGaussian()). The spread of the distribution doesn't mean that -5.25 and 7.8 are *impossible*—they are just quite unlikely.

The textual description above might be clearer with some images. Let's generate a bunch of random numbers from each of these two distributions, then generate *histograms* from the numbers—we'll count the number in each of various ranges (*bins*) in order to see how likely the different ranges are from the distributions. First, let's generate 500 random numbers from a uniform distribution.

Example Java Code 159: Generating random numbers from a uniform distribution

```java
import java.util.*;   // Need this for Random
import java.io.*;   // For BufferedWriter

/**
 * Class to generate a uniform distribution of numbers
 * @author Mark Guzdial
 * @author Barb Ericson
 */
public class GenerateUniform {

  public static void main(String[] args) {
    Random rng = new Random(); // Random Number Generator
    BufferedWriter output=null; // file for writing

    // Try to open the file
    try {
      // create a writer
      output =
        new BufferedWriter
        (new FileWriter("C:/dsBook/uniform.txt"));
    } catch (Exception ex) {
      System.out.println("Trouble opening the file.");
    }

    // Fill it with 5000 numbers between 0.0 and 1.0,
    // uniformly distributed
    for (int i=0; i < 5000; i++) {
      try {
        output.write("\t" + rng.nextFloat());
        output.newLine();
      } catch (Exception ex) {
        System.out.println("Couldn't write the data!");
        System.out.println(ex.getMessage());
      }
    }

    // Close the file
    try {
      output.close();
    } catch (Exception ex) {
      System.out.println("Something went wrong closing " +
        "the file");
    }
  }
}
```

How It Works. This class is another example of creating a class just to have a main method that does what we need. We create a file-writing stream on some file. In a loop for 5000 times, we get a random nextFloat and write it out to the file. (By writing out a tab character first, we force a string conversion, and thus avoid having to deal with conversions ourselves.) We have the requisite try-catch to deal with possible file errors.

Now we want to figure out the number of random values that fall within each of 0.0 to 0.1, then 0.1 to 0.2, then 0.2 to 0.3, up to 1.0. Below is a class that can create a histogram in several different ways and write the results to a file.

Example Java Code 160: Generate a histogram

```java
import java.util.*;
import java.io.*;

/**
 * Class to generate a histogram
 * @author Mark Guzdial
 * @author Barb Ericson
 */
public class HistogramGenerator {

  /** the map to hold the values */
  private Map<Double,Integer> valueMap =
    new TreeMap<Double,Integer>();

  /**
   * Method to read a set of values from
   * the inputFile and create
   * bins based on the array of keys.
   * This will count the number
   * of values in each bin.  Any value
   * larger than the last key
   * will be put in the last bin.
   * @param inputFile the file to read from
   * @param keys an array of key values to use
   */
  public void countValuesForKeys(String inputFile,
                                 double[] keys) {

    BufferedReader reader = null;
    String line = null;
    double doubleValue = 0.0;
    boolean found = false;
    int lastIndex = keys.length - 1;

    // put the keys in the map using a count of 0
    for (int i = 0; i < keys.length; i++) {
      valueMap.put(keys[i],0);
    }

    try {
      // open the file
      reader = new BufferedReader
        (new FileReader(inputFile));

      // loop reading from the file
      while ((line = reader.readLine()) != null) {
```

```java
48          doubleValue = Double.parseDouble(line);
            found = false;
            for (double key : keys) {
50              if (doubleValue < key) {
                  valueMap.put(key,valueMap.get(key) + 1);
52                found = true;
                  break;
54              }
            }
56          if (!found)
                valueMap.put(keys[lastIndex],
58                          valueMap.get(keys[lastIndex]));
          }

60
          // close the file
62        reader.close();

64      } catch (Exception ex) {
          System.out.println(ex.getMessage());
66        ex.printStackTrace();
        }
68    }

70    /**
       * Method to read a set of values from
72       * the inputFile create even
       * bins based on the passed factor.
74       * This will count the number
       * of values in each bin.
76       * @param inputFile the file to read from
       * @param factor the factor to use to break the values
78       * into bins
       */
80    public void countValues(String inputFile,
                              int factor) {
82
        BufferedReader reader = null;
84      String line = null;
        double doubleValue = 0.0;
86      double key = 0.0;
        int currCount = 0;
88
        try {
90        // open the file
          reader = new BufferedReader(
92                      new FileReader(inputFile));

94        // loop reading from the file
          while ((line = reader.readLine()) != null) {
96          doubleValue = Double.parseDouble(line);
            doubleValue = doubleValue * factor;
98          key = Math.ceil(doubleValue) / (double) factor;
            if (valueMap.containsKey(key)) {
100           currCount = valueMap.get(key);
              currCount++;
102           valueMap.put(key,currCount);
            }
104         else {
              valueMap.put(key,1);
106         }
          }
108
```

```java
                         // close the file
110                      reader.close();

112                  } catch (Exception ex) {
                         System.out.println(ex.getMessage());
114                      ex.printStackTrace();
                     }
116              }

118          /**
             * Method to output the keys and values in the histogram
120          * to a file
             * @param fileName the name of the file to write to
122          */
             public void writeFile(String fileName) {
124
                 BufferedWriter writer = null;
126              double key = 0;
                 int value = 0;
128              Set<Double> keySet = null;

130              try {

132                  // create the writer
                     writer = new BufferedWriter(new FileWriter(fileName));
134
                     // get the keys and loop through them
136                  keySet = valueMap.keySet();
                     Iterator<Double> iterator = keySet.iterator();
138                  while (iterator.hasNext()) {
                         key = iterator.next();
140                      value = valueMap.get(key);
                         writer.write(key + "\t" + value);
142                      writer.newLine();
                     }
144
                     // close the writer
146                  writer.close();

148              } catch (Exception ex) {
                     System.out.println(ex.getMessage());
150                  ex.printStackTrace();
                 }
152          }

154          /**
             * Generate the histogram from the uniform data
156          */
             public static void genUniform() {
158              HistogramGenerator histGen = new HistogramGenerator();
                 double[] keyArray = {0.1,0.2,0.3,0.4,0.5,
160                                  0.6,0.7,0.8,0.9,1.0};
                 histGen.countValuesForKeys("C:/dsBook/uniform.txt",
162                                           keyArray);
                 histGen.writeFile("C:/dsBook/uniformHist.txt");
164          }

166          /**
             * Method to generate the normal histogram
168          */
             public static void genNormal() {
170              HistogramGenerator histGen = new HistogramGenerator();
```

```
172    double[] keyArray = {-1.0, -0.9, -0.8, -0.7,
         -0.6, -0.5, -0.4, -0.3,
         -0.2, -0.1,0.0,0.1,0.2,0.3,0.4,
174      0.5,0.6,0.7,0.8,0.9,1.0};
       histGen.countValuesForKeys("C:/dsBook/normal.txt",
176                                 keyArray);
       histGen.writeFile("C:/dsBook/normalHist.txt");
178    }
     }
```

This can be executed by typing the following in the Interactions Pane.

```
> java GenerateUniform
> HistogramGenerator.genUniform();
```

The file that this generates lists the bin size in one column, and the number of random values in that bin in the second column. That's a perfect form for generating a chart in any spreadsheet program. So, now we can take a look at the histogram for these 5000 uniform values (Figure 17.2). Yes, that looks pretty flat and uniform.

Now, let's do the same thing with our Gaussian, normal distribution.

Example Java Code 161: Generate normal random variables

```java
   import java.util.*;   // Need this for Random
2  import java.io.*;     // For BufferedWriter

4  /**
    * Class to generate a normal distribution of numbers
6   * @author Mark Guzdial
    * @author Barb Ericson
8   */
   public class GenerateNormal {

10
     public static void main(String[] args) {
12     Random rng = new Random(); // Random Number Generator
       BufferedWriter output=null; // file for writing

14
       // Try to open the file
16     try {
         // create a writer
18       output =
           new BufferedWriter(
20             new FileWriter("C:/dsBook/normal.txt"));
       } catch (Exception ex) {
22       System.out.println("Trouble opening the file.");
       }

24
       // Fill it with 5000 numbers
26     // normally distributed
       for (int i=0; i < 5000; i++) {
28       try {
           output.write("\t" + rng.nextGaussian());
30         output.newLine();
         } catch (Exception ex) {
32         System.out.println("Couldn't write the data!");
           System.out.println(ex.getMessage());
34       }
       }

36
```

```
        // Close the file
38      try {
            output.close();
40      } catch (Exception ex) {
            System.out.println("Something went wrong closing " +
42              "the file");
        }
44    }
    }
```

■

Again, we generate the histogram, now with bins from −1.0 to 1.0, since that's the range of the standard deviation of the built-in normal distribution in Random. When we graph it, we see the bell-shaped curve that we associate with a normal distribution (Figure 17.3)—except for those weird spikes at either end of the histogram! What are those? Recall that *most* of the values are between the mean +/− the standard deviation. The values that are lower than −1.0 are all mapped to our first bin. The values that are bigger than 1.0 are mapped to the last bin.

Generating Useful Random Distributions

We hope that we have now convinced you that uniform and normal distributions *are* different kinds of random, and that we have shown you how to generate each from Random. The next step is to figure out how to make each of these useful. We will be using these random numbers to represent real values in the world, like the height of a person or the probability of developing cancer. In order to do this we will need to be able to develop random numbers within a specified range, beyond 0.0 to 1.0.

We have already seen how to generate uniform random distributions in a certain range.

- You simply add the lower bound of what you want to the value returned from nextFloat(). If you want values to start at 4.0 for the variable that you are modeling, then adding 4.0 to nextFloat() gives you a value between 4.0 and 5.0.

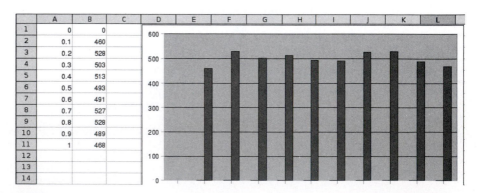

	A	B	C	D	E	F	G	H	I	J	K	L
1	0	0										
2	0.1	460										
3	0.2	528										
4	0.3	503										
5	0.4	513										
6	0.5	493										
7	0.6	491										
8	0.7	527										
9	0.8	528										
10	0.9	489										
11	1	468										
12												
13												
14												

FIGURE 17.2
A histogram of 5000 random values from a uniform distribution.

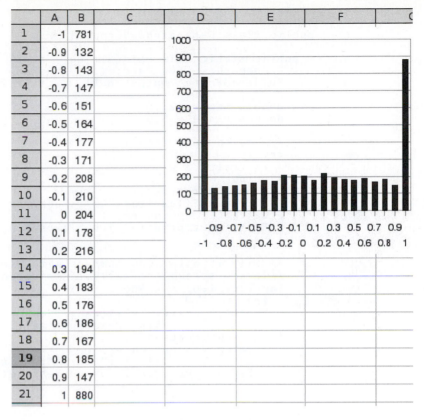

	A	B	C	D	E	F	G
1	-1	781					
2	-0.9	132					
3	-0.8	143					
4	-0.7	147					
5	-0.6	151					
6	-0.5	164					
7	-0.4	177					
8	-0.3	171					
9	-0.2	208					
10	-0.1	210					
11	0	204					
12	0.1	178					
13	0.2	216					
14	0.3	194					
15	0.4	183					
16	0.5	176					
17	0.6	186					
18	0.7	167					
19	0.8	185					
20	0.9	147					
21	1	880					

FIGURE 17.3
Our histogram of 5000 normal random values.

- You multiply nextFloat() by the maximum size of the *range* of what you want. Let's say that you want values between 4.0 and 6.0. Your range is then 2.0 (6.0 − 4.0). 2.0*nextFloat() will give you a value between 0.0 and 2.0. Add that to 4.0, e.g., 4.0*(2.0*rng.nextFloat()), and now you get a random value between 4.0 and 6.0.

The process is *exactly* the same for normal random distributions. You add the *mean* value, and multiply by the desired *standard deviation* to get the right *range*. In code, that is (range * rng.nextGaussian())+mean). Let us test that, by generating a new normal random distribution, where we specify the mean and range.

Example Java Code 162: Generating a specific normal random distribution

```
import java.util.*;  // Need this for Random
import java.io.*;  // For BufferedWriter

/**
 * Class to generate a normal distribution of numbers
 * with a mean and range specified
 * @author Mark Guzdial
```

```
 8      * @author Barb Ericson
        */
10    public class GenerateNewNormal {

12      public static void main(String[] args) {
        Random rng = new Random(); // Random Number Generator
14      BufferedWriter output=null; // file for writing

16      double mean = 25.0;
        double range = 5.0;
18
        // Try to open the file
20      try {
          // create a writer
22        output =
            new BufferedWriter(
24            new FileWriter("C:/dsBook/normal-new.txt"));
        } catch (Exception ex) {
26        System.out.println("Trouble opening the file.");
        }
28
        // Fill it with 5000 numbers with a mean of 5.0 and a
30      //larger spread, normally distributed
        for (int i=0; i < 5000; i++) {
32        try {
            output.write("\t"+((range *
34                          rng.nextGaussian()) + mean));
            output.newLine();
36        } catch (Exception ex) {
            System.out.println("Couldn't write the data!");
38          System.out.println(ex.getMessage());
          }
40      }

42      // Close the file
        try {
44        output.close();
        } catch (Exception ex) {
46        System.out.println("Something went wrong " +
                              "closing the file");
48      }
      }
50    }
```

When we generate the histogram via our bin-counting program and spreadsheet, we see that we do get a fairly normal curve, with a mean of 25.0 and with most of the values between 20.0 and 30.0 (Figure 17.4).

Common Bug: Beware of combining in main

Class HistogramGenerator has a main method which generates one of the distributions. Don't try to simply add in the other methods. All three will simply be summed together. Run them separately.

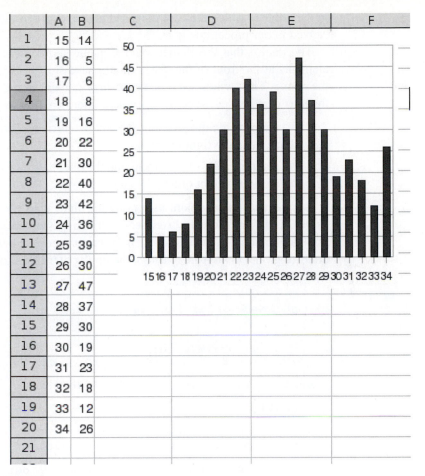

	A	B
1	15	14
2	16	5
3	17	6
4	18	8
5	19	16
6	20	22
7	21	30
8	22	40
9	23	42
10	24	36
11	25	39
12	26	30
13	27	47
14	28	37
15	29	30
16	30	19
17	31	23
18	32	18
19	33	12
20	34	26
21		

FIGURE 17.4
Histogram drawn from a normal distribution to our specifications.

17.4   ORDERING EVENTS BY TIME

As we mentioned at the start of this chapter, it is important to keep time straight in a discrete event simulation. Since we do not generate every moment in time, we use our random distributions to come up with realistic lengths of time between events. In our simulation, we might have a moment where Truck A leaves the factory on day 3.0, going on a trip that averages 2.5 days, with a standard deviation of 0.5 days. Rather than simulate the 2.5 +/ − 0.5 days, we roll our random die, and might find that this truck will take 3.2 days. (It happens.) We queue up Truck A to arrive on day 6.2 (call it "early in the morning on day 6"). Now, Truck B leaves on day 3.5 and the random die comes out as 2.0. We queue up Truck B to arrive on day 5.5. "But wait!" you say. "Using a normal queue means that Truck B comes *after* Truck A!"

You are right. According to the order of time, Truck B passes Truck A somewhere on the road and shows up a day before. How do we fix it so that we process the trucks in the order in which they are supposed to arrive, not in the actual order in which they arrived in our processing queue?

The goal is that the elements in the queue should always be in *sorted order*. The elements at the front of the queue should have smaller event times than those later in the queue. Then, when we process the first element in the queue, we are sure to have the *next* (earliest) event being processed. There are two ways to achieve this goal:

- We can *sort* the queue after each element arrives. Sorting involves putting all the elements in the right order.

- We can *insert* the new element into the queue in *sorted order*, so that the queue is *always* in the right order.

Let's set up the problem as a program, first, then try each of our solutions. Let us set up an event queue exerciser—something we can use to test our event queue implementations, both versions. Our exerciser creates a bunch of events, in the *wrong* order (e.g., not always increasing), then pulls them back out. Our goal is to get them back out in sorted order.

Example Java Code 163: Event Queue Exerciser

```java
/**
 * Class to try out the EventQueue
 * @author Mark Guzdial
 * @author Barb Ericson
 */
public class EventQueueExercisor {

  public static void main(String[] args) {

    // Make an EventQueue
    EventQueue queue = new EventQueue();

    // Now, stuff it full of events, out of order.
    SimEvent event = new SimEvent();
    event.setTime(5.0);
    queue.add(event);

    event = new SimEvent();
    event.setTime(2.0);
    queue.add(event);

    event = new SimEvent();
    event.setTime(1.3);
    queue.add(event);

    event = new SimEvent();
    event.setTime(1.1);
    queue.add(event);

    event = new SimEvent();
    event.setTime(7.0);
    queue.add(event);

    event = new SimEvent();
    event.setTime(0.5);
    queue.add(event);
```

```
38      event = new SimEvent();
        event.setTime(1.0);
40      queue.add(event);

42      // Get the events back, hopefully in order!
        for (int i=0; i < 7; i++) {
44        event = queue.pop();
          System.out.println("Popped event time:" +
46          event.getTime());
        }
48    }

50  }
```

■

How It Works.   There's not much to this code. As you can see, we are using SimEvent, an instance of which represents a simulation event. We will see how that is implemented, in just a few pages. In the exerciser, we create some SimEvent instances with the times not in order and add them to the EventQueue instance. Then we pop them off. If we do it right, we should see this:

```
Welcome to DrJava.
> java EventQueueExercisor
Popped event time:0.5
Popped event time:1.0
Popped event time:1.1
Popped event time:1.3
Popped event time:2.0
Popped event time:5.0
Popped event time:7.0
```

Now, let's look at our event queue implementation.

Example Java Code 164: EventQueue (start)

```
    import java.util.*;
2
    /**
4    * EventQueue
     * It's called an event "queue," but it's not really.
6    * Instead, it's a list (could be an array, could be a
     * linked list)
8    * that always keeps its elements in time sorted order.
     * When you get the nextEvent, you KNOW that it's the one
10   * with the lowest time in the EventQueue
     * @author Mark Guzdial
12   * @author Barb Ericson
     */
14  public class EventQueue {

16    /** a linked list of elements */
      private LinkedList<Object> elements;
18
      /// Constructors ////////////////
20
```

```java
22    /**
       * No argument constructor
       */
24    public EventQueue() {
        elements = new LinkedList<Object>();
26    }

28    /**
       * Add the event.
30     * The Queue MUST remain in order, from lowest time
       * to highest.
32     * @param myEvent the event to add
       */
34    public void add(SimEvent myEvent) {
        // Option one: Add then sort
36      elements.add(myEvent);
        this.sort();
38      // Option two: Insert into order
        //this.insertInOrder(myEvent);
40    }

42    /**
       * see the first element but don't remove it
44     * @return the first element in the queue
       */
46    public SimEvent peek() {
        return (SimEvent) elements.getFirst();
48    }

50    /**
       * remove the top element from the queue and
52     * return it.
       * @return the top element
54     */
      public SimEvent pop() {
56      SimEvent toReturn = this.peek();
        elements.removeFirst();
58      return toReturn;
      }

60
      /**
62     * Return the number of elements in the queue
       * @return the number of elements in the queue
64     */
      public int size() {return elements.size();}

66
      /**
68     * Check if the queue is empty
       * @return true if empty else false
70     */
      public boolean empty() {return this.size() == 0;}
```

■

How It Works.   An EventQueue is like a queue only in the sense that it will insert at the end and pull from the front. Most of the methods, like pop() and peek(), are the same as in our previous Queue implementations. The tricky part is add(). First, we'll explore the first option: doing a normal add(), then sorting the events.

Sorting Objects

Sorting a collection of items is a task that computer scientists have explored for a long time. It's trickier than one might think. There are lots of ways to do it, and many are smarter (and thus, faster) ways than others. The obvious but inefficient ones take $O(n^2)$ time—if there are n elements in the collection to be sorted, it takes (roughly) n^2 steps to sort the collection. The best ones take $O(n * log_2(n))$ steps to do it.

Let's think it through:

- Here's a simple way to sort a collection of items: start with the second item in the list and compare it to the first. If it is smaller than the first time, insert it before the first item. If it is bigger, leave it alone. Now move on to the third item in the list. Insert it into the correct place in the sorted list so far. Do the same with each of the remaining unsorted items in the list.

- Here's a different way of thinking about the fastest way to do it. Remember when we talked about searches in trees, and pointed out that the fastest search is $O(log_2(n))$? Imagine if you could take each of the n items out of the tree and then insert them into the sorted tree in $log_2(n)$ steps. The end result is that you would do the whole sort in $n * log_2(n)$ steps—$O(n * log_2(n))$.

There are also sorts that are better than $O(n^2)$ in some cases. We are going to implement one of those to do our sort. We are going to implement an insertion sort. The basic idea of an insertion sort is to slowly grow the part that is sorted as you go along. Here's how an insertion sort works:

- Consider the event at some position, starting at 1 and ending at n.

- Start with the previous index to the current position. This is the event to compare to.

  1. If the comparison event time is *less than* the time in the event we're considering, then shift the comparison event down to make room.

  2. Wherever we stop with this process of comparing and shifting, that's where the considered event goes. Once the comparison event is greater than or equal to the considered event—stop.

- Now consider the next event from $(1..n)$, until done.

Here's the code, for `EventQueue`, that implements this.

Example Java Code 165: Insertion Sort for EventQueue

```
/**
 * Sort the events in the linked list using an insertion
 * sort
 */
public void sort() {

    // For comparing to elements at smaller indices
    SimEvent considered = null;
    SimEvent compareEvent = null; // Just for use in loop
    // Smaller index we're comparing to
```

```
12      int compare;

        // Start out assuming that position 0 is "sorted"
14      // When position==1, compare elements at indices 0 and 1
        // When position==2, compare at indices 0, 1, and 2, etc.
16      for (int position=1; position < elements.size();
          position++) {
18          considered = (SimEvent) elements.get(position);
            // Now, we look at "considered" versus the elements
20          // less than "compare"
            compare = position;

22
            // While the considered event is greater than the
24          // compared event ,
            // it's in the wrong place, so move the elements up one.
26          compareEvent = (SimEvent) elements.get(compare-1);
            while (compareEvent.getTime() >
28                  considered.getTime())   {
            elements.set(compare,elements.get(compare-1));
30          compare = compare-1;
            // If we get to the end of the array, stop
32          if (compare <= 0) {
              break;
34          }
            // else get ready for the next time through the loop
36          else {
                compareEvent = (SimEvent) elements.get(compare-1);
38          }
          }
40          // Wherever we stopped, this is where "considered"
            // belongs
42          elements.set(compare,considered);
        } // for all positions 1 to the end
44    } // end of sort()
```

If all of the events are in sorted order already, we do $n - 1$ comparisons and no swapping. This is called *the best case* and will be $O(n)$. However, the best case is quite unlikely. If the collection is *exactly sorted in reverse order* (e.g., largest one is at the front), then we do $(n - 1) * n$ comparisons and lots of swaps— so in the *worst case*, the insertion sort is $O(n^2)$.

Inserting into a Sorted List

If after every time we add an event, we then sort it, we can be sure that the event queue remains in sorted order. However, this is a particularly time-consuming (and dumb) way of doing it. If we keep sorting the list then we know that only the new element is out of order. Think about it this way: You are holding a collection of numbered cards, which you have in an order from smallest-to-largest. Someone hands you a new card. Do you put it at the end, then re-sort the whole deck? Of course not! Instead, you take the new card, and figure out where it fits into your hand. That is, and it is much more efficient than sorting after every addition.

In order to try this new approach, we're considering this other option for Event-Queue's add():

```
/**
 * Add the event.
```

```
   * The Queue MUST remain in order, from lowest time
   * to highest.
   * @param myEvent the event to add
   */
  public void add(SimEvent myEvent) {
    // Option one: Add then sort
    //elements.add(myEvent);
    //this.sort();
    // Option two: Insert into order
    this.insertInOrder(myEvent);
  }
```

Inserting into an ordered list is much simpler. We simply figure out where something goes, then move (shift) the elements to make room.

Example Java Code 166: Inserting into a sorted order (EventQueue)

```
   /**
2   * Add the new element into the linked list of
    * elements, assuming
4   * that it's already in order.
    * @param thisEvent the one to add
6   */
  public void insertInOrder(SimEvent thisEvent) {
8   SimEvent comparison = null;

10    // Have we inserted yet?
      boolean inserted = false;
12    for (int i=0; i < elements.size(); i++) {
        comparison = (SimEvent) elements.get(i);
14
        // Assume elements from 0..i are less than thisEvent
16      // If the element time is GREATER, insert here and
        // shift the rest down
18      if (thisEvent.getTime() < comparison.getTime()) {
          //Insert it here
20        inserted = true;
          elements.add(i,thisEvent);
22        break; // We can stop the search loop
        }
24    } // end for

26    // Did we get through the list without finding something
      // greater?  Must be greater than any currently there!
28    if (!inserted) {
        // Insert it at the end
30      elements.addLast(thisEvent);
      }
32  }
```

■

Using a Min-Heap

We really don't need to keep all the data sorted in ascending order all the time in our event queue. We just need to make sure that the smallest item in the queue is the one we pop off next. There is a data structure that is perfect for this situation. It is called a min-heap. This type of data structure is often used to implement a priority queue, which can be used to schedule jobs sent to a printer.

A *min-heap* is a kind of binary tree that is complete and where the value at each node is less than or equal to the values stored at its children nodes. A complete binary tree is one in which all levels are filled except the last (deepest) level and all nodes at that level are filled from left to right (Figure 17.5).

When items are added to a min-heap, they are added at the next open position at the deepest level of the tree (Figure 17.6).

Next, a method is called to check that the new added value is less than or equal to the parent node's value. If it is not then the values are switched (Figure 17.7).

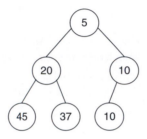

FIGURE 17.5
An example of a min-heap.

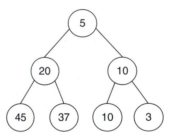

FIGURE 17.6
Adding a new value to the min-heap.

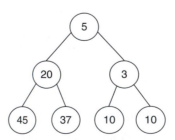

FIGURE 17.7
After switching the 10 and 3 values.

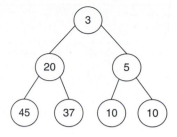

FIGURE 17.8
The final min-heap after adding a new value.

This is continued until the value is less than or equal to the parent node's value or the root of the tree is reached (Figure 17.8).

Java has a class called `PriorityQueue`, which uses a min-heap to return the smallest element in the queue each time you **pop** the queue. As usual, you can also **add** elements to the queue. The elements in the queue must implement the `Comparable` interface in order to determine which is the smallest. We could have simply used a `PriorityQueue` instead of creating an `EventQueue` class, but we wanted to demonstrate the need for a priority queue and cover both sorting an ordered list and inserting into a sorted list. Java defines many classes and before you write a new class, you should check to see if there is an existing Java class that does what you want.

17.5   IMPLEMENTING A DISCRETE EVENT SIMULATION

At this point, we know all that we need to implement a discrete event simulation. This is a big project using many of the data structures that we have learned about in this book, such as:

- Queues: For storing the agents waiting in line for some resource.
- EventQueues: For storing the events scheduled to occur.
- LinkedList: For storing all the agents.

We will run our discrete event simulation like this:

```
Welcome to DrJava.
> FactorySimulation fs = new FactorySimulation();
> fs.openFrames("c:/temp/test1/");
> fs.run(25.0);
```

When we run the simulation, we will see a screen like Figure 17.9. The turtles (representing agents) do not move from place to place in this figure. They simply appear in each of the locations: at the factory, at the warehouse, at the start of the marketplace, and leaving the marketplace. Since we do not simulate the moments in between these discrete events, we do not see the motion that would (in the real world) occur between those moments. Basically, the animation is not very useful in the discrete event simulation.

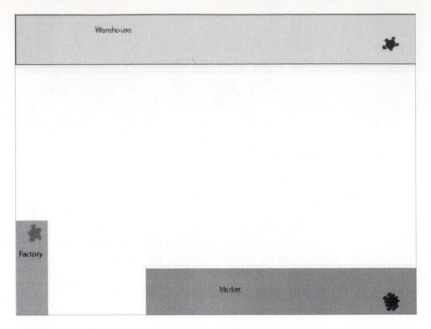

FIGURE 17.9
Screenshot of factory simulation running.

All the useful information coming out of a discrete event simulation is in the details, either stored to a file or appearing in the console. For example, here are some lines from the console during a run of the factory simulation:

```
Time: 0.3842370395847543, Distributor: 0, Arrived at warehouse needs 21
Time: 0.3842370395847543, Distributor: 0, is blocking
>>> Timestep: 0
Time: 1.104921081542508, Distributor: 3, Arrived at warehouse needs 14
Time: 1.104921081542508, Distributor: 3, is blocking
>>> Timestep: 1
Time: 1.5431456642843075, Truck: 2, Arrived at warehouse with load 13
>>> Timestep: 1
Time: 1.7428695489888186, Distributor: 1, Arrived at warehouse needs 22
Time: 1.7428695489888186, Distributor: 1, is blocking
>>> Timestep: 1
Time: 1.7864299413396005, Distributor: 4, Arrived at warehouse needs 11
Time: 1.7864299413396005, Distributor: 4,
  Gathered product for orders of 11
>>> Timestep: 1
Time: 3.3538468937044357, Truck: 1, Arrived at warehouse with load 19
Time: 3.3538468937044357, Distributor: 0, unblocked!
Time: 3.3538468937044357, Distributor: 0,
  Gathered product for orders of 21
>>> Timestep: 3
Time: 4.260574628277275, Distributor: 2, Arrived at warehouse needs 6
Time: 4.260574628277275, Distributor: 2, is blocking
```

```
>>> Timestep: 4
Time: 4.26374539037954, Truck: 0, Arrived at warehouse with load 19
Time: 4.26374539037954, Distributor: 3, unblocked!
Time: 4.26374539037954, Distributor: 3, Gathered product for orders of 14
>>> Timestep: 4
Time: 4.726820817399738, Distributor: 0, Arrived at market
>>> Timestep: 4
Time: 5.329512576401011, Truck: 2, Arrived at factory
```

...

Let's spell this out a bit, to explain what's happening here:

- The first distributor (number 0) appears at the warehouse at about time 0.384 (call it "early on the first day of the simulation"). There is nothing in the warehouse yet, because no trucks have arrived, so the distributor blocks, waiting.

- Early on the second day (time 1.10), distributor 3 appears at the warehouse at about time 1.10. It also blocks waiting for product to arrive. What happened to distributor 2? In the real world, it might be traffic or car trouble. In terms of the simulation implementation, the variance in the random number generation means that the distributors can arrive in any order.

- Later the second day (time 1.54), truck 2 arrives with a load of 13 items. But, this is less than either distributor 0's or 3's needs, so they continue waiting.

- Distributor 1 arrives at about 1.74 and also waits since it needs 22 items.

- Distributor 4 arrives (time 1.78) and only needs 11 items and there are more than 11 items, so it takes 11 items leaving two items and leaves.

- Truck (number 1) arrives on day 4 (time 3.35) with 19 items, meaning that there is a total of 21 items and now distributor 0 can take 21 items and leave. This leaves no items at the warehouse. What happened to day 3? No events occurred that day so it doesn't show up in the simulation.

- Distributor 2 arrives on the fifth day and blocks, since there are no items at the warehouse.

- Later on the same day, truck 0 arrives with 19 items and so distributor 3 can finally take 14, which leaves five.

- On the same day distributor 0 arrives at the market to sell the product.

- On day 6, truck 2 arrives at the factory to pick up more product.

- And so on...

Once you have a simulation like this for any real situation that you might want to model, and you are convinced that the model is pretty accurate, there are lots of questions that you can ask which might be hard to answer in the real world.

- How long do distributors wait? If we recorded the time when they block (get stuck in line), then when they unblock, we could get the difference and write it to a file.

We could then average those differences to get a sense of the time the distributors wait.

- How much product sits in the warehouse? Given the above snippet of the simulation, we get the idea that the warehouse does not have to store much at any time. Maybe we need more of a backroom than a whole warehouse? We could compute the maximum amount of product being stored by simply computing the amount in the warehouse at each time a distributor leaves, then writing it out for analysis after the execution.

- How long does the queue of distributors get at the warehouse? Just how many of our salespeople are hanging out the local Motel 6 awaiting trucks? Each time that a distributor blocks, we could save the number of people in the queue.

- Finally, the most interesting question for the owners of the system: Can we move more product by having more distributors? Or more trucks? Or maybe bigger or faster trucks? We can easily make these changes and see what happens.

Building a Discrete Event Simulation

Figure 17.10 is a UML class diagram describing the classes in our discrete event simulation package. You see that these are an extension of the simulation package classes we have created previously.

- Class DESimulation represents a discrete event simulation, which is an extension of Simulation. An instance of DESimulation has a field for now, which always stores the time of the latest event pulled from the EventQueue referenced by the field events. A DESimulation has a different kind of run(), one that takes a floating point value as the stopping time, and stops when now goes past the input time.

- A DEAgent represents an agent in a discrete event simulation, which is an extension of Agent. An instance of DEAgent knows if it is blocked (e.g., waiting in a queue), and it has a set of methods that can be queried to determine if the agent isBlocked() or isReady() (to execute again). An instance of DEAgent will waitFor() some resource, then become unblocked() and will likely then processEvent(). Processing events is actually the main activity of DEAgent instances, rather than act().

- There is also a class Resource that represents some resource that the agents want, produce, or consume in a discrete event simulation. A Resource instance has a field blocked which points to an instance of a Queue for storing blocked agents. Agents are blocked by calling addToList() on that resource. A Resource instance knows how to tell the amountAvailable() of itself, and can be told to consume() that resource or add() to that resource.

Figure 17.11 extends the earlier class diagram with the classes needed to implement our factory simulation. There are only four new classes.

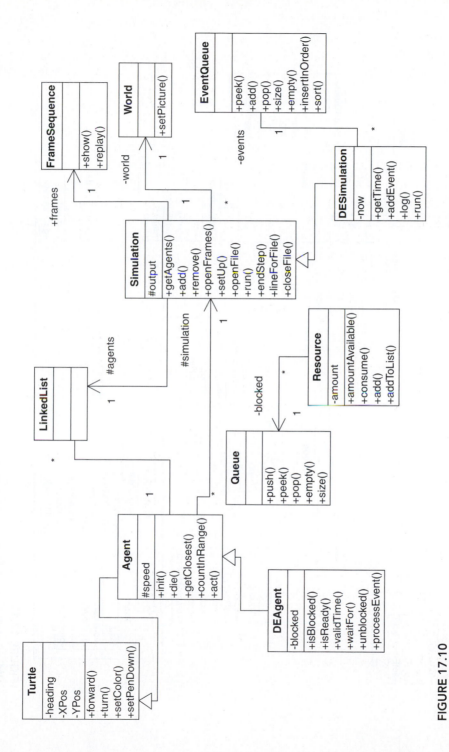

FIGURE 17.10
UML class diagram of the discrete event simulation package.

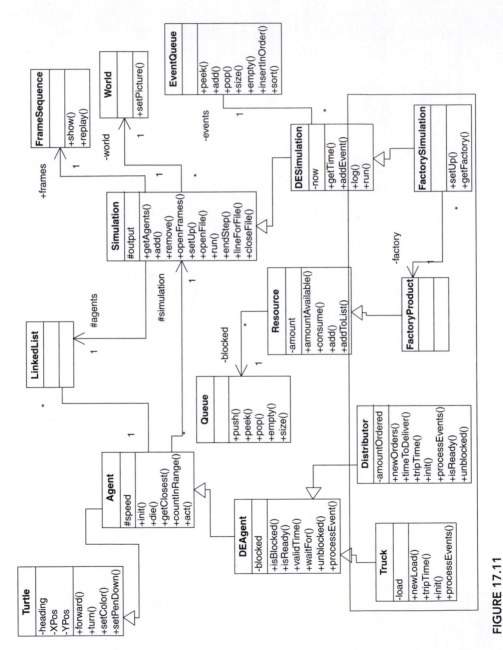

FIGURE 17.11
UML class diagram with factory simulation classes.

- The class `FactorySimulation` extends `DESimulation`. It defines its own `set-Up()` method, and it knows how to `getFactory()`.

- The `factory` is just a reference to a `FactoryProduct` class, which extends `Resource`—but that's all it is. (It doesn't need to be there at all—it just allows us to talk about "Factory Products" rather than "Resources.")

- The `Distributor` class defines what distributors do, as a subclass of `DEAgent`. An instance of `Distributor` has its own `init()`, `processEvents()`, `isReady()`, and `unblocked()`. Its methods `newOrders()`, `timeToDeliver()`, and `trip-Time()` use random distributions to generate (respectively) the number of new orders taken, the time to deliver product, and the time to travel between the marketplace and the warehouse.

- The `Truck` class defines what trucks do as a subclass of `DEAgent`. An instance of `Truck` has its own `init()` and `processEvents()`, but not the others that `Distributor` overrides since trucks never block. A `Truck` does know how to compute its `newLoad()` (from the factory) and `tripTime()` (between the factory and warehouse).

The heart of any discrete event simulation in this package is the subclass of `DESimulation`. A `DESimulation` instance:

- calls `setUp()` to create agents and schedule the first events,

- provides `log()` for writing things out to the console and a text file,

- executes `run()` by processing each event in the event queue and tells the corresponding agent to process a particular message.

Here is the heart of the `run()` method in `DESimulation`:

```
// While we're not yet at the stop time,
// and there are more events to process
while ((now < stopTime) &&
        (!events.empty())) {
  topEvent = events.pop();

  // Whatever event is next, that time is now
  now = topEvent.getTime();

  // Let the agent know that its event has occurred
  topAgent = topEvent.getAgent();
  topAgent.processEvent(topEvent.getMessage());

  // repaint the world to show the movement
  // IF there is a world
  if (world != null) {
    world.repaint();
  }

  // Do the end of step processing
  this.endStep((int) now);
}
```

How It Works.   This section of code reads pretty close to our definition of how a discrete event simulation works. As long as there are events in the queue, and we're are not at the time to stop, we (1) grab an event from the event queue, (2) make the new event's time "now," and (3) process the event. Next, we repaint the world (if there is one) and do any end-of-step processing.

You may be wondering what our `SimEvent` instances look like. There really isn't much to them.

Example Java Code 167: SimEvent (just the fields)

```
 /**
2 * SimulationEvent (SimEvent) -- an event that occurs
  * in a simulation, like a truck arriving at a factory,
4 * or a salesperson leaving the market
  * @author Mark Guzdial
6 * @author Barb Ericson
  */
8 public class SimEvent implements Comparable<SimEvent> {

10  ////////////////////// Fields //////////////////////////

12  /** the time that the event occurs */
    private double time;
14
    /** the discrete event agent that the event occurs to */
16  private DEAgent whom;

18  /** the type of event */
    private int message;
```

How It Works.   An instance of `SimEvent` consists of a `time` when the event should occur, an instance of `DEAgent` describing to whom the event should occur, and an integer `message` which should have meaning to the agent. That message will be sent to the agent, who will know the meaning of the number that is that message. It could be a string, or just about anything—we simply decided to model it as a number.

All action within the simulation occurs within `DEAgent` as it processes events. The subclasses of `DEAgent` define the constant numbers for messages, in answer to the question, "What will be the main events for this agent?" If an agent needs a resource, it asks to see if it's available, and if not, it blocks itself. It will be told to unblock when it's ready. The most critical aspect of any `DEAgent` is that each agent is responsible for scheduling its own events. The `DESimulation` class doesn't decide when agents come and go—the agents themselves cause their next activity to occur by creating the appropriate events and pushing them onto the event queue.

Let's take the `Truck` class as an example of a kind of `DEAgent`.

Example Java Code 168: Truck

```java
import java.awt.Color; // For color

/**
 * Truck -- delivers product from the Factory
 * to the Warehouse.
 * @author Mark Guzdial
 * @author Barb Ericson
 */
public class Truck extends DEAgent {

  ///////////////////// fields //////////////////////////

  /** an arrive at factory event */
  public static final int FACTORY_ARRIVE = 0;

  /** an arrive at warehouse event */
  public static final int WAREHOUSE_ARRIVE = 1;

  /** The amount of product being carried */
  private int load;

  /////////////////////// Constructors ///////////////////
  // not shown here (see the class)

  ///////////////////// methods //////////////////////////

  /**
   * A method to create a new load.  The returned amount
   * will be between 10 and 20 on a uniform distribution
   */
  public int newLoad() {
    return 10 + randNumGen.nextInt(11);
  }

  /**
   * Calculate and return the total trip time
   * @return the total time of the trip in days
   */
  public double tripTime() {
    double delay = randNumGen.nextGaussian() + 3;
    DESimulation sim = (DESimulation) getSimulation();
    if (delay < 1)
      // Must take at least one day
    {return 1.0 + sim.getTime();}
    else {return delay + sim.getTime();}
  }

  /**
   * Method to arrive at the factory, load up,
   * and schedule the event to arrive at the warehouse
   */
  private void arriveAtFactory() {

    // move to the factory
    this.moveTo(30,350);

    // Load up at the factory, and set off for the warehouse
    load = this.newLoad();
```

```java
60         ((DESimulation) getSimulation()).addEvent(
             new SimEvent(this,tripTime(),WAREHOUSE_ARRIVE));
62
       }
64
       /**
66      * Method to arrive at the warehouse, unload,
        * and create the event to arrive at the warehouse
68      */
       private void arriveAtWarehouse() {
70         // change location to warehouse
         this.moveTo(50,50);
72
         FactorySimulation sim = (FactorySimulation)
74           getSimulation();
76         // Unload product -- takes zero time (unrealistic!)
         sim.getProduct().add(load);
78         load = 0;
80         // Head back to factory
         sim.addEvent(
82           new SimEvent(this,tripTime(),FACTORY_ARRIVE));
       }
84
       /**
86      * Set up the truck
        * Start out at the factory
88      * @param thisSim the simulation
        */
90     public void init(Simulation thisSim) {
92         // Do the default init
         super.init(thisSim);
94         this.setPenDown(false); // Pen up
         this.setBodyColor(Color.GREEN); // Let green deliver!
96
         // show up at factory, load up, and leave for the
98         // warehouse
         arriveAtFactory();
100
       }
102
       /**
104     * Process an event.
        * @param message the type of event
106     */
       public void processEvent(int message) {
108       DESimulation sim = (DESimulation) getSimulation();
         switch(message) {
110         case FACTORY_ARRIVE:
             // Show the truck at the factory
112           sim.log(this.getName() +
                                   ", Arrived at factory");
114           // show up at factory, load up,
             // and leave for the warehouse
116           arriveAtFactory();
             break;
118
           case WAREHOUSE_ARRIVE:
120           // Show the truck at the warehouse
             sim.log(this.getName() +
```

```
122          ", Arrived at warehouse with load "+load);
             arriveAtWarehouse();
124          break;
         }
126    }
```

∎

How It Works.   The Truck class has two constants representing event messages: one for arriving at the factory, and the other for arriving at the warehouse. The only other field of a Truck is its load.

- The init() method sets up the truck. A bunch of housekeeping is done for the sake of the graphical representation (e.g., setting body color, and moving the turtle), but those are really pretty unimportant. The important part is that every truck gets an initial load (newLoad()), and then schedules itself to arrive at the warehouse. Let's take apart that line a little bit.

    ```
    ((DESimulation) thisSim).addEvent(
        new SimEvent(this,tripTime(),WAREHOUSE_ARRIVE));
    ```

    The simulation object is passed into init() as the parameter thisSim. We cast it to DESimulation in order to add an event (addEvent) to the event queue. We create a new simulation event (SimEvent), that speaks to this agent, is scheduled to occur at tripTime(), and whose event is "Arrive at the warehouse."

- The tripTime() method computes the delay as:

    ```
    double delay = randNumGen.nextGaussian() + 3;
    ```

    That makes it between 2.0 and 4.0 days to arrive. Now, while that is unlikely, it is possible for that number to be less than 1.0. We assume that it is possible to make the trip in one day (by speeding and avoiding all speed traps), so the trip time is the current time (((DESimulation) simulation).getTime()) plus the normally distributed delay *or* 1.0.

- A newLoad() is a simple uniform distribution, between 10 and 20.

- The method processEvent is called when a message is popped off the event queue for this agent. The agent is told to process the event, with the message number as input. We use a switch statement to choose what to do, based on the message input.

    1. If we have just arrived at the factory, we log() that information and move the turtle. We then compute a new load, and move back to the warehouse.

    2. Once we get to the warehouse, we log() that information and move the turtle. We then ask the factory to accept our product: ((FactorySimulation) simulation).getProduct().add(load);. Note that there is actually a big flaw in the veracity of this part of the simulation: it takes no time to empty the truck. Wouldn't you expect the time to empty the truck to be a function of the size of the load? In any case, our truck now has nothing in it (load = 0;), so the truck schedules a new event to arrive back at the factory.

Instances of `Resource` keep track of what amount they have available (of whatever the resource is). They maintain a queue of agents that are `blocked` on this resource. They can `add` to the resource, or have it `consume`(d). When more resource comes in, the agent at the head of the blocked queue gets asked if there is enough resource for it to continue, by asking it if it `isReady()`. If so, it can unblock. The code that does that last part looks like this:

```
/**
 * Add more produced resource.
 * Is there enough to unblock the first
 * Agent in the Queue?
 * @param production the amount produced
 */
public void add(int production) {
  amount = amount + production;

  if (!blocked.isEmpty()) {
    // Ask the next Agent in the queue
    // if it can be unblocked
    DEAgent topOne = (DEAgent) blocked.peek();
    // Is it ready to run given this resource?
    if (topOne.isReady(this)) {
      // Remove it from the queue
      topOne = (DEAgent) blocked.pop();
      // And tell it it's unblocked
      topOne.unblocked(this);
    }
  }
}
```

Let's now look at the more complicated agent in our simulation, the `Distributor`, since it does block on resources.

Example Java Code 169: Distributor

```
   import java.awt.Color; // To color our distributors
2
   /**
4   * Distributor -- takes orders from Market to Warehouse,
    * fills them, and returns with product.
6   * @author Mark Guzdial
    * @author Barb Ericson
8   */
   public class Distributor extends DEAgent {
10
     //////////////////// fields ////////////////////////////
12
     /** message that means things have arrived
14     * at the market */
     public static final int MARKET_ARRIVE = 0;
16   /** message that means the goods have left the market */
     public static final int MARKET_LEAVE = 1;
18   /** message that means items arrived at the warehouse */
     public static final int WAREHOUSE_ARRIVE = 2;
20
```

```java
       /** AmountOrdered so-far */
22     private int amountOrdered;

24     ////////////////// Constructors /////////////
       // not shown here, see the class definition
26
       ///////////// Methods ////////////////
28
       /**
30      * return the number of new orders
        * @return the number of new orders
32      */
       public int newOrders() {
34       // Between 5 and 25, uniform
         return randNumGen.nextInt(21)+5;
36     }

38     /**
        * return the time to deliver
40      * @return the time to deliver
        */
42     public double timeToDeliver() {
         // On average 5 days to deliver, normal distr.
44       return validTime(randNumGen.nextGaussian()+5);
       }
46
       /**
48      * return the trip time
        * @return the trip time
50      */
       public double tripTime(){
52       // On average 2 days to travel
         // between market and warehouse
54       return validTime(randNumGen.nextGaussian()+2);
       }
56
       /**
58      * Initialize a distributor.
        * Start in the market, taking orders, then
60      * schedule arrival at the warehouse.
        * @param thisSim the simulation
62      */
       public void init(Simulation thisSim) {
64
         //First, do the normal stuff
66       super.init(thisSim);
         this.setPenDown(false); // Pen up
68       this.setBodyColor(Color.BLUE); // Go Blue!

70       // Show the distributor in the market
         this.moveTo(600,460); // At far right
72       // Get the orders, and set off for the warehouse
         amountOrdered = this.newOrders();
74       ((DESimulation) thisSim).addEvent(
           new SimEvent(this,tripTime(),WAREHOUSE_ARRIVE));
76     }

78     /**
        * Method to check if we are we ready to be unlocked?
80      * @param res the resource
        * @return true if ready else false
82      */
```

```
      public boolean isReady(Resource res) {
84      // Is the amount in the resource more than our orders?
        return (res.amountAvailable() >=
86        amountOrdered);
      }
88

      /**
90     * I've been unblocked!
       * @param resource the desired resource
92     */
      public void unblocked(Resource resource) {
94      super.unblocked(resource);

96      // Consume the resource for the orders
        ((DESimulation) getSimulation()).log(this.getName() +
98        ", unblocked!");
        resource.consume(amountOrdered); // Zero time to load?
100     ((DESimulation) getSimulation()).log(this.getName() +
          ", Gathered product for orders of "+amountOrdered);
102     // Schedule myself to arrive at the Market
        ((DESimulation) getSimulation()).addEvent(
104       new SimEvent(this,tripTime(),MARKET_ARRIVE));
      }
106
      /**
108    * Process an event.
       * Default is to do nothing with it.
110    * @param message the message to process
       */
112   public void processEvent(int message) {
        Simulation simulation = getSimulation();
114     switch(message) {
          case MARKET_ARRIVE:
116         // Show the distributor at the market, far left
            ((DESimulation) simulation).log(this.getName() +
118                                  ", Arrived at market");
            this.moveTo(210,460);
120         // Schedule time to deliver
            ((DESimulation) simulation).addEvent(
122           new SimEvent(this,timeToDeliver(),MARKET_LEAVE));
            break;
124       case MARKET_LEAVE:
            // Show the distributor at the market, far right
126         ((DESimulation) simulation).log(this.getName() +
                                   ", Leaving market");
128         this.moveTo(600,460);
            // Get the orders, and set off for the warehouse
130         amountOrdered = this.newOrders();
            ((DESimulation) simulation).addEvent(
132           new SimEvent(this,tripTime(),WAREHOUSE_ARRIVE));
            break;
134       case WAREHOUSE_ARRIVE:

136         // Show the distributor at the warehouse
            ((DESimulation) simulation).log(this.getName() +
138                            ", Arrived at warehouse " +
                             "needs " + amountOrdered);
140         this.moveTo(600,50);
            // Is there enough product available?
142         Resource warehouseProduct =
              ((FactorySimulation) simulation).getProduct();
144         if (warehouseProduct.amountAvailable() >=
```

```
                              amountOrdered) {
146                               // Consume the resource for the orders
                                  warehouseProduct.consume(amountOrdered);
148                                 // Zero load time?
                                  ((DESimulation) simulation).log(this.getName() +
150                                   ", Gathered product for orders of "+
                                      amountOrdered);
152                               // Schedule myself to arrive at the Market
                                  ((DESimulation) simulation).addEvent(
154                                   new SimEvent(this,tripTime(),MARKET_ARRIVE));
                              }
156                           else { // We have to wait until more product
                                  arrives!
158                               ((DESimulation) simulation).log(this.getName() +
                                                                  ", is blocking");
160                               waitFor(((FactorySimulation) simulation).
                                      getProduct());}
162                           break;
                          }
164                   }
```

■

How It Works.   The class `Distributor` has three kinds of messages: arriving at the warehouse, arriving at the market (where the distributor delivers product and collects new orders), and leaving the market. The only other field it has is `amountOrdered`.

- In the `init()` method, the `Distributor` instance is just leaving the market. It computes a number of `newOrders()` that it has just collected, and it schedules itself to arrive at the warehouse.

- There are three kinds of events to be handled in `processEvent()` for `Distributor` instances.

  1. When arriving at the market, the distributor logs the activity and moves the turtle. The distributor then schedules the departure from the market.

  2. When leaving the market, the amount of new orders is computed, and then arrival back at the warehouse is scheduled.

  3. Here's where it gets more interesting. When the distributor gets to the warehouse, it asks how much product there is by asking the simulation for its resource `getProduct()` and asking the resource for the amount `amountAvailable()`, then asks if there is enough product available to fill its orders. If so, the distributor consumes the product, logs the activity, then schedules the trip back to the market. If *there is not enough product*, the distributor blocks, waiting on the resource.

- The distributor `isReady()` to go on when there is enough product: the amount available is greater than or equal to the amount ordered.

- When the distributor is `unblocked()`, it consumes the product and schedules the trip back to the market.

After seeing all of this, the `FactorySimulation` itself does very little. Instead, it merely sets up the pieces and lets it all go.

Example Java Code 170: FactorySimulation

```java
/**
 * FactorySimulation -- set up the whole simulation,
 * including creation of the Trucks and Distributors.
 * @author Mark Guzdial
 * @author Barb Ericson
 */
public class FactorySimulation extends DESimulation {

  /** the product the factory produces */
  private Resource product;

  /**
   * A constructor for the factory simulation
   */
  public FactorySimulation () {
    // Let the world be setup with a background picture
    super(new Picture(
        FileChooser.getMediaPath("EconomyBackground.jpg")));
  }

  /**
   * Get the product
   * @return the product
   */
  public Resource getProduct() {
    return product;
  }

  /**
   * Set up the simulation
   */
  public void setUp() {

    // Let the world be setup
    super.setUp();

    // get the world
    World world = getWorld();

    // Create a warehouse resource
    product = new Resource(); //Track product

    // Create three trucks
    Truck myTruck = null;
    for (int i=0; i<3; i++) {
      myTruck = new Truck(world,this);
      myTruck.setName("Truck: "+i);
    }

    // Create five Distributors
    Distributor sales = null;
    for (int i=0; i<5; i++) {
      sales = new Distributor(world,this);
      sales.setName("Distributor: "+i);
    }
  }

  /* main for testing */
  public static void main(String[] args) {
    FactorySimulation fs = new FactorySimulation();
```

```
           fs.openFrames("c:/temp/test1/");
62         fs.run(25.0);
        }
64    }
```

■

17.6   THE FINAL WORD: THE THIN LINE BETWEEN STRUCTURE AND BEHAVIOR

We have now completed an entire course on data structures. We have covered a lot of material about representing structure and behavior. Here are some of the things we have learned about data structures and their properties:

- **Arrays** are memory efficient, since everything is packed together serially. They are very fast for accessing any individual element. They are hard to insert and delete with, since you have to move elements in the array. Arrays, by their nature, cannot be grown—they have a fixed size.

- **Linked lists** are slightly less memory efficient, since every element has an additional piece of memory that points to the next element. They are great for insertion and deletion—one merely disconnects and reconnects the links to the next element. Accessing any element is costly in terms of time. One basically has to search to find any element. Linked lists can expand as much as available memory allows.

- **Circular linked lists** are good for describing data that has a natural loop in it. However, be careful traversing them using normal methods, or one could end up in an infinite loop.

- **Trees** are terrific for describing data that has hierarchy or clustering to it. They are a form of linked lists that use branch nodes to connect to children. In binary trees, *every* node is both data and branch, since every node can have both a `left` and a `right` branch. Trees have the insertion, deletion, and expandability strengths of linked lists. While a general tree also has to be searched to find things, trees can be structured to allow for faster access than a linked list.

- **Graphs** are like trees, but allow for arbitrary linking. Any node can link to any other node, allowing for looping. Graphs are great for representing structures that do loop, like transit systems and pipes and blood paths.

- **Stacks** are last-in-first-out (LIFO) lists. We defined them using an Abstract Data Type (ADT). Our use for stacks was reversing a list or undoing commands.

- **Queues** are first-in-first-out (FIFO) lists. Our use for queues was for representing agents awaiting a resource.

- **Min-heaps** are complete binary trees where the value at each node in the tree is less than or equal to the values at the children nodes. Min-heaps are often used to implement priority queues such as printer queues.

Let's step back a little. This book uses Java as its language for implementation and description. Java is an *object-oriented language*, which means that it is structured around *objects*. Objects have fields and methods. They specify both structure (of data, through fields) and behavior (process, through methods). They combine both of these ideas in a single computational entity. Each instance of a class has all the data of the class and all the behaviors of the class.

Objects are not the only computational entities that combine structure and behavior. In fact, several of the data structures that we built in this book combine structure and behavior in fairly complex ways. Consider the branches in our trees that scale (for sounds) or move or horizontally/vertically place other pictures. Rendering of those sound trees or image trees was changed based on where those special scaling or moving branches were in the tree. The resultant sound or image was dependent upon the structure of the tree that created it. The *behavior* was determined, in part, by the *structure* of the data.

In a real sense, this thin line between structure and behavior is exactly how computer viruses work. A computer virus typically loads into your computer as data. It just so happens that the data that gets loaded is actually executable code. The virus enters into your computer (through techniques like *buffer overflow*) as data, but is structured in such a way that the executable instructions can get executed. That structuring is typically based on some insight about some flaw about your computer—some place where data can get handled in such a way that some of it can become behavior. Once your computer is executing instructions that the virus writer wrote, all is lost. Your computer's behavior belongs to the virus writer, who snuck in his or her behavior through some flaw in the computer structure.

These complicated interactions between stuff (structure) and how it works (behavior) are difficult to describe. A program describes them, but only by tracing or executing it. We often want ways of thinking about these interactions without having to read the whole program.

That is where our UML diagrams come in. They give us the ability to see the *model* (which is defined both in terms of structure and the behavior of that structure), without getting stuck in implementation complexity. It's pretty hard to trace through the interactions between agents, resources, and event queues in the actual execution of a discrete event simulation. The class diagram makes it so much clearer.

Here is the interesting question to ponder: Where is the program? In languages like Python or Basic, the program is often in one big file, defined through a set of functions, that one can point at. In Java and other object-oriented programs, the program is spread across many objects, many files, where the flow of behavior moves between all these pieces.

The insight that we hope that you come away with, at the end of this book, is that the *actual* program, what really happens, is a mixture of all of that, plus data structures. The definition of what the program does can also be structured by what is in the data, like our special branches in our sound and image trees. The program, thus, is distributed across many computational entities. Programs are distributed across all your representations of structure and behavior.

EXERCISES

17.1   What are the differences between a continuous simulation and a discrete event simulation? Explain a situation in which you would use each.

17.2   Explain what a uniform random distribution is and give an example of data that fits this type of distribution. How can you create data of this type in Java?

17.3   Explain what a normal (Gaussian) distribution is and give an example of data that fits this type of distribution. How can you create data of this type in Java?

17.4   How would you generate numbers using a uniform random distribution between 50 and 100? How would you generate numbers using a normal (Gaussian) distribution between 20 and 40?

17.5   Explain what a Poisson distribution is and give an example of data that fits this type of distribution.

17.6   Create a `MinHeap` class. You should be able to add items to the min-heap and remove the minimum item from a min-heap. Items in the min-heap must implement the `Comparable` interface.

17.7   Create a `MaxHeap` class. You should be able to add items to the max-heap and remove the maximum item from a max-heap. Items in the max-heap must implement the `Comparable` interface. A max-heap is like a min-heap except that the value at a node is greater than or equal to the values stored in the children nodes.

17.8   Modify class `DESimulation` to use a `PriorityQueue` object instead of an `EventQueue` object. Does this change the simulation in any way?

17.9   Run the `FactorySimulation` five times. What is the average length of time a distributor is waiting for product? Add more trucks to the simulation. How does that change the average wait time?

17.10 What happens if you use larger capacity trucks in the simulation? Does it change the average wait time?

17.11 How can you change the simulation to create more small orders?

17.12 Create a simulation of a gas station.

17.13 Create a simulation of airplanes and airports.

17.14 Create a simulation of people and elevators at a hotel.

17.15 Create a simulation of patients in an emergency room.

Bibliography

1. HAROLD ABELSON AND ANDREA DISESSA, *Turtle geometry: The computer as a medium for exploring mathematics*, MIT Press, Cambridge, MA, 1986.

2. ADELE GOLDBERG AND DAVID ROBSON, *Smalltalk-80: The language and its implementation*, Addison-Wesley, 1989.

3. MARTIN GREENBERGER (ed.), *Computers and the world of the future*, MIT Press, 1962.

4. ALAN KAY, "The early history of Smalltalk", *ACM SIGPLAN Notices*, 28(3), 69–95, 1993.

5. M. RESNICK, *Turtles, termites, and traffic jams: Explorations in massively parallel microworlds*, MIT Press, Cambridge, MA, 1997.

6. SVETLANA YAROSH AND MARK GUZDIAL, "Narrating data structures: The role of context in CS2," *J. Educ. Resour. Comput.* 7(4), 1–20, 2008.

Index